INDIAN VOICES

INDIAN VOICES

The First Convocation of American Indian Scholars

THE INDIAN HISTORIAN PRESS
SAN FRANCISCO

THE INDIAN HISTORIAN PRESS, INC.

AMERICAN INDIAN EDUCATIONAL PUBLISHERS
SAN FRANCISCO, CA.

THE First Convocation of American Indian Scholars brought together Native scholars, professional people, artists and traditional historians. Ten nonIndian scholars representing various disciplines attended. Participants were selected by a Steering Committee named by the American Indian Historical Society, sponsors. The Convocation was limited to 200 participants, and every effort was made to get a good cross-section of the Native peoples as to tribe, locality, academic discipline and profession.

Held in March, 1970, at Princeton University, it involved 36 Native students on an equal footing with academicians. The four-day Convocation heard four major presentations during the morning General Assembly sessions. Panels were held during the afternoons. Two evening sessions were held. The Convocation was conceived, organized, and directed entirely by Native Americans. No Federal or other governmental agency was involved in any part of the preparations, organization, or conduct of the Convocation. No political organization, social agency, or church was involved in any way.

The challenging thought, creative ideas, and the high level of both Presentations and Discussions will be an effective tool for the Native Peoples for years to come, and will affect the affairs of this nation more than appears possible today.

Indian Voices: The First Convocation of American Indian Scholars is a record of the Assembly Presentation, Papers given at panels, and discussions held at the Convocation. A comprehensive report of the Proceedings has not been attempted, since this would have necessitated several volumes. However, the Presentations and Papers are intact. The spirit and sense of the discussion is faithful to the record. The routine "business" has been eliminated in the interests of space.

The Convocation was a milestone in the history of the Native Americans, and indeed it was a milestone in the history of this nation. The event proved beyond doubt that leadership exists among the Native American people, for all the purposes of education, administration, economic development, and the general betterment of the American Indian.

This event will be continued, bringing together broader representation of the Native scholars, professionals, artists and Native historians in all disciplines, and increasing the participation of our elders, linguists, and religious leaders. Our goals are quite simple: to form a solid basis for educational accomplishment, and to unite our scholarly forces on behalf of our people.

Chapter headings throughout this book are greatly reduced photographs of the Wampum Belts, sacred property of the Iroquois people.* Wampum was used by the Iroquois to "vouch for the integrity of a speaker, to give responsibility to an office, to assuage sorrows and heal spiritual wounds, or to lend their aura of authority to the proceedings of a council."**

The strings of Wampum shown on this page were sacred to the Iroquois, and were displayed to give authority to a meeting or observance.

Other illustrations, used consecutively as chapter headings, are: the Washington Covenant Belt (over chapter 1), the Hiawatha Belt (over chapter 2), the Wing Belt (over chapter 3). This latter belt was displayed whenever the Constitution of the Six Nations was recited, and represents the ever-growing tree.

The return of the Wampum Belts, now in possession of the State of New York, was the subject of a resolution passed favorably by unanimous action of the Convocation. It seems fitting that they should be representative of this historic event.

*Photographs courtesy of the New York State Museum
**"Wampum Beads and Belts," Charles E. Gillette

Contents

Call for a Convocation

NEVER before in the history of this country has there been so much popular, scholarly, and governmental attention devoted to Indian affairs as during the past several years. As a consequence, there have never been so many challenges and so many opportunities for the Indian people. To be sure, some voices are being heard, both from the right and from the left, voices both of Indians speaking as individuals of their respective tribes, and as members of political groups; and voices of people who claim to speak for the Indian.

As always before in the past, however, there is very little true representation of Indians on the highest levels, where conclusions are drawn, decisions made, and long-range policies formulated. This is why the First Convocation of American Indian Scholars is called, to bring together not only scholars but Indian students, tribal leaders, and nonIndian friends, to explore the issues as these bear on the Indian people as a whole.

This is a call for Indian scholars to come together and take the lead in formulating clear-cut stands and goals on the issues. This is a call for Indian scholars to look to the mountaintops and to greatness in seeking a better life for our people; to demonstrate that we are not the inarticulate masses about whom so much benevolent concern has been voiced in the past.

The Indian people cannot afford not to take advantage of what is probably an unprecedented national mood of goodwill; for it will pass, as other such moods have passed before.

Members of the American Indian Historical Society Comprising
THE STEERING COMMITTEE

Rupert Costo, President; Alfonso Ortiz, Convocation Chairman; Edward P. Dozier, Joseph Senungetuk, Bea Medicine, Fritz Scholder, Robert Kaniatobe, Jeannette Henry.

Listening and Learning are two student participants at the Convocation. Left to right are James West, and Richard West, Jr. Both are college seniors soon to graduate.

2

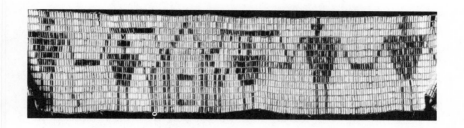

1

Moment of Truth for the American Indian

RUPERT COSTO
Keynote Address

THIS is a moment of truth for the American Indian—a moment when we stand on the threshold of great change. We have it in our power now to overcome the disasters of centuries, and to perform a miracle of change in favor of a better life for our people.

Our history in this land has a force of thousands of years' duration, and cannot be overlooked. Our profound concern for this land and for our people, has a force so ancient and all-absorbing that it cannot be ignored. Yet we are indeed ignored and we are overlooked, in all the practical elements of life as it affects our people. Somehow, despite the many promises, and despite the many evidences of concern, the Native American lives in poverty, receives a complete and fruitful education only by the exercise of the greatest personal sacrifices, and dies in squalor.

At this moment in our history, our American Indian Historical Society conceived the idea of calling a Convocation of American Indian Scholars. Our purpose is to set in motion a responsive leadership that can give effective help in performing that miracle of change so desperately needed for our people. We entered upon the planning and organization of this Convocation with a sense of great pride in our people. In spite of centuries of being cheated out of our land, defrauded of our rights, and denied every privilege accorded all others in this nation, we have survived as a people. We have among us distinguished Native Americans who possess magnificent leadership qualities. Among us there are scholars who have contributed to knowledge, as well as those who, without formal education, have managed to help their people, and with utmost dedication. Above all, there is an upsurge of student population in higher education. Indeed it is in these young people that the hope of our race resides.

It is not the purpose nor the intention of this Convocation to dictate policies or to make decisions which will affect all of our people, or to impose upon the sovereignty of the tribes. It is our purpose only to point out a direction, to provide the help needed to reach certain necessary goals, and to support our own people wherever and whenever they need us.

Among us, traditionally, the scholars are the servants of the people. The *People* reign supreme, by virtue of their right to approve or disapprove actions in all areas of life, and by reason of their prerogative to protect individual and tribal rights. And so we say—let the people come for help to their own scholars. And let the scholars spend *their very lives* and energies in the service of their people.

To perform this miracle of change, we must, however, deal with our own problems and our own situations. The problems that disturb us—the issues that we need to talk about openly— the *facts of life* that beg for a meeting of our minds, these are the things we must deal with in our tribal meetings, and in our organizations, if we are to achieve our goals. We need to ask questions of ourselves, and of one another. We need to explore areas of concern, and come to mutual and unified decisions. It is not true that Indians cannot unite. We have united for years in our immense effort for sheer survival. In matters of practical need, it is enough if we can unite on a point no larger than the head of a pin, in order to make gains. In matters of the larger concern, it becomes a matter of exploration of thought and ideology, of ideas . . . and the use of creative intelligence. Let us ask ourselves some of these questions . . . questions of profound concern for ourselves as a people.

Is there, truly and honestly, anything left of our Indian cultures, traditions, and lifeways? I know there is, and you know it too. Therefore, let us pinpoint these areas of remaining Indian heritage, preserve the remaining cultures, traditions, philosophy, and the languages of our people. Indeed we have a duty to our historical heritage. I don't believe there is anybody here who would disagree.

Just the same, there is a tendency to vulgarize our cultures and history, even among our own people. For example, there is a class being conducted in Native history, at California State

College at Hayward, in which the white students are given "cute" Indian names, are assigned to imaginary and "cute" Indian tribes, and who then conduct themselves as though they are "real Indians." This is a class taught by an *Indian*. We all know about some of the things that are taught by white teachers, degrading to our people. But when an Indian pursues this type of vulgarization, then we must stop and view the whole situation, and we must begin to teach the true history of our people, teach it with respect and scholarly interpretation both to our own people, and to the American public at large. Among us, we have been remiss with respect to our children. We should have had, long ago, practical schools for our children, to keep the languages alive, to keep the beauty of our heritage alive. It is not too late to do this even now.

Another question: Shall we allow tribal society and leadership, tribal autonomy and rights, to be wiped out? Or, shall we fight to preserve our ancient sovereign rights. The present situation, I grant you, is bad, and the present leadership in many tribes has been criticized, especially by our young people. Is it not time to make a stand, and change this situation, to change this leadership if change is needed?

If we do not improve our tribal leadership, by action of the people themselves, we are faced with total destruction of Indian life and cultures. What is left of Indian culture, when the tribal entity is gone? I ask this question of our young people who are so active on the urban front, who find it impossible to act on the tribal front, and who have forsaken their own Indian people in favor of a struggle with windmills and shadows. For, if tribal life disappears, so too does the Indian as an Indian. This is our political entity. This is what remains of our social structure and lifeways. And this is where it is *at*. In my opinion, tribal society has been deformed and degraded by the Bureau of Indian Affairs. I think this should be changed, and I think it can be changed— but only with the greatest courage and single-mindedness, and only by our young people.

Let me pose another question . . . Shall we continue to allow our scholars, artists, and leaders to be overlooked and overshadowed, and even completely ignored by educational institutions, cultural programs, and institutional projects? Is it not time that we refuse to allow ourselves to be exploited for the sake of the self-interest of an ambitious intellectual, an ambitious city or state, or a Chamber of Commerce seeking to develop tourist attractions?

I say that we must insist, that wherever Indian programs are considered, Indian scholars and tribal people shall be dealt with, and shall constitute the leadership of such programs. We are continually confronted with ready-made programs that are carbon copies of programs for blacks, Chicanos and other ethnic groups. These programs have no relationship to our history and culture, nor to our situation today, and they are absolutely worthless, either for teaching about Indians, or for teaching Indians themselves.

I would like to deal more directly with some of the profound questions with which we are faced in this moment of truth, at this time of change. And these questions can find answers only if the Indian scholars work well with the Indian people, and if the Indian people will turn to their *own* scholars for help.

The Bureau of Indian Affairs has dominated the Indian world for nearly a hundred and fifty years. It has stultified our initiative, corrupted our society, and caused a creeping paralysis to set in among our people—economically, and socially as well. Notwithstanding this fact, I don't know any Indians who want termination to take place. It would automatically abrogate our treaties, which are valid under international law, and valid in the constitution of the United States of America. Despite the seriousness of this question, there is no unanimity of opinion as to the course of action that should be taken to rid ourselves of this incubus of Bureau domination. I submit to you, that the method of *supplanting* Bureau controls of programs, *by Indian Tribes and organized groups*, is one good way to accomplish this.

The greatest and most important problem for us is the development of support for one another, as tribes, as organized groups, and as individuals. Some practical consideration as to the method of developing such support should be given. It is not enough simply to support one another, regardless of the quality of any program, or its administration. Support should be given after one is permitted the right to be consulted, to be informed, to be assured that there is a responsible intelligence at work. We must have a standard of leadership, and we must insist upon the highest standards. We should make it clear, to ourselves, to our own people, and to the general public, that leaders are chosen by the people, and that no one has a right to this status unless he is so chosen. This is an internal problem, and how we shall solve it is for ourselves to determine, and nobody else.

I would like to say that most of our so-called internal problems are not part of our heritage, nor are they part of our philosophy of human relations. To take one example—that of factionalism among Indian peoples and tribal groups. This is a condition that has been elevated by certain anthropologists and

Factionalism, as it is understood in the western sense, is not an Indian tradition. It was not a normal way of life for the Native American. It is a European influence, a result of the disruption of Indian life, standards, and of the total destruction of distinctive Indian tribal land bases. In OUR tradition, man lived in peace with his brothers. Only when tribe after tribe was pushed off their land into the land of another tribe, did inter-tribal conflict occur. The ideology of THIS type of European or western civilization and its influence must be wiped out of our Indian society if we are to survive and prosper, in any area of our lives.

I say, let us be aware of these influences. Let us put a stop to it. Let us DEFEND one another, protect and help one another in our relationships both individually and as a race. This is not to say that Indian people who are wrongdoers should be covered up for their evils. But surely we can handle these things ourselves. Not all Indians are noble . . . not all Indians are little red angels.

I think the time has come when we must consider the question of land usage, land development, and land reclamation— *as a whole.* It seems rather foolish to fight for the reclamation of land in purely general terms. It seems foolish, too, when one considers that many Indians are being forced to SELL, at lowest prices, their land, now currently held by tribes or individuals. A glance at the Pine Ridge or Rosebud situation is an example. These people have only a small fraction of their land left to them, and an effort should be made, to help them out of their poverty, to develop them economically, so that they are not confronted with the loss of their land. This too, is one of the questions which scholars, students, and tribal people should be able to discuss and develop programs about.

The Native American population is small, compared to that of the whole country. It would appear that efforts should be combined, expended wisely and with the greatest promise of effectiveness. I know there are some who have become stupefied with the public interest, the publicity, the headlines. By itself, it will not solve anything. Together with a sound program of change, it will help enormously.

Where shall we look for help, to cause a miracle of change to happen? Certainly not from the federal government. Neither the Eisenhower, the Johnson, nor to date the Nixon administration has developed a single effective and successful program leading to the practical improvement of our condition. We ourselves will have to take positive and effective action to make this change possible.

In this great effort, those who are scholars, those who are students, and those of us who are tribal activists, must unite all our energies and talents, so that the people may once again be the leading force in our lives and in our destiny.

Today's society is being torn apart by internal struggle.

There is destruction ahead. Already there are forces in motion, questioning the whole fabric of American society, questioning the form of government here in this country, struggling and fighting—but truly they don't know for WHAT, and often they don't even know WHY. This land is rotting to death. It is corrupt in so many ways and in so many places that water pollution is secondary to spiritual pollution.

Poverty is rampant in this nation, and the Indian is suffering most from this disease. I don't see any way to help, other than by our own people helping one another. We have to be aware of the current tumult in this land. *Every value* is being questioned, and many are already discarded like a dirty rag. The government that exists in peace today, may be confronted with questions of mere survival tomorrow. The society that has been happy with its porcelain bathtubs, its television sets, automobiles, and all the supposed comforts of life, is no longer happy to own an automobile and a television set, while also *being owned* by a finance company. In the intellectual world, the same turmoil is taking place, and perhaps even more. Because all the beliefs of western civilization are now being challenged. The honors that men receive with such gladness today, may well be the shame of tomorrow.

I think that the true Indian values, however, persist. And I am proud to know this, and to know that MY people still hold to their spiritual life and their love of their land. I believe in their deep and profound goals. I believe that WE INDIANS have more to offer this world than any other section of society.

2

American Indian Philosophy: Its Relation to the Modern World

ALFONSO ORTIZ
Assembly Presentation

WEBSTER'S dictionary defines *philosophy* as "the knowledge of the causes of all phenomena and matter." But it also defines it simply as "practical wisdom." My purpose today is to discuss with you that segment of American Indian philosophy known to me through experience and book learning . . . in this second sense, as practical wisdom, as providing assumptions or premises about the nature of reality. Since I may say little that most of you have not experienced, felt, or thought at one time or another, let me cast my hopes in the widest possible context, both in terms of the Convocation and in terms of what I see by my own set of premises about the nature of contemporary reality, to be the immediate future of our people. I come to this subject by a curious path. Most important, I guess, was my own growing sense of disenchantment at wandering around from Indian meeting to Indian meeting in which nothing was said about Indian philosophy and spiritual values after the invocation.

To me, it was like trying to define the nature of the iceberg from just the part that was above the water. Also, although I have taught in three colleges over four years, I have never, despite being an anthropologist as well as an Indian, offered a course on the American Indian. I have not done so, in part, because I have felt inadequate to the task of teaching such a course in the way I believe it should be taught. But I refrained, mostly, because I felt that neither the colleges involved, nor the students in those colleges, were ready for such a course. I felt it would be far too traumatizing to them, because if done right, it would force them to question not only their cherished values and beliefs, but perhaps the very point of their career plans. I have since changed my mind and shall attempt to teach such a course in the Fall. I would like to share with you my reasons for this change of mind and heart, because they set the tone for the remainder of my discussion.

The primary determinant was the very nature of the period in which we live. In these times, when, as one Time Magazine cover story laments, "nothing seems to work well anymore;" in these times of seemingly unending racial tensions, when non-Indian Americans shoot down their leaders, when urban people go hacking and coughing through their daily lives in the cities, and when the military of this nation has to lie about poisoning some sheep with nerve gas in Utah . . . when this same military, supposedly the most powerful machine for warfare the world has ever known, gets bogged down in a hopeless war with a tiny country in Southeast Asia; in these times, when, finally, the only clean air and water left in this country seems to be in the National Forests and on Indian reservations . . . then at long last, there seems to be emerging out of the collective American subconscious a realistic sense and recognition of both the tragic and the comic in life, of both the glories and the bear traps that comprise our common lot as human beings. With this recognition, White America can at last talk with Indian America with some hope of understanding. At long last, they know how it is. At long last, also, pure reasoning and technology no longer command everyone's faith as providing the best hope for solutions to all of our problems, much to the detriment of the nobler aspects of the human spirit. One detects a relaxation of the previous standards of blind headlong growth, unbridled dog-eat-dog competition construed not as setting goals from within, but as elbowing people out of the way as you try to win as many of life's things for yourself as possible, and of hoarding material goods as an end in itself.

I think all Indian people can understand and sympathize with the man who recently took a sledgehammer to a vending machine which had cheated him once too often. He seemed to be saying, "Enough! There must be something better than this!" Nowhere is this attitude more common than on college campuses, as a third of you delegates who are intimately involved with colleges know.

These are some of the reasons for my own change of mind and heart. The time has come for the spiritual heritage of America to be scrutinized closely for the profound insights it holds, if not for resolving some of these modern dilemmas, at least for understanding them more clearly. And make no mistake about this; modern America is at long last ready to listen to the "practical wisdom" of the Indian people, as well as to share in our spiritual heritage. Indeed, modern America desperately needs to listen and to share. As long as the attitude prevailed that only whites have religion while Indians have superstition, that only whites are civilized while Indians are primitive, that whites have beauty spots while Indians have warts, then one could reasonably ask, "Why bother? Why share any knowledge, however poor and incomplete it might be, of the loftier, more noble aspects of our common heritage?" We anthropologists cannot continue year after year mindlessly reciting in the classrooms our litany of Indian exotica and assorted trivia. This time is now at an end. Speaking as an anthropologist, the Indian people will no longer permit us to get away with it. Speaking as an Indian, the students will no longer permit anthropologists to get away with it. They need and demand far more. More important, they have access to first hand knowledge which sharply, disturbingly, runs counter to some of our most cherished anthropological assumptions about the nature of Indian reality. Two weeks ago, Thomas Banyacya, the Hopi man, came through here with a simple message of peace and gentleness. He found an enthusiastic response among all students who heard him, and he struck an enduringly responsive chord with his appeal for respect for nature, and with his urging that everyone return to basic spiritual truths to guide his life. As a result, a group of my students are laying plans for a gala "mother earth warming festival" to be held here in the spring. It will be one based on a composite model copied from various Indian spring fesitvals. Perhaps, the songs of the Delawares may yet be heard again in the woods around Princeton.

The point to all this is if it could happen here, in an institution which has not had more than two Indian students at a given time in almost two hundred years, in which the level of ignorance and unconcern about matters Indian was initially so profound that I regard my first year here on the faculty in retrospect as a lonely odyssey; if it could happen here, then it could happen anywhere.

Let me now turn to some examples of this practical wisdom, and examine them briefly in the light of contemporary events. Let me begin with the notion of tribe or tribalism, a notion which is being relentlessly drilled into the consciousness of both Indians and nonIndians these days, and yet one which is still so poorly understood by nonIndians. When Marshall McLuhan writes about it, he seems to mean one thing; when someone else writes about it in the context of Indian affairs, he seems to mean quite something else.

11

This being so, let me begin with the simple precept of Jeffersonian democracy: "That government is best which governs least." Translated into social science terminology, it would mean simply, "That social structure is best which is most unconfining." Unconfining in reference to the individual; unconfining in the sense that, while providing the security and comfort of the group, it leaves the individual with as much free rein as possible to create and realize his full potential as a human being. It is a vision of group existence in which hallowed notions such as freedom, personal autonomy, and responsibility are given expression in their purest forms.

I can pause here for some off the cuff examples. In the Pueblos where I grew up, there is very little need for parents to say "Don't!" And there is very little need for children to ask, "May I?" In every Pueblo language, these words are irrelevant. They have no point, because all Pueblo people have, to the best of my knowledge, the Indian belief that freedom is not theirs to give. There is also a striking passage in the writings of Standing Bear, a Sioux, to the effect that when he was eleven years old, recruiters came to his reservation from the Carlisle School in Pennsylvania. He decided to apply. He went by himself without telling anyone and without asking anyone. The recruiter, of course, would not accept his application because he didn't get permission from his parents. So they called his father, and his father said permission is not for me to give. "He is an individual. If he wants to go, he can go." It didn't matter that he was only eleven years old. This is the sort of thing I mean. In contemporary America, nonIndian America, these cherished notions such as freedom, responsibility, autonomy, seem to have been encrusted through centuries of misuse.

On another score, the question of whether individualism and tribalism are compatible, is one being agonized over these days. Let me state in this sense, Indians are said to be tribal, and whites are trying to become at least partially so. The signs seem to be all around us. The Hippies, the rock festivals, the growing popularity of communes, the pervasive sense of community among other minorities, members of common movements— even women and Wasps. These and others are cited as examples of the resurgence of some primeval, tribal soul, presumably inherent in us all—in all Americans anyway. In our discussion this afternoon, we might even consider the question of whether these and other contemporary phenomena are realistic, and whether they have anything in common with the ancient Indian sense of community.

I started with the Jeffersonian precept, because implicit in it is the premise that someone in those early days, at the birth of this country, must have known about some form of government somewhere which governed little, and yet which worked well; in which people were happy. As we all know, Indian tribal governments, particularly that of the Iroquois Confederacy, deeply influenced the original framers of the constitution. How deeply, we may never know, but the paths of American democracy and Indian tribal governments soon diverged completely in practice, and all of America has been the poorer for it. Thus, one of the ways in which current protests can be understood, is that they urge a return to a more ordered relationship between tribal values and the irreversible commitment to technological advancement. In this sense also, Indian models for this return are readily available, as they have always been, and many of the most reflective and visionary of American people are beginning to realize this, once they encounter it, if Princeton is any indication. This is true not only in the political sense, but in the quest for other life models as well. The process is just beginning; it may be that the Year of the Indian which people have been talking about at least since 1968 will carry through most of the decade. Indeed, if it is anybody's year—a long, long year—it is the Year of the Indian. One day, when we look back on it all, we may regard it as an even more serious threat to our survival than military force. That failed, but we can still be loved to death.

Let me just sample the remainder of my text, and thereby save something for our deliberations this afternoon. Let me try, simply, the notions of space and time. There is no Indian language of which I am aware that has abstract terms for the notions of space and time. Space is only meaningful as the distance between two points. Time is only meaningful as the interval between events. Yet, there are profound differences in the way these simple and basic notions are applied. So basic are they in fact that they underly all reality for all peoples. The general American view seems to be that empty space is intolerable. It must be filled with objects. It never ceases to amaze me how white Americans can never gaze upon a landscape without wanting to fill it with sheep, barns, plowed fields, or something else. They just can't seem to let it be; to just look at it and enjoy it for what it is. The tract homes which are now rapidly gobbling up the countryside are the most frightening aspect of it. Most Indian people can still let an "empty" landscape be, and enjoy it. Most of them can still infuse it with meaning and order without infusing it with objects. There is no compulsive need to make it useful. And the examples are legion. Those of you who come from the Southwest (and I only choose my examples from there, because that is my home), have been struck on entering a Pueblo, how you never know it's there until you are almost on top of it. Here is truly a human use of space. Every Pueblo seems to be planned and laid out very carefully. Even when you are talking about a place like Santo Domingo, which houses over two thousand people now, the very location and the way the buildings are constructed blends right into the landscape. In these times of urban blight, I think there are some very important lessons to be drawn here. Also, not to leave our numerous and good Navajo friends out of the picture here entirely, driving through the interior of the northern part of their reservation, I have never ceased to be impressed by this same thing—how difficult it is to find a hogan, how they are set off nicely in little pockets and blend right in with the landscape. Again, the magnificent knowledge of the use of space for habitation or other things. The interior, I note, is also so magnificently organized, that the wife and mother sitting before the fire cooking, can reach out and bring everything to her.

The next notion is time. Again, the general American view seems to be that if it is empty, it must be filled with activity, even if it is just busy work, or even if it becomes compulsive or neurotic. We seem to have lost—and I am afraid I include myself in this indictment—the ability to just be. This orientation, as you know, this attitude towards time has been one of the most enduring sources of misunderstanding between Indians and nonIndians in this country from the beginning. Even doctors have long believed that Indians are more impervious to pain, because Indian children just sit and look straight ahead when they are being vaccinated, or when they undergo other painful treatment. The question is, why jump up and down and scream about it? Sure it hurts, but yelling is not going to make it feel any better. Indians recognize this, but those who would presume to understand Indians attribute it all too often to racial differences.

Now, is this a different way of orienting ourselves to reality? Very different. Quite simply, Indian people know how to sit still and enjoy things. As Dorothy Lee points out in her *Freedom and Culture*, Indians also still know how to look even where there is "nothing" to see. Consider the use of words, which is another universal aspect of cultural reality, since we all use words. I am forcibly reminded of the magnificent parody done by Scott Momaday. Speaking through the Priest of the Sun, in his Pulitzer Prize-winning novel, "House Made of Dawn," he repeats the beginning of the story of Genesis: In the beginning was the Word and the Word was with God. The Priest of the Sun argues that Western man went wrong when he started compounding words. Words upon words, upon words, upon words. He should have left well enough alone, when he said in the beginning was the Word, and then contemplated the implications of what he said. Words should not be substituted for meaning, and I think Scott makes this point splendidly.

Again on the question of time, my tribal brother Herman Cata, who is also here at this Convocation, and I have both listened to an old storyteller back home in San Juan when we were growing up. When this old man sat down on a winter night and started reciting the oral narratives of the tribe, it was almost as if he were looking at a book on the ceiling, because when he got going, he could give forth with the most lucid prose, the most word-perfect display of memory, hour after hour, all night. It was said of him that when he sat down, lit up his hand-rolled cigarette, and looked up at the ceiling, it was as if there were a book up there, and he could turn the pages by flicking his eyelashes. For him and his listeners, truly, there was no time past, no time future, and no time present. All time was fused into one. He was reliving the traditions he was narrating. His words lived for him in a way that those of Western man no longer do. They had a pervasive and literal quality about them which is all but lost in the modern world. Of this Indian heritage of America, I think we can truly say that if there is any difference today, it is only that we are articulating it more. It is being discussed much more out in the open. We are more conscious of it, these assumptions about the nature of reality, gorging them up from tribal subconsciousness.

Other things, once over lightly. There is a group of theologians, we might call them "theologians of joy," who are urging a return to medieval models for worship and festivity, like what all tribal people in this country still have. They see as one of the great national needs, expressed primarily through the churches, to be a return to fantasy and celebration in life and worship. I ask simply, "Why?" Why go back all the way to the medieval ages for these models, for a source of inspiration, when people have been truly festive and having fun and fantasizing all around us in this country without interruption, for thousands and thousands of years. If only white America would look, there are plenty of home grown native models to serve as guides to strike a new balance between solemnity and joy in religion.

The most all-inclusive and convincing example of the sort of thing I am talking about is provided by an experimental program conducted in 1966 to teach traditional Navajos to make movies of themselves and their lives. This was conducted by Sol Worth of the University of Pennsylvania and John Adair, an anthropologist at San Francisco State College. Worth gave the Navajo people a minimum amount of technical instruction. The results, in seven films, are all fascinating from any number of perspectives. One in particular awakened a long-dormant understanding in me, in a very vivid rush of imagery. It was a fifteen-minute film on the sand-cast method of making silver jewelry, done by a community leader. The film starts out unexpectedly with a man leaving his hogan and walking through an open area at a leisurely pace, with many shots of the sky and trees interspersed. It continued in this way for several minutes, with all of us in the audience beginning to wonder what it all had to do with making silver jewelry. Suddenly, the man came to an open pit, took out a paper bag from his hip pocket, unfolded it, and put some small stones from the backfill into it. He then returned to the hogan, left this bag of ''nuggets,'' and started out again, this time to get some sandstone blocks for the mold. By the time he returned home a second time and we get to the presumed subject matter of the film, we have scarcely a minute left. This was a fifteen-minute film, and for fourteen minutes he was just walking about and doing seemingly unrelated things. But as you know, the challenge here is to stand back and ask what does all this mean? The question is, just what was going on here? Surely, it was not accidental, since the maker was in complete charge of editing the film. Rather, it demonstrates a completely different view of reality, a completely different style of orienting oneself to reality from the Western norm. Whereas we have come to expect a man sitting at his bench, casting jewelry by a series of carefully demarcated steps, we are instead, shown a man gathering the material and the sky and trees; on nature itself. It did not matter to him, when told that silver had never been mined on the reservation. How myopic we have become in forgetting this! There is a forceful reminder for Indian and nonIndian alike. As one of my students observed in an uncharacteristic moment of cynicism, a nonIndian film maker would have devoted fourteen and a half minutes to depicting the silversmith trying to peddle his products.

As I conclude here, many of you may be thinking: ''All right, this guy has told us how good we are. Now we shall have to go out into the rain again and face reality.'' I submit that I have spoken about reality, the most enduring kind of reality, because it has sustained and survived, despite everything that American and European civilization has thrown at us for almost four centuries. It is this kind of reality, based on thousands and thousands of years of experimentation and observation, that modern Americans have ignored through short-sightedness, much to their discredit. The simple fact is not recognized that for many, many problems, this Indian view of reality can hold so much more—for eliminating modern dilemmas. But that, of course, is not our primary concern here. Nor is this a pipe dream because, as you know, anything which is thinkable and enduring, anything that is conjured up in a logical and coherent fashion by the mind of man can be attained. As we go forth now, and proceed to consider the pressing and immediate prob-

lems facing all of our people—in education, economic development, health, discrimination, and others—let us not forget the
philosophical and spiritual values which underly them all and
which in the end, must help guide their solution.

In the larger context, nonIndian America would be wise to
turn to the Indian for guidance. Mankind needs what most of
us have kept only in our hearts until the present time.

Are you ready to share it?

DISCUSSION

American Indian Philosophy and its Relation to the Modern World

Alfonso Ortiz, *Chairman*

JEANNETTE HENRY: I would like to raise a question in
connection with your presentation, Dr. Ortiz. I think your
presentation is perhaps primarily concerned with the philosophy
of the Tewa people. However, I would agree that many general
concepts would apply to most if not all Native American tribes.
I think, too, that perhaps some distinction might be made as
to just when, or at what period in our cultural history, such
ideas persisted, and such concepts held. Too, what remains in
the present philosophy of the people? What has been corrupted,
changed, distorted? I think a comprehensive study of Indian philosophy is long overdue, and I don't know of such a study, do
you? I know that during the course of man's history, any period
of sharp or revolutionary change was always preceded by very
basic and profound conflicts in philosophical theory. Such change
is now upon us in this era, and I do not see any basic or profound dialogue in philosophical concept. It would be most valuable too, if some study were made, of a comparative nature,
of concepts held by original Indian tribes or peoples, and those
held by other societies throughout world history.

ALFONSO ORTIZ: There isn't such a study as you indicate.
I would restate my message in this way, however. In times of
stress and turmoil, values or philosophical precepts—call them
what you will—assume center stage in the national consciousness.
I believe that the rape of the environment, of nature, goes hand
in hand with the rape of the human spirit. The devastation of
our natural resources is followed closely by the devastation of
the human spirit. Rupert said, and I agree, that there is a great
spiritual hunger and drought in the country, and I think we can
supply part of what is missing with our heritage.

17

RICHARD WEST: I was wondering, in terms of trying to relate it to other concepts, if you could comment on what you might have discovered as to what the Indians feel of man's relationship to nature. As an example, they see themselves as a part of nature, as opposed to the basically white European and Christian doctrine based on Genesis, in which man is supposed to dominate.

ALFONSO ORTIZ: One of the underlying premises here is that we have never been a people to export our beliefs or to force them on anyone. This is a very basic problem, yes, but I think other people are examining their beliefs, and we are in this together with our many nonIndian friends. This is the only country we've got, and we can't push each other out of existence. We have to share what we each have, and we have something that is desperately needed in the modern world. That is my belief. That is why I wrote a book despite the fact that I knew half the councilmen in my tribe would get mad at me. It's the kind of decision each one of us has to make for himself.

RICHARD WEST: I would like to restate the question. I was asking what information you found on the Indian's view of man. What his nature is. Because from what I found, it's very different from those held by the white Christian church, as to the doctrine of man, or the nature of man.

ALFONSO ORTIZ: Nothing, really. I think I understand what you mean, although I am not a philosopher but an anthropologist, and I am discussing philosophy as practical wisdom. But I don't know of any clearly formulated doctrines of man in the Indian literature with which I am familiar. Philosophical speculation seems to be applied to other problems.

RICHARD WEST: Isn't the role in which he defines himself on the same terms as being part of his environment?

ALFONSO ORTIZ: Yes. There was a quotation I was looking-for. A very haunting and moving statement made by an Eskimo. Perhaps I can recapture it from memory: "No bears have come because there is no ice, and there is no ice because there is no wind, and there is no wind because we have offended the powers . . ." Very introspective, inward looking, and all-inclusive. This illustrates what you just said. Perhaps a better example of this, in these days of talk about the environment, is one based on my personal experiences: Our people in the Rio Grande Valley of New Mexico have long been worrying about the atomic research center at Los Alamos, which is near our area in the mountains. We note with increasing dismay that the bullfrogs and crickets no longer chirp along the Rio Grande, and certain kinds of birds no longer come, since the establishment of the atomic facility there. We note that there are only a few species of desirable fish left in the Rio Grande. This is a continuous process, and yet our older people blame themselves, saying these things happen because we do not live according to tradition anymore. They do not blame Los Alamos. To me it's obviously Los Alamos, because among the hills around Los Alamos they have technical labs dug into the canyons, where they seem to work around the clock. You can't see them, and no one knows precisely where they are because they are fenced off. They may have radiation dumping areas also. But it is precisely in this area that there are great groups of pine and pinon trees dead, or dying. There is something happening here, something very sad, very mysterious, and very unusual.

When we were small, and we went to sleep at night, we listened to the sounds of the bullfrogs and the crickets along the Rio Grande. It was like an exchange of choral groups at night. They are all gone now, but we just blame ourselves.

RICHARD WEST: In talking about the concept of space, do you have any thought as to how one might apply the Indian concept of space and society to where it is urban and there are large concentrations of people?

ALFONSO ORTIZ: Take a close look at Habitat '67, erected for the Montreal World's Fair. It is but a picture of North Pueblo, at Taos. It's just a crooked version of a multi-story Pueblo house block, and these go back well over a thousand years. This is the most concise answer I can give you. Beyond that, there are experiments going on in cities to create smaller, face to face neighborhoods. Obviously, the means of production is not and cannot be localized there, as it was in the Pueblos. This is why I say that we cannot get the technological monster off our back. But the question is, is technology incompatible with tribalism? Will technology prevent us from sustaining at least some tribal values?

GARY KIMBALL: Sir, are you suggesting that this process by which tribal thought is developed is intuitive, or are you suggesting that it might be economy of intuition, and say it's illogical? A second question. How can you reconcile your answer with the concept that . . . and I will give you an example, Einstein's final conclusion in relativity was reached by intuition alone, as was reported in Time magazine?

ALFONSO ORTIZ: On the first question, is it intuitive? I would like to rephrase that: Does it have to be expressed and explained with words, through words? There is no need, when you have a tribal society, to respond always with words, but everyone subscribes to it and believes anyway. It is only through years and years of what I found to be a very exacting intellectual discipline that I was able to stand back and see the broad contours of a Tewa philosophy and express it in words. But, you see, I react to the word "intuitive" only because on one hand it can mean that perhaps it can't be used by anyone else, or communicated outside the group. We just have to bring it up to consciousness and make it comprehensible to others. I think that is the real question. Now, on the second part of your question, I have no reaction at all.

GARY KIMBALL: Well, sir, the only reason I proposed it is because by an intuitive process we develop wisdom. It seems to me that we are in a tough bind to explain that when Einstein was asked, how it was that he did it, he said—through intuition, because I think it would be correct to say that Einstein's contention is that the apex of our technological thrust is based on intuition.

ALFONSO ORTIZ: Actually, you're saying something very profound. It's even more sustaining as a tribal way. Let me reach it from another angle. Let's not forget that it's based on centuries and centuries of experimentation and contemplation and so on. To go back to the Pueblos, most of them have been where they are since the 13th century. They have not been occupying the same villages, but the same general vicinity. Can we assume that they have learned nothing about the nature of reality, about the nature of nature, about the nature of man, and about harmony with all things, human and non-human? Even beings without life in the conventional sense? We have to presume that they have, before we are ready to believe anything else about them.

DICK WILSON: I have seen the area, from the south of Albuquerque. Getting back to this statement about seeking solutions or accenting the calamities from the dying of pine trees, disappearance of bull frogs, crickets and so forth, this brings up a question. Isn't that sort of thing self-defeating? Who is going to stop them from drilling deep holes into the earth? It all sounds very impossible, but the truth of the matter is, we have got to stop it.

ALFONSO ORTIZ: Well, it scares the hell out of me, too. I left out a whole list of other examples of this kind of thing. I agree with you. The technological monster is something we have to live with. You know, there are even inflatable communes now. Madison Avenue and technology pick up what is a very good idea and mass produce it. And in so doing, it's probably going to defile it and render it useless for the purposes of people getting back together again.

CHARLES LOLOMA: I don't want to get out of here without making this statement: Generally, the whites do not know what they want. And, in not knowing what they want, and the direction in which they are going, they have unbalanced completely earth and its natural ways. What anybody can do about it is something else. Their solution seems to be that a person thinking about these forces or their correction, has to change his ways. Otherwise the sun can't shine through the earth anymore.

ALFONSO ORTIZ: We have a lot of points in this area to discuss, and we shall be looking for you in particular, Charles, to inform us as far as you can, about the truth among the Hopi people.

(At this time, a recess for lunch was called.)

ALFONSO ORTIZ: Let us proceed with our discussion. The best part of this presentation, which now becomes a panel discussion, is that I can abandon this chair, and let somebody else make a statement.

WILFRED WASSON: I am from Washington State College. This morning, you stated that you hadn't taught Indian courses. And for the last two years, I have been experimenting, trying to teach an Indian course, in contemporary Indians in the United States. Primarily, teaching the teachers who are working with Indian children. Of course, my aim has been to change their attitudes and opinions. What you were speaking of this morning was probably the problem I ran into, because there is a difference in value systems between Indian and nonIndian. I find a great deal of difficulty in discussing values. I think it's primarily because all of my life, no one around me has valued the things that I value. Therefore, I have had to hide my values inside, rather than have people laugh at them. This has become so set with me, that I can't verbalize things. But then, somebody brought up that perhaps you can't verbalize values. Perhaps this is an abstraction that you cannot describe. One of the problems I run into is teachers wanting me to list Indian values. They want it all packaged, set out nice and neat for them, so that they can go back and refer to it. I can't do that.

ALFONSO ORTIZ: I concur. Let me expand in one new direction on what you just said. It is this: I've seen many non-Indian audiences addressed, particularly in California, by a really fiery Red Power type and, you know I think nonIndian Americans have become so mesmerized in being insulted that many of them actually enjoy it. This is frightening, you know. They would rather be insulted than informed or intellectually stimulated. Again, another reason for re-ordering our sense of reality itself, we are trying to find new areas of reality. It's incredible to me, and frightening, when a thousand people are insulted left and right. . . four letter words and so on . . . and then stand up afterwards and applaud. But, I use the word "mesmerized" because I think that it really doesn't touch them inside.

A SPEAKER: It doesn't cost them any money.

ALFONSO ORTIZ: It's a great game.

A SPEAKER: In a sense, are they applauding a performance for violence, or . . . ?

ALFONSO ORTIZ: Maybe so. Like our sun dances, pow-wows, corn dances and squaw dances. It seems to be the same kind of thing to them, except it's in the violence. This is Ken Hale, a linguist from Massachusetts Institute of Technology.

KEN HALE: I don't know where to begin, but all kinds of things that I have been thinking about for the last two years have to do with the kind of linguistics I do. I am known as a "methodological linguist," that is, a linguist that works in all kinds of languages. For about ten years, I have been fascinated by American Indian languages. But I have been bothered by the fact that only recently have I come to focus on what I think the problem is. It's a matter of fact that in the study of American Indian languages, a field that has associated with it a great deal of honor and so forth, most of the honor has gone to outsiders. It hasn't gone to the American Indians. More recently, I have looked at it from a purely linguistic point of view, and discovered that even from that point of view, from the science of linquistics, we are going to have to change the situation. I think maybe it's too much to ask the American Indian community to actually transform our society for us. I think we have plenty of models, the American Indian communities serve as an excellent model for a society I would like to see. What's going to have to happen is that the Anglo community will have to recognize what its real interests are and attempt to adequately reform or change this society that we live in. For that reason, the answer for a lot of people is in radical politics.

SPARLIN NORWOOD: I read in *The Indian Historian* about the linguistics program at M.I.T. I am Cherokee from Oklahoma. We are studying our language now, and we are finding great difficulty. The alphabet or syllabary — 86 sounds — is learned, and then phrases are learned. Somebody comes along who supposedly knows how to speak it, but it's ending up phonetic, rather than the language that has beauty and feeling. The Eastern Cherokee, for instance, will dispute the way we talk in Oklahoma. We think we're right, and they think they're right.

A SPEAKER: We're both right.

ALFONSO ORTIZ: That's the way it is. But how do we get people involved with M.I.T. in the program?

KEN HALE: It's something I would like to see. Last year, I brought a friend to M.I.T. from the Papago community who worked with me. He taught me how this would work. When I first thought of bringing him there and teaching him something about formal linguistics, I conceived the idea of getting up to the blackboard and saying this is a phoneme and so forth. But it became evident that this wasn't going to work, and what we should do is to use *his* knowledge and let *him* figure out the best way to develop a program for the study of his own language. I think the answer resides in the communities. They have to make certain decisions. This has happened in other parts of the world where there are differences in pronunciation, where they had to settle the question of dialects. The vocabulary differs also in many cases. It may be necessary to settle definitely on a common dialect or two. Or to have conferences with people from different areas in order to arrive at such decisions. They decide for the purposes of technical literature, let us say, what the language is going to be, what form to develop. What I tried to do was to give my friend an idea of what the problems were, what it means for different dialects to be spoken, and that very often this is a matter of regular rule. Changes can be stated once for all. You can pick up a writing system, for example, to which that rule can apply, and some people speaking other dialects can learn the rule and convert it to their own dialect. This doesn't solve the problem of vocabulary difference. There you have to make some decisions as to what terms will be used for the community at large. It takes a long time, quite often. But what is so encouraging is that people are facing this problem at all, really thinking about it, using the language.

A SPEAKER: Are you suggesting then, that a standard kind of usage or dialect for a given Indian language could emerge on the basis of a series of conferences? Among people such as the Eastern Cherokee and Western Cherokee . . . so that when Cherokee talk in their language, there is some kind of an agreement on standard usage, as we have in English? Or as the French have?

KEN HALE: Not quite. I think the solution has to be decided by the communities. It may be appropriate for Eastern Cherokee to do one thing and the Western to do another. I didn't address myself to the question of how the language should be taught in the schools, because I have some ideas of my own about that. It goes something like this: I think one very good way to do it is particularly in the areas where the people speak the language, to develop the teaching materials themselves. I think in the case of Navajo, for example, the best material will probably be drawn out of the actual teaching situation. I don't know how to face the problem in areas where people no longer speak the language.

A SPEAKER: I think you're talking about a very complicated thing, and I know very little about it. But I am interested in it. Are you talking about a partnership arrangement between an anthropological linguist and a native speaker? But even the native speaker couldn't work constructively with his linguist unless there was some agreement on the part of his own people as to what the language should be.

KEN HALE: You see, you're asking an extremely difficult question. But these languages are being initially introduced and some of the colleges and universities I know are showing an interest. How do you design a program of this nature? My answer is that when you bring a person in to learn something about linguistics, that in the course of working with that person the program will develop. I found that in one situation, the native linguist began to structure the program, and taught me a tremendous amount. The idea as to how it should develop should, of course, have come from him in the first place. So I would be led to suggest that there should be this kind of open structure.

A SPEAKER: In terms of the relationships and emotions of our language, they are obvious. I would like to know my tribal language. What about the mainstream, instrumental, or practical Anglo-Saxon advantages? If you want to sell a program, you must get it funded and so forth. How would you construct a program with justification for a broad development of Indian language training?

KEN HALE: This is something I might be able to answer. It's been demonstrated that the use of native language in schools, for example, is not detrimental at all, but helpful. I think, personally, that the ultimate answer to the question of maintaining and strengthening American Indian languages really has to do with fundamental changes in the so-called mainstream, and that's a long, long struggle.

A SPEAKER: You're working with Indian languages. I would like to see someone do a study of the way Indians speak English, because there is a great lack of communication between Indian students and teachers. Quite frequently, the way in which a question is phrased will give it a specific meaning, and one which is lost on the teacher. There is a lot of non-verbal communication among white people that's lost on Indian students.

KEN HALE: There is some work being done in this direction.

A SPEAKER: I am speaking of using a completely different language. Using the same words. The English that was learned from Indian parents with Indian concepts and thought patterns behind them. It isn't the same linguistic pattern.

KEN HALE: Yes. I was speaking from the other point of view, Anglo teachers turning students on and off without the message. If you look at it from a detached point of view, that's very true.

ALFONSO ORTIZ: Jeannette, would you like to come down and give a spirited statement, as I am sure you will?

JEANNETTE HENRY: I would like to come back to philosophy. I oppose the position of Mr. Kimball, who stated something about intuitive, instinctive development in Indian philosophy. In the first place, I think it's improper when you talk about philosophy and the American Indian to consider it as though it was one smooth concept or system of thought. It is not so. I think you will find there is considerable diversity among various tribal entities, as to how they view themselves in relation to nature, and how they view nature in relation to man . . . and how they view the nature of man in general. It's a philosophical concept, certainly, but you cannot put the whole thing in one bag. The way the Navajo consider themselves, and have considered themselves in relation to nature is just not the same as the concepts of other tribes . . . the Cherokee, the Sioux, the Iroquois, as examples.

The second point I would like to make, is that if you consider a philosophical concept as an instinctive thing, or an intuitive thing merely, you fall into the category of the Anglo historian, who has degraded Indian life, Indian thought and Indian contributions in areas apart from those of material culture. Indian contribution in thought was considerable. If you explain this contribution as an intuitive one, well, so are animals instinctive . . . intuitive. What else is meant by the concept of the "noble savage," so highly advertised by concerned Anglos? This "noble savage" is just a glorified animal. Over the thousands and thousands of years of our development, thought has been as painful a developmental process as the working of the soil or the utilization of the land, or material products of the land. This does not come instinctively, intuitively. It comes as the result of the development of man in his highest and most complex nature, side by side with his material or technological development, if you will. The Indian, when he was first seen by Europeans, was a highly complex human being. If this is understood, you are confronted with the fundamental error of the Anglo historian who is capable of putting the Indian in a separate bag because he is presumed to have merely an intuitive philosophy . . . not a very superior mental development.

A SPEAKER: I think I can defend Mr. Kimball this way: That while Indian thought patterns are not biologically inherent, they are learned; the way you view the world is learned from your parents at a very early age. To this extent, it acts in the same way as something that is biologically inherited. As it acts the same way in an Indian because it is learned so early, this is why the Bureau of Indian Affairs failed in their attempt to stamp out Indian culture by sending Indian children off to boarding schools at an early age, to educate them out of being Indian. It failed, because these patterns had already been set.

ALFONSO ORTIZ: Hold on. I think you raised another thorny issue, for which I would like to take you on myself.

HERB BLATCHFORD: I think our struggle in trying to get at the root of an oral philosophy might be meaningful in a broader sense. It has revealed a tremendous amount of technical knowledge which may or may not be applied according to who is revealing the application. But when things were brought up about values, it seems to meet the very confused source of languages. In place of it, we have learned to use "customs" instead of "values," because the whole concept of what man is in relation to his environment and his ecological counterparts brings together certain things that we know are concrete. We know it. The meaning of certain rituals are not known very much beyond our own group, yet we know them and whether we can express this knowledge is another piece of linguistics. When we talk beyond the point of mentality, we don't know what else to call it, because it's an intangible part of reality. That intangible, using the English language, is a pretty messy affair. But when you go beyond this, the actual native disciplines of leadership, of medicine, social custom . . . you find that they definitely have a method that goes beyond this intangible point, because the European ethic is saying, so far, that they believe in something objective. If you are not objective, then you are subjective. But the real life of the fact is that the fulfilled method of dividing up all concepts in Indian reality tend to follow. They start from a tangible point of view and work towards the intangible, while the European method would start from the "objective" the physical being, then the mental being, then you crop out to infinity.

When we talk about spiritual discipline, we are not talking about religion. The simple fact that you have to tie your shoe and to put your clothes on in the morning: These are basic beliefs that come from discipline, where Indian people have been labeled for years as historically unbending in situations. They will not get involved in these anxiety games, is really what is behind this, that these Europeans feel to be so necessary. But I can see more and more out of our training processes that we are working from a point of intangibility to a point of tangibility, and when you finally get to the mentality, this is where the discipline comes out of our ritual practices. We understand them, and it's difficult to get anybody else to understand, who is not part of the custom out of which these rituals grew. And so, consequently, because we don't understand them, we play them down. Or the academic gods or groups tend to play them down, because *they* don't understand them. Yet it seems to me there is a completely ordered system out of tradition, that has gone from a spiritual base to a mental base, and to a point of physical reality.

ALFONSO ORTIZ: One quick question. Would you include, when you say to the kids at home . . . you are working with spiritual things, (you say they head the list), would you also include in this—under the spiritual umbrella, having fun, playing? You say they include everyday kinds of things, everyday spiritual values and realities . . . shall we say, commonsense mysticism, like the implications of waking up in the morning?

HERB BLATCHFORD: It is part of it. Festivity is part of this release of the spirit. To be a spirit, rather than a mental thing, or to be a physical thing. Or even linked to a mental thing. If you want to get entirely intuitive about it. But one thing we found out, probably has the greater survival value to the Indian. Whatever has been done with him, they always kept him in a group, and they haven't been able to break up that group very well. But leave the job to a group, and let them do it as a group, as an extension of their clans and an extension of their families. If you can keep that matter of spirituality together, then your function seems to be in an efficient area which you can work with. But in European ethics, you're dealing with something else.

BILL BYLER: I think the speaker may not have wanted to identify as closely as the statement here identifies them. The thought is not biologically derived intuition, but rather intuition may be something that . . . taking whatever evidence is available . . . makes imaginative and experimental solutions, and then tries these out against reality. If it works, that's a working intuition. I think all peoples move this way, and perhaps this is really the only way for basic or scientific progress, for social change.

ALFONSO ORTIZ: To that I can only add, that I reacted in the way I did because the image that was conjured up in my mind was of something that was much more individual and capricious and hard to pin down. Very possibly it's reality such as space or time. You almost have to begin with those, because they comprise two of the primary axis of orientation to reality for all peoples. That's why philosophers are spending so much time with notions such as these. And I reacted, because for it to be useful, for it to be transformed into a driving force for constructive social change, for the forming of a new kind of identity appropriate to new kinds of circumstances, it must be derived from the old, sustained by the old. But if you have to do this, you have to have the kinds of precepts which are shared and historically transmitted. Ideal with what I like to think as a philosophy, with thought that takes place out there in the market place, in the fields, and where women gossip, rather than in some murky private sanctuary.

ROSALIE NICHOLS: I have two points. The first is to ask, are you suggesting that the Indian philosophy be accepted, let's say, by young Indians and also by nonIndians, because it is better, or because it is traditional? Secondly, if the Indian culture is the result of learning from parents as this gentleman here suggested, which is, in other words, purely traditional, what allowance does is make for innovation, and how do you expect something like the Iroquois Confederacy to fit in? Where and how was that learned?

KEN HALE: I wasn't saying that these things are taught, but they are learned. They are not taught by parents; they are learned by children from parents. A child from the time he's born, sees his parents acting in a certain way, towards certain relatives, towards certain things, towards animals, the world around him. He learns to act in the same way.

ROSALIE NICHOLS: Isn't the learning an acting process of the individual, whereby he decides what is good and what is bad, what's right and what's wrong, out of what's presented to him? He doesn't necessarily have to accept something just because his parents tell him or show him that particular way. He sees that it's good. He senses it. If he thinks it's bad, he rejects it.

KEN HALE: Most children are going to accept the way their parents do things as good. It isn't conscious learning. I wouldn't give our value systems . . .

ROSALIE NICHOLS: You don't think anybody ever thinks?

KEN HALE: I mean, did you think . . .

ROSALIE NICHOLS: I think.

KEN HALE: But do you think and decide how you want to view the world?

ROSALIE NICHOLS: I think we do that all the time.

KEN HALE: Or basically competitive or cooperative with other people?

ROSALIE NICHOLS: I think and I have thought about this continually.

A SPEAKER: Since when?

ROSALIE NICHOLS: Two years old.

A SPEAKER: Five years old.

A SPEAKER: Luckily, I wasn't raised in an authoritarian enviornment. I was encouraged to think. Of course, you may say otherwise, but I think when you accept something, you must accept it on the basis that it can be validated, it's in accordance with reality; secondly, is it logically validated. Third, if the first and second points are true, then it is reality. You should be able to demonstrate it by putting it into action and making it work.

A SPEAKER: This is why it is natural for children, because it does work. It is in accordance with reality for their parents, because it does work for them.

A SPEAKER: But this is tradition, and we ought to believe in it, because it is tradition. This is the way Indian life is. Indian culture is very much alive.

JEANNETTE HENRY: I feel that our religion is not providing our young people with the directions they need. Our Indian religion braces us up to a certain point and leaves us dangling there. Maybe it's because of that, we have a high alcoholic rate and a high suicide rate. Those who can move into other religions, don't seem to have that problem, because they are filling this gap that you might say Catholics and Protestants provide, while our Indian religion, because we don't intellectualize it and we don't consciously teach it, regresses. It just brings us up to a certain point.

A SPEAKER: It depends on why you move into another religion. Do you accept it because it makes more sense, or do you accept it because your particular authoritarian background proves inadequate, so you turn to some other and hope it will work entirely?

ALFONSO ORTIZ: I think that, perhaps we go into alternative religions or belief patterns, because we have not understood why there might have been a few stumbling blocks in the way for a matter of years. So we try another avenue. We say, well, we will use any method, but we will still use this as a jumping off point, because the Indian tradition is still the springboard to whatever point they want to reach. I think the biggest question they are answering is: Is it functional or not?

A SPEAKER: Not in just the material sense.

A SPEAKER: But, is it pragmatic in the sense that the Europeans would use it?

A SPEAKER: Right. As a discussion point?

ALFONSO ORTIZ: There is something else. I dispute any contention that it must be capable of being rendered intelligible, be validated, that it be logical and coherent and so on. Who are the people who have had the greatest ideas? The mystics, the dreamers. We are in such a pickle these days that I think we need some dreamers. I don't think we have exhausted reality and I don't think we have rendered everything very logical, rational, useful, coherent, and verifiable.

A SPEAKER What is real?

ALFONSO ORTIZ: What is reality? You read a book, regardless of its real use. You read a book like Carlos Castaneda; some say it's a product of his mind, rather than being "real." I don't know. But the question is not really pertinent. I believe that because it was thinkable, it's real. Here is at least a glimpse of a completely different reality.

A SPEAKER: Reality that exists, or reality that somebody imagines?

JEANNETTE HENRY: What's the difference?

SAM DELORIA: We have a whole bunch of people here who make a good living off anthropology and linguistics. Reality is completely conditioned by your world views from the beginning, by the language you speak and by attitudes you pick up, you don't necessarily know how. To talk about authoritarianism and traditions and customs as if it's a complete blank up to one day, when Granny brings you in and sits you down and starts to teach you the world view, and says, "This is reality," is unreal. Then there is some way to make an objective decision. She's right or she's wrong about reality. All that is nonsense. I am surprised that all these guys that make their living in this field haven't brought this up. Why the hell have they been studying Indians all this time?

SAM BILLISON: I don't know if this is a valid question or not, but are you insinuating that philosophy should change after you leave the native base, which is the reservation? In the case of the Navajo, I don't think you can theorize that the Navajo philosophy changes. This, to me, is all theory. I don't know whether it's philosophical or what it is. But what you stated was that once you leave the reservation, you have a different philosophy. You mentioned Indianism and Pan-Indianism. What are you talking about?

ALFONSO ORTIZ: That's a strange notion. I, myself, still don't understand that. But this is the sort of thing I mean: I tried to get Charles Loloma to give the invocation last night. He wouldn't do it because he couldn't do it. He was out of the Hopi world. It would have been invalid. You, as Navajo, Sam, have the belief that your world is enclosed by four sacred mountains, and as Tewa, we do too. There was a time when, if you went out of this area, you had to purify yourself. You were in alien land, the "non-world," occupied by non-people, and so forth. You were in a perpetual state of danger and pollution. If you have this concept, it's kind of a neatly bound world, and everything is in order within it, and if you go outside of it, obviously you are going to have to change your idea of where your world ends, and of its boundaries.

SAM BILLISON: I would rather think that if I leave the reservation, I leave the Navajo philosophy there, and I pick up a new philosophy which is Anglo. I won't insist that this is a continuation of Navajo philosophy, because I don't think you can read about Navajo philosophy.

ALFONSO ORTIZ: You have another very powerful point there, Sam. You see, it comes down to individual choice. The only reason I raise the other point is that people don't seem to be doing it. They are trying to. The Indians are not melting into the cities. They refuse to melt or drift into the middle class.

DON WANATEE: You covered quite a span of subjects here, but I would like to say this: Language is important to the Indian, because it's the basis of what he is. In my tribe back home, we still practice our old native religion, we still have our medicine man—but we are losing these because of loss of our language. We have to go to a white man in Washington to find out what our language is, what we have lost. Dr. Voorhees, at the Smithsonian Institution, is the expert in the Algonquian stock. The Kickapoos have a more archaic language than we do. sometimes we can't even understand them. The Mesquakies have all but lost their language now, except for the older ones. I think language is important to all existing tribes which have still retained their traditional values. I hope some day we can get back our school at Tama, Iowa, where I come from, so that we can educate our children, because they have been told not to speak Indian in the public schools. "It has no value," is the reason given. Whatever philosophy it is you're looking for, you will find it there. Every year, most of the traditional tribes are beginning to stir. You can hear the drums; you can almost see the fires. I think this is what most Indian tribes in the United States are wanting to go back to. This is a good sign. I have nothing against Christianity. I respect it. As a matter of fact, every year the whole tribe gathers in an old rundown school building operated by the Bureau of Indian Affairs.

We gather together as a tribe, to celebrate for somebody whom we pay respect to every year. But do you see what people gathering together means? A whole town gathering together in one big building to celebrate? I think this is what I am trying to say, that our religions, regardless of whether they are being taught in one language or another, have a value. And they form some sort of a philosophy that you can live by, be a person by. The Mesquakies know back home what I am talking about. I carry with me all the time the Indian tobacco that has been given to the Indians long ago, even from the time we came from around the Quebec area. We migrated, and through the entire migration, we still kept our medicine mugs. Some of them we have lost completely, but I think through fasting, through prayers, we can get them back. And possibly through self- re-education. Because I think one of these days, even the white men will turn against each other, for religious reasons. I am not speaking for the entire tribe; this is what I believe myself.

ALFONSO ORTIZ: You know what Chief Joseph replied when he was told that various missionaries were coming to work on his reservation. He said, "No. You will not send them. You are not going to teach us to fight about God. You have taught us to fight about everything in this world. You are not going to teach us to disagree about God, about what is in the next world."

FATHER BROWN: I was just going to toss my two cents into this thing. About a year ago, we had a meeting in Denver. The B.I.A. called together about thirty Indians, to listen to what they had been doing to try and revise the social studies in the Indian schools. Two questions were discussed: One was the Indians in the cities and the other was some of their BIA schools, and some in Oklahoma, where they have different tribes and so on, and their experience at the school in Santa Fe, different religions and different art forms and so on. They were trying to teach Indian youth in a place like Santa Fe, where they were encouraging them to keep their own cultures. The anthroplogists call it a cultural program. Well, they read all these things to us for a while and we were supposed to make comments. Dr. Dozier and Mr. Costo were there, and immediately pointed out the difficulties in the so-called concepts. The approach of these BIA people who were drawing up the curriculum revision, categories of thought, and questions they asked, were all out of their white, middle class experience, rather than out of the Indian experience. Mr. Costo pointed out that the Indian and his cultures didn't appear in these curriculum proposals. He said that no Indian kid could be computer-programmed and it just wouldn't work. While they could be considered in certain cultural areas, the tribes remain unique. They discussed what happens when the Indians move out of their environment. Is he supposed to say, "We do like they do in Los Angeles; in Rome, you know, do as the Romans do?" As though there was something wrong with that Indian, or he wasn't objectively real. That wasn't the idea at all, in moving to an urban area. At least, it shouldn't be, although in the Anglo tradition, that is the case. They say, that which is objective is valid if it's been written, not just spoken. So they would label the Indian "without a valid culture," because he did not have a written language. The Anglos are as out of touch with reality as though they were in an insane asylum. Indians recognize from other tribes those things that might have a different viewpoint, and be of a different tradition. Whereas, in the colleges, which follow the European tradition, no differentiation is made. A culture is an absolute thing. With us as Indians, of course, one tribe will see it one way, another will see things quite differently.

The Anglo schools are trying to prove that all they have to do is to find a common denominator among Indians and tribes. While, for purposes of classification, this is nice and tidy, it is not true to life. A good many studies have been made about cross-cultures. They aren't valid. We have an entirely different approach. The Indians, regardless of tribe, were in themselves a whole people, not only in their intellect, but in their imagination, in every way. As one example, they would cooperate rather than compete. They talked, at this conference, all *around* the main question, which was WHAT to teach in the BIA schools, the content of the subject areas. We insisted on finding out what kind of *content* they were going to put into the courses.

I saw a big report put out by a team sent out to check on the Navajo Rough Rock school. Even before they left home, they knew what they would be looking for. Well, they reported their findings. The Navajos disagreed, and made their own evaluation. Finally the University of Minnesota issued a report reviewing both. Their conclusion was that the members of the first group were victims of cultural shock. As one example of what happened: The school had brought in parents to work in the dormitories. One of the kids had an earache. The first team reported that the parents were very callous, because they just watched the child and walked out of the room. After awhile a nurse came in and took care of the child. The team thought that was terrible. Any kind-hearted person would have done something for the child! On the other hand, the Navajo report pointed out that Navajos have their own people to take care of such sickness. But the Public Health Service had told them to leave it to the doctor and nurse. So they didn't interfere. But they were actually working on the case. However, this team just "observed," and what they saw, they misinterpreted.

ALFONSO ORTIZ: You hit on something there. We happen to have a member of the Rough Rock school here. It would be of value if he told us what they objected to in this evaluation. Because I think it illustrates the head-on clash between the different sets of assumptions involved here.

DILLON PLATERO: It's true, that certain people had preconceived ideas. Those arrived at were probably acquired prior to whatever decision was made on the study. I understand that even today there are seminars and conferences at which one of the persons who made the first study still makes a classic example of this, not knowing that he himself is the classic. But our team made a different evaluation, an objective one, utilizing a different approach and different techniques. The principal investigator from the first evaluation asked: "What the hell was wrong?" Well, look at your staff, he was told, that's what was wrong. He said, "I should be able to crack the whip." "Well," I said, "I had enough of that in the Navy."

MARY BYLER: I just want to add to the discussion of the Navajo evaluation. A couple of years ago, an evaluator went to the Pueblos to evaluate their Head Start program, and came back with the report that the children were too quiet, too well behaved, really too nice in class. They should be running around and jumping and fighting like normal children. Who defines what is normal? Those children were behaving as their parents expected them to behave in that situation. One of the big problems in Indian affairs is who can find what is proper for an Indian. When? We are constantly being told what we are. I'm glad that the Navajos fought back, because it's the only way we will get the fact across that we are not like the general population in this country, and they cannot go on telling us what we should be, because the definition always comes out negative.

SAM DELORIA: I would like to point out the difficulty in expressing many of the ideas that we want to express, by virtue of the fact that we are using the English language. I suspect (perhaps our linguist or someone else who knows more than I about this can confirm), that there are certain patterns in the English language tending to focus communication into certain ways against the whole complex of the world view and the language reflecting it. I suggest that this, plus the habits that one learns, as one is educated, may cause some crucial changes in trying to bring an Indian world view into what I understand you to mean by a conscious, systematic philosophy. I think that we should, at the very least, be aware of this problem, and perhaps even entertain the possibility that articulating an Indian philosophy is not worth it. It's doomed to be made nonIndian by virtue of being articulated in a systematically foreign way.

SPARLIN NORWOOD: I can't believe that, and I am a school teacher. I teach that any time you think something, somebody usually thought of it before you. I don't believe that there could be an Indian philosophy per se, cold hard words on a piece of paper. But I do believe that there are aspects that we should touch on, that we all know about reality, and so, as a teacher, let me ask some questions. How many of you have ever seen an Indian or known an Indian who has not in some manner been in touch with this universe that we live in, or multiverse, whatever you want to call it, in a spiritual outlook? The metaphysics of an Indian is a subject that we need to touch on more fully. Every Indian seems to have basically within him, the knowledge that he is one with the universe. He has a reverence for life. I remember hearing about Albert Schweitzer. As a young man, I used to laugh when I thought about him stepping over an ant crossing his path. But he had a reverence for life that I soon came to appreciate. If you look, I know some of you have some knowledge of Indian prayers. If the Indian had a religious system, rather than merely being superstitious, then we must look at his prayers. Because embodied in his prayers is a real deep feeling, and we say that prayer.

JEANNETTE HENRY: What do you mean by prayers?

Are you thinking of a formal prayer as in the Christian religion?

SPARLIN NORWOOD: No. But in songs, too. Perhaps you know some songs that have this universal attitude. A Ponca prayer that I recall, is one in which the speaker was praying to the stars in the heavens, and he was immediately casting himself out upon that expanse, putting himself at one with it. In the same sentence, he talked about the grass under his feet, which brought him right back to where he immediately was. Time and space concept. But I do believe that if we had an intimate working knowledge of these prayers of our people, we could find here an embodiment for some rather cold, hard facts, that our people have been and are at one with the universe.

ALFONSO ORTIZ: Let me read a brief quotation from a statement put out some years ago by the people of Taos Pueblo, when they were first appealing for help to regain control of their sacred Blue Lake area, some 48,000 acres. That is one of the big battles, dating back to 1906, when it was first taken away. I mean it as a reaction to what you just said, and as an answer to Mr. Sam Deloria about whether the English language, in a sense, defiles it. I think we must try whether it could be rendered into English and still have approximately the same meaning it did to the people. My hope that it does is bound up in finding little things like this:

"Our tribal government is responsible to this land and to the people. We have lived upon this land from days beyond history's records, far past any living memory deep into the time of legend. The story of my people, and the story of this place, are one single story. No man can think of us without also thinking of this place. We are always joined together."

A very eloquent statement, and in the English language. I think it can provide the incentive to go just a little further. Let me give a most extreme example, and observe how threatening this example must be, particularly to a child of our people in the Southwest in the recent past. Most of them believe that the world is bounded by four sacred mountains. Beyond that there is no world, at least there is no real world.

Furthermore, they believe the earth is flat, and that these four sacred mountains hold up the sky. The upper level is like an inverted bowl, and if you could only float up there, you could tap at the roof of the whole world with your finger. To have this view, and have it taught to you as an oral tradition, and have it sustained in your art forms, and then to have this belief at six years of age in a school where you first encounter a teacher with a circular globe, who puts her finger on it and spins it, and tells you the earth is round . . . ! That it is not the sun that revolves around the earth but the earth revolves around the sun . . . how very threatening it must be! It's that kind of battle, and your question, Mr. Deloria, I think is confronted. I believe that the cost of giving up, in trying to translate these our most deeply felt beliefs, because of this difficulty, is too great. We cannot give up the fight.

SAM DELORIA: I think what we need is to define more precisely what we are talking about in articulating an Indian philosophy. Those of us who hear you read that, can see behind the words to the experience that these people are talking about, and because we have some experience with Indian religions to a greater or lesser degree. Take that statement as it is, and read the same thing in a completely nonIndian context. To people who haven't had that experience, it sounds like the typical Indian "nature," . . . imaginary stuff that they just can't relate to. Is there necessarily a conflict between their view of the world and the scientific view? Or, have we arrived at a point where we can recognize different kinds of truth that don't have to be reconciled with each other. Do we still believe that there is one truth?

Is it the job of science or religion to discover that one truth, and throw everything else out? I hope that what Indians can do is to lead the world to believe there isn't one simple truth. There are equal truths of equal validity, whether it is expressed in such terms of not precisely equal validity, but of validity within their own terms. We have to define more precisely what we are talking about when we say Indian philosophy. Are we going to compete with other philosophies? Or, are we going to try to expand everybody's mind to open themselves to a spiritual dimension of which I do believe, they probably have a very limited experience.

ALFONSO ORTIZ: The latter, I hope.

BILL BYLER: I think, in the statement that has been read, there is an interesting touch, in connection with the whole question between the two different cultures. This was written for a nonIndian audience, as a political document. It may have expressed some sincere feelings; no doubt it did. Expressing these thoughts to themselves, the Indian people would have chosen different words, and it would have been in the language of the people. As a political instrument, it was an attempt to translate it into what would make sense to the nonIndian who is going presumably to act on this. Some kind of common ground of experience was needed, so that they could identify with that statement, have something that was meaningful to them. And in fact, it is perhaps not so much an expression of their philosophy, but of what the white man's philosophy is.

A SPEAKER: A logical extension of that is the other phraseology, which we have heard before, the one stating that the Blue Lake is our "cathedral." You don't litter your cathedrals. You don't desecrate your cathedrals. The people have demanded and pleaded: Please leave our sacred area alone. Another phrase: "Custer died for your sins." Phrases and statements of that type go back to philosophical ideas of an entirely different culture and era. There are certain philosophical crudities going on. We must recognize the need to make a re-statement, or to find some equation of the philosophies. I don't see English as a language that can become equated with an Indian language, since an Indian language has a certain tangibility. English does not have this. European languages don't have this, because their religions came afterwards, after the process. Christianity in its modern form is really a minority religion in the world. All these other philosophies, I think, eventually became an expanded version of what is meant by world view. I believe, in all the Eastern philosophy, you will find much the same thing as in Indian philosophies around this country. There is a certain degree of compatibility. Let us take what Dr. Ortiz said about our world view as shown in the belief about the four mountains. But that doesn't mean that time and space were limited to them. Because, now and quite suddenly . . . after so many years of hearing of these four mountains, I suddenly find within these four mountains the entire universe.

And so, eventually, I get to the stage that the world is no longer confined to the four mountains. But this comes out of your own experience and process of thought, your own development and belief in a philosophy. With knowledge, you come to this point. And then there is included the stars, the moon, (everyone wants to go physically to the moon), but for us, there is no purpose in going to the moon. The fact is, that the big argument was that the moon was originally ours . . . that Coyote had a way of getting it up there. However, this is one philosophical concept of what a world view can do. It can make the world so real to you, that you don't have to touch it in order to know that it is real. But the concept found in the English language is a retreat from that. I don't know whether we not only need to expand the vehicle by which we are expressing the philosophy onto a base that has already expanded the realities of what others see. Because the realities, as the Europeans sense it is, don't allow a great amount of subjectivity. When you reach subjectivity in a discussion point, then it becomes synonymous with the religious ritualistic thing. You get to the place where philosophy and religion appear as one and the same, so to speak. You don't think of philosophy and religion as a daily process, in which you have to face the world and make some real effort, for which you can say at the end of the day: It has been good.

ALFONSO ORTIZ: I would like to toss this question about the inherent limitations of the English language to Ken Hale.

KEN HALE: That is really a tough question to answer. But my feeling is that it's not that any language is inherently incapable of expressing ideas. But that some people are incapable of understanding certain ideas. Going at it from the opposite direction, and trying to express, let us say, a technical or theoretical concept in linguistics, I found that it was not only possible, but very revealing to learn that with some thought, once the concept was understood, the native speaker of Papago was able to not only devise a set of technical terminology, but also one that we found to be far superior to one we have now, which is basically a set of terms we have attached, between the concept and the word. Indian languages don't differ much in ability to express ideas. It's the ideas that differ in some ways. Once you have a common understanding, you can probably express it. There are, of course, opposing positions.

SAM BILLISON: I'd like to disagree to this extent: Regarding the Taos prayer. I don't think it has the same meaning as "prayer." I don't think it can be explained in the English language for the reason that there are some Indian words that just don't have counterparts in English. For instance, the word "intelligence." There is no word for this in Navajo. So I don't believe you can rely on the English language for interpretations, to the extent that is being stated here. There is no true counterpart for whatever the Indian would say, whether the word is "prayer" or whatever.

KEN HALE: I would have to agree with your position to this extent: that a particular concept given a name in English or in Navajo or another Indian language, doesn't have an exact translation in the Indian language. But I believe that a language is an instrument which is capable of expressing any idea that man can think.

SAM BILLISON: What I am saying is that you can come close to it, but I don't think you can really get the feeling as expressed in Indian.

KEN HALE: There are inherent limitations in either language. But it has to do with people's ability to grasp an idea. You see the real problem, taking the Taos prayer as an example, is that the way Anglos would interpret it is not the way the Navajo would. It's not the fault of the English language. It's due to the inability of Anglos to understand that kind of thing.

A SPEAKER: I don't see the distinction you're making. Aren't you saying that it's not the fault of the language but the fault of the people who speak the language and fail to understand what the language conveys? Are you abstracting the language from the people, so that the language no longer exists, in effect, to all intents and purposes, except as a listing of words?

KEN HALE: That's the reason.

A SPEAKER: If a word carries certain associations to a speaker of that language, and if that's the only word that you can use (or set of words), that will even come close to a concept in another language, but some of the associations are unfortunate, and change their meaning in translation to such an extent, then it seems to me that you have to say that it cannot convey that concept.

KEN HALE: That's true. But suppose you take that word which fails to capture the meaning of the word in the Indian language, and refine it. You see, that's basically how the language is changed. The people who speak the language that fails to match the other one, come to re-define that term so that it is consistent with the meaning of the other language.

A SPEAKER: I think now we are getting down to the problem. Let's say there are two alternatives. One is to re-define the English word so that it matches the Indian word. Another is for the English speaking people to be able to invent a whole new word and understand what it means as much as possible (and this is a question), in the way the Pueblo people understand that word, as an example. It seems to me that if we accept what Dr. Ortiz was saying this morning, that two different cultures have unique world views, it may be that if these world views are present, if they start from the beginning of man, even before birth, it may be that there is absolutely no way in which to fully convey that concept.

KEN HALE: If that were the case, what you said a minute ago, if world views or conditions are even somehow biologically inherited, that that would be right.

A SPEAKER: I don't mean necessarily biologically. I don't mean genetically.

KEN HALE' How can it be any other way, if it's before birth?

A SPEAKER: Well, here we are running into another cultural problem.

KEN HALE: Right.

A SPEAKER: Then, if I am to pose the possibility that the total cultural experience could start even before birth by some kind of physical, chemical reaction, and then go on to the beginning of postbirth, consciousness . . . and continue from there to become more consciously articulated, do I have to prove scientifically that that is an existing influence before we can talk about it? Or, do you have to prove that it's not an influence, before we can talk about it?

A SPEAKER: As soon as you start discussing it, you have to be aware of the limitations as to how you can talk about it. Such a discussion is necessary.

BILL BRANDON: Let me make one other comment on how not to talk about it. I would like to make this point: I visited the Taos Pueblo council last year, and I don't speak Tiwa. The proceedings were carried on in Tiwa. I found out that I communicate better in a language that I don't understand than in a language I do understand. There are a great many "signals" and when we are speaking the language we understand, we don't see those signals. They are ready to use, but we are on the surface. I understood what these Tiwa people were saying. Every question I asked was interpreted and answered, down through the council. I literally knew what everybody was saying. I knew by all sorts of signals, that I wouldn't have seen if they were speaking English.

ALFONSO ORTIZ: I attended that council once, and it can be one of the most unnerving of experiences. There is this bare room with no electricity, and a fire burning in the corner. And sitting around the room, with their blankets up over their noses, are the councilmen, with their eyes just flickering back and forth. But in this context, they arrive at consensus. They know each other so well, an answer seems to find itself.

BILL BRANDON: May I make another comment? The difference in these so-called philosophies has been mentioned. I think the term "philosophies" is undfortunate. It seems to me that the "attitudes" of this world, or that world would be better.

ALFONSO ORTIZ: World view, is the term most often used.

BILL BRANDON: Well, that expression bothers me too, because it's a word that you anthropologists have developed. A point that hasn't been raised, is that none of this is static. It's always moving back and forth from one world to another. I have read a great deal in history of the 16th and 17th centuries, and I find that there is a lot of influence in the history of the non-Indian world, from the Indian world, that's been largely overlooked. The gist of this idea first came to me from something written by D'Arcy McNickle, who is sitting here. It goes that the idea of freedom became so pronounced . . . even in the 16th century, let alone in the 17th. A great deal of work was done in France on this matter from the fantastic voyages, and the stories of the new world. All this idea of freedom came from the discovery of the new world, as far as I can determine. In Dante you do not find the term "freedom" mentioned once. Loyalty, however, is all through Dante. Freedom is not there.

MARY BYLER: I say you don't find eggplant either.

A SPEAKER: I agree with you. I think freedom was omitted on this continent.

ALFONSO ORTIZ: If you had it, you didn't have to worry about it. You didn't have to talk about it.

BILL BRANDON: They didn't have freedom, nor did they

even think of it. But freedom became a very active ingredient in thought by the time Mr. Shakespeare was writing and using this term. It was a point Dr. McNickle mentioned, I think an excellent one, about the freedom of the new people in the new world. Shakespeare put it into *The Tempest*. This is the kind of thing that created the attitudes. It's not conscious philosophy; it is rather on an unconscious level. The important things that we believe, we do not know we believe. It comes to us by a Shakespeare, it doesn't come to us by sitting around in a group and deciding that we believe this or that. I think it's very possible to use the Indian influence on the nonIndian world. Not just in this hemisphere, but in the whole world, also, from the American Indian world almost from the very beginning of contact in 1492. I believe, that in times to come, your historians will recognize it as a field of study. I did some work on this at the University of Massachusetts, and it's a very serious subject that will have a lot of literature in time to come I'm sure.

ALFONSO ORTIZ: It seems that one way of translating what you just said for myself, is that we need to be able to envision the world as it was in the past. This is one of the challenges in this new field of Indian philosophy. Because if there is anything you convinced me of anew, it is of the urgent need to get out in the open, to try to experience together, talk together. To be able to envision the world as it was when Columbus first landed. If we are going to save it, we have to know what it was. And if it takes founding local chapters of the first earth society to do it, maybe that's the way we should go.

BILL BRANDON: I will be a charter member.

HERB BLATCHFORD: There is something that disturbs me about this language bit, and about this expression of philosophy. For instance, if we are going to have to wait for the English adherents, for the English speakers to come up with the English fragments to have new meanings, and it took, as you say, a hundred years before the word "freedom" got into the books, then I just wonder how much longer we have to wait. What I am really trying to face, in my own mind, is the responsibility of language. We are using the common language of English. Indians have been revising the means of English to suit their own purposes and they do this. But if the burden of proof is on the Indian to catch up with something that they have to somewhat confine themselves within, or wait for the English counterparts to develop, then we have to slow down, while they catch up. Now where is the burden of responsibility going to end, if this will be continually tossed back and forth?

SAM BILLISON: It would be hard for the linguist to really describe the language, unless he speaks the tongue. Like somebody was saying, that the Navajo coin a lot of words as time goes on. Comes a new invention, we coin a word for it. So when something new comes in, there is a consensus of the people in what to call it. I guess every part in the automobile has a Navajo name now. So like Blatchford said, we can't wait for the English language.

HERB BLATCHFORD: If you assume, from a logical standpoint, that ideas have to change the meanings attached to the words, that means that the ideas have been expanded to the further extent of the Indian philosophy, because it's a cosmography, and everything else combined . . . all your ecological precepts and everything. In fact, it's proven by the simple fact that you have pollution. That somehow the non-pollution resides on federal forest reserves and Indian reservations. This has been the last holdout. When you talk about pollution, well there is a set of values and a set of philosophies that did not allow this pollution to occur. Now that you have polluted this land, how do you "unpollute" it? Waiting for ideas to set it about?

KEN HALE: Your point is very well taken and that's the whole thrust of the kind of thing I have been interested in recently. Because I have learned, after studying Indian languages for 15 years, that I will never really understand them myself.

HERB BLATCHFORD: Then you are putting the burden of responsibility for doing this on the people who are being confined by this responsibility.

KEN HALE: Yes. I see what a bind I am getting myself into. But I feel a sense of helplessness. At one time I thought I could learn a lot about American Indian languages. But the more I learn about it, the more I see that will not happen.

HERB BLATCHFORD: You see what a difficult problem it is for us, after rubbing shoulders with the Europeans for 475 years. We are still at an impasse as far as communications go, simply because of the refusal of some linguistic stocks to get out of their insulating shells.

BILL BRANDON: Isn't this similar, though, to the experience the translator had in translating Dante? He was an American-Italian, and he grew up in an Italian family. But he grew up in it, and also came in contact with English early. Because he is a poet, he's done a pretty tremendous job of translating Dante, because he's Italian, and he's at home with Dante, with his thoughts and with Italian thought. He knows he is capable of poetic expression in English. So he does a better job for this kind of thing than I would do. Maybe this is what you're talking about. You could do a better job if you're working with the Navajo language, if you know Navajo and you know English.

HERB BLATCHFORD: It's logical, fine. But when you're dealing with English and Italian, you are dealing with related language stocks. But from English to Navajo, you're dealing with a considerable separation in language stocks.

BILL BRANDON: Well, I don't know if the "separation" is real, or due to an Indian mysticism.

HERB BLATCHFORD: It's real. I know it's real.

BILL BRANDON: I think we can all agree that a culture that would not place a high value on abstract thought does have a great deal of difficulty in putting that thought into words of the English language, but I would like to get back to something else. We were discussing the size of your world as you learned it as a child. I don't think the size is really the important thing, but the way you view that world and the world in general. No matter what the size, the way you treat your world, the way you react to things in your world, is important. I'd like to hear some discussion on that.

ALFONSO ORTIZ: That was a new vista to me. It came up more than once. Herb Blatchford mentioned it this morning and earlier this afternoon. Sam Billison mentioned it in a different way.

A SPEAKER: Well, this particular thought just came out concerning how you deal with your world. It's like dealing with the Bureau of Indian Affairs education budget. I mean, it's a violent world. You can't change it. The beauty of thought is fine, but you've got to jump in. I don't like it, but you've got to get into it.

A SPEAKER: But the world is something to be defeated, something you have to overcome, and as an Indian, I don't see this coming.

A SPEAKER: What about all the testimony before the hearing on education? It's budgeted wrong for education. They are jumping right back into the old pattern. This is a world that the whites live in and like, and won't change, certainly not on behalf of the Indian. So it seems to me that it's a bit of accommodation that must be made from the Indian to the other world. On the other hand, it can work both ways.

A SPEAKER: This is something that we may have to decide: Do we have to change, or can we continue the way we are now, or how much of real difference is there? Some of these things we have got to look at. In my viewpoint, there are many differences . . . differences in the way I see the world, the way I treat the world, where I live. Differences between that and the way white people act. I don't know whether these things are common to you people or not. Is this common to most of us, or all of us, or any of us?

HERB BLATCHFORD: I think this is becoming a real problem for a traditional people. What we are looking at now, judging from the BIA budget as an example, is a plastic-wrapped world. But the distortions are there, and we want to feel it is a world that our philosophies can grow up on. On the other hand, when you consider coming in direct contact with it any more . . . there is some kind of separation that has occurred. The interpretation as to what we can find in it isn't real. I mean, we escape them and have to escape them, just to find out where the sky is.

ALFONSO ORTIZ: We have one young white radical here, who has been saving up a mouthful.

MR. VENTERS: I would like to ask the person who remarked about radical policies: What connections do you make in your mind with this Indian philosophy, which I see really hasn't been put into a paragraph yet . . . and the possibility for radical actions? In my opinion, there are many young white people who look into what they think Indians are, and a lot of them don't know what that is. But they can read, and they can truly know that something is happening there that is a lot better than what they have known. My experience in Oklahoma showed there has been a lot of misunderstanding on the question. What about Viet Nam? What about the draft? Racism, which is being put out of the suburban world, or in my case, the South. These are problems I'd like to hear talked about here, because if you have something, you can't just keep it to yourself and merely get into a dialogue about language. I won't presume to understand what you mean. When I read anthropology, I don't just read; I am trying to read and understand the informants, because it seems to me that that is the important thing to get out of those books.

At this point in the history of the American university. who wants to be intelligent in terms of footnotes? I am there to try to find out, despite the inability of language that you have talked about. I am being totally selfish here, but I think selfishness is necessary, given white middle class racism, pollution, Viet Nam, youth. Part of the whole psychodelic drug thing that has occurred, was an attempt through an experience to encompass a world that you never found out about in words. I do think there is something there, and I try to understand what, maybe, an Indian philosophy is, even if you have to say it in English, because it seems to me that is valuable. What I am concerned about is the planet itself. I have nothing to tell you myself, but I ask you to say what an Indian philosophy is, just in terms of what it is if somebody desires to see the world as beautiful.

HERB BLATCHFORD: I have this problem right at my front doorstep. There are going to be more realistic approaches on the problem of drugs. I know, for taking trips of several varieties and trying to reach some kind of meaningful, compatible explanation of what Indian philosophy is. They know something is there. They have been held out from getting pollution everywhere. How come it's happening? What philosophy do you go by, to resist this encroaching defecation of years? But the problem was the insulated shell around the institutions that perpetrated this. And now, you want to break out of it, and in the result of breaking out of it, you need something to carry you further, beyond that point of insulation. You think you've been misled on a lot of information about philosophy. Granted. We realize that this has been happening, and we have spoken out against it. All the literature, from the time of Red Jacket on forward, has expressed this neglect of facing reality, rather than merely viewing reality through a mirror.

Now, you expect us to express what we have been saying all these years? Even before the time of Red Jacket, when he expressed things such as to "take care of the earth. This is our mother." If you want to understand Indian philosophy in a nutshell, so to speak, we have the belief that we are in a family with the world, in a family with the earth. There is a sky-mother and the earth-mother, and we are all children of that. Whatever grows in the mother is to be respected, not to be manipulated in your self-interest, or whatever you may want to do with it. But that's the simple crux of the whole philosophy. You can find that basic philosophy in almost every tribe across the country, such as when you listen to the White Roots of Peace. They express it very well, in terms of who is the father? Respect the birds, the seas, and so on as they go through the whole bit. Is that burden of understanding upon us, to have you understand it? Or is the burden upon you to expand yourself to where you can understand?

MR. VENTERS: The burden is for me not to get arrested in the attempt. In terms of what I can do, you see, I have different problems with the United States government. I don't want to go to Viet Nam. I don't want to be busted for smoking pot or dancing in the streets. I want to kind of shiver in the corner in a way, because I want to have peace, freedom, beauty.

HERB BLATCHFORD: But we were treated the same way.

A SPEAKER: I am very interested in what you said. There is a word used, overworked, when older folks talk to younger people. They say: "You say that you have your rights, but we take your responsibilities." There is another word I would like to offer. It's in the Book of Genesis. People have overlooked it, and this shows the Indian's point of view, because I never overlooked it. When I first saw and looked around in Oklahoma and saw fences, it offended me. Because I saw this was a travesty on what I believed should be: that men should be able to move freely. It took thousands of acres to support a small tribe, because of the way they took life. When we say, support earth, we don't mean to plow it up and fill it with garbage and buried atomic waste, because they walk over it gently. But there is a word in Genesis that we should find again, because the politicians got hold of the word "ecology." It says, "Be fruitful and multiply." It also says, "Replenish the earth." For most Indians, to live here was the whole thing. Just to live here. The white man's word was progress, progress. It's not my word.

DILLON PLATERO: I want to mention an area that I think is quite interesting. It has a great deal to do with what is not written. Books like the one by Deloria are one way of getting a philosophy across. But this certainly doesn't describe EVERY Indian philosophy! The individual Indian describes it for himself. It should be understood that not necessarily is this true for all. Even in our own Navajo group, philosophies may and do vary. Basically, I think what we are looking for now, is what is written Navajo. Whatever philosophy people might express in Navajo, I would ask, "Which Navajo philosopher . . . has expounded this or that?" As another example, some of the Navajo creation myths are very difficult to explain from one point of view, but yet are easy from another. Certainly a discussion of this type isn't resolved in one day. The people are just kind of looking at one another here and feeling each other out, because this Conovcation is really just the start.

ALFONSO ORTIZ: The important thing is that a lot of us are meeting for the first time here, and we can continue. The point is well taken that we do not have a sort of "nutshell" treatment. Did anyone think we would? We can make a list of notions, like freedom, space, time, tribe, tribalism, color, numerical classification and so on. These are games we play to try and see if we can arrest something very neatly in experience, for just a little while, and then see what behavioral manifestations it has. I like space and time, because they are so uniquitous.

WILFRED WASSON: I don't have anything in a nutshell either. But there is one thing I would like to say to the young man over here. Every time I tell white people the way I see them, I get all kinds of tolerant smiles. "No," they seem to be saying, "we are really not like this." But the way I see white people is that they reduce everything to its lowest common denominator, which is the dollar. This is the way I see white people. And this is why we have the pollution problem, because it costs more not to pollute. The city of Bellingham, Washington, is dumping sewage into the bay because it would cost more money to treat that sewage. You can't eat clams out of the bay any more. Georgia Pacific is dumping its waste into the bay, because it would cost more money to treat that sewage. You see, this is the way I see white people.

46

MR. VENTERS: That's why we have to have radical politics, I say.

A SPEAKER: That's *his* problem. I think he doesn't quite know what to do about it.

ALFONSO ORTIZ: One word on the matter of drugs. I see it as comparable to using dynamite to get into church, when the door is open. I believe, because of the Puritan ethic, modern man's soul has become so encrusted with greed and violence that he really cannot fully enter a spiritual realm without a crutch.

Thank you. The panel now stands adjourned.

N. SCOTT MOMADAY, ''The Man Made of Words''

3

The Man
Made of Words

N. SCOTT MOMADAY
Assembly Presentation

I want to try to put several different ideas together this morning. And in the process, I hope to indicate something about the nature of the relationship between language and experience. It seems to me that in a certain sense we are all made of words; that our most essential being consists in language. It is the element in which we think and dream and act, in which we live our daily lives. There is no way in which we can exist apart from the morality of a verbal dimension.

In one of the discussions yesterday the question "What is an American Indian?" was raised.

The answer of course is that an Indian is an idea which a given man has of himself. And it is a moral idea, for it accounts for the way in which he reacts to other men and to the world in general. And that idea, in order to be realized completely, has to be expressed.

I want to say some things then about this moral and verbal dimension in which we live. I want to say something about such things as ecology and storytelling and the imagination. Let me tell you a story:

One night a strange thing happened. I had written the greater part of *The Way to Rainy Mountain*—all of it, in fact, except the epilogue. I had set down the last of the old Kiowa tales, and I had composed both the historical and the autobiographical commentaries for it. I had the sense of being out of breath, of having said what it was in me to say on that subject. The manuscript lay before me in the bright light, small, to be sure, but complete; or nearly so. I had written the second of the two poems in which that book is framed. I had uttered the last word, as it were. And yet a whole, penultimate piece was missing. I began once again to write.

During the first hours after midnight on the morning of November 13, 1833, it seemed that the world was coming to an end. Suddenly the stillness of the night was broken; there were brilliant flashes of light in the sky, light of such intensity that people were awakened by it. With the speed and density of a driving rain, stars were falling in the universe. Some were brighter than Venus; one was said to be as large as the moon. I went on to say that that event, the falling of the stars on North America, that explosion of meteors which occurred 137 years ago, is among the earliest entries in the Kowa calendars. So deeply impressed upon the imagination of the Kiowas is that old phenomenon that it is remembered still; it has become a part of the racial memory.

"The living memory," I wrote, "and the verbal tradition which transcends it, were brought together for me once and for all in the person of Ko-sahn." It seemed eminently right for me to deal, after all, with that old woman. Ko-sahn is among the most venerable people I have ever known. She spoke and sang to me one summer afternoon in Oklahoma. It was like a dream. When I was born she was already old; she was a grown woman when my grandparents came into the world. She sat perfectly still, folded over on herself. It did not seem possible that so many years—a century of years—could be so compacted and distilled. Her voice shuddered, but it did not fail. Her songs were sad. An old whimsy, a delight in language and in remembrance, shone in her one good eye. She conjured up the past, imagining perfectly the long continuity of her being. She imagined the lovely young girl, wild and vital, she had been. She imagined the Sun Dance:

There was an old, old woman. She had something on her back. The boys went out to see. The old woman had a bag full of earth on her back. It was a certain kind of sandy earth. That is what they must have in the lodge. The dancers must dance upon the sandy earth. The old woman held a digging tool in her hand. She turned towards the south and pointed with her lips. It was like a kiss, and she began to sing:

We have brought the earth.
Now it is time to play.

As old as I am, I still have the feeling of play. That was the beginning of the Sun Dance.

By this time I was back into the book, caught up completely in the act of writing. I had projected myself—imagined myself—out of the room and out of time. I was there with Ko-sahn in the Oklahoma July. We laughed easily together; I felt that I had known her all of my life—all of hers. I did not want to let her go. But I had come to the end. I set down, almost grudgingly, the last sentences:

It was—all of this and more—a quest, a going forth upon the way of Rainy Mountain. Probably Ko-sahn too is dead now. At times, in the quiet of evening, I think she must have wondered, dreaming, who she was. Was she become in her sleep that old purveyor of the sacred earth, perhaps, that ancient one who, old as she was, still had the feeling of play? And in her mind, at times, did she see the falling stars?

For some time I sat looking down at these words on the page, trying to deal with the emptiness that had come about inside of me. The words did not seem real. I could scarcely believe that they made sense, that they had anything whatsoever to do with meaning. In desperation almost, I went back over the final paragraphs, backwards and forwards, hurriedly. My eyes fell upon the name Ko-sahn. And all at once everything seemed suddenly to refer to that name. The name seemed to humanize the whole complexity of language. All at once, absolutely, I had the sense of the magic of words and of names. Ko-sahn, I said, and I said again KO-SAHN.

Then it was that that ancient, one-eyed woman Ko-sahn stepped out of the language and stood before me on the page. I was amazed. Yet it seemed to me entirely appropriate that this should happen.

"I was just now writing about you," I replied, stammering. "I thought—forgive me—I thought that perhaps you were . . . that you had . . ."

"No," she said. And she cackled, I thought. And she went on. "You have imagined me well, and so I am. You have imagined that I dream, and so I do. I have seen the falling stars."

"But all of this, this imagining," I protested, "this has taken place—is taking place in my mind. You are not actually here, not here in this room." It occurred to me that I was being extremely rude, but I could not help myself. She seemed to understand.

"Be careful of your pronouncements, grandson," she answered. "You imgaine that I am here in this room, do you not? That is worth something. You see, I have existence, whole being, in your imagination. It is but one kind of being, to be sure, but it is perhaps the best of all kinds. If I am not here in this room, grandson, then surely neither are you."

"I think I see what you mean," I said meekly. I felt justly

rebuked. "Tell me, grandmother, how old are you?"

"I do not know," she replied. "There are times when I think that I am the oldest woman on earth. You know, the Kiowas came into the world through a hollow log. In my mind's eye I have seen them emerge, one by one, from the mouth of the log. I have seen them so clearly, how they were dressed, how delighted they were to see the world around them. I must have been there. And I must have taken part in that old migration of the Kiowas from the Yellowstone to the Southern Plains, near the Big Horn River, and I have seen the red cliffs of Palo Duro Canyon. I was with those who were camped in the Wichita Mountains when the stars fell."

"You are indeed very old," I said, "and you have seen many things."

"Yes, I imagine that I have," she replied. The she turned slowly around, nodding once, and receded into the language I had made. And then I imagined I was alone in the room.

Once in his life a man ought to concentrate his mind upon the remembered earth, I believe. He ought to give himself up to a particular landscape in his experience, to look at it from as many angles as he can, to wonder about it, to dwell upon it. He ought to imagine that he touches it with his hands at every season and listens to the sounds that are made upon it. He ought to imagine the creatures that are there and all the faintest motions in the wind. He ought to recollect the glare of noon and all the colors of the dawn and dusk.

The Wichita Mountains rise out of the Southern Plains in a long crooked line that runs from east to west. The mountains are made of red earth, and of rock that is neither red nor blue but some very rare admixture of the two like the feathers of certain birds. They are not so high and mighty as the mountains of the Far West, and they bear a different relationship to the land around them. One does not imagine that they are distinctive in themselves, or indeed that they exist apart from the plain in any sense. If you try to think of them in the abstract, they lose the look of mountains. They are preeminently an expression of the larger landscape, more perfectly organic than one can easily imagine. To behold these mountains from the plain is one thing; to see the plain from the mountains is something else. I have stood on the top of Mt. Scott and seen the earth below, bending out into the whole circle of the sky. The wind runs always close upon the slopes, and there are times when you can hear the rush of it like water in the ravines.

Here is the hub of an old commerce. A hundred years ago the Kiowas and Comanches journeyed outward from the Wichitas in every direction, seeking after mischief and medicine, horses and hostages. Sometimes they went away for years, but they always returned, for the land had got hold of them. It is a consecrated place, and even now there is something of the wilderness about it. There is a game preserve in the hills. Animals graze away in the open meadows or, closer by, keep to the shadows of the groves: antelope and deer, longhorn and buffalo. It was here, the Kiowas say, that the first buffalo came into the world.

The yellow grassy knoll that is called Rainy Mountain lies a short distance to the north and west. There, on the west side, is the ruin of an old school where my grandmother went as a wild young girl in blanket and braids to learn of numbers and of names in English. And there she is buried.

> Most is your name the name of
> this dark stone.
> Deranged in death, the mind to
> be inheres
> Forever in the nominal unknown,
> Who listens here and now to
> hear your name.
> The early sun, red as a hunter's
> moon,
> Runs in the plain. The mountain
> burns and shines;
> And silence is the long approach
> of noon
> Upon the shadow that your name
> defines—
> And death this cold, black
> density of stone.

I am interested in the way that a man looks at a given landscape and takes possession of it in his blood and brain. For this happens, I am certain, in the ordinary motion of life. None of us lives apart from the land entirely; such an isolation is unimaginable. We have sooner or later to come to terms with the world around us— and I mean especially the physical world, not only as it is revealed to us immediately through our senses, but also as it is perceived more truly in the long turn of seasons and of years. And we must come to moral terms. There is no alternative, I believe, if we are to realize and maintain our humanity; for our humanity must consist in part in the ethical as well as the practical ideal of preservation. And particularly here and now is that true. We Americans need now more than ever before—and indeed more than we know—to imagine who and what we are with respect to the earth and sky. I am talking about an act of the imagination essentially, and the concept of an American land ethic.

It is no doubt more difficult to imagine in 1970 the landscape of America as it was in, say, 1900. Our whole experience as a nation in this century has been a repudiation of the pastoral ideal which informs so much of the art and literature of the nineteenth century. One effect of the Technological Revolution has been to uproot us from the soil. We have become disoriented, I believe; we have suffered a kind of psychic dislocation of ourselves in time and space. We may be perfectly sure of where we are in relation to the supermarket and the next coffee break, but I doubt that any of us knows where he is in relation to the stars and to the solstices. Our sense of the natural order has become dull and unreliable. Like the wilderness itself, our sphere of instinct has diminished in proportion as we have failed to imagine truly what it is. And yet I believe that it is possible to formulate an ethical idea of the land—a notion of what it is and must be in our daily lives—and I believe moreover that it is absolutely necessary to do so.

It would seem on the surface of things that a land ethic is something that is alien to, or at least dormant in, most Americans. Most of us in general have developed an attitude of indifference toward the land. In terms of my own experience, it is difficult to see how such an attitude could ever have come about.

Ko-sahn could remember where my grandmother was born. "It was just there," she said, pointing to a tree, and the tree was like a hundred others that grew up in the broad depression of the Washita River. I could see nothing to indicate that anyone had ever been there, spoken so much as a word, or touched the tips of his fingers to the tree. But in her memory Ko-sahn could see the child. I think she must have remembered my grandmother's voice, for she seemed for a long moment to listen and to hear. There was a still, heavy heat upon that place; I had the sense that ghosts were gathering there.

And in the racial memory, Ko-sahn had seen the falling stars. For her there was no distinction between the individual and the racial experience, even as there was none between the mythical and the historical. Both were realized for her in the one memory, and that was of the land. This landscape, in which she had lived for a hundred years, was the common denominator of everything that she knew and would ever know— and her knowledge was profound. Her roots ran deep into the earth, and from those depths she drew strength enough to hold still against all the forces of chance and disorder. And she drew strength enough to hold still against all the forces of change and disorder. And she drew therefrom the sustenance of meaning and of mystery as well. The falling stars were not for Ko-sahn an isolated or accidental phenomenon. She had a great personal investment in that awful commotion of light in the night sky.

For it remained to be imagined. She must at last deal with it in words; she must appropriate it to her understanding of the whole universe. And, again, when she spoke of the Sun Dance, it was an essential expression of her relationship to the life of the earth and to the sun and moon.

In Ko-sahn and in her people we have always had the example of a deep, ethical regard for the land. We had better learn from it. Surely that ethic is merely latent in ourselves. It must now be activated, I believe. We Americans must come again to a moral comprehension of the earth and air. We must live according to the principle of a land ethic. The alternative is that we shall not live at all.

Ecology is perhaps the most important subject of our time. I can't think of an issue in which the Indian has more authority or a greater stake. If there is one thing which truly distinguishes him, it is surely his regard of and for the natural world.

But let me get back to the matter of storytelling.

I must have taken part in that old migration of the Kiowas from the Yellowstone to the Southern Plains, for I have seen antelope bounding in the tall grass near the Big Horn River, and I have seen the ghost forests in the Black Hills. Once I saw the red cliffs of Palo Duro Canyon. I was with those who were camped in the Wichita Mountains when the stars fell. "You are very old," I said, "and you have seen many things." "Yes, I imagine that I have," she replied. Then she turned slowly around, nodding once, and receded into the language I had made. And then I imagined that I was alone in the room.

Who is the storyteller? Of whom is the story told? What is there in the darkness to imagine into being? What is there to dream and to relate? What happens when I or anyone exerts the force of language upon the unknown?

These are the questions which interest me most.

If there is any absolute assumption in back of my thoughts tonight, it is this: We are what we imagine. Our very existence consists in our imagination of ourselves. Our best destiny is to imagine, at least, completely, who and what, and *that* we are. The greatest tragedy that can befall us is to go unimagined.

Writing is recorded speech. In order to consider seriously the meaning of language and of literature, we must consider first the meaning of the oral tradition.

By way of suggesting one or two definitions which may be useful to us, let me pose a few basic questions and tentative answers:

    (1)   What is the oral tradition?

          The oral tradition is that process by which the myths, legends, tales, and lore of a people are formulated, communicated, and preserved in language by word of mouth, as opposed to writing. Or, it is a *collection* of such things.

(2) With reference to the matter of oral tradition, what is the relationship between art and reality?

In the context of these remarks, the matter of oral tradition suggests certain particularities of art and reality. Art, for example . . . involves an oral dimension which is based markedly upon such considerations as memorization, intonation, inflection, precision of statement, brevity, rhythm, pace, and dramatic effect. Moreover, myth, legend, and lore, according to our definitions of these terms, imply a separate and distinct order of reality. We are concerned here not so much with an accurate representation of actuality, but with the realization of the imaginative experience.

(3) How are we to conceive of language? What are words?

For our purposes, words are audible sounds, invented by man to communicate his thoughts and feelings. Each word has a conceptual content, however slight; and each word communicates associations of feeling. Language is the means by which words proceed to the formulation of meaning and emotional effect.

(4) What is the nature of storytelling? What are the purposes and possibilities of that act?

Storytelling is imaginative and creative in nature. It is an act by which man strives to realize his capacity for wonder, meaning and delight. It is also a process in which man invests and preserves himself in the context of ideas. Man tells stories in order to understand his experience, whatever it may be. The possibilities of storytelling are precisely those of understanding the human experience.

(5) What is the relationship between what a man is and what he says—or between what he is, and what he thinks he is?

This relationship is both tenuous and complicated. Generally speaking, man has consummate being in language, and there only. The state of human *being* is an idea, an idea which man has of himself. Only when he is embodied in an idea, and the idea is realized in language, can man take possession of himself. In our particular frame of reference, this is to say that man achieves the fullest realization of his humanity in such an art and product of the imagination as literature—and here I use the term "literature" in its broadest sense. This is admittedly a moral view of the question, but literature is itself a moral view, and it is a view of morality.

Now let us return to the falling stars. And let me apply a new angle of vision to that event—let me proceed this time from a slightly different point of view:

In this winter of 1833 the Kiowas were camped on Elm Fork, a branch of the Red River west of the Wichita Mountains. In the preceding summer they had suffered a massacre at the hands of the Osages, and Tai-me, the sacred Sun Dance Doll and most powerful medicine of the tribe, had been stolen. At no time in the history of their migration from the north, and in the evolution of their plains culture, had the Kiowas been more vulnerable to despair. The loss of Tai-me was a deep psychological wound. In the early cold of November 13 there occurred over North America an explosion of meteors. The Kiowas were awakened by the sterile light of falling stars, and they ran out into the false day and were terrified.

The year the stars fell is, as I have said, among the earliest entries in the Kiowa calendars, and it is permanent in the Kiowa mind. There was symbolic meaning in that November sky. With the coming of natural dawn there began a new and darker age for the Kiowa people; the last culture to evolve on this continent began to decline. Within four years of the falling stars the Kiowas signed their first treaty with the government; within twenty, four major epidemics of smallpox and Asiatic cholera destroyed more than half their number; and within scarcely more than a generation their horses were taken from them and the herds of buffalo were slaughtered and left to waste upon the plains.

Do you see what happens when the imagination is superimposed upon the historical event? It becomes a story. The whole piece becomes more deeply invested with meaning. The terrified Kiowas, when they had regained possession of themselves, did indeed imagine that the falling stars were symbolic of their being and their destiny. They accounted for themselves with reference to that awful memory. They appropriated it, recreated it, fashioned it into an image of themselves—imagined it.

Only by means of that act could they bear what happened to them thereafter. No defeat, no humiliation, no suffering was beyond their power to endure, for none of it was meaningless. They could say to themselves, "yes, it was all meant to be in its turn. The order of the world was broken, it was clear. Even the stars were shaken loose in the night sky." The imagination of meaning was not much, perhaps, but it was all they had, and it was enough to sustain them.

One of my very favorite writers, Isak Dinesen, said this: "All sorrows can be borne if you put them into a story or tell a story about them."

Some three or four years ago, I became interested in the matter of "oral tradition" as that term is used to designate a rich body of pre-literate storytelling in and among the indigenous cultures of North America. Specifically, I began to wonder about the way in which myths, legends, and lore evolve into that mature condition of expression which we call "literature." For indeed literature is, I believe, the end-product of an evolutionary process, and the so-called "oral tradition" is primarily a stage within that process, a stage that is indispensable and perhaps original as well.

I set out to find a traditional material that should be at once oral only, unified and broadly representative of cultural values. And in this undertaking, I had a certain advantage, because I am myself an American Indian, and I have lived many years of my life on the Indian reservations of the southwest. From the time I was first able to comprehend and express myself in language, I heard the stories of the Kiowas, those "coming out" people of the Southern plains from whom I am descended.

Three hundred years ago the Kiowa lived in the mountains of what is now western Montana, near the headwaters of the Yellowstone River. Near the end of the 17th century they began a long migration to the south and east. They passed along the present border between Montana and Wyoming to the Black Hills and proceeded southward along the eastern slopes of the Rockies to the Wichita Mountains in the Southern Plains (Southwestern Oklahoma).

I mention this old journey of the Kiowas because it is in a sense definitive of the tribal mind; it is essential to the way in which the Kiowas think of themselves as a people. The migration was carried on over a course of many generations and many hundreds of miles. When it began, the Kiowas were a desperate and divided people, given up wholly to a day-by-day struggle for survival. When it ended, they were a race of centaurs, a lordly society of warriors and buffalo hunters. Along the way they had acquired horses, a knowledge and possession of the open land, and a sense of destiny. In alliance with the Comanches, they ruled the southern plains for a hundred years.

That migration—and the new golden age to which it led— is closely reflected in Kiowa legend and lore. Several years ago I retraced the route of that migration, and when I came to the end, I interviewed a number of Kiowa elders and obtained from them a remarkable body of history and learning, fact and fiction —all of it in the oral tradition and all of it valuable in its own right and for its own sake.

I compiled a small number of translations from the Kiowa, arranged insofar as it was possible to indicate the chronological and geographical progression of the migration itself. This collection (and it was nothing more than a collection at first) was published under the title "*The Journey of Tai-me*" in a fine edition limited to 100 hand printed copies.

58

This original collection has just been re-issued, together with illustrations and a commentary, in a trade edition entitled "*The Way to Rainy Mountain*." The principle of narration which informs this latter work is in a sense elaborate and experimental, and I should like to say one or two things about it. Then, if I may, I should like to illustrate the way in which the principle works, by reading briefly from the text. And finally, I should like to comment in some detail upon one of the tales in particular.

There are three distinct narrative voices in "*The Way to Rainy Mountain*"—the mythical, the historical, and the immediate. Each of the translations is followed by two kinds of commentary; the first is documentary and the second is privately reminiscent. Together, they serve, hopefully, to validate the oral tradition to an extent that might not otherwise be possible. The commentaries are meant to provide a context in which the elements of oral tradition might transcend the categorical limits of prehistory, anonymity, and archaeology in the narrow sense.

All of this is to say that I believe there is a way (first) in which the elements of oral tradition can be shown, dramatically, to exist within the framework of a literary continuance, a deeper and more vital context of language and meaning than that which is generally taken into account; and (secondly) in which those elements can be located, with some precision on an evolutionary scale.

The device of the journey is pecularily appropriate to such a principle of narration as this. And "*The Way to Rainy Mountain*" is a whole journey, intricate with notion and meaning; and it is made with the whole memory, that experience of the mind which is legendary as well as historical, personal as well as cultural.

Without further qualification, let me turn to the text itself.

The Kiowa tales which are contained in "*The Way to Rainy Mountain*" constitute a kind of literary chronicle. In a sense they are the milestones of that old migration in which the Kiowas journeyed from the Yellowstone to the Washita. They recorded a transformation of the tribal mind, as it encounters for the first time the landsape of the Great Plains; they evoke the sense of search and discovery. Many of the tales are very old, and they have not until now been set down in writing. Among them there is one that stands out in my mind. When I was a child, my father told me the story of the arrowmaker, and he told it to me many times, for I fell in love with it.. I have no memory that is older than that of hearing it. This is the way it goes:

If an arrow is well made, it will have tooth marks upon it. That is how you know. The Kiowas made fine arrows and straightened them in their teeth. Then they drew them to the bow to see that they were straight. Once there was a man and his wife. They were alone at night in their tipi. By the light of a fire the man was making arrows. After a while he caught sight of something. There was a small opening in the tipi where two hides had been sewn together. Someone was there on the outside, looking in. The man went on with his work, but he said to his wife, "Someone is standing outside. Do not be afraid. Let us talk easily, as of ordinary things." He took up an arrow and straightened it in his teeth; then, as it was right for him to do, he drew it to the bow and took aim, first in this direction and then in that. And all the while he was talking, as if to his wife. But this is how he spoke: "I know that you are there on the outside, for I can feel your eyes upon me. If you are a Kiowa, you will understand what I am saying, and you will speak your name." But there was no answer, and the man went on in the same way, pointing the arrow all around. At last his aim fell upon the place where his enemy stood, and he let go of the string. The arrow went straight to the enemy's heart.

Heretofore the story of the arrowmaker has been the private possession of a very few, a tenuous link in that most ancient chain of language which we call the oral tradition; tenuous because the tradition itself is so; for as many times as the story has been told, it was always but one generation removed from extinction. But it was held dear, too, on that same account. That is to say, it has been neither more nor less durable than the human voice, and neither more nor less concerned to express the meaning of the human condition. And this brings us to the heart of the matter at hand: The story of the arrowmaker is also a link between language and literature. It is a remarkable act of the mind, a realization of words and the world that is altogether simple and direct, yet nonetheless rare and profound, and it illustrates more clearly than anything else in my own experience, at least, something of the essential character of the imagination—and in particular of that personification which in this instance emerges from it: the man made of words.

It is a fine story, whole, intricately beautiful, precisely realized. It is worth thinking about, for it yields something of value; indeed, it is full of provocation, rich with suggestion and consequent meaning. There is often an inherent danger that we might impose too much of ourselves upon it. It is informed by an integrity that bears examination easily and well, and in the process it seems to appropriate our own reality and experience.

It is significant that the story of the arrowmaker returns in a special way upon itself. It is about language, after all, and it is therefore part and parcel of its own subject; virtually, there is no difference between the telling and that which is told. The point of the story lies, not so much in what the arrowmaker does, but in what he says—and indeed that he says it. The principal fact is that he speaks, and in so doing he places his very life in the balance. It is this aspect of the story which interests me most, for it is here that the language becomes most conscious of itself; we are close to the origin and object of literature, I believe; our sense of the verbal dimension is very keen, and we are aware of something in the nature of language that is at once perilous and compelling. "If you are a Kiowa, you will understand what I am saying, and you will speak your name." Everything is ventured in this simple declaration, which is also a question and a plea. The conditional element with which it begins is remarkably tentative and pathetic; precisely at this moment is the arrowmaker realized completely, and his reality consists in language, and it is poor and precarious. And all of this occurs to him as surely as it does to us. Implicit in that simple occurrence is all of his definition and his destiny, and all of ours. He ventures to speak because he must; language is the repository of his whole knowledge and experience, and it represents the only chance he has for survival. Instinctively, and with great care, he deals in the most honest and basic way with words. "Let us talk easily, as of ordinary things," he says. And of the ominous unknown he asks only the utterance of a name, only the most nominal sign that he is understood, that his words are returned to him on the sheer edge of meaning. But there is no answer, and the arrowmaker knows at once what he has not known before; that his enemy is, and that he has gained an advantage over him. This he knows certainly, and the certainty itself is his advantage, and it is crucial; he makes the most of it. The venture is complete and irrevocable, and it ends in success. The story is meaningful. It is so primarily because it is composed of language, and it is in the nature of language in turn that it proceeds to the formulation of meaning. Moreover, the story of the arrowmaker, as opposed to other stories in general, centers upon this procession of words toward meaning. It seems in fact to turn upon the very idea that language involves the elements of risk and responsibility; and in this it seeks to confirm itself. In a word, it seems to say, everything is a risk. That may be true, and it may also be that the whole of literature rests upon that truth.

The arrowmaker is preeminently the man made of words. He has consummate being in language; it is the world of his origin and of his posterity, and there is no other. But it is a world of definite reality and of infinite possibility. I have come to believe that there is a sense in which the arrowmaker has more nearly perfect being than have other men, by and large, as he imagines himself, whole and vital, going on into the unknown darkness and beyond. And this last aspect of his being is primordial and profound.

And yet the story has it that he is cautious and alone, and we are given to understand that his peril is great and immediate, and that he confronts it in the only way he can. I have no doubt that this is true, and I believe that there are implications which point directly to the determination of our literary experience and which must not be lost upon us. A final word, then, on an essential irony which marks this story and gives peculiar substance to the man made of words. The storyteller is nameless and unlettered. From one point of view we know very little about him, except that he is somehow translated for us in the person of an arrowmaker. But, from another, that is all we need to know. He tells us of his life in language, and of the awful risk involved. It must occur to us that he is one with the arrowmaker and that he has survived, by word of mouth, beyond other men. We said a moment ago that, for the arrowmaker, language represented the only chance of survival. It is worth considering that he survives in our own time, and that he has survived over a period of untold generations.

DISCUSSION

The Man Made of Words

A SPEAKER: Would you deal more with the oral tradition.

SCOTT MOMADAY: The tendency is to regard things in the oral tradition as dead, but they are not. They are very much alive, and it's important to see the way in which they are alive, the way in which they are relevant to what we are doing. And what is being done to us.

A SPEAKER: What difficulties were there to try to get Kiowa translated?

SCOTT MOMADAY: Many difficulties. And I had to rely to a great extent on people who were much more conversant with the language than I am. My father speaks it very well. He did some of the interpreting for me.

A SPEAKER: I am interested in terminology. Such terms are being used, as "literature, American Indian, oral tradition, or oral history." There is this differentiation made between literature and history. We do have a literature, you know. What do you consider the definition of the word "literature" to be?

SCOTT MOMADAY: These terms, I think are only useful as conveniences. People talk about oral literature, but sometimes it's convenient to distinguish between the tradition that is created by word of mouth and one that is set down in writing. If you consider literature, we ought to take that word to indicate writing.

A SPEAKER: But what you have described is literature, if even oral literature. You would not object to the term?

SCOTT MOMADAY: Not at all.

A SPEAKER: The body of literature of the American Indian.

SCOTT MOMADAY: I use that term, yes. It is important to realize that there is a great body of oral literature among the various tribes. It consitutes an incredible wealth of material, and it is being lost at a very great rate. It should be preserved, I think, as much as we can, for its own sake. It is eminently worth preservation. And I became convinced of that several years ago, and since that time, have done something about it. I hope that those of you who have access to oral traditions and bodies of literature will try to preserve them. The time is now. A great deal remains and I hope I can interest the people in preserving it.

A SPEAKER: I have listened to a lot of people from various parts of the country. One of the things that I have noted, both in your talk and others, is the topic of ecology. I think that what we are talking about in ecology does not really describe the concept of what our Indian people are talking about when they use similar words. Particularly now, many of our people from different parts of the country, have said that the end of the world is now in sight. It could be sometime within the next thousand years or sooner. So, I then tried to explain that American people are becoming aware of ecology, and the things of which you are speaking. But we have difficulty separating that which is truth, and that which is just words. I think what they are saying is that the word ecology is being used in a monetary or political sense, just like so many other words in the white society. And they say, you know, that the end of the world is imminent. I was wondering if you have any further insight into this, which I haven't been able to gain.

SCOTT MOMADAY: I do firmly believe that the extinction of life as we know it on this planet is threatened. I don't know about the word "imminent." I am not sure what that means, but I think we have polluted our atmosphere and spoiled our land to the extent that survival itself is necessarily brought into question. And unless we become aware of that danger, unless we change our style of life, we are on a disaster course.

A SPEAKER: My understanding is that it's too late.

SCOTT MOMADAY: I have heard that too. And I am in no position to judge. I certainly want to believe that it isn't so. The thing that I wanted to stress was that I think one begins to change his style of life by changing his frame of mind, to begin with. And this is one way in which I think the Indian has set an example that the rest of the world can benefit from. The Indian has always lived on the best of terms with the natural world. Western man and Western European civilization has always been at odds with nature. We are reaping now the consequences of that tradition, if that's what it is. We have to change our attitude towards the land. We have to develop, I think, an ethic—a land ethic.

A SPEAKER: One of the main hang-ups that most of us have is the restriction that the English language places on the attempt of native authors to translate. To a certain extent, each individual author will have to make his own decisions on how to overcome this. But I wonder if you had this difficulty.

SCOTT MOMADAY: Well, I think the question you are asking is a very complicated one. If you mean that there are intrinsic difficulties in the English language, I am not sure whether I would agree. Or to put it another way, I am sure there are limitations, but I don't think we have begun to exhaust the possibilities. If you mean that a man who has grown up speaking a native language, the use of English as the language which he's using to write a book certainly presents grave problems. Not only do you have to change languages, but you have to change the mentality which brought each language into being. And that, of course, is a difficulty which depends upon the nature of the two languages . . . English on the one hand, and whatever the other language may be. That's a complicated question. There is no ready answer.

A SPEAKER: Scott, there has been, I think many of us know, a program instituted by Navajo where they have taped and gathered together all their old historians, and I think Carl was one who did a lot in taping much of this oral history. I believe that Mr. Cassadore, who is here, has also worked among the Papago, and some of the Sioux also, and other people. There has been some work done among our people, and we still have our ceremonies at certain times of the year, when the history of our people is still being told. Sometimes it takes all of it and parts of another language to tell the whole story of creation, and it's still available. It is being worked upon in many areas. We are not losing, as a matter of fact, we are reactivating it, which is good. Because in answer to the gentlemen here on the question of translation, we may lose some of our story in translation. But the main body of what we wish to express is still available.

A SPEAKER: In your book, "*The Way to Rainy Mountain,*" and in relation to the destroying of the insects, and pesticides and insecticides, you wrote a very beautiful passage where you relate how the moon appeared in the night and the insect came towards your vision. Would you recall that to mind and talk a little bit about that?

SCOTT MOMADAY: That happened when I retraced the migration route. My grandmother, who lived just outside of Mountainview, Oklahoma, near Rainy Mountain, had just died. She had died in the Spring, on my trip. And when I visited her grave at Rainy Mountain, it was quite a touching experience for me. The first time I went back to the house in which she lived, was at night. I remember sitting on the porch outside the house, and it was a beautiful moon-lit night. The moon was full. And it was casting that moonlight upon the whole landscape. And I sat there full of mourning, and memory. I was sitting on the steps of the porch and there was a handrail to my left, and I happened to glance in that direction, and there was a cricket perched up, as it happened, in my angle of vision. The cricket was perfectly framed by the full moon. And I wrote about that in the introduction to Rainy Mountain.

HAROLD DRIVER: I am from Indiana University, and I want to tell you about certain archives we have there that may be of interest to some of you. We have the largest archives of tradition, one of the largest in the world, and the largest of music. It's accessible to any scholar, and if you are looking for a safe place to store a copy of anything you have, whether it's analyzed or not, we will take it.

(Adjournment for Lunch)

SCOTT MOMADAY: To resume our discussion about oral tradition and its relevancy to our time and place. I would repeat that I think there is a certain urgency to our consideration of preserving American Indian literature. I know for a fact that very few young Kiowas, to name but one tribe, are learning to speak Kiowa. It is a language that is dying very quickly. And it's very sad to contemplate that, because so much will be lost in terms of human imagination, as it is brought to bear upon a long history, and a very rich experience.

The only way that this experience has been reported is in terms of an oral tradition. And when the language goes, a lot of the experience itself will have been lost to us. I can't help thinking that the more time we can spend in convincing young people, particularly, that they have access to this material, and they had better make the most of that, the better off we will be, not only as Indians, but as human beings. I know that the oral literature of the Kiowas is very valuable in terms of human wisdom, the passing on of enlightening wisdom, the benefit of experience to future generations. I am sure that what is true of the Kiowas, is true of other tribes as well. And so we stand to benefit a great deal by looking into the oral tradition, into the various literatures and preserving as much of that as we can.

There are ways in which to go about it. It costs very little in terms of resources. Any one of you can arm yourself with a tape recorder and a box of tapes and do an inestimable amount in preserving tradition. If the Indian is to be defined in terms of his tradition, then it becomes a matter of asserting one's self and preserving one's identity. And that, I think, particularly now in this technological society, is worth doing.

CHARLES LOLOMA: Since you brought up the question of convincing the youth of our people that it is necessary to preserve our oral traditions, and to learn their language, can you give us an idea of *how* to convince young people of this? I really think that we just have to do it, and immediately. Because youth is demanding to know just what are we talking about in oral literature. I really appreciate, that a person like yourself is here to discuss this. Not because I am in the arts. Because you too are in the arts, if you please. There are many art forms that can say a lot. We need to find different ways of communicating. For instance, your words ring a lot of bells, and I can't help thinking, when you said that a person who tells a story is not much in white society. But he is to me, a dignified person in his own native society.

These things touch you inside. And also, you mention that if in a story you brought forth the sorrow, and if it is projected effectively, the storyteller can really make you see it. And if a story is told in laughter, then, of course, you can laugh. And other forces are used effectively. All this is done in a verbal sense, not written. Which to me is very related to life itself, and how I think and feel, and react. It is a whole system of profound and effective communication. And, also, if the story-teller gets stuck at times and some part of his story is weak, in a long storytelling, and if he catches himself doing it (mind you, he's not a trained professional man in this society) he acts this one out. How marvellous that is! He is acting in such a way that he could make you see it and feel it, and taste it. Behold, he now tones down his voice; now he makes a hollow sound; now he makes whatever sound that animals may perhaps do. And if you are an intelligent listener, you know he's using the art of pantomime.

I cannot help but recollect and compare with the Kiowa situation, also experiencing somebody whom I greatly appreciated meeting. And he is really good. He was portraying a mask scene and that ties into our discussion of myths. I heard about this man, and saw him in his own home, his own theater. His name is Marcelle Marceaux. This was in Paris, France. Seeing him doing what he did, you say to yourself, ha ha, he's a perfect clown. Saying nothing, but using his hands to make you laugh, to make you cry, to make you mad. I thought this is a great indication that we Indians have done as well, and that this our native art is not dead.

SCOTT MOMADAY: No, it is not dead.

CHARLES LOLOMA: The clowns perform. In this case, it is not necessarily the mask, but this guy is doing it with his hands. When they perform, they portray everything as to what the people in reality might be. Having met this man, I realized this is *communication* that really could be colorful to a fellow. In the pantomime, I sometimes do it in the Kiva, because I was chosen to do it, it's something that we Hopi take pride in.

Many forces are alive today for us to use in our Indian way. We have not analyzed all parts of it, certainly. I am sure the youth could develop ideas and techniques in this part of the art area. I know that, because the force of words, communication, is enormous. I believe a young Indian could possibly with this rich heritage become so great, beyond other people in this art. Because the source is very rich. At least where I come from this is alive.

SCOTT MOMADAY: I think that's true. I think that it is alive in more places than we realize. The native traditions are very widespread, and they are vital. We think of them as being lost. And there is no doubt that a great part of that wealth has been lost, but so much remains, that it really is an inconceivable kind of wealth. I sometimes think that everybody is required at some point in his life to manifest his spirit, to express his spirit as he understands it. And for the Indian, I think that's one thing, as opposed to what it is for other people. He does that by keeping alive his traditions, by returning to them, by continually expressing them over and over again. He works within the verbal dimension, but there are other ways, which you have touched upon, Charles. He does it by dancing, painting.

CHARLES LOLOMA: This is what I'm getting at.

SCOTT MOMADAY: And certainly, all of those expressions are valid, and I wouldn't put one above the other, so long as you know you express the spirit.

CHARLES LOLOMA: What you get back to then are the forces of communication that you could examine and use in such a way that you don't lose your tradition. Really you can't talk to anybody. How can you communicate? I maintain that we act all the time, because whether we like it or not, whether we know it or not, it is a matter of how well you express yourself.

SCOTT MOMADAY: The question you asked about young people, about how you convince the young people of the necessity for action at this point is a difficult one to answer. I think there are many aspects to that. In my experience, I would say that a great many young Indian people now as never before are becoming aware of their native tradition, and they're seeing it for what it is. They are recognizing the value of it. And I think it's fair to say that there is a growing kind of tribalism. A sense of tribalism that we have not had before. There are many implications in this. It would seem that there is a real chance for unification now.

CHARLES LOLOMA: Do you know of an immediate way of convincing young Indians to think in such a way that they would choose sort of immediately; because if they don't, we are going to have young kids crying. And they are already.

SCOTT MOMADAY: I think you have to tell them. I think that each of us who realizes that the native traditional values are important has a great obligation to convince the young of that, who may be wavering with alternatives. I think that a number of young people are coming to that realization on their own. They simply see what's going on around them, and they look at the world and look at the dominant society which is destroying the world in which it lives. I think it doesn't take a great deal of experience or intelligence to see that, as an alternative, it's a very bad one. Surely there is a better destiny available to man. I don't think they have to look much further than that to see that they have one at their fingertips, and it's the one in which they've grown up and have a blood interest. But beyond that, I think it's really up to the older people. Those on the reservations, and those who are not on the reservations. You know, there is, of course, an intrinsic and primary obligation on the part of the parents for their children. I think that this business of becoming aware of this, the danger of superficial existence in the modern world, is not lost upon the older people, even the elders on the reservation, who have had relatively very little experience with the outside world. I think they have a sense of the kind of dangers that exist out there in that smog-filled horizon. They have a primary obligation to tell their children and grandchildren about the traditional world, and to try to show them by example and tell them explicitly that there is an option available to them, and that they're damn fools if they don't avail themselves of it.

For a long time, the Indian culture, the traditional values in the Indian world, have not been valued in the terms of the modern dominant society. We've always, I think, thought of acculturation as a kind of one-way process in which the Indian ceases to be an Indian and becomes a white man. That's been an objective, whether we want to admit it or not, in historical diplomacy. I think, for the first time, that it is not a one-way process at all. Acculturation means a two-way, a reciprocal kind of thing in which there is a realization of a one world, or is composed of both elements, or many for that matter. I think many young people are aware of this. I think certain others are completely lost, because there are so many alternatives on the horizon. But I think more and more we ought to educate the white man. We ought to reconstruct the institutions within the dominant society, so that the Indian values are available to the dominant society. This could be done in many ways.

I teach at the University of California on the Berkeley campus, and I am working now on the institution of a program in American Indian literature within the Department of Comparative Literature there. This has not been done before, as far as I know. It's the only program of its kind. The only one that has this kind of literary focus which is very, very tight, very narrow, if you will. To deal with literature, and the oral tradition and the way in which it works in the academic framework. The more that can be done in this way, the more we can include within the existing academic framework, things that are peculiarly native, and unique, the more we are making the horizon of opportunity for young Indian people wider, and all others as well.

At the University of California, the academic world stands to gain in this venture, just as much as the Indian does. The contribution accrues to both sides, and that's exactly the way it should be. But I would like to see many more programs of this kind. Not only in literature, but in art, history, sociology, economics, philosophy, religion. There is room for all kinds of experiments in education. They ought to be made. I sat in a panel yesterday in which the whole business of Indian studies programs came under discussion. But, you know, we talked about what could an Indian studies program be, and I think there is no single answer. I think there are a great many alternatives. We have a terrific opportunity at this point. And I think the more directions we can take, the better off we are.

A SPEAKER: There seems to me to be a small contradiction here. It may be I do not understand. One of the problems is mainly between traditional ways or making them more than available; as opposed to going to school with, say, white college kids. Education, for what? It is a big problem. If you have that problem, that's one thing. But then you just said a very interesting thing about the Indian's teaching the more dominant culture, and if they stay in Oklahoma, how are they really going to do that. I think that white kids now are really open to that.

A SPEAKER: Two days ago I said I wanted to hear about Indian philosophy. And someone pointed out to me that people have been explaining about Indian philosophy for a long time, for example, Red Jacket. But now, some people are actually listening among the whites. San Francisco is a good example of that; Berkeley, too, I would think. But I would be deeply saddened to think that you have to lose who you are to become educated, because I don't think that needs to be true at all.

A SPEAKER: I don't think you have to stop being who you are. Your talk today was very beautiful. I thought it really got to the question of becoming a man, becoming who you are by birthright. And I don't really think that when you leave a place you have been in all your life, that you have to 'become' the place you're going to. If you can recognize that there are certain bad elements say in Princeton or Columbia or Radcliffe, that doesn't mean you have to "become" that bad element. As a matter of fact, you must be strong enough not to do that. Actually, you have the advantage over people. I would be insulted to think that getting a college education now means that a person simply takes what is offered, without giving what is *in* him. I think it would be an advantage to go to school, but you have to know who you are before you leave for school. I don't know about art. But you see the kind of contradiction I am worried about. How are you going to get this learning without giving up who you really are?

SCOTT MOMADAY: Well, I think that it is good to go into the enemies' camp. I think that's part of the educational process.

A SPEAKER: It is an educational process?

SCOTT MOMADAY: Yes, I don't think this is necessarily a contradiction. The Indian, in order to discover who he is, must do that on a comparative basis. It does him no good to know who he is, so long as that knowledge isolates him . . . alienates and shuts him off from the possibilities that are available to him in the world. No. He must take advantage of the possibilities, recognizing the opportunities and taking advantage of them, retain his identity. We don't want to "freeze" the Indian in time, to cut him off at a certain point in his development. We don't want to end up with a 19th century man in the 20th century. He doesn't want that, and neither do any of us. It's just simply not among the available and desirable possibilities. He has to venture out, I think, beyond his traditional world, because there is another very real world. And there are more worlds coming, in rapid succession. But it is possible for him to make that adventure without sacrificing his being and identity.

A very good point was made about the fact that the world at large is ready to listen to what the Indian has to say. It is ready to appreciate the traditions and the values, as it has never been before. Berkeley is a prime example of that. I have students in my classes who would give their left arm to be Indians.

To be an Indian on the Berkeley campus now, is to be *some-body*. Everybody listens to you. They are curious about you, and they look at you with a great deal of respect. That's not necessarily good, in the long run, but it is an opportunity of which the Indian should avail himself. And I think that's not limited to Berkeley. Alcatraz is good as an example. I had very little hope for it at first. I was very skeptical about it, because I thought it was going to be terminated very quickly, and that the Indian would be left holding the bag, and simply the scape-goat in that whole venture. It turned into something rather more serious than that, and there is no way at this point to realize just what it's going to be. But *symbolically*, it's very important at this moment, and the kind of sympathy for the Indian that has been generated in the Bay Area is really quite remarkable and quite impressive. It's a sign of the times.

MR. LYONS: I am a member of one of the Six Nations Confederacy. The question that arose here about how do you teach your children is very real to us. We are very traditional people. And yet, at the same time, we have managed to co-exist. We go out and we come back. The thing that we have had to be very careful of was the dominance of this larger society which has a great deal of pressure and power so that it can bring to bear the way of the dollar bill, and its values: Material values as opposed to what you said earlier this morning about the value of your land; your heritage is in the land. It's always the land.

We base our whole Confederacy, our whole religion around this. And how we teach is by example: You set an example and they will learn. You can't tell somebody what to do. If you don't do it yourself, they are not going to listen to you. So you teach by example.

A SPEAKER: And they believe in it?

MR. LYONS: They believe in it. How many times do you do it a day? After awhile they don't think. They do it along with you. And you bring *this* up, and you bring *this* through. Simple things really. For example, you just don't interrupt other people. Yet we do operate in the outside world very well. I my-self have been working in New York for ten years, and yet, I am a Chief of the Confederacy. I believe in it whole-heartedly, and I find that all the things that I have learned are nothing but fictions. I know we are right. Now, the people are turning back, as you might say, and looking for somebody to tell them what to do. Show us the way, they say. They don't know par-ticularly if it is going to be an Indian. It could be anybody. But it so happens that we *do* have the way, and we should show them. It's for the benefit of mankind. There are two hundred million people here and we are very small in comparison. Yet, we have maintained our identity up to this point. And it's really because our basis is the land. I mean, if the economic values of this United States should disappear, how many people are going to disappear with it? What else do they have? That's why they are searching for something stronger and more lasting. We have it. You have the land under your feet. And it's your duty to subsist on this land. If something is going to happen, and you can raise your own food, then you are not going to have to worry about that supermarket down on the corner with the empty shelves. And then the dollar bill does not rank supreme. I am very happy to hear the way you spoke this morning.

SCOTT MOMADAY: I think you have the responsibility not only to teach your children, but to reach the rest of us who have not had the same experience. You know you have been able to retain your traditional values in the most urbanized society of all in this country. And that the knowledge of how to do that and the conviction that can be developed is worth a great deal, because most Indian people in this country don't face the conflict in the same way that obviously you have. To realize that you can maintain your own identity in New York City—it ought to be terribly revealing to the rest of us, and we ought to be informed about how you do it. I wonder if you would tell the story that you told me earlier.

MR. LYONS: I will go to the story Dr. Momaday asked me to tell. About the question of "who are you?" What is an Indian? I went fishing with my uncle, he's an old chief from home, and we are out there in a boat in the middle of the lake and talking about this and that. I had just graduated from college at that point, you know. And I was kind of feeling my oats a little bit. And we were talking and he said, "My, you are pretty smart, you know. You learned a lot of things." I said, "Yeah." I was surprised. And he said, "Good. Then you ought to know who you are then." "Sure," I said. "I am Farland Lyons." He said, "Yeah. That's who you are, I guess. Is that all?" So, I started to suspect right away something is going on here. Here I am in a boat, and I can't get out. And we were out in the middle of the water. He said, "That's your name alright. We know that. Is that all you are?"

Well, then I started thinking. I started to feel a little track already, and I went to my father's line, my mother's line, my clan. I searched, and he chased me all over that boat for two hours. He wouldn't let me out. I was ready to swim. I was getting mad. Then I said, "Well, who the hell am I then?" And he said, "Well, I think you know, but I will tell you. If you sit here, and look out right over there; look at that. The rocks: the way they are. The trees and the hills all around you. Right where you're on, it's water." And he said, "You're just like that rock." And I listened. He said, "You're the same as the water, this water." I waited and listened again, as he said, "You are the ridge, that ridge. You were here in the beginning. You're as strong as they are. As long as you believe in that," he said, "that's who you are. That's your mother, and that's you. Don't forget." I never have.

CHARLES LOLOMA: Not long ago, the power people from the electric company were coming in on our land and they put the poles in by force. Somehow something happened, and the people came out and pulled the poles all back out. These people don't want the electricity. I mean, it's not really clear why a lot of people who are termed progressives want electricity and stuff. I think what the older people are pointing out, is they would—if they could afford it, welcome electricity. Their point is, if they want it, they will buy it. And it comes from you yourself and you will respect it.

MR. NORTH: University of Arizona. Its precisely because of this split among adults that we are not learning our oral history, and it's their responsibility. I have uncles who will not teach me our history. And they are the conservatives. I would like to learn from them. Our own people will go out of the community rather than communicate with me about our oral history, they will go out and tell the white man about our history. But they won't tell me.

SCOTT MOMADAY: Why do you suppose that's true? And I think you're right. That's been my experience too. I know of cases like that. I wonder if you have any idea of why they shut up at a certain point like that, why they won't talk to you.

MR. NORTH: Well, this is because of factionalism. I don't want to go into heavy history, but it's precisely the fact that we are living in close communities; families are close, but as a unit it works in reverse. As a result, we the young aren't learning our history. There are so many factors that enter into this. This is a proposal that I would like to make—talking about Indian Studies Programs yesterday. Why couldn't we have something like an Indian Studies program within our reservations, and particularly, in the communities where we have the opportunity to do so? We have a Navajo girl, who is at the University of Arizona. She's an anthropologist, and she's tired of reading books in anthropology, and what they have to say about the Navajo. I mean, I am an anthropologist, myself. Why couldn't we go out and collect our history ourselves and tell it from our viewpoint? This is her point, too. She's hiring youth, and she will have these kids go out to the hogans and interview older people. They are transcribing the tapes. This is really a great idea, because we have the need to teach oral history to our own youth.

A SPEAKER: You see, I work in a museum, and they said to me, you catalog this. It's a Hopi dress. I said yeah, okay, I can. This is my first reaction: They say, it's named such and such, and this the description. But they are also telling me how it's made, and it is not wholly correct. And, of course, I disagree. I look at the old catalog system, and see how they describe it. I use the same terms. Then, I think, well, that's not right. I am going home, and ask someone what this was for. Then it begins to make a lot of sense. With a project like the Hopi history, you have also to consider ceremonies and a cultural center. At this center, I would like to see something done like this. Have an anthropologist ask for research, and try development, hire Indian youth in the summers to do a project in language. I am interested in language. And, collect oral history. There are a lot of other possibilities, and there are kids in geology, biology and anthropology, now. This would be done by the Hopi people themselves.

SCOTT MOMADAY: There is no reason this can't be done. I mean, there ought to be, I think, from people like you, a lot of agitation for that. It certainly is desirable. In a cultural sense, it's absolutely necessary. I would love to see that done by the Hopi, and everywhere else.

A SPEAKER: But we are fighting among ourselves. Whether electricity is going to come into our communities or not. You say something like that is desirable? Something like this? It would probably threaten the community more than it would electricity. So, you mean—

SCOTT MOMADAY: You mean with devious methods?

A SPEAKER: Right.

SCOTT MOMADAY: I suppose there is that risk. And I think maybe that risk is always going to have to be run. But I think it's time to run those risks. The alternative is that we are going to lose a lot of that tradition, and we cannot afford the loss of it. I am just talking off the top of my head, now. Some of you have a much better sense of this, as regards your own communities, but I think it may be worth it. If you are going to run the risk of alienating a certain section within the community, that's just the way it has to be. We're thinking of something in longer terms of time, and of greater importance, as far as posterity is concerned. Some of you may have different ideas.

BEN BARNEY: We have been talking about convincing students or young Indian people, just as well as—I guess, younger people across the country. I am Navajo, and my training is sort of different from other Navajos. My background is, that up to about the age of about eight, I had a teacher who taught me Navajo tradition, and it ended, because he died. It was my grandfather, and ever since then, I have been going around at a loss. He sent me out to a school, because that was the only possible way I could go. So I have been going around all over, trying to find Indians, older people especially, who can take somewhat of a position that he had, and it's really hard for youth to be able to figure this out, to be able to find people. I don't mean to throw this whole thing back on the older people, but in a way, I guess I am doing that. I think, you know, this is the first time the whole picture could be seen. We come out here to this Convocation, and hear not only from Navajo, but from other tribes too.

A SPEAKER: We say that it's hard to find old people who will talk to you, and it's also hard to get them to give you the oral literature or old tradition. Well, my grandfather died, and he was one of the last men in the village who knew the whole ritual cycle or songs. He died without letting me or my father, or any of us record any of it. I think he felt that this thing that he had was too precious to just give out, and have it exposed to someone whom he never knew well. And he'd rather die with it than have that happen to it. It seems to me that he was saying, you're not going to live it. You're one of these people that's fighting for the electricity. (I am not, in fact.) But he was saying, you're one of these people who are fighting for this. My people never had electricity. We never lived that way. And if I give you my lifeway, if I tell you my life-way, you're going to sit and laugh at me, because you're laughing anyhow just by your behavior. Naturally, they are not going to tell you. I mean, they can't. I can see why he felt there is no way to communicate experience; the essence of it, the reality of it. I believe he was saying: I could give you words, and you could put them down, but that wouldn't mean the same thing. It's an entirely different thing.

SCOTT MOMADAY: I think there is no doubt that we had some very valuable contributions to this discussion, and I am very pleased that some of you have shed some very important light upon the business of oral tradition, and other kinds of tradition that are beyond any question worth our very careful scrutiny and preservation. We haven't heard from some of you who represent some very important areas of experience and expertise. I wonder if, Mr. Morgan, you would say something about the Navajo Community College.

WILLIAM MORGAN: I am from the Navajo tribe in Arizona and from the Navajo Community College which is located at Chinle, Arizona, about twenty miles from the Rough Rock Demonstration School. The only thing that I think I could contribute at this time is that we have a program going on at the

Navajo reservation, and we think this is quite a step forward. I try to put the Navajo language in written form. Finally, this was done between 1936 and '39 as a start. But we have done it, and it has worked. So now, we have several books published. It's mostly reference books, and one is entitled, *The Navajo Language*. This was mainly written for linguists. It's used for teaching. And then, when we got this program going, we had a newspaper which we put out monthly. This is a bi-lingual newspaper, both in Navajo and English. And we named this newspaper *Hitoni*, which means *The Current Events*. Mainly, the idea was to pass any information to the Navajos who are able to read it, to the people who can't read their own language. But due to the fact that the government didn't renew our funds for the publication of this monthly newspaper, why then it just stopped. But we continued to work on the Navajo language and a form of book like I mentioned. We finally got the book published by the Bureau of Indian Affairs, and with a minimum amount of money that was allowed us, we only printed about five hundred copies.

And, of course, these books went out like hotdogs, and they were gone in a few days. And we haven't been able to get any more money from the federal government to republish this book. But, while this was going on, missionaries started coming in and wanted to learn to read and write the Navajo language, and wanted to get this orthography that we use in writing Navajo. So, the Mormons got hold of this book, and they have reproduced it, as it was written by us, and these are available at the Deseret Press Company in Salt Lake City, Utah. So, if you are interested in getting a copy of it, the title of it is *The Navajo Language*.

Then, of course, several other denominations of the Christian churches adopted this type of written language. A bible translator at Farmington, New Mexico, has published it. He has published the New Testament in this system of writing. Anyway, as time went on, we had a program set up where the Navajo tribe just decided to have a small college for the Navajo students, who could have this basic training, so that they can go on to college. This small college is called the Navajo Community College, since it was established on the Navajo reservation. The older people, our leaders, thought this Navajo Community College should put emphasis on Navajo culture, and language. Right now we are still at the beginning stages of this college. We have the facilities that we need, but people are still working on it. The location of the college has been selected, surveyed, and construction will be starting somethime this spring. The contract for construction of the establishment has been let, so that all they need to do now is to start the first phases of construction, as soon as the weather permits. And then when Navajo students come to this small college, they take Navajo history as one of the basic courses. I happen to be the Navajo language instructor. They're using the system that I just mentioned, established about 1939. There have been quite a few people interested in learning how to read and write. Especially those Navajos who are more inclined to be Christians, and because they want to read the New Testament in Navajo. Of course, they have some hymn books which are written in Navajo, with the same orthography. All this has created quite a lot of interest.

Then we found out that when the Navajo students came to their Community College, there wasn't as much of an interest as we thought there would be. The reason is, because there weren't enough books in the library written in Navajo. So we are now working on some of the mythology, and the legends of the Navajo tribes as told by our older people. We sit down with them, and some of them come to our college for American Indian Seminars and talk bout certain topics. Tapes have been made, and they are stored away. All we need to do now is to transcribe these and translate them into English. These are some of the things that hopefully our students will be doing. Then we begin with our culture study. We start out with the creation of the world or story of creation. The Navajo people believe that we came up through the surface of the earth into this world. Of course, the scientists and the anthropologists say we came from Asia to the Bering Strait and then came down from the north; but the Navajo people believe that we originated right within the Navajo country. So these are some of the things that our people tell us, and these will be written bi-lingually, both in Navajo and in English, so that they could be passed on to the young people. In order to create interest among the students, we have several, what we call sacred places. There are four sacred mountains that surround the Navajo country, and we make arrangements so that some of these sacred places could be visited by our students. And then they can determine for themselves whether they want to believe these things. We also take our students to some of the ceremonies that go on throughout the year, like the dances. We take students there who are in the cultural class. Some of them participate in these ceremonies, so that they can get the feeling of being part of the ceremony. I guess most of you have heard about the ceremonial sand paintings that are made, and some of our students participate in making the sand paintings and performing the dances, the mask dances. We think this is a great opportunity for them to learn. I would like to tell you a little about myself.

When I came to school, I was about sixteen years old, and I didn't know a word of English. And I was scared of the white people. When I first came to class the lady who was our teacher was a white woman, and everything was strange. I looked at the ceiling, looked around, and I just wondered, what keeps the rooms warm? And there was no fire. There wasn't anything, but after a few days—well, some kids were running around. They had been there before I came. I guess this was at a recess time in the morning. One girl was fooling around with something, and, I guess, they kept turning it, and it came off. And then the steam came out. And this was what it was that was providing heat. I never knew there was any water or steam in that, the thing that was sitting over there in the corner. So that's how I found out that the steam came from that big piece of iron sitting in the corner. So I began to learn a lot of things just by actually seeing some of these things work. Then the surrounding was entirely new. What we learned during the first year in school through the nine months that I was there, didn't interest me at all. I tried to learn, but everything was new to me. And, of course, I may not have been so bright. When I came home after nine months for the summer vacation, well, my brothers and sisters came out to meet me, and they wanted to know what I learned. The first thing they wanted to know was how do you say water. The word for water is toe-hee in Navajo. How about o-roy-yas, this very common in the Navajo country. You see, o-roy-yas and canyons and rock, rock formations and everything like that. But I didn't know what o-roy-yas was, because this wasn't taught in school. Well, how do you say clouds? I don't know what clouds were, because this wasn't taught in school. And then they asked me how about sheep? Well, I said, I don't know what they call sheep. But I know what lamb is. Because the book that they gave us to read had *Mary had a Little Lamb*, and the *Little Jack Horner* story. These had no connection with our way of life back home. But these were some of the things that I learned first. The books were very disappointing, because I didn't know how to say *canyon*, and I didn't know how to say *rock*, or how to say *cloud* or *rain*. And just things like this.

Finally, we started to learn some of these things, after many years of this sort of teaching. The federal government and the schools that we had on the reservation in those times began to feel, I think, that Indian children would learn more if they were in a classroom with a home atmosphere. Nowadays, the kindergarten students are being taught with some kind of environment. Maybe a Navajo rock in one corner and maybe a saddle over there, and a Navajo rug and loom, and a fireplace, maybe some cooking utensils. Then they know they can point out these things and say: That's a saddle, that's a Navajo rug, and that's a loom, that's wool, and that's a picture of sheep up there. And they could learn a lot in a very short time, instead of learning about Jack Horner, and so on like that. And then you can just build your vocabulary fast with this home environment. But we really struggled through—and I was telling my friends, the white people, that it took me twelve years, or maybe more, to learn a few words in English, and I still have problems. I can listen to white-man talk. I can understand what he says, but in return, I can't express myself the way I am thinking. A lot of times they wanted me to tell them about something, and I said, I can tell you in Navajo, because if you are going to make me tell it in English, that's not fair, because that's not my language. So you're the one that is supposed to learn Navajo. If you want to know something about Navajo mythology, you better learn. Some things are pretty hard to translate. As time went on, after my graduation from high school, I started working for the branch of education in the Bureau of Indian Affairs. Then I had a chance to do quite a bit of interpreting. And when you interpret for a branch of education, I feel more competent, because I worked in the branch of education for a long time and I knew just what they'd be talking about.

In my later years, when I started working for Cornell University Medical College, who were doing some research work on the Navajo reservation, I learned a lot more medical terms. So now I feel confident that I can interpret for medical doctors. And, of course, as we went along, why we had to create some new terms to mean what the doctors were talking about. Of course, they already have some of it in our language, for instance, the body anatomy, how our lungs and heart work. And the Navajos already knew about these things, but what makes us sick, what bothers us when we are sick, what's wrong with us, well, to the Navajos, it's nature, and it means that we have done something that was not in line with nature, so we have pains. This had to be counteracted by certain healing ceremonies, and the Navajo still strongly believe some of these things. But working with the doctors has given us a lot more information about the body parts, and how different parts function. And so we have to formulate new terminology for it. We are still struggling with some of the things, because as time goes on, there are new things that are discovered in medical fields, because last summer I was talking to one of the medical doctors at the hospital in Gallup, New Mexico. He told me that there was a kind of a current of electricity in our heart which makes the body function. It supplies blood throughout the body. He said your heart would run down just like a car battery would, and it needs electricity. So this could be restored, and this is possible.

Now, how do you explain that in Navajo? We still have to find out how to explain it. You sit down with a Navajo parent or some old people who need this kind of service, and how do you explain it to them? And he, naturally, will say no. I don't want any electricity in me, because we will never know what will happen. So these are some of the things that we have to learn, and we still have to find words for. These are some of the things we are trying to work out so that we can pass this information, the new things, to our older people. And then in time, we are trying to get their old stories of mythologies on tape, and put them in black and white so that these could be printed and passed on to the younger generation.

When I first came out of school, I had learned a certain amount of English, and I had a certain amount of Navajo, my own language. So, because I have been away from school, I have been away from my home, I have been away from my parents and all my relatives. I spent nine months trying to learn English. When I went back, I found out that I didn't have very much vocabulary in Navajo either. So I have a little of this and a little of that, and I am lost right in the middle. Finally, after I finish school, I started working with the Navajo tribe as a community worker. I went to different areas on the reservation and met with people about community development, community government, and so on. Here older people talk, and a lot of times the government people would come in, and I would translate for them or interpret for them; from this, I learned my Navajo again. Like the rest of them. So, I think I know more Navajo now than I do English. These are the sort of things that individuals get into. The world is going so fast, and you can't keep up with these things. Yet, the world is going so fast that we have left a lot of things behind. I think we are in a position where we will be able to pick up some of these things, some of these stories, these old legends that are being lost. I believe that the Navajos are lucky enough now so that we have a written language. And if you are interested, I might show you examples of some of the ways that we have developed this system.

We use the ordinary English alphabet, so that some of these words and stories can be typed on an ordinary typewriter, as well as on the ordinary printing press. And this could be put into books and could be read. Except that there are only a few sounds which English doesn't have that we have, and so a special symbol was made to indicate these. And this is all I want to say at this time. Unless there is a question that you might want to ask.

SCOTT MOMADAY: Thank you, Mr. Morgan. It's a pleasure. Are there any questions?

A SPEAKER: Sir, you have chalk there that he could write with. Write "man, woman" in Navajo.

WILLIAM MORGAN: Sure. I said we use the regular English alphabet. And here we have—I'm going to write it a little larger, so that you can see it better. When we say "greeting," we say "ya-at-tay." That's pronounced ya-at-tay; this means *greetings*. The Navajo is a language—that although some of the words are spelled the same, the sounds are different. Like—like this word here. This means "you." "Nee." All right. Then this one here is, with this little mark over it, this means that this is pronounced neee, a little higher. This is "nee" and that is "neee." Then here, we have another word that spells almost the same, this means *you*, this means *he said*, or *she says*. Another thing about the Navajo language is that we don't have any special form to say *he* or *she*. So when I speak English I say this is—this is Mr. Kessler, he's sitting here. And she comes from San Carlos. I said *she*, but we don't say that. Because we don't have any special form to indicate gender. So we have difficulty with English from that point of view. Or, my father is fifty years old, or she works in Gallup. Like that. So this means, *he says*. And this means *the ground*. You see, the ground we stand on. So these are different sounds.

SCOTT MOMADAY: What is the sound of the last one there?

WILLIAM MORGAN: *Mee* and *neee*. Mee and neee. She can —and there is a way to place these little marks, that when you speak, you have to fill your lungs with air before you make sounds. You have to put some air in it, then you produce the sound. If there is no air in your lungs, you can't produce any sounds at all. So, right here, is a little opening right here. Up here, and it goes—it closes like this.

Now, I want you too—I want you to say something for me. I want you to say—this word here. The word at. A-t. That's an English word. When I drop the chalk you say at. Don't say anything until I drop the chalk. Now, ready,—now, what are you doing now? You're holding your breath. You have this thing closed. You're holding your breath before you say at. Because, all I want you to believe is that you hold your breath before you say anything. So, when this is closed, when this thing is closed, then—and then every time it's closed, this little thing comes in like this. So, then you open—and then you say *hah*. And here you have "at." Now, if you are going to say the word hat, h-a-t, now watch the chalk drop. Now, you're not holding your breath, because you are watching the chalk drop. And that's what it means. This only means that the tone on those letters is high. So these are some of the symbols that made it possible to have the Navajo language written.

I was asked to write the word for woman or something. So we call woman, *a-son-nee*. This means this one syllable here. *A-s*. And then you have *d-s*. And then you have *nee*. A-son-nee means woman. You can say ash. It looks like *as*, like that. But that's pronounced *ash-keee*. It means *boy*.

A SPEAKER: Mr. Morgan, I want you to write a word, keeen.

WILLIAM MORGAN: Okay. Keeen means horse.

A SPEAKER: What do those words mean?

WILLIAM MORGAN: That means woman.

A SPEAKER: I thought so.

SCOTT MOMADAY: Better explain that.

WILLIAM MORGAN: We have a sound which the English language doesn't have. And that's the letter right here, and it's pronounced *look*, just like the English language. And then we pronounce another sound which is voiceless. This is a sound that we make with our tongues in the same position to make the L sound. So it's *L-L*. You put your tongue here, against your front teeth. But you don't make any sound. You say L-L-L. Nothing going on here. But you say L-L-L. You can see that the voice box here is open, and it's functioning. So you say L-L-L-L, like this. But when it's closed we call it voiceless. And we say Lu-Lu-Lu. There's nothing going on here. So what we do is make the L sound by just ssh the air out on both sides, or either one side or both, it doesn't matter. Just so you pronounce the sound. So in order to make that symbol, we just put a cross here and then here is your "eye." Another high tone. And that we pronounce *shee-sleenk*. This means horse, also. Also we have another sound like this. We pronounce that, click. Like that. Now, in order to produce that, all of us can say click. But when you say that, you suck the air in. The next thing you do is just make the same sound, but reverse the air. And that's pretty hard to do, so then, we have this word. Which means goat. *Gesssa*. So we have this sound here, which the English language doesn't have. And the English also has a sound that we don't have. And that's the R sound. When I first came to school, there were pictures of rabbits all the way around during Easter. And they said those are rabbits. And I would say labbits. Because that's the closest I could get, because we don't have the R in our language.

Boy, we had a hard time saying rabbit, but we can say lamb. That's easy. Then we don't have the sound F. I had a hard time saying for. I would say poor. With my lips closed. It's as close as I can get. But eventually with a lot of practice and study, you can produce these sounds. I heard last summer, I had a chance to listen to some of the tape recordings of some of the Indians up in Alaska. I think this was the Tlingit that

I was listening to. We have a sound that is produced here, here, and here. And this is as far as we go. But they have a sound that is produced way down here. And I couldn't get it. So there are different areas on the inside of your mouth where these sounds can be produced. But there was a sound that the Tlingit was making, and making it way down. I couldn't say it. Maybe with a lot of practice I could.

That's how the Navajo language was made possible to be written, and we turn out quite a few books now. Most of our material would be bi-lingual. As the years go on, hopefully, we will create interest for young people so that they can look back on these written books, and into their old mythology and legends which could also be kept this way. So that's all I have to say.

SCOTT MOMADAY: Now, I know why it is that every Navajo carries a piece of chalk around. When you were talking about going to school the first time, I couldn't help thinking about Quincy Tahoma who was quite a fine Navajo artist, who is dead now. But he used to come, and he and my dad would paint together. And Quincy was telling me about the first time he went to the Santa Fe Indian School. He was just off the reservation, and very green. And I don't know what the custom is now, but I was certain that when he went to Santa Fe, everybody there was required to go to church on Sunday morning. And I guess there were several kinds of services there, but he ended up at a Catholic mass, the first Sunday he was there. He didn't know at all what was expected of him, and he just did everything that everybody else did.

He was telling me about this. The time came for the distribution of the hosts, communion, and everybody got up and went to the communion rail. So did he. He said, "Well, it's chow time." Regretfully, our time is up. I wonder if there are any final questions or comments?

A SPEAKER: I wonder if we could get all the Indians who are present in various languages to say out loud, as loud as they can the word *woman* in their language. Do we have time to do that? Would they be willing to?

A SPEAKER: Do you mean woman singular or woman plural?

A SPEAKER: Either one.

A SPEAKER: Do you mean an old woman or a young one?

A SPEAKER: He's pretty preoccupied with woman, isn't he?

A SPEAKER: Not necessarily. It's a word that is so common in sound. Usually, linguistic studies start off from this word.

SCOTT MOMADAY: In succession, you mean? Each one?

A SPEAKER: Well, I don't know if I can say it. But it's the same as it is in Sioux. I think it's practically the same as Sioux. Wee-yon.

SCOTT MOMADAY: All right. Who's next?

A SPEAKER: Stann-naa.

A SPEAKER: Isn't that plural?

A SPEAKER: No, it's just a different form.

A SPEAKER: In our Navajo language, we don't have any plural system. We say woman.

SCOTT MOMADAY: Everybody knows that woman covers a variety of forms. Right?

A SPEAKER: How about the Apaches over there?

A SPEAKER: Sann

A SPEAKER: Woo-dee

A SPEAKER: What tribe?

A SPEAKER: Hopi

A SPEAKER: Tewa is kwee.
San Juan Tewa, kwee.

A SPEAKER: Oh, yeah. Kwee-wen-na

A SPEAKER: Koo-sha-tee.
Koo-sha-tee is Miccousukee.

A SPEAKER: Moc-ka-saa.

A SPEAKER: Mine are the same as Victor's. Woo-dee.

A SPEAKER: How about you?

A SPEAKER: Bee-ya. The Cree word for woman is bee-ya.

A SPEAKER: That's like mother in Comanche.

A SPEAKER: Are there others?

A SPEAKER: I was just trying to think of which form to use.

A SPEAKER: If it's a married woman, it's another thing.

A SPEAKER: Women in general. Well, I suppose that the nearest thing to general terms would o-kee-ya. O-kee-ya. Any others?

A SPEAKER: Mother. Because everybody mostly says mother

A SPEAKER: I think you should have asked for mother rather than woman.

A SPEAKER: Well, I will give you ours. We-ya. We-ya. Sioux.

SCOTT MOMADAY: This discussion has been much more interesting than I dared to hope for. Okay. I think maybe we are about fifteen minutes over-time. Thank you very much. Let us adjourn.

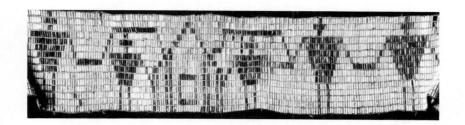

4

Implications of the 1968 Civil Rights Act in Tribal Autonomy

VINE DELORIA, JR.
Assembly Presentation

IN considering the implications in the expression "tribal autonomy," we think we ought to try first of all to define this term in its contemporary sense. In doing so, when federal-Indian relationships are considered, and when an attempt is made to analyze some of the case law involved, you immediately run into incredibly sloppy terminology. So that what appears to be relatively simple, as the words "tribal autonomy," breaks into a number of very separate and distinct doctrines, so that I don't think tribal governments today understand fully what rights they have within the 1968 Civil Rights law. In addition, they don't understand the rights they have under their treaties. By the same token, I don't think any federal agencies understand what has happened legally in America's past, as far as federal-Indian relationships are concerned.

I look at the current scene in terms of two legal concepts: "Tribal Rights," and "Individual Indian Rights," (as members of a tribe). It's pretty much an open ball game right now as to defining the Indian's relationships, both individual and tribal. The 1968 Civil Rights law, in connection with the American Indians, was motivated by two things. In the first place, a series of conflicts occurred between members of the tribes of the southwest, culminating in three legal cases. These dealt with religious freedom. This included a case in which the Native American Church was not permitted to function on the Navajo reservation, because the tribe was not considered subject to the Bill of Rights in tribal relationship with its members. Consequently, there was no way to force the issue. Another strand emerging to create pressure for the provisions of the Civil Rights law in reference to the Indians, was the situation on the Fort Belknap Reservation, where, in 1965, the right of habeas corpus was sustained by the federal court. And so this was the type of application of the rights of an Indian individual: a right to due process in criminal procedure. Prior to that time, I can find only one case in law, and this was with regard to the airport in New York State. The right of habeas corpus has been available to Indians of New York State's reservations.

I would like to dwell primarily upon what we call tribal autonomy. The Handbook of Federal Indian Law lists certain attributes of tribal autonomy. It says that tribes possess all the powers of sovereign states, that tribal rights are derived from treaties, and that the treaties limit only external powers. So when the United States was formed, the Indian tribes in this country had power to sign with *other* nations than the United States, and also had the right to regulate their internal affairs. Thus, we have the United States in direct relationship with the tribe, and this is primarily on a treaty basis, or in other words, with the tribes treated as sovereign nations. In 1871, when treatymaking ended, the third doctrine that Cohen describes in his Handbook of Federal Indian Law should be considered, as to tribal sovereignty; that is, the doctrine of tribal sovereignty by statute and by treaty. And so, looking at it simply from the tribal point of view, it is an evolution from an independent nation capable of exercising all aspects of sovereignty, scaled down (first) in external powers to sign treaties with governments other than the United States; and then, with limitation of powers. In one court case, the court ruled that the government has absolute power to do anything it wants with Indian tribes. What then emerges is the United States as a power with the ability to completely ignore the tribe as a political entity, concentrating all of its efforts upon its powers over tribal members as individuals.

Now, I am going to re-draw that diagram, because I think this is where the confusion exists. If you read the case law carefully, and check the statutes on federal Indian law, you find that the United States government has two principal concepts of what a tribe is. In the treaty relationship, the tribe is a corporate organization. In other words, the tribe has identity in and of itself. The United States, signing a treaty with the Navajo nation, for example; or a conglomerate of tribes, on a one-to-one basis, one nation to another. But, in 1831, we have the major cases on the Cherokee nation. What the courts and the

VINE DELORIA, JR. explaining that the "next step for Indian tribes, or Indian individuals, is a reaffirmation of the basic cultural behavior pattern and value system of the Indian Tribe."

lawyers are talking about here is the concept of the tribe as a conglomerate. In other words, a lot of the language in Worcester and Cherokee Nation vs. Georgia describes a Federal-Indian relationship, and it states that their relationship and status is comparable to that of "Ward and Guardian." In this case, the tribes are being considered as a conglomerate of *individuals*, and not a tribe with an existence and a political entity all its own. And so, if the tribe is so considered as a conglomerate of individuals, then it is fairly easy to move over into another status and innovate the "ward" relationship, as in Worcester vs. Georgia, to describe this status and relationship of the tribe, thus actually and in fact completely ignoring the tribes in their corporate status. But the TRIBE is the original signer of treaties.

These are the two major developments that can be seen in connection with historic federal-Indian relationships as to the Native American tribes. And this is what must be considered when discussing the question of tribal autonomy generally and even in the contemporary sense. Paralleling this is the relationship of the states of the union with the tribes.

In 1812, in one case, New Jersey vs. Wilson, the fact is expressed that a state once contracting by treaty with tribes, could not then break that treaty or amend that relationship, because this would be an impairment of contracts under the Constitution of the United States. Thus, in this specific case, the position of the Indian tribe, insofar as its corporate ability to act is concerned, is frozen at that point in its relationship with the state. And yet, you take a case in Nebraska, where the state attempted to assume jurisdiction over individual members of the tribe. It was ruled that the state had no right to come in and act against the individual members of the tribe, because they had maintained a tribal relationship. The courts have consistently ruled that if the members have tribal relationships, then they are still "wards" as a distinct entity of the United States government, and the state cannot act unless the United States government authorizes them to do so. And so now, basically, there are three *types* of relationships. In applying the 1968 Bill of Rights to the members of Indian tribes, I think there are some real questions on constitutionality, whether or not the United States can do this. Because, what we are dealing with, I believe is the frozen situation that exists, and legislation has in some cases been interpreted as if it was a treaty. For example, the Sioux tribes sued the United States government in an attempt to get a reversal of the 1887 Allotment Act in regards to reservations. The case went to the Supreme Court, and in its decision the Court said that in regards to the Sioux nation, the 1887 Allotment Act should be construed as a treaty. So again, in this case, where Congress had said after 1871, that they would not deal with Indian tribes on a tribal basis, there is a determination (in the Sioux decision) that many statutes pertaining to Indian tribes must still be construed on the basis of treaties. Whether the Sioux decision can be made to affect contemporary Indian affairs in relation to the Bill of Rights, is still a question. I would suggest that in a number of cases, this whole confusing set-up has been reversed; the most spectacular reversals are in fact being seen today. In 1872, the State of New Mexico passed a statute saying that Indians in New Mexico, particularly the Pueblo Indians, were not to be regarded as Indians in other areas are regarded: They were to be regarded as citizens of New Mexico, with all the rights of citizens, including the right to sell land and the right to be taxed. In 1912, this was overruled. And so, on the one hand an Indian was being considered in the conglomerate sense as an individual person, capable of being a citizen—paying taxes and selling land. But in 1912, in the Santa Fe decision, Indians are considered in the sense of a group of people living in the Pueblo, exercising certain tribal or community rightss the rights of an identifiable political entity. This created the Pueblo land problem. Because, through all of New Mexico, which had originally been occupied by the Pueblos, every sale by individual Indians that has been made during the forty years between 1872, when the first legal decision was made, to 1912, when the second decision was rendered, the title of such land was clouded, thrown completely into the air. I think Joe Sando can tell you more about this than I can, with reference to the situation in New Mexico. That is one good cause in favor of the situation in connection with Blue Lake now. It switches back and forth, and the rights guaranteed in 1912 are guaranteed to the Pueblos as a corporate governing body, which is really the first theory of Indian law.

I know this is confusing as hell, and technical beyond recall, but there are any number of side avenues that can be taken, and so if we are talking about the legal power of the United States to unilaterally put the 1968 Bill of Rights into operation over the Indian tribes, I believe there is a great question of constitutionality in terms of forcing the tribes to be placed under this Act . . . because these definitions have never been cleared up in any point of law. Specific cases and particular litigation runs into immediate confusion.

I would like to talk a little about the Congressional hearings on constitutional rights of American Indians, so that you can see the confusion that is created in this situation. I will refer to a memorandum of one hearing. They are discussing guardianship of the federal government over Indians residing on reservations, and guardianship of Indian members of a tribe when the tribe is considered or interpreted as a conglomerate. In other words, all of you have a treaty relationship and there is no conceivable way in which you can have wardship, so-called, if the tribe maintains its corporate status. It has been interpreted in Worcester vs. Georgia, and in other cases, as if the tribe was a conglomerate people, with the United States as responsible for each individual of this conglomerate. And thus the Solicitor of the Department of the Interior is talking about guardianship, and he says this guardianship is extended to all Indians within the reservation. In the early days after the Allotment Act, there was a tendency to withdraw from federal guardianship. This tendency was later reversed. Federal guardianship, or responsibility of a sort, over tribal members was recognized. A recent case in court also gave far-reaching recognition of administrative and supervisorial guardianship. This case made a determination of the rights, the powers, and the duties of Congress as a guardian of the Indian "wards," unless there is some determination on the part of Congress, in the form of legislation, plainly indicating the purpose of Congress to change or further implement or alter the relationship of the U. S. government with the tribes. Unless this is done, Indians of tribes under patent must be held as wards.

In another case, in connection with Indians who had received fee patent land under the Allotment Act, it was determined they were to be terminated for all practical purposes, even though they had status which the United States government and Congress had clearly defined as "unrestricted Indians" because they had retained tribal relationships. This concept had another facet, in which the United States is placed in the relationship of guardian over Indians who in essence had no Indian rights or relationships whatsoever, since their relationship with the government had been terminated. Another case still resulted in determination that the guardianship of the United States, and of course that of the Secretary of the Interior, extended beyond the termination point. This case came up in court only two years ago. And so I am placing some really basic questions before this assembly of Indian scholars, questions involving three separate and distinct ideologies running through federal laws concerning Indians, any one of which has tremendous implications for us. It is going to be incredibly difficult to determine just how it will affect tribal governments, or tribal autonomy if you will. I believe this can only be resolved in a suit against the United States to prevent the United States from enforcing the 1968 Civil Rights Act upon tribal members. In such a case, I see that we stand at least a fifty-fifty chance of success.

There is a case in which the first amendment was not enforced against the Cherokee Tribe, because it was in existence before the United States of America came into being, and since it possessed sovereign status and the rights of a sovereign nation, it could only be limited by special wording of Congress to limit. The question that ties all this together is in one 1912 court case, which determined that once the rights of Indian individuals are vested, once these rights are capable of being exercised by an Indian individual, then no subsequent legislation by Congress can take away that right. Thus, it would appear to me, that all the rights that we have and exercise as Indian people, derive from our membership in the Tribe. I believe these rights have been vested in us, so far as we in our lifetime can exercise them, because *and only because* we are members of our tribe.

What has been happening is that the tribe is considered to be a conglomerate, with Congress having guardianship over this conglomerate. Therefore, it has not been possible to have property rights vested, taxation rights, or any other so-called rights of citizenship, until Congress passes legislation directly affecting the members of the tribe. When you examine the termination statutes, this confusion becomes incredibly clear. There is one person present in this Convocation, Gary Orfield, who did the most sensational research into the nature of Termination Acts. Here is another thing to ponder over . . . in preambles to termination legislation, it is stated that this legislation is for the purpose of making the Indian people first class citizens, and to bring the Indian up to the level of the white citizens. But when you read this, and get to the last part of the Act, in Section 23, it is stated that nothing in this Act shall in any way change the status of these people as United States citizens.

And so, they are running in confusion back and forth. Because in termination, what you are doing is, you are jumping your logical train, and you're affecting the vested rights of tribal members, insofar as they are tribal members. Yet, the intent of the termination statute is to affect tribal membership status. So, the preambles in termination statutes deal with definitions of what membership is. The concluding clause uses an entirely different concept of membership, and an entirely different concept of Indian rights. And so, it seems to me, this is a legal problem. It will affect just about any kind of research that we can be doing in the next few years. Because when you get into the Bill of Rights, you are dealing, I believe, primarily with equitable doctrines of Anglo Saxon law, and these have been construed over a period of close to a thousand years. And they are construed primarily in terms of one value system and what the justice in that value system would be, regardless of what the law is. What I would suggest as the next step for Indian tribes, or Indian individuals, is a reaffirmation of the basic cultural behavior pattern and value system of the Indian tribe. Because, if we can wipe out this interpretation, (I think it could be very easily done, and I think the case in 1968 did) and transfer jurisdiction to the federal government, the autonomy of the tribe is intact. It's the jurisdictional change. There is a real question of constitutionality here, as to whether the United States has the right to unilaterally extend its own laws over the tribes at the corporate level without the tribe's consent. And so the 1968 Act didn't make any difference with those tribes. I am talking about the tribes that have a very serious question as to how the Civil Rights Act is going to apply to them. If we wipe out this interpretation, concentrate on the constitutionality of the Act, as to relationship of the federal government, it seems to me that our Indian courts and tribal councils can create an Indian common law to clearly and justly define this relationship. I think we have a chance to develop a contemporary, very sophisticated, and very modern concept of law, because law and every other social area in non-Indian America is going steadily away from retribution, and all of the Anglo-Saxon Old Testament concepts. Most of you know, from your personal knowledge and studies, that much of Indian law is based on compensation and not retribution.

I think all I can do this morning is to outline for you where I think the next action will be, and how I think we can define how the 1968 Act can be interpreted. Upgrading the tribal courts and tribal council knowledge of their people in all aspects, is extremely necessary. We can create an Indian common law to define this relationship, and in effect not only nullify the unilateral extent of the Bill of Rights beyond the tribal government onto the individual Indian people, but we can develop an incredibly sophisticated law which will be of much more use to our people, and an example to all other people. Non-Indians will begin to copy it, and so on. I think one of our purposes is not just to talk about it, but to begin to find out how we can cross tribal lines and begin to map out an area in which we can jointly contribute as scholars. I know it sounds incredibly technical, but I think I gave you enough of an idea, so, as you are working in your other discipline, you can begin to see those elements in your own field that might relate to it. Until we clarify the incredible confusion of words existing in federal Indian law, I think it would be virtually impossible for anyone to define the 1968 Civil Rights Act and its implications for tribal autonomy or for individual Indians. Basically, we will have to see what the Indian courts do on the reservations. We will have to encourage the Indian judges not to make any but the simplest opinions on the minor situations that come before them. We will have to be of great assistance to these people. They will be thoroughly close to scholarly doctrines, and it will record much of the history and much of the folk ways that other people and anthropologists and sociologists have been and are recording, simply for their own information, certainly not for our use. But now, we as Indian scholars have an opportunity to combine all these disciplines and help to develop Indian common law, tribe by tribe, eventually on a national basis. And so that's the situation as I see it.

I will answer any questions, but this, I think, is a pretty complicated situation. I hope that in the next year, you will be able to see things in your own discipline that will help construct a total body of knowledge to help us practically in this endeavor.

DISCUSSION

Implications of the 1968 Civil Rights Act in Tribal Autonomy

A SPEAKER: In a very practical sense, do you feel that there should be a movement back to tribal corporate structure, and the defining of membership from the tribal courts other than allowing it to be done elsewhere?

VINE DELORIA: Yes, I do. As an example, let's take something that is pretty hot in the news, the Indian fishing rights issue. The fish and game people continue to oppose the Indians, breaking up their nets and boats. The state, through the Fish and Game Commission, is enforcing the public policy. The public policy doctrine is presumably "the greatest good for the greatest number of people." It means that you can do anything you want, in the name of this doctrine. You can sacrifice a small group of people in order to do something for the larger. But the Indian claim is based on treaty rights. What we have there is a direct relationship of the state and the individual Indian in a conglomerate sense. And yet, when the Indians hunt and fish, they are going off the reservation, because their tribe signed a treaty with the federal government guaranteeing them this right. Now, individual Indians didn't sign the treaty. The tribe signed the treaty. All that the Indians are doing is exercising their tribal rights. It would be my contention, that the state cannot make a forcible entry against individual Indians. It should not. The only remedy that the state has is to go through the federal government, with the treaty as a center of legal reference, to get a restraining order or some type of declaratory judgment against the tribe.

In other words, the only remedy the state would legally have would be to go into federal court, and act with the help of the federal government. I think this is where the confusion arises. You see, because the northwest people are acting as if the tribe were conglomerate, and each one of them had individual hunting and fishing rights. You don't see that situation logically until you begin to exert legal reasoning.

A SPEAKER: Mr. Deloria, we recently had an incident in Montana. The state court ruled that they had jurisdiction over the tribal courts on those matters involving the individual on the reservation. How will this affect your argument?

VINE DELORIA: I would think that this ruling could be broken. Unless your tribe has accepted the concurrent jurisdiction of the state, I think they can break this ruling. I think some of the tribes have different types of concurrent jurisdiction with the state on different things. But I think if the tribe is wholly federal then legally we can get a finding that the reservation is Indian country.

A SPEAKER: I was wondering about most of the cases that have been brought out in the last four or five or six years. Efforts were made to put federal and tribal relations on an individual basis, in order to prevent a specific case from going out of tribal jurisdiction. On the other hand, there have been cases where tribes or individuals have tried to act as a tribe, in legal cases.

VINE DELORIA: Yes. This is the trouble, you see. The Sioux tribe, in 1956, stated: "The Federal government has the responsiblity to act." So we went to the Supreme Court, which said in effect: "This is less than a nation. We had no responsibility whatsoever when that treaty was signed." In other words: "Wait a minute, man. You are a ward of the government. You didn't even have a standing to begin with." If you are going to start out on these theories in the criminal courts, you defend the nation, and one nation's going all the way to the court. If you start out on the wards, you are talking about individual members. What you are talking about in connection with wardship is really a last action. You have to have recognition of one nation against another, one recognizing the identity of the other as a nation, and vice versa. When you get to the Supreme Court, the Court very candidly says that if you accept the wardship theory, we will wipe you out, because you are a dependent nation. The words "tribal autonomy" in referring to a relationship with the United States, imply a relationship with the reservation itself.

A SPEAKER: There have been no cases where they could maintain any sense of tribal autonomy, up to the completion of the case.

VINE DELORIA: Yes. This is the weird thing. In Kansas, the tribal governments are dissolved for all practical purposes. So right before the Civil War, the State of Kansas comes in and introduces taxation, and includes the Shawnee, as well as a whole series of small tribes. Individually, they are cases of the Supreme Court. Now, in many cases, the treaty declared that tribal government was to become extinct, and a civilized (or Western) language was to be adopted. And yet, they get up to the Supreme Court, and the Supreme Court says, so long as you have a tribal relationship, the state has no right to tax you. And this Dewey County thing that I read, the essence of that case is that there is no way out of the tribal relationship. Because if you have allotments, and a fee patent on it, and are regarded as a competent person, the federal government still has a wardship relation with you, because you have a tribal relationship. And so, one of the keys to resolving the whole thing is to take this concept of tribal relation and examine it, and what is it? Is it a relationship between individuals, a conglomerate, or is it a tool we haven't used yet to find the corporate situation? What I am really saying is that I don't see any conceivable way to develop an interpretation of the 1968 Civil Rights Act as to its implications for tribal autonomy. We are simply going to need more initiative from tribal people, their courts, and their councils, to get more legal doctrine so that we can go in and define this. But I think if you compare Worcester vs. Georgia, the Kansas Indian case 1956, Lone Wolf, and then Native American Church vs. Navajo, you will find all the ideologies run through the law that I outlined here today. And I think it's our task, as Indian people, to work in all these aspects of the law.

A SPEAKER: Going back to the earlier illustrations, the ward theory, and the question of dependent nations. Do you know of any instance of a case tried on a trusteeship theory? The theory of such relationships? Put it in a different dimension, could this be construed so as to give that relationship a different light? A trust relationship?

VINE DELORIA: I think that's where the word and the concept come from.

A SPEAKER: But the words "guardian relationship" seem to indicate an inferior position. Which the courts have dealt with over the centuries. I was just wondering if this could be argued, if treaties can be construed that way.

VINE DELORIA: I would think it could. I think the only problem you have there is the relationship itself and the words "a ward, guardian," but they've been used a hundred and twenty-eight years.

A SPEAKER: But given a set of facts on a particular treaty, it seems to me that at least it should be attempted in court.

A SPEAKER: Mostly in the area of water rights and land rights, because it's been obvious where legal title is held by the United States in trust for the particular tribe. It seems to me that we could work up a case. We could get a trustee-beneficiary relationship. We might be able to move it into other areas and distinguish the ward-guardian relationship.

VINE DELORIA: The more I think about it, the more I like the idea. I really haven't thought of it before. But there is a case, I know, that indicates the Statute of Limitations can't be revoked because of the tribal relation. And, you know, certainly I think that is something to look into. I am happy that you brought it up.

A SPEAKER: I have a second question. If you are going to develop Indian common law and you can crack this system by using remedies which are guaranteed under the constitution, aren't you in effect saying that you are going to use the constitution, but that ultimately you won't be bound by it? Or are you suggesting the possibility we could develop our own constitution.

VINE DELORIA: I think a certain development in this country has moved the constitution quite a ways from the original interpretation as to Indians, merely because of the cases on Welfare and Non-residence, and all the Civil Rights business. A number of them are beginning to interpret individual rights in the group sense. If you go through the Civil Rights cases you might say the Blacks shall have the same rights as the superior race, but all the way along it's a group situation. I think today we are in an ideal situation to move, and reinterpret the interstate commerce clause of Congress's relation to the tribe. Because in the constitution, where you have the commerce clause in the 14th amendment, all you really have is the right of Congress to regulate commerce among the Indian tribes. You don't have justification for the bureaucracy existing today. Nor do you have justification for Congress coming in and doing anything it wants on the reservation. I recognize the problem, but I think that with research and litigation programs, we can define the terms. And that's why I can't really define tribal autonomy at this point.

JEANNETTE HENRY: During the settlement of the California Claims cases, one of the attorneys told us that Congress, when it passes a law which is in opposition to treaty conditions, the law takes precedence over the treaty conditions automatically if the law was passed after the treaty was signed. In other words, Congress can pass a law which in effect abrogates a treaty. Where are we then?

VINE DELORIA: I think that has been bugging the Indian people for a long time. I think the way, which we never tried, is to go into the immigration treaties, because there are definitions, and very specific ones, about how a treaty can be amended or changed. Maybe Bob Bennett or some others who have been in law longer than I have can quote the cases. I have gone through a lot of them. At any rate, it says that a government and the nature of society can change in one part of the treaty relationship, and the treaty is still valid. I can think of another doctrine of interpretation. Just because some part of the context of a treaty is abrogated, does it mean the whole treaty falls? I feel that the Indian community just never had a clear shot at defining the law itself. We have always been so under-educated and struggling to define what our rights are, that many times we have had to accept whatever people said about Indian law. I think that we have got to restrict what we are talking about and really make the treaty operative as a *treaty*. In other words, if the United States and Canada had a treaty, we should support that treaty under the same ideology. For example, in immigration treaties referring to China, the government of China changes several times during the life of the treaty. But the basic rights guaranteed to Chinese individuals are maintained under that treaty. And so I think what we have to do is to use international law concepts to define our own treaties that now affect us in domestic relations inside the country.

A SPEAKER: Can you discuss something about Alaska? Regarding what is happening there.

VINE DELORIA: No, I really wouldn't know much about that situation.

A SPEAKER: One more question. What bothers me, is that I think the present supposition is that this idea of yours will work, if the government permits us to maintain the treaty relationship. Now, I think that's always been an Achilles heel. And I don't think our condition is such, with the leverage that the government has, that this could be a workable system. It seems to me, and I suggest this to you, that a better idea, although it may be at this time unrealistic, is to negotiate more new treaties. If our land setup is a commonwealth or territory, a permanent commonwealth or territory, we could re-enact the common law into our own system with our own courts and our own judges interpreting our evaluation of the common laws that exist in the United States today. I suggest that to you, only for discussion.

VINE DELORIA: I am just thinking in terms of what has happened in connection with the termination act. I think it would be extremely dangerous at this point to open up new treaty negotiation situations. If we take the decision on the allotment act in reference to the Sioux tribe, that subsequent legislation after the treaty making period is to be construed as part of a treaty, then we have to go back to the treaties and we will find that there are guarantees of how this is affirmed. If you study all the treaties, you find that the requirements almost universally were that three quarters of the adult males of the tribe must agree before the treaty relationship could be valid.

SAM BILLISON: I'm from the University of New Mexico. Where did you conceive this idea of Indian common law? Many times we have Indian leadership who take the route of litigation, and once they go to court and get involved with the BIA, we lose their effectiveness. We also lose their effectiveness when they go to work for the BIA. I am thinking, are you interpreting from the Bureau standpoint in connection with the law? The reason I state this, is that I understand you, Mr. Deloria, may be considered as a candidate for one of the Bureau's positions.

VINE DELORIA: You really know how to hurt a guy. No. I think we have a lot of case law for reference. In 1895, there was a case in which Indian marriage laws were determined by tribal custom rather than by civil law. In 1911, there was an

Oklahoma case in connection with divorce. Bob and some others can correct me. But I think that in the majority of domestic and individual relations of tribal members, most of the cases have been decided on this basis: that if the Indians applied their own law to the situation, it was upheld, and in the complete absence of Indian law, you had a definition of state law applied to the Indians. So, I think there has really been an Indian common law in the state and federal courts for a long time. What I am suggesting is that our tribal judges do not render formal decisions, but go back to the definitions used in the old days, and there have been a lot of papers done on the way the tribes would avoid executing a murderer, as one example. I think the Yanktons have four different ways to let a person off the hook before they killed him. And I am suggesting that we use our scholarly talents in all areas and rebuild a concept of Indian law out of it. Because I think we can go through the recorded cases now, to obtain a pretty good basis for an Indian common law. But these are at another level. They are not at the tribal level. (We've got to have some coffee at some stage of the game. I know I do anyway.)

A SPEAKER: One question. I was wondering if I understood you correctly when you said one of the advantages of letting common law develop, is that, historically, Anglo American law has been retributive and Indian laws have been compensatory. What we are talking about when we are talking about the 1968 Civil Rights law, isn't this mostly a question of pre-Civil Rights laws? Does the fact that we are talking about applying the Civil Rights law to tribes have that much to do with the difference between American common law and tribal common law?

VINE DELORIA: I think it does, in the sense that we have all the particular situations we want. Let's take the case of a father of seven, who seriously injured a father of five. Give the accused person his due process. And the council goes through the whole thing of civil law: search and seizure, and so on. But if the man is found guilty, then what you are doing is taking the father of seven away from his family and putting him in some federal penitentiary. The father of five is in the hospital. And you have two mothers and twelve kids who have nothing. What I am suggesting in connection with Indian common law is that we use the law build up to the point where through due process procedures the person may be found guilty or innocent, but the actual sentence that he is going to have is to be just and humane. You see, the thing of it is, that in some tribes, a man would be required to stay and provide for both families until the man he had injured is well enough to support his family again. I think that the approach in Anglo-Saxon law is irrational and unjust. And I think the Indians are the only people who can improve this. What I am really worried about, is that we will not be able to fill this gap quickly enough with Indian ideology, and what will happen in the next ten years, is a tremendous definition of criminal procedural practice in tribal courts. So that what we will have is speedy justice in the white man's way of meting out justice, but in effect we would be destroying our communities. In all the things we are doing in the Indian movement, we are going to be blocked, if we put a basically formal type of language into legal decisions. I have no quarrels with procedural guarantees. But I think that they should be heavily founded on native culture and ideology.

JEANNETTE HENRY: I think it's about time. Vine is trying to tell us, what he's proposing is that we strengthen our treaty rights, and retain the Indian culture and ideology that we had in the past. And I believe that he proposes to strengthen this for all the tribes. I think it is a fine idea, rather than block out that area he has designated on the board. I believe that is what he is trying to tell us, and I think he's correct. I think there was something brought up yesterday in regards to looking into our treaty rights.

WILLIAM DEMMERT: I'm from Alaska. I would imagine some of you know the situation, but for those of you who don't, the Alaska Indians and natives were conquered and they never signed a treaty. When Alaska became a territory, and later a state, the land that Indians used and claimed, were not to be infringed upon. This is the basis for our Land Claims Act which is now in Congress.

VINE DELORIA: I am not familiar with the Alaska situation.

D'ARCY McNICKLE: I wanted to ask Vine a question. The Claims Commission Act authorizes lawsuits against the United States in the name of tribes or identifiable groups. It seems the United States tribe and treaty relationship reaffirmed the obligation to the tribe with respect to treaty provisions. Now, we're winning judgments, and we're winning many cases, if not all cases. Congress, in appropriating money established by the judgments, often stipulates the conditions by which the tribes can get that money. Often, there are limitations against the right of the tribe to make per capita payments or to stipulate a certain percentage in payments. In some cases it is stipulated that the tribes terminate federal relationship. And my question is, whether or not this isn't a good area in which to bring action against the United States which would reaffirm that corporate tribal status.

VINE DELORIA: I think it is. I think there is a case in court now, concerning a tribe which terminated in 1954 and part of the government liability in it, is that they set up an Affiliated Ute Corporation, and at the same time, the trusteeship relationship is continued. A suit is pending in the name of the Affiliated Utes, but the class action is on behalf of those Utes, because not all of the physical assets in the reservation were specifically mentioned, (and Congress has not spoken on the subject) they still retain those rights. I think that, at the present time, there will be cases that might do us more harm than any good. I think the whole subject has to be approached very cautiously and very selectively in terms of litigation, until a lot of consistent logic can be built up. If you are familiar with the litigation that the Black community undertook between 1937 and '54 to defeat the Board of Education, they completely reversed the Supreme Court decision. But this was done step by step on the basis of logic. I am not suggesting that we go into one major suit in the next year and try to break the whole issue open. A consistent theory of reaffirmation of tribal sovereignty must be built up, and substantiated. I think that the United States has a certain liability as trustee in the Affiliated Ute case. If you can establish liability of the United States, for the way the Ute assets are handled, then you can use that as a stepping stone to limit the power of Congress to tell the tribes what to do in distribution of Claims Commission awards.

There is a ruling that states, as to the Sioux, that in cases where the tribal council refuses to act, an individual Indian may act as plaintiff on behalf of the tribe. This introduces a different concept as to what sovereignty is, and might constitute an element that severely limits what I suggested here today. I think it would be very applicable in Oklahoma, where you have the tribal government appointed by the Secretary of the Interior. Individual Indians in that state might approach the issue on the basis of representing the tribe, and a class action could be made applicable. At least such action might rebuild certain sovereignty for the Five Tribes. Bob, I wonder if you could speak to this point, because I think it's very relevant.

ROBERT BENNETT: The whole Indian society, and the individual who commits a wrong against their society, knows when it is a wrong. They know the difference between right and wrong. Also, they are prepared for the consequences of their actions. As a result, the statistics on the criminal offenses which come before tribal court systems, show a large number of convictions per thousand population. This is because of the fact that these people in almost every case (at least ninety-five per cent of the cases) plead guilty to the offense, having committed a wrong against the society, and are willing to suffer the consequences.

Now, as the various legal procedures of Anglo society move

into tribal society, you will find a development of criminal case procedure in which an officer must, for example, knock on the door three times before entering, and sustain a violation of procedure for example, in not spelling the name right, and a few other things. These young individuals alleged to have committed some crime are going to get off, and not be convicted of their wrongs. This is going to have a very serious and traumatic effect on tribal society, because it will act to change the whole concept of justice in the fact that they are only wrong if they are proven guilty. Which is not their traditional concept, still existing at the present time, because they know they are guilty when they commit a wrong against their society.

And so, many young Indian people are taking the consequences of their actions. However, outside interests have been moving in and saying that you no longer have to take these consequences, because this is a violation of your civil rights. Further, I think that such individuals will have some hangups. We already know of young Indian people writing to the Circuit Courts and saying: Why didn't you punish me, because now I go with this criminal act on my mind all through my life, because I wasn't punished for what I did. So I think this is another aspect of this situation, quite apart from the legal aspects, which also will have an affect.

HERB BLATCHFORD: Vine, In your concept of Indian common law, I have a feeling that a great deal more should be done for the corporate status of the tribe, but I am not really sure as to how this could be accomplished. For instance, perhaps a termination bill has been signed, or the approach of termination confronts a tribe or reservation, as examples. The procedural approach could be that, first you get hold of the assets and the tangible value of the tribe. And in return for those assets or whatever valuable consideration it may be, you have to sign for termination now. This places, it seems to me, the tribal corporate entity under a situation of duress, not so much different from that of duress in a treaty situation. Somewhere along the line the corporate entity structure should be strengthened along with the common law element. I was wondering if you could give us some possible approach to that?

VINE DELORIA: You can't develop one without the other. My suggestion would be to examine the early treaties. You will find in sections of the earlier treaties, I would say from the very beginning up to about 1830, that the phrase applying to the contracting parties continues throughout the text. Many of the provisions enclosed in that phrase, implicit or stated, are in terms of two parties contracting with each other. So, to strengthen the sovereign corporate aspect of the situation, I think there would have to be a dual interpretation of treaty and contract, simultaneously, so that specific provisions, of a contractual nature, can be enforced against the United States. But, the major emphasis would have to be one that would protect the tribes in connection with termination, and would involve an appeal to the equity of the situation. The doctrines of interpretation of Indian law, I think, spell this out, except that we haven't put it together and articulated it. For example, one doctrine is that if Indians aren't specifically mentioned in legislation, then the legislation does not apply to them. This raises a real question in taxation matters because of the questions raised as to the rights of Indians in 1912, and the Income Tax Amendment in 1913. Certainly, there is no evidence that any tribe signed legislation agreeing to pay income tax. Indians aren't mentioned in the Income Tax Amendment. They are mentioned in the 14th Amendment as "Indians not taxed." The whole thing is an incredible can of worms. Once it's opened up, it will cause endless debate. I think part of the answer to this is to go to the treaties in the claims areas. Any Indian wishing to settle down into an agricultural mode of life, signs his name in the government book, and the agent allows him to locate some place on the reservation, according to regulations previously enforced.

And so, I think the tax exemption, the right to allotment, would then be derived from your corporate tribal status. I think you are certainly going to have to go in on specific sections of legislation well, since 1906, and hit specific points and develop a new concept of tribal powers.

MR. NORWOOD: How many law students do we have here, or people who are involved in court cases, litigation, and so forth? There must be some. The rest of us then are laymen, as far as legal language, is concerned. But what I am interested in is, that you raised great hope here that we will be fortunate enough to find the evidence and legal justification necessary to push some of these cases through court, and thereby take a definite Indian stand on common law and other matters. How successful have we been in the past in this . . . without having them blocked by people who are as shrewd as we? Who, perhaps, sense a danger in allowing a minority to come to the fore?

VINE DELORIA: I would say that we have never had Indian lawyers who are not motivated entirely by pecuniary needs or desires. I see John Echohawk and his new generation of young Indian people coming up, and these people are going to create a new legal ideology. I think we have been very fortunate in the past, to have some of these decisions fall our way even though we were totally helpless to create any type of defense. I realize that if there is any significant movement towards a redefinition of Indian rights that would give us a clear case against the United States, and particularly against Congress, there would be immediate moves to block or to nullify such a victory. That's why I suggested a broad legal examination of such cases as Immigration Treaties and other issues. We've got to expand our thinking. We've got to expand the concepts that have been used.

For example, take a good look at the treaties made about 1808 when the United States goes up the Missouri River. These treaties are formulated on just one page. They provide that the United States as a sovereign nation, and the particular Indian people, will be friends forever. I think that type of phrase has been used to mean that the Indian tribe gave up its sovereignty and became a totally powerless nation. But I think you've got to start writing briefs using the material gathered from all disciplines, so that we can take those particular treaties with the help of historians and others, and show that the United States was in great fear that the Indian tribes on the frontier would become allies with Great Britain, in the coming war of 1812, and that this phrase and those treaties should not be interpreted as Indian tribes giving up everything. But rather as the fact, that at this point and at that time in history, they acknowledged the United States, as an ally, as opposed to Great Britain. So I am not talking simply in a legal sense. This is our first Convocation of Indian Scholars. There are a lot of Indian historians and others who can help. But I certainly think that if we start making our point, only on a legal basis, we are going to find ourselves blocked over and over again.

Actually, I am at the same stage that most of you are. You know, I am just finishing law school. But when I was in North Carolina, I realized we were virtually helpless without a knowledge of court strategy. We could put tremendous political pressure on Interior and Congress. But we could not hold a united front for very long. And some of you who were in tribal government in '67 know that we had a lot of telegrams blocking Stampede Dam, and we held up the second series of the issuance of rules and regulations for its construction for about six weeks. But our united front began to disintegrate as time went on. If we had had a well developed court strategy and worked with political action in another direction or in a series of court actions in another way, we would have been much better off.

So all I am trying to do here is throw out some ideas to think about. We have to start some place; we have to outline some kind of a route and go as far as we can go, and then re-evaluate. If we could correlate such plans nationally, I think we could win in different areas.

A SPEAKER: How can we use such a tactic when you see what happened in the state of Washington where the judge, about two weeks ago, ruled that another judge's decision of last year wasn't valid. He said it was nonsense. He refused to even recognize that the tribes exist. This is their tactic now, that the tribes don't exist. And that, therefore, they have no rights. This completely ignores any federal court decisions in the state of Washington. How do you fight this kind of thing?

VINE DELORIA: I think you have to coordinate a series of national organizations and national programs that have different emphases, so that you can build up a lot of pressure on one particular point, and you give them certain alternatives to the situation. For example, take the Presidential Proclamation of 1819, and the statement passed by Congress, in which the President of the United States has authority to initiate programs to prevent the extinction of Indian tribes on the frontier. This does not say anything about "on or off reservation," "urban" or anything. It provides for upholding their treaties' rights. What I am trying to say is that we always have an option of how we go into court. Take the state of Washington, and if that state is compelled to provide services for Indians which might break the state budget, they might consider alternatives. What would be the effect, for example, if an Indian group starts bussing unemployable Indians into the state of Washington? And the state can't refuse them, because of the present nonresidency rule on welfare. I think that all kinds of strategy can be worked out, but I certainly don't have a lot of the answers.

A SPEAKER: There were many Indians in court for fishing illegally, in which we won. We got a ruling that we did have the right to fish. But then when we went back and fished again, we were arrested on a civil action, and charged with contempt of court. So a jail sentence of 90 days was the result. How do you react to this?

VINE DELORIA: There is no doubt, you know, of the harrassing powers of the state. There is also a good chance we can use some of the Civil Rights provisions in such cases. Thank you my good friends. Let us adjourn this panel.

5

The American Indian
in American History

JEANNETTE HENRY

IT is not my purpose, nor is it possible in this short paper, to present a comprehensive study of the American Indian in American History. We can only approach some salient points for purposes of discussion and indicate certain areas of study. A critical view of how the Native is dealt with in the history of this nation is needed before proceeding with the story as it really was, as it really is. Such a critical overview comes readily to this discussion, since Indian scholars have assembled their own study of the subject, some of which was dealt with in various Memorials, articles, and oral statements of the Natives in the early part of this century; most of it in the comprehensive study published by the American Indian Historical Society titled *Textbooks and the American Indian*.

To briefly enumerate the failures of the educational system and the educators in relating the role of the Indian in the history of this nation: Omission of the contributions and role of the Native occurs in most cases, federal-Indian relations are not dealt with, slanders and degrading statements are made against the Natives, inaccuracy exists in most textbooks, there is general misconception, misinformation concerning the history, cultures, and current situation of the American Indian. The fact that the Native American culture and history is the only original culture and history of this land should guide historians in their treatment of their subject. The undisputed contributions of the Indian in all phases of national and world economy, technology, medicine, and arts, should have guided the historians in their telling of the story of America. Instead, the historians have on the one hand exhibited racism, and on the other have denied the role of the Indian in our history. That this is no accident, but the result of a philosophy of historiography among the historians of the United States, will be dealt with later in this paper.

The subject of this panel, *The American Indian in American History* could just as well have been titled *A History of Indian Americans.* While the two are certainly inter-related, the treatment of each really needs to be different. The interesting thing about both subject titles, however, is that neither has received a comprehensive, scholarly treatment to this day. Fragmented histories of the Native Americans have appeared in the works of anthropologists, historians, sociologists and popular writers. But there is not even a working and workable chronology of events in connection with either the Native's role in the history of this nation, or that of the history of the Native himself as he emerged from his isolated pre-history to take up his place in national and world evolution as a prime contributor to economy, medical science, naturopathy, conservation, and philosophy; to influence the fate of this nation in her most crucial historic moments; and finally to persist in the face of all obstacles as this nation's Achilles heel, the conscience of America.

This paper cannot fill the void created both by a failure of the academic community and a failure of the Indian himself to perform the task of clearly delineating his history, analyzing and authoritatively portraying his role in the life of this land. We can only approach some strategic concepts, create some ideas around them, explore and examine them as a means to identify an objective point of view which can stand the test of analysis.

Let us briefly trace the philosophy of historiography, and identify some of the historians whose work has falsified the history of this nation and that of the Native. Among the early historians, whose work is clearly racist and exhibits the most blatant prejudice, we can name George Bancroft, John Fiske, R. Carlyle Buley, and David Saville Muzzey. The latter is still utilized in classrooms all over the nation. His book is used even by the Bureau of Indian Affairs to teach Indian children that their ancestors were "always at war, nomads," a concept so palpably untrue that a search of the specialized literature could disprove it. This concept is utilized in an effort to disprove Indian claims to their land. Indians were certainly no more nomadic than the early Europeans whose restlessness impelled them to move from one area to another across the nation, in a search for riches, for gold, for better land and a "better living." That they moved

Emplaning from San Francisco, this group of Participants. Left to right: Frank La Pena, Edmund Ladd, Rupert Costo, Rosalie Nichols, Bea Medicine, Barney Hoehner, Lowell Bean, Rick West, Robert Kaniatobe.

Cross section of Participants at the General Assembly sessions. Listening, learning, weighing all sides of a question, appeared to be the general reaction.

illegally upon Indian lands is never mentioned. It is also not mentioned that Oraibi, for instance, in Hopi country, is the oldest continuously inhabited area in the United States, and is older than Berlin or Moscow. It is not mentioned that the race of peoples now known improperly as "Indian" constitute the oldest and most persistent, continuous, occupiers of their land in the world; and that each tribe and nation had its well-known and well-delineated lands.

Among those historians who entirely ignore the role of the Indian in our history are Charles Beard, Lincoln Steffens, Carl Becker, to name only a few. A recent book by Arthur M. Schlesinger, Jr., "The Age of Jackson," ignores the Indian, Jackson's crimes against the Indians, the Trail of Tears . . . all of which marked Old Hickory's administration as one of the most evil and punitive in history. The list of such "falsifiers by omission and commission" is voluminous and includes many modern writers.

In 1893, Frederick Jackson Turner, a young history instructor at the University of Wisconsin, read a paper at the American Historical Association Chicago meeting. "The Significance of the Frontier in American History" was Turner's contribution to the philosophy of historiography in the United States. Since then, historians of the United States have argued the "Turner Thesis" back and forth, for and against. Many eminent historians have supported the Thesis, which rejected the view that the United States political system was Anglo-Saxon in origin, and advanced the idea that the determining role in American history was the colonization of the territories of the West, and westward expansion. Turner's concept, with its principle that the expansion of the United States was one of the primary and basic determinants of its development both past and future, served also as the geopolitical foundation for the idea of American world domination. The Turner Thesis influenced historians from then on, and as one writer has stated, it "reigned almost unchallenged during the first quarter of the 20th century." Opposition to the Thesis developed thereafter on the part of United States historians, but that is another story and one which we will not explore in this paper. Suffice it to say that adherents of the famous Thesis are still working in the discipline of history. This concept has influenced American philosophical and historical thought, and has certainly influenced the writers of textbooks. Aside from the concepts propounded by Turner in connection with the development of this country, of special interest to us is the Turner concept as it affects an understanding of the position and role of the Native American in the history of the United States. Let me quote from Turner's work, above referred to, for an illustration of this point:

"Up to our own day American history has been in a large degree the history of the colonization of the Great West. *The existence of an area of free land,* its continuous recession, and the advance of American settlement westward, explain American development."

"In this advance (westward expansion), the frontier is the outer edge of the wave—the meeting point between savagery and civilization."

"The most significant thing about the American frontier is, that it lies at the *hither edge of free land,*" (Emphasis supplied.)

Thus the concept of Indian land as "free land," "unoccupied land," was woven into the philosophy of historic interpretation. In this way it was denied that the Native American had rights to his land, both under international compact between the European nations, and through legal actions of the United States government in the very fact of national recognition of Indian tribal land rights in treaty making actions with the tribes. Thus, from a position in colonial and later Gold Rush times, that the native had to be exterminated in order to make way for progress and civilization, was developed the more sophisticated philosophy of *nonrecognition* of Indian land rights. In more modern times, there is the historian Ray Allen Billington, who describes the taking of Indian land as an element of the "continual rebirth of society." Billington is a supporter of the Turner Thesis. His references abound with phrases of "free, unoccupied land."

"The frontier army post, serving to protect the settlers from the Indians, has also acted as a wedge to open the Indian country . . ." says Turner in the above mentioned paper. He gloats, "Every river valley and Indian trail became a fissure in Indian society, and so that society became honeycombed." He explains and describes his philosophy of imperialist expansion at the expense of the Native peoples in these words, "The Indian was a common danger, demanding united action." Thus, if one wishes to *understand why* the textbooks are filled with misconceptions and distortions, we must look to the philosophy of historiography developed by the historians of the United States. On the other hand, let me say that every dominant political class in any society attempts to control the ideology of the people most particularly through the learning process in the schools. It is not to be wondered at that *this* American society does the same. The school boards and curriculum commissions which control the adoption and purchase of textbooks usually adopt books to support the dominant political class. So too do the professors in universities, departments of various disciplines. Indeed they are not presented with alternatives to these books. In the case of the Native American, to date there has been no effective resistance to this philosophy and these books. Without resistance, and particularly with no alternative books submitted for adoption, we have ourselves to blame for this condition.

The study and evaluation of the history of the Native Americans is confronted by another difficulty. With the exception of highly specialized works in anthropology and archaeology, the works of historians and other scholars are bound hand and foot by preconceived concepts of world history and its beginnings. It is recognized generally, that the North and South American continents developed independently of Asia, Europe and Africa. Historians concern themselves largely with the known world of Europe and Asia prior to the knowledge of the American continents. Known history ("known" through the development of the art of writing) begins, in the minds of western scholars, with Egypt in the Nile Valley and Sumer in the Tigris-Euphrates Valley. This point of historic reference is wrong to begin with. There already exists a large body of knowledge about the western hemisphere, and this body of knowledge should be incorporated into that of the world as a whole. The practical application of this position can be shown in several ways. Let us take the question of the existence of slavery as a political and economic stage of society. While slavery existed in Asia and Europe in the centuries before Christ, it did not exist here. The upheavals and revolutionary destruction of slavery in the Han empire in Eastern Asia during the second and third centuries A.D., and the collapse of the slave-holding system in the Roman empire in the fourth and fifth centuries A.D. occurred at a time when North America was building a completely different, diffuse, varied society based upon the direct relationship of man to his fellows and man to nature. In this area, investigation is still to be done. It seems highly probable that if left alone, Native American society could have developed in an entirely different way and in a different direction from that of the rest of the world.

We need to examine the concept of history as a whole, the history of mankind, and not alone that of some group of peoples or countries, in order to understand our own history and to make it understood to others. Even the terminology in the historic sense (a terminology which we ourselves accept without question), is unrealistic and unreliable for an understanding of the historic process. Concepts such as Europe, Asia, Africa, East, West, are also unreliable in the study of history. For the Chinese today, the West is Europe and America. For the ancient Romans, the East was Syria, Palestine, Persia, Armenia, and Mesopotamia. And so, if we wish to examine history and understand the process of history as it took place on this continent, we need to take as our subject-matter the history of all mankind, and within that framework the history and development of our own people can be made clear, and some understanding can be achieved.

We have opened up several avenues of thought here, and I will leave you at this open door and proceed to deal with certain specific areas of our history. For those of you who expected a precise chronology of events in our presentation, this is not our intention. Our goal here is to stimulate thought, encourage serious study, and disclose some fruitful areas for scholarly work.

One of the most important elements to be found in the history of this nation, as well as in the history of the Native races of this country, is that of conflict between the Europeans and the Indians from the time of first contact, through the ages and until the end of the 19th century. Nearly four hundred years of such conflict occurred, perhaps the longest period of war and near-war in human history. While it is perfectly true that blood has been spilled on *both* sides, even the most biased of historians must admit that ours has been enormously the greatest loss . . . especially when considering the facts of genocide, foreign diseases, the destruction of our culture and the loss of our country. The whole story of this conflict has still not been told. From Philip to Joseph, we have fought the intruders. Every step of his march across our land we fought him. Today, our posture is that of a defeated people, yes. But a people who did not bend, and had to be broken. And even when broken, we are a people who arose again and again to fight once more. Today, in a different arena and with tools of policy, strategy, and legal negotiation, we are fighting still. We often read about Indian ''terror, wars, resistance to progress.'' Nowhere has there been told in full the story of courageous Indian resistance to the onslaught of the European, or the open and brutal attacks upon the Native by the white invaders. For the sake of historic overview, let us see the brief, bare facts of this chronology of bloody conflict:

> 1537: Pequot war in Northeastern U.S., in which Indians were burned alive.
> 1580: Pope revolt of Pueblo Indians.
> 1675-6: Philip's war against white intrusion.
> 1769: Revolt of Indians at San Diego Mission, California
> 1782-7: Wyoming Valley conflict in Pennsylvania
> 1790-5: Conflict with the Northwest Indians. Mingo, Miami, Wyandot, Delaware, Potawatomi, Shawnee, Chippewa, Ottawa.
> 1811: Continuing conflict with Indians
> 1812: Beginnings of Seminole conflict.
> 1813: Peoria Indian war in Illinois.
> 1813-14: Creek conflict, Alabama, Georgia, Mississippi, Tennessee.

1817-18: Seminole conflict in Georgia and Florida.
1823: Arikara conflict, upper Missouri river.
1824: Chumash rebellion, California
1827: Illinois Indians at Fever River conflict.
1827: Winnebago, Wisconsin, conflict.
1828: Revolt of Estanislao, California
1831: Sac and Fox war in Illinois
1832: Black Hawk Indian war, Illinois and Wisconsin
1834: Pawnee conflict in Indian Territory.
1835-36: Toledo boundary dispute
1835-42: Seminole conflict in Florida, Georgia, Alabama.
1836-37: Creek conflict in Alabama
1836: Missouri and Iowa line conflict
1836-38: Cherokee removal
1837: Osage conflict in Missouri
1847-48: Cayuse conflict, Oregon
1849-55: Indian conflict in New Mexico and Texas
1849-50: Yuma Indian revolt
1849-55: Apache, Navajo, Utah conflict
1849-61: Navajo conflict, New Mexico
1849-52: Gold Rush conflict with California and Oregon Indians.
1849-61: Conflict with Comanche, Cheyenne, Lipan, Kickapoo in Texas
1850: Attacks on Pit Rivers in California
1850-53: Utah Indian conflict
1851-52: Rogue River Indian conflict, Oregon
1854: Open warfare in Oregon
1855: Yakima conflict in Washington Territory
1855: Oregon and Idaho sees conflict with the Klamath and Salmon River Indians
1855: Oregon continuous conflict—Snake Indians
1855-56: Nebraska Territory, Sioux conflict
1855-56: Cheyenne and Arapaho conflict
1855-58: Florida war continues
1857: Sioux conflict in Minnesota and Iowa
1858: Spokane, Coeur d'Alene, Paloos in conflict with whites
1858-59: Wichita Indians in Indian Territory conflict
1859: Colorado River in California, conflict
1859: Pecos, Texas conflict
1860: Kiowa and Comanche conflicts in Indian Territory
1860-61: Navajo in New Mexico
1861-64: Cheyenne Indians, conflict
1862-63: Sioux Indian conflict, Minnesota and Dakota
1863-69: Open conflict against Cheyenne, Arapaho, Kiowa, Comanceh in Kansas, Nebraska, Colorado, Indian Territory.

1865-68: Southern Oregon, Idaho and northern California Indians, conflict

1867-69: Indians in Kansas, Colorado and Indian Territory subjected to attack.

1867-81: The Lipan, Kickapoo and Comanche Indians sustain attacks.

1874: Sioux attacked in Wyoming and Nebraska

1872-73: Modoc Indian war, Oregon and California

1873: Apache Indians in Arizona and New Mexico, conflict

1874-75: Kiowa, Cheyenne and Comanche Indians in Indian Territory, conflict

1875: Conflict against Eastern Nevada Indians

1876-77: Wyoming and Montana conflict

1876: Battle of the Little Big Horn, in which Custer was defeated

1876-79: Northern Cheyenne in Indian Territory, Kansas, Wyoming, Dakota, Nebraska, Montana, conflict

1877: Nez Perce conflict in Utah

1878: Bannock Indian conflict in Idaho, Washington Territory, Wyoming Territory

1878-79: Cheyenne Indians in Dakota and Montana, conflict continues

1879: Ute conflict in Colorado

1879: Snake Indians, in Idaho, conflict

1879: White River conflict against the Utes in Utah and Colorado

1890-91: Sioux conflict in South Dakota

1898: Chippewa conflict at Leach Lake

This is a very incomplete listing of the conflicts between the whites and Indians since contact. Still, it provides an insight to the resistance shown by the Natives to encroachment upon their land; and a complete history will show the conflict as erupting between tribes as well as between whites and Indians. Such fratricidal conflict arose when the Indians of various tribes were forced upon lands already occupied by other tribes. This history of continuing conflict and open warfare gives us an entirely different picture of Indian history and should be explained and described in textbooks as well as in all studies of the history of this nation.

History will ask, in the face of this 400 years' conflict, could it have been prevented? Considering that the demands and needs of the *Europeans* have always dictated policy towards the Indians and their lands, without considering Native demands and needs, the question itself is purely academic and the answer is self-evident. First, in early history of white-Indian contact, the co-existence expedient was dominant and based on a need for a friendly and co-operative Native. Next historically, the attempt was made to obliterate the Native once he showed resistance. A policy of genocide and extermination was then "justified" by religion, white supremacy, and racial expediency. Following this, the removal policy held sway, ugliest and most rampant result of that philosophy which negated the very principle of democracy and law, on the basis of which the Nation had purportedly been founded. And finally, the brazen and outspoken philosophy of the apologists for the American Imperialist land-grab as enunciated in the Thesis of Frederick Jackson Turner. With the philosophy of "free, unoccupied land" as propounded by this authoritative scholar, homesteaders and land grabbers could feel free to continue overrunning Indian land, treaty or no, legal or illegal. In capsule form, these are some of the highlights of the history of Indian America, and that of the American Indian in American history. What we need now is an exposition of the role of the Indian at the various stages of this nation's history: the colonial period, Revolutionary war, the war of 1812, civil war, and so on to modern times. Such a history would develop the story of legislation such as the Dawes Act, the Indian Reorganization Act, relationships between the Federal government and the Indian tribes, movements of tribes throughout the years on reservation lands at first, and latterly to urban centers as a result of the Relocation policy of the United States government.

Indeed we have fought defensively and offensively, not only on the battlefields of this land. We have fought as well in political negotiation, as recognized nations signing treaties with other recognized nations. The story of these treaties is also known only in a fragmented way. Felix Cohen surveyed our legal conflicts from the viewpoint of a jurist. But the full implications, national and international, of this arena of our struggle, remains to be told. No one has yet traced the treaty-making of a specific tribe or conglomerate of tribes, with its effects upon the tribal economy and society, through the hundreds of years' history of that tribe since white contact. Indeed all history to this date has been written from the European point of view, the view of the foreign intruder. Even today, history is still being written from the viewpoint of a dominant political class. The question may be asked: Is it possible to deal with history in a purely objective way? Is it possible to tell it like it was and like it is? It is possible. It is scholarly, and it must be done.

Let us take another example of historic treatment of our subject. Let us take one practical aspect of the story of our people. I will take that part of it having to do with white contact in and of itself. Take the history in modern times, of the Pueblos. The Indians of the Southwest, particularly the Pueblos, practiced a form of agriculture in which they diverted enough water for their needs from the great Rio Grande River, and conserved its waters by small dams, developing intensive cultivation during the dry seasons. In 1846, white settlers came upon their lands, bringing huge herds of cattle and sheep, which denuded the vegetation. The result of this was erosion, huge quantities of silt carrying the stream bed of the Rio Grande off. In 1943 it was reported that two-thirds of the arable land of the Rio Grande Valley had been lost. Overgrazing of the uplands, lack of such care as was exercised by the Native Pueblo people, caused this condition. Today the Rio Grande is a mere trickle; the land is dry; both Indians and nonIndians suffer the results. Now *this* is history of a different order than the conflicts we have enumerated. But it is history of a most important kind, and should be dealt with, if for no other reason than as a lesson for the future.

I have merely indicated areas of research and study, teaching and writing about our people. A massive amount of work is to be done, and must be done objectively, with scholarly care and accuracy. It is a fact not to be ignored that our people—who have spent their lives, their meager earnings, and their energies in the struggle for the rights of their own people—have become bitter, sometimes soured and cynical. It is not to be wondered at that when the Astronauts stepped upon the moon for the first time, and the news of this great scientific feat was broadcast all over the world, one Indian wag could only mutter ''I wonder how long it will take them to get rid of the Natives *this* time!''

I wish to make only one more point, to raise one more question, before closing this paper. The question is one of identification of the Native American in this modern day. According to the Bureau of Indian Affairs, an Indian is one who is enrolled on a federal roll of Indians, in some cases of one-qurter quantum Indian blood. In other cases, such as that of California, the Bureau accepts one-two hundred and forty-sixths degree of Indian blood (Mr. Leonard Hill's statement in hearings in California). For ourselves, we need some clarification on this matter. First of all, we believe that the tribes themselves and they alone have the right to determine Indian membership on a tribal roll. But then, what should be done with the thousands of Indians in the state of California, as one example, whose tribes have been decimated, massacred, who have been mixed with other races, but who consider themselves to be Indians and whose communities have always considered them to be Natives? This question has caused a good deal of conflict among Indian peoples, and deserves to be treated. I will say only this: There are two sides to this matter; and both sides involve the question of assimilation. Racially, the Native American has been assimilated, and any other ideas are foolish. The bloods are mixed so much, and inter-mixed again and again, so that the full-bloods can be counted in the mere few hundreds. Even the full-bloods now have relatives representative of some part of Caucasian or other racial strain. Nationalistically, however, the Native race is further from the European immigrants than we have been in 200 years. A peculiarity exists as well in the fact that generally the whites who intermarry with Natives become imbued with Indian nationalism so quickly that they are indistinguishable in their attitudes from the blood-Natives. Culturally, the situation is even more complex. Languages, religions, ritual observances, the arts . . . these, in their purity and original form, are largely lost, the pitiful remnants almost painful to look upon.

Politically, the Indian remains a thorn in the side of the American ship of state, whose flag will always fly at half-mast whenever the so-called "Indian problem" comes to the forefront, a place it holds today without any doubt. Thus, from the posture of a Native People whose nationalism is still intact and growing, from the position of a people united in their demands for historic justice and reclamation of their lands from some specific date in history, can we proceed to examine, study and evaluate the facts of our history as a race, and the story of our people as we have affected and been affected by the development of the United States of America.

I call to your attention a case in point, which brings the problem fully in view and frankly ready for consideration: The case is that of the Lumbee Indians of the middle Eastern seaboard, who have no language, no culture of their own, no enrollment with the Bureau of Indian Affairs, and no per capita payments for lands taken from them. All they have by which they can be recognized as Lumbees, is the fact of their own knowledge that they are Indian, and the fact of the discrimination and prejudice shown them by the state of North Carolina, which did not permit their children to attend the public schools, forced them into segregation, and finally wrote into the laws of the State, that they are Lumbee Indians! How shall we view this question, as Indians? Well, we have, as one of the discussants in this panel, a Lumbee educator, Dr. Adolph Dial, who will pursue the matter further.

Finally, let me say this: The Greeks left us Homer; the Trojan War left to posterity the character of Hector; the wars with the Saracens gave us Roland; the English peasant movement gave Robin Hood to the world; the folklore of Iceland produced Grettir; the Scotch border poetry brought the Douglas; the Spanish epic brought Don Quixote. But the American epic, even more elemental, more passionately moving, more filled with color and the heart-throb of humanity, has given us Tecumseh, Logan, Sitting Bull, Philip, Joseph, Estanislao, Osceola, to name but a very few, the noblest heroes of them all. Shall their story remain untold? That is for _you_ to say.

ADOLPH DIAL, _Discussant_

How many of you know anything about the history of the Lumbee? Six. I am safe in assuming that most of you know very little. Let us then approach it from this angle. In Robinson County today, which is in the southeastern part of North Carolina, there are some thirty-five thousand Lumbee Indians. These are a people who were never wards of the United States government . . . a people who never lived on a reservation . . . a people who were speaking the English language many, many years ago . . . a people who have been living in European-type homes. I could go on further. We believe, and historians believe, that the Lumbees are descendants of the Lost White colony of 1587. You should know the story of this lost colony, so I won't take the time to go into it. Out of a total population today of 100,000 people, there are some 35,000 Lumbees. Sixty per cent of the Lumbees are part Black. Forty per cent are part white. The two groups actually make up a clear majority, but yet you wouldn't think so. Registration for voting is poor, consequently it is very difficult to get a man in government office. I have a brother who serves on the County Board of Commissioners. In the area of maximum population we have many, many Lumbees, and we vote pretty much a solid ticket in that particular area.

Many of you remember the Lumbees from the Catfish Ku Klux Klan movement in 1958. We put the Klan on the run once for all, and I am quite sure that the Klan will never again return to Robinson County. We came out with guns in self-defense; we came out to prevent the Klan from getting into our country; and we won against them.

Now about the history of the Lost Colony, briefly. White's colony came to the Lumbee country in 1587. When he returned in 1591, the colony had disappeared. They had had a previous arrangement, that if the Colony was in trouble, they would "write on the tree," to make it known. And if they left the area, they were to "write on the tree," and if they were in serious difficulties, they would do the same, and make a cross. Upon the return of the group, there was no cross, but there was the word C-R-O carved in one place, and on the tree there was the word cooctroan, which gave no cross, showing no sign of distress. In the early 18th century, when Europeans came again to this area, they found a group of people there, the Lumbees. In 1754, the Governor wrote to the North Carolina governor, asking for the census of the Lumbee Indians in that state. The North Carolina governor replied that there is a group of Lasnees living on the Lumbee river who have taken their land. He was speaking of course, of the group we know today as the Lumbees. We find these people during the early American Revolution, serving also in the war of 1812, but in 1835 to 1887 this became a dark period in Lumbee history. This was so, because due to constitutional revisions, North Carolina in 1835 did something to the people. You see, we were not "wards" of the government, and therefore we were completely ignored in every way, although it was generally known about our race and our background. During this "dark period," or the dark ages, as I call it, there was a gang, from 1864 to 1874, led by Henry Barlower and his brothers, and seven others. This man's father was forced to dig his own grave and was then shot. And so Henry started out for revenge. I think, what is significant is, why were these people killed, and why would a young man in his early twenties begin to really fight for his people. He set out to make the people responsible for the murder of his father and brother, pay the penalty. The government had $10,000 reward for this man, dead or alive. To this moment, no one has collected a penny for the body of Henry. An interesting thing about this gang, was that it was an integrated gang. Doc McLaughlin, one of its members, was a white man. Alfa White was a black man. Henry, Steve, and Tom were Indians. Calvin Knox and Hendrickson were Indians. William Charfice was Indian. We now expect to begin some kind of Henry Memorial Fund in honor of this man. We feel today that the "Lowery Gang" should be viewed as a group which did something for the Indian people. After all, we view the boys who raised the flag on Iwo Jima as great heroes. In the same way every Indian in Robinson County today sees the Lowery gang as men of honor, men who fought for a cause.

In 1885, the North Carolina legislature designated the Lumbees as "Croyden Indians." A white legislator had this done, because he believed the Lumbees were descendants of the Lost Colony, which then blended with the local Indian population. This name was used in such a way, from 1885 to 1911, that if you walked up to a man and called him a "Croyden" in Robinson County, the way the whites were using it, you were subject to prejudice and prejudicial acts of all kinds. So they got to the politicians in 1911 and demanded that something be done to recognize this group of Indians in another way. So, in 1913, the North Carolina legislature changed the name again . . . this time to Cherokee. We went on this way until 1935, when the state legislature of North Carolina again took up the matter and gave the people the name Lumbee. And that was a good name;

it was perhaps the name they needed all the time, because geographically they were residing on the Lumbee river. In 1954, Congress followed up with the same recognition.

Fortunately or unfortunately, we never had to contend with the Bureau of Indian Affairs. We built our own schools, and my own grandfather gave something like $500 for this purpose, to build the first one-room school for the Lumbees. The state legislature appropriated another $500 to run the school. We started with 15 students, and out of that school, which was known then as Croyden-Navajo school, grew the Pembroke State University as it is today . . . a school of about 1600 students, with a faculty of 107, eleven of whom are Lumbee teachers. The university president is a Lumbee; so too is the head of the history department, and some other administrators. I believe we now have only about 150 Lumbee students out of approximately 1600 total enrollment. There are about thirty Black students. Once this school was for Lumbee students only. Now the situation is changed; we had to desegregate, and our people began to panic. Actually, the total number of Indians there today is not much more than what it was in 1943. A great deal of discrimination exists in Robinson county today. It would take a week to tell about it.

Our public schools are all of 95% plus, Lumbee. For a long time we wanted money for schools, and we didn't get it. We never did have federal money for schools, until very recently. So out of our own pockets we began to make our own way. I feel that we made considerable progress. I am proud of the Lumbee people who now hold high positions in government, in education, in various agencies. While we have a Lumbee on the Indian Claims Commission, we ourselves don't have any claims. So, if this Lumbee judge doesn't treat you right, let us know, and we will get him down home and work him over. I believe at this point, I will open up for questions.

DISCUSSION
The American Indian in American History

DON WANATEE: You stated you spoke the English language. Is this your primary language?

ADOLPH DIAL: Yes.

DON WANATEE: You have no native language?

ADOLPH DIAL: No, we haven't.

LEW BARTON: We have remnants of the Algonquian among our people.

RAY CROSS: I want to ask about Pembroke State University. You say it started to educate the Indian. Why did it lose its orientation, and how do you justify that in terms of educating American Indians in history?

ADOLPH DIAL: Maybe this was bad.

RAY CROSS: I think it was bad.

ADOLPH DIAL: In the early 1950's, when we integrated the institution we never thought the whites would swallow us up. We thought it was a good idea at the time. But the whites did swallow us up. Maybe we would have served a better purpose if we had gone around the country and looked for Indian students, and traveled in that direction. Pembroke State University is the only existing state university that once was all Indian. I think I am right on this.

A SPEAKER: Does Pembroke actually recruit Indian students today, or are they subject to the same individual motivation?

ADOLPH DIAL: Here is the problem. One day, when we started pulling in students from New York, New Jersey, all over the place, the kids who attended these poor high schools, they just couldn't make it in college; they didn't do well in the college level. So what do they do then? They go to work in a factory, or move away.

RAY CROSS: I think this was an unfortunate move.

ADOLPH DIAL: I think so too. And I argue with them around Pembroke about this.

EMERSON ECKIWARDI: I am Comanche, southwestern Oklahoma. I understand that Lumbees, in addition to a few other tribes, are not recognized as an Indian tribe as we understand it. I am wondering what criteria, if any, were used by the government in not recognizing you people as Indian tribes.

ADOLPH DIAL: If you're saying: Do you have the Bureau of Indian Affairs there; do have a reservation; do you have the United States Government looking after you, then the answer is no. We do not have them. In 1954, by congressional action, we were recognized as Lumbee Indians.

EMERSON ECKIWARDI: I guess, what I mean specifically, is—for instance—do you have a language of your own? Do you have a special culture?

ADOLPH DIAL: Well, you could get into a definition of a culture. But I know what you are asking. You are saying are Lumbees like Comanche. Right?

EMERSON ECKIWARDI: Yes.

ADOLPH DIAL: And Navajo or some other groups. And I would say that we are quite different. On the other hand, I would like to point out that with all the obstacles, we have been one of the most progressive groups in the United States, and I am not trying to take anything away from anyone. We have in our public schools, out of eight or ten thousand students, about three hundred and fifty Lumbees in Robinson County with college degrees. They are teaching in public schools, and have received their degrees from all over the country. A Lumbee is head of the Health and Physical Education Department at Temple University. I can tell you that Bobby Brayboy just received his Ph.D. from the University of New Mexico. And so on.

JEANNETTE HENRY: I think the question is being asked: how do you determine that any individual is a Lumbee Indian?

ADOLPH DIAL: Okay, alright. The question is, how do you determine whether an individual is a Lumbee. One writer said once that a Lumbee is what he says he is. How do you like that one?

JEANNETTE HENRY: The question in the minds of the participants is this: If you do not have treaty rights with the United States government; if you do not have a tribal form of society or any vestiges of it; if you do not have a language; if you do not have any parts of your culture remaining . . . if, in other words, you could pass right out of here and become a white man, then what are you? I think this is the crucial point, because the Lumbee may be what everybody else is going to become in twenty or fifty years.

ADOLPH DIAL: We have thirty school systems today. I was a principal of Prospect Union School, grades one through twelve, about seven hundred students. Forty per cent of them were Lockleer and I will give anyone a thousand dollars to show me a Lockleer that doesn't trace back to Robinson County. And those Lockleers are Lumbees, as long ago as ten thousand years. What you are saying, though is that because of our origin, because of our Lost Colony origin, when we lost many things that other tribes have, we may not be considered Indian?

A SPEAKER: We lost, yes, including favor with our own people.

ADOLPH DIAL: I think the important thing is that we share your problems. And I say further, that until all Indians are ready to work together and fight for a common cause, nothing good will come of it. I am sure there is no one in the country today doing any more than the Lumbees for Indian people.

A SPEAKER: Mr. Kaniatobe, I don't think anybody is quite satisfied with the answers being given so far to the question, which is: How do we know we're Indians, and particularly how do the Lumbees know?

ADOLPH DIAL: All right. If you come right down to it, I know you look at me, and you say, you look a little bit Indian. But I can tell you, that you show a little white. Yes! So let's get right down to it. How many, acutally how many pure people are left in this country today? Pure Indians? Just like any other group of people, what happens to the Indian when he moves to Chicago or any other urban area. They often intermarry. But the point is *today*—how much significance are you going to put on this thing? The significance is that the American Indian is being mistreated. We need to work together for a common cause. We need to be somebody.

RAY CROSS: You speak of discrimination, common causes. I think you miss one small point with the problem we are facing in the American Indian in our history. The program in the Historical Society is to preserve culture, language, Indian identity, tribal identity. Sure, we can preserve what is left of the Lumbee culture, if you can find it.

ADOLPH DIAL: Yes, we can preserve what is left of it, which is the people who are left.

LEW BARTON: That is what we are trying to do, and we are fighting for all we are worth.

JEANNETTE HENRY: I think we should sum up this discussion.

ADOLPH DIAL: I would like to make one other point. That is, that many people have come into Robinson County, and they have written about the Lumbees either of the county, or Baltimore, and so forth. And I sit down and read this stuff and laugh. . . . He was funded by the John Doe organization, or by the Mary Brown Foundation, and to the best of my knowledge there has never been any Lumbee funded to write about his own people, even though we know more about it than anyone else, and can write about it more accurately. . . . Take for example, Bruce Toeberry. If he came into Robinson County, no one knows it. I have not been able to find one person to whom he has talked, who has met this man, and he writes about a group called Almost White. He doesn't know a darn thing about Lumbee Indians. I hope he's here.

DON WANATEE: The name itself does not make the tribe, because back home we are known as the Tami Indians and we are not Tami Indians. We are not even properly named "Indians," . . . we are the People. We are Mesquakie People . . . People of the Red Earth. But they continue to call us second class folks—Tami Indians, because we live geographically near Tami. I told him, "Man, right where you're standing, you're located closer in proximity to Monitor, and if you care to step over a hundred yards or so, we'll be near Toledo, Iowa. If you step into this car, I will drive you a quarter mile this way, and we'll be near the Grande. Why don't you call us the Tami Rocoli Indians? But you don't call us Mesquakie, why not? I don't think it's the name. I think it's the person. Like the good man over there said if he's a Lumbee, he's a Lumbee. I believe him.

JEANNETTE HENRY: Well said. There's no doubt that he's a Lumbee, and there is no doubt about the existence of this group of people, that they are Indian people. The tragedy of it is that there is no other way to describe the predicament in which native people find themselves. The Lumbee people are now where they have been for hundreds of years. They have recognized themselves always as Indians. They are mixed. There is so much difference between the Lumbee and Comanche situations that here there is room for other and broader work. But the situation is alike in this sense: the Lumbees are ignored in the literature, just as the Comanches are. I can show you areas in California where the Indians there don't know who they are, yet they know they are Indians. They have been wiped out as tribes during the Gold Rush. Some of them say they are "Mission Indians." There is no such tribe as a Mission tribe. However, I must agree with Mr. Cross, I think it was a mistake to integrate the Indian school at Pembroke.

DON WANATEE: I know the Comanches quite well. We used to fight them many years ago. Now we don't have any cause to fight them. What I would like to say is that you asked, how many of you are full bloods. I am not a full blood. My great-great grandfather, during the time of the American Republic, when he was an infant, somehow came across an Englishman. And so now my middle name is Wellington. My first name is Donald. In the 1930's a duck was made popular by that name, but my last name is derived from my great-great grandfather in the language that he spoke. He spoke, and he lived, and he died, a Mesquakie. So that I am just as proud of being an Indian as being an Englishman. I say, further, if you have a language, preserve it. If you have a culture, keep it. If you have a history, tell it.

ROSALIE NICHOLS, *Discussant*

First of all, I don't consider myself a qualified historian. I am just beginning to study history. So if you have any questions about history, please don't ask me. But I have some basic ideas about history that I would like to bring up. One point, just in passing, is the fact that we are dealing with government-controlled education. I would like to suggest that part of the problem is the existence of state education itself. It's part of what we are up against.

Secondly, I agree with what Jeannette said about the need not to just criticize, but to offer something better. This was really brought home to me the first night we arrived here, and we had that pre-Convocation dinner. There was a student from Princeton sitting next to me, a white fellow, who was studying economics, and we got into a discussion. Those of you who are Indians, sitting around, many were criticizing history as told by the white historians. His first response was, "Well, are there any better books?" No. So what could I say? And it rested right there.

Third, I think we are not just up against white misconceptions about Indian history, but we are also up against our own ignorance and our own misconceptions about our own history. I think that many of us have received these misconceptions from the white history books, certainly. But then, on the other hand, the white historians and anthropologists have gotten these misconceptions originally from us, too. So you have a kind of circular transfer of misinformation going on. A lot of it becomes just folklore, really. We need to have a more objective substantiation of our data about Indian history and Indian culture, not just rely on individual opinions, experience, or whatever, which may be valid, but may not be part of the authentic picture. Or even part of the total picture.

Fourth, we actually need two kinds of histories. We need the Indian history, especially about Indians, and the Indians in Indian schools so that we can know about our own history. This is not a question of one or the other, but we need both. Because if we only write about Indian history, it will only reach Indian people. The white people are not going to be interested in the writing only about Indian history. We need Indian history as it has affected and been affected by the white history, the history of the nation as a whole. To do this, it is going to take a lot of scholarship—it will take broad scholarship. I feel the size of this task, particularly since I started studying history seriously. It's a huge field, and to try to sit down and write a history book requires much more than simply an understanding of our own history. We are also going to have to know European history, United States history, besides having an understanding of philosophy, economics, and even aesthetics. All of these things impinge upon the study and writing of history. So it's a very very broad job of scholarship, and not something to be approached lightly. This sort of relates to the idea that many people have now, about having separate ethnic studies in school. I think this is a wrong approach, because of the fact that what we really need to do is to get Indian history into American history, rather than only separate the subject off by itself.

At the university which I am attending, there is no Indian history taught as part of American history. Of course, this puts me at a disadvantage, both from a scholastic standpoint and probably as well from an emotional standpoint; because I can't react to the attitudes of my professors. I am at a disadvantage, because their interests are different from mine, and their view of history is different from my view. I think it's probably true of all our young people who want to study history in public schools; they are going to come up against this problem too. But I don't think ethnic studies programs is the answer.

Somehow we have to infiltrate the history department and get our history into it. So that we won't be under this disadvantage. Then we also have to learn their history. You see, they are telling it from their side, and we might react from this and fall into the category of being subjective in just telling our side, and that's not going to develop any understanding. It's only going to cause reactions back and forth.

My final point is the idea that a sound philosophy precedes the study of history. I think we must have a basic philosophy ourselves before we can approach the study and the writing of history, because you have to understand the different aspects of the subject itself. When you are writing about human beings and human actions, you must have some principles for analyzing what takes place between and among human beings and between different races of human beings.

ROBERT KANIATOBE: I grew up in southeastern Oklahoma, and this is Choctaw country. And yet, the only history taught when I was a student, was Oklahoma state history, which I managed to avoid taking. But we had no course in Choctaw history, even though this is our country. When I got out of eighth grade, I went to Haskell. Even though this school is one hundred per cent Indian enrollment, we had no courses on American Indian history. They do teach United States history, however. I was so turned off, that I can't remember anything I learned. Later I went to school at Chilocco, and I graduated there. And at *that* Indian school (this was in the 1950's), they did not offer American Indian history courses either. Perhaps this had changed by now, but I don't hear anything to that effect. Now I would like to read one quotation, from *Time* Magazine. This article came out February 9th, 1970. "Prejudice is a painful fact to the Indian, as it is to Blacks. Indians suffered just as harshly from biased history books. One text observed that it is probably true that all American Indian tribes in the course of their wandering lived for some generations on the frozen wastes of Alaska. This experience deadened their minds and killed their imagination and iniative." What I would like to know, is what does this sort of thing do to the minds of Indian children? And the minds of the rest of the population?

JOHN BATES: I am from State College, Oklahoma. I would like to know, as a student, whether there is any format where you can discuss freely with the administration, Indian policies, Indian studies, to be incorporated into the curriculum, whether as a separate entity, or within the history studies. How are the students to go back to their campuses and fight for independence and to bring these text books into the studies, to discuss such subjects? Where can we get information about what textbooks are available? What can be done about it . . . because a meeting like this is fine, but how are we to go back and express our view of what we learned here?

JEANNETTE HENRY: How do *you* thing it should be done? Nobody can give you a ready-made answer, because your situation is going to be different from another situation. A Native American studies program will not at one blow solve the situation.

RAY CROSS: How are we going to get the Bureau of Indian Affairs, or public schools generally, not to adopt textbooks that are derogatory about Indians? What type of approach should be used in this kind of program? How would you have us insist that the true story should be told, and what kind of materials can we utilize to tell this true story?

JEANNETTE HENRY: You just have to get your feet wet. You have to get into the issues, raise the questions, discuss it in classes, discuss it with the professors and even with administration. And when you get your feet wet, you will find all kinds of ways. We first went to the State Curriculum Commission, and there we got the floor and raised the question of the inaccurate text books. We were told by the superintendent to go ahead and evaluate the textbooks for the next adoption period. And then we received by parcel post 123 textbooks for evaluation. I feel sure he had no idea we were such fools as to go ahead and attempt to do it. Because after the first shipment another 120 came. They came in crates. But we did evaluate those books, and we told the superintendent that as a result of that evaluation, we would like to develop a Criteria as to what should be in the books, so that when the publishers present books for adoption, we will be able to have a standard of judgment. They will have to meet the conditions of those Criteria. We ourselves presented a list of Criteria. We worked with teachers, both Indian and nonIndian. We worked with pupils, and we worked with an Indian boy of 11 years, in the fourth grade. He was a very good evaluator, by the way. On the basis of our evaluations and our Criteria, there was not one book that we could accept or recommend. We also evaluated the books used in Indian schools under the direction of the Bureau of Indian Affairs. If possible, these books are worse than those used in the public schools.

But the thing of it is, that now we are confronted with the eye of the needle, so to speak. There are no books with which to replace those that we have rejected. We presented teachers' guides, and some materials that we had mimeographed, for use in the classrooms. There are no good books. How long this situation will last, I don't know. All I do know is that we feel very keenly in the American Indian Historical Society, that a good share of this situation is our responsibility, and we have to write and study and do the research and get the books out.

We have the brains among us. We have the scholars. And we must insist that our scholars write books for use by the educational community. I certainly agree with Rosalie Nichols: it is not easy. But there are all kinds of people who are willing to help us. We are not using our own talented people, writers, illustrators, poets. You people who have children. Don't you ever tell them stories? We need those stories, about Indian things. It's a pleasure to write, really. And if you begin, you too will find it to be a pleasure. Surely we cannot any longer shirk our responsibility in connection with supplying accurate and exciting educational materials about our own people.

With that, the Panel was adjourned.

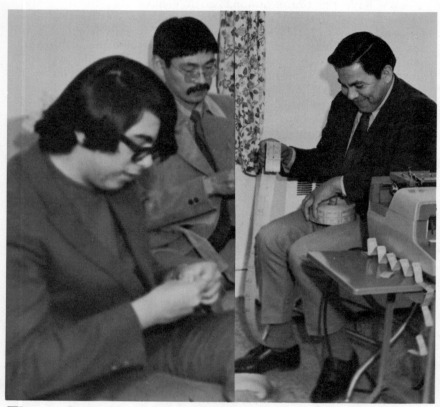

These three Native Americans were part of the Registrations team, and helped prepare the Convocation, left to right: Michael Galvan, Ohlone of California; Joseph Senungetuk, Eskimo of Wales, Alaska; and Michael Paul, Salish of Washington.

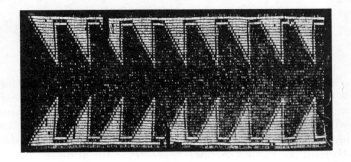

6

Innovations
in Education

SAMUEL BILLISON

I would like to introduce the Panel members. Mr. John Compton is a Sioux, a teacher at the University of Iowa. Mr. Herschel Sahmount is Kiowa, the head of the Human Relations Commission under the Oklahoma State Department of Education. Dillon Platero, Navajo, is Director of the Rough Rock Demonstration School at Chinle, Arizona, and Frank La Pena is a Wintun Indian of California, a teacher at Shasta Junior College. I am Samuel Billison, Navajo, candidate for Ph.D. at University of Arizona. Briefly, I would like to comment on our Panel subject.

Perhaps Senator Fannin of Arizona was right when he paraphrased, "There are more conclusions about what is right and wrong with Indian education than there are Indians," but a change in attitudes towards Indian education must be our immediate goal if we are to contribute to our society. In 1967, Congress expanded Elementary and Secondary Education Act (ESEA), to provide needed monies for schools teaching Indians. The ESEA is designed to encourage educational innovation; the major portion of the funds goes to poor school districts. One of the major forces of influence of Indian educational innovation is the recent special Senate Labor Subcommittee Study on Indian Education, wherein specific recommendations were made. Another, yet to be released, and a very recent research study, (funded by the U. S. Office of Education), on Indian education, by Dr. Robert Havighurst of the University of Chicago, is directly concerned with the status of Indian education nationally.

We can no longer continue merely to criticize the educational system, because we now have Indian scholars to get involved in the process of improving education on a positive basis. We can no longer depend on non-Indians to dictate our course of destiny. The Bureau of Indian Affairs must trust the Indians to operate their own schools. The vast potential of Indian scholars awaits the delegation of authority of local autonomy. Although the innovations are few and slow, credit must be extended to those who have taken the plunge against formidable odds because of lack of funds, and in many cases because of the administrators who are against change. Some of the significant recent innovations made are these:

The Santa Fe Institute of American Indian Art, under BIA direction, was primarily established to encourage Indian students to express themselves through all forms of art.

During the 1962 school year, scholarships for higher education were made available in the amount of $600,000, but this was not all used. This year, there is approximately $4,000,000 which has already been exhausted. This indicates the increase of Indian youth attending colleges. Although the Bureau has authority to grant monies to graduate students, it is being used up by undergraduates. The Bureau of Indian Affairs officials headed by Commissioner Bob Bennet called in educators, Indian leaders, sociologists, and other professionals to help plan a vocational school in Albuquerque to the tune of 13 million dollars, but only 9 million dollars were allocated, which eliminated many important programs originally planned. This school is for grades 9 to 12, with special emphasis on adult education in the evenings and during the summer vacations.

We have eight public high schools with elected Indian board members, and the first Navajo superintendent. These schools are endeavoring to innovate with an oral language English program, using child-centered activities to produce the teaching of the English language. Earphones and recorded tapes are utilized to have students talk about subjects which are of interest to them. The use of home visitors for liaison work is replacing the traditional attendance officers.

The most prominent innovation in Navajo education is the Rough Rock Demonstration School, which I will mention briefly. The political community relation aspect entrusts policy-making to the local elected school board, which does not exist in BIA schools. The RRDS concept has shown the people a model of a school, in which Navajo culture is not given a second place in priority. The arguments for and against Rough Rock are these:

"Opposed: The position is held that RRDS is doing the same thing that BIA does, except that they are going in the opposite direction. You cannot educate people to live in the past, which is RRDS' total philosophy, it is said, in the opposing viewpoint. Another position of opponents of RRDS is that the achievement level and the grade levels are not comparable to other schools. Some opponents say that not all Navajo wanted this concept. I cannot help but reply to this position by pointing out that the immediate question, it seems to me, is where else have the Navajo experienced such a school, in which they can constructively oppose? One has to experience in order to know. It is also stated by the "Con" advocates, that "well, eventually, all the Navajo will be assimilated anyway." To answer this, you and I know that no group of any significant size among the Southwest Indians has been totally assimilated, and very few, if any, elsewhere. The condition in the Southwest is one of strongly cultural pluralism which definitely tends to work against any idea of assimilation; a school that prepares students for pluralism is realistic.

Still another "Con" objection, is the high cost per pupil of RRDS, and instruction of the child by heavy community and parental emphasis. Still another, is the claim that the continued dependency of the child upon the parents, contains the germ of parent-teacher conflict in disciplinary matters. Mr. Platero, in his presentation, will certainly reply in detail to such objections. But I am purposely mentioning these opposing comments because I strongly believe that you will see for yourself that the "Pro" will far outweigh the "Con," and that many of these questions can be answered with ease in the actual functioning and results of the school itself.

For positions in favor of the Rough Rock Demonstration School, I might summarize by saying that the concept has many advantages, and only a few are: It creates and freely allows community involvement, with emphasis on the teaching of tradition and language. There is low teacher-pupil ratio. Thus more and extensive personal attention is given, which helps create comfortable learning experiences for the child. There is use of indigenous teachers, of which the majority is Navajo, who stand side by side of well-oriented and trained non-Navajo teachers who must to some extent be morally obligated to share the knowledge gained.

These comments are purposely directed to those who seek an alternative—an alternative that is Indian. We feel positive that it will take courage to innovate Indian education, and it can only be Indian if it is planned and implemented by Indians

. . . Indians like you scholars. It is an instrument to gain independence and local autonomy in education.

I would now like to introduce Mr. Dillon Platero, director of the Rough Rock Demonstration School.

Dillon Platero

In 1965 like-minded persons from the Navajo Tribe, governmental agencies, and institutions of higher learning came together and were able to propose, and get funded, an experimental school. A demonstration school if you will, which would show to the many skeptics that Navajo people could run their own educational affairs, *now*. Unfortunately the mechanics of establishing such a school made it necessary to place a dual staff in an existing Bureau of Indian Affairs boarding school, with the result being an obvious source of friction. What resulted was essentially two schools operating in one plant and with one student body. With allegiance thus divided, with the federal employees responsible for functioning under their rules and regulations, however well meaning, and the demonstration staff seeing their responsibility to the people of the community and their children, misunderstandings, friction, and ill-will were inevitable. The school was not then successful, and its supporters agonized over this apparent failure, as the decision to terminate the project was seriously considered. However, everyone understood what had happened. The principle underlying the experiment was felt still to be sound. Only the manner of attempted implementation needed improvement.

And so we tried again, this time with a more experienced administrator and in a locale where only the demonstration school would be functioning. A new facility was turned over to the Navajo people, only the broadest restrictions were imposed as to its use. A private, non-profit corporation was formed, as the legal entity which could accept funds from government agencies as well as from private sources for the operation of the Rough Rock Demonstration School. This was accomplished in the Spring of 1966 and on July 1 of that year, the experiment began anew.

From the very beginning, cooperation and even more importantly, freedom, have characterized our relationships with other involved agencies. Rough Rock now truly became responsible for its own school. With the election of a five-member board of education in June, 1966, the governing body was ready to begin functioning by the time the school came into being.

The Navajo people of Rough Rock wanted to accomplish two things: (1) the development of educational experiences comparable to those offered in the federal and state schools, in order to equip Indian children with knowledge of English, and the subject areas usually taught in any elementary school in the state of Arizona; (2) the development of educational experiences in Navajo-oriented subjects in order to enrich our children's academic work and enhance their total educational program.

When Rough Rock first began operation, the community had been used to having their school serve children from the ages of six through the highest grade taught. Not even a kindergarten program existed, to say nothing of a nursery school. In 1966-67, for the first time, a Head Start unit was established, affiliated with the Demonstration School. These children were among the most enthusiastic in the entire educational community. Our gravest problem is how to keep the class to a reasonable size. The Office of Navajo Economic Opportunity set up a unit to provide for 20 children. in its first year, average daily attendance in that was 20.9. In 1967-68 it was 19.7; in 1968-69 it was 22.8. In response to increasing pressure from local parents to extend the entrance age downward, Rough Rock began a nursery school, accommodating 2, 3, and 4-year-olds. The kindergarten program bridges the gap between this group and the regular school age children. Just last week our nursery school had an average attendance of 26.4 and it has recently been as high as 29.6. A third pre-school section currently is our kindergarten class, with an average daily attendance of about 25. Serving as a transition between the less highly structured nursery school and the more formally constituted beginning phase (our school is ungraded), kindergarten at Rough Rock functions as do kindergartens in other parts of the country. There are two notable exceptions; (1) Instruction is in the Navajo language; (2) emphasis is placed on the relevancy of education to the children's Navajo home milieu.

In this fashion the child's self image and feeling of worthy personhood is not shattered so mercilessly as often happens, when the difference between what is actual life and what is taught in school strikes the child at the age of six. School at Rough Rock is an extension of the child's normal world, in which he is competent to communicate and react in fashions sanctioned by his community and culture. Recently, the community has also begun a child care center for infants. It's so new that no general statement can yet be made about it.

Rough Rock is a bilingual school. We believe this term embraces the concept of fluency in two media of communication: in our case in Navajo and in English. This is a little different from the usual "bilingual" programs at other schools, that merely treat the language other than English as a necessary evil. All students receive instruction in the Navajo language one period a day. The school was thus firmly committed to the concept of equality of value of the two most commonly used languages in the community. At the same time, thought was seriously being given to actually providing instruction in Navajo to certain children for certain periods of time. In 1968-69, our "Follow-Through" students, at the early primary grade level, began receiving all their teaching in Navajo, with exception of a daily English lesson. Today we have six classes being taught in the Navajo language, in addition to our kindergarten and nursery school. As the children gain confidence in their ability to handle the intricacies of school learning, Navajo gives way as the basic medium of instruction, and English replaces it—by the end of the third grade age level.

The Rough Rock community, through their elected school board, hold to the philosophy that we teach the Navajo language for the reason that proficiency in it is a tool needed by our children and a skill worthy of formal education efforts. Just as there is a wide range of fluency in the speaking of English, so in Navajo some handle the language better than others. All too often in the past the Navajo child has been removed from his home environment at an early age and thrown into a completely alien cultural milieu and language. Great efforts were made to inhibit the speaking of such Navajo as he already knew, which not only stunted the quality of his native tongue, but actually made him ashamed of himself and of his language, as something inferior to English. The result was often a person who was fluent in neither language—one who was handicapped linguistically. Once the parents at Rough Rock actually had control of their school, the Navajo language ceased to be considered as a patois to be eliminated, or suppressed, and instead took its rightful place as the co-language of the school, a place it continues to hold with dignity.

Navajo culture is taught daily at Rough Rock. But we recognize that there is no clear cut dichotomy, with Navajo culture occupying one compartment and non-Indian culture another. Recognizing and accepting the inevitability of our children's biculturalness, the school board emphasizes the values found in each and helps our students understand that neither is "right" nor "wrong" as such.

The school board also realizes that our children's familiarity with Navajo culture needs to be systematically expanded, and the nonIndian culture taught as well. The early primary grade levels find what is probably the best teaching done in this area, inasmuch as these children all have Navajo-speaking teachers whose knowledge of Navajo culture is better than any non-Navajo's could possibly be. Speakers from the community who have special knowledge of various aspects of Navajo culture spend an entire day at the school, lecturing to the older students on their specialty, once a week. These presentations are followed with vocabulary study, composition, and consideration of the specific topic during the following five days, in the social studies classes and homerooms.

Such extensive and systematic teaching of Navajo language and culture calls for both texts and teaching aids. In this respect the school's Navajo Curriculum Center has proved to be invaluable. Rough Rock has found that there are teachers of Navajo language and culture . . . and others, who merely think they can teach. Too often a person not professionally trained to teach has attempted to provide instruction only to find himself running out of pedagogic steam within a few weeks. This is one explanation for our school's attempt to hire as many Navajo teachers as possible: They have both the knowledge of Navajo language and culture and the professional acumen to organize and present their subject. During the past three and a half years the Navajo Curriculum Center has published such texts as Black Mountain Boy, for intermediate grades, several beginning readers, and a book of Navajo biographies for older students. Emphasis at the present time is being placed on getting more works in the Navajo language. The Center has also completed materials explaining the school, and the principles upon which it is founded, and such ancillary teaching aids as film strips, puppets, and dramatic presentations.

We need leadership, of course. And, in cooperation with the Navajo Community College, the Chinle Public School District, and Arizona State University, we have had four teacher aides in full time training for the past year. These are people who spent several years as practical aides in our classrooms and showed such potential for the teaching profession that the opportunity was given them to upgrade their skills and prepare for entrance into the profession. We have also been able to provide rotating employment opportunities for parents in the community whose lack of special, non-Indian skills makes it impractical to engage them on a full time basis. The U. S. Office of Education has provided funds for this purpose.

Since the school began in 1966, Rough Rock has had dormitory parent aides. They have functioned as less experienced instructional aides and have the same benefits as our classroom parent aides. It is recognized that a most sensitive point with parents is the way their children are treated in the dormitories. At Rough Rock our community parents have nearly all had the opportunity to actually work in the dorms and find out for themselves what is involved in group living with large numbers of children. The dormitory program itself may slowly go out of business, but right now the Navajo communities don't have facilities such as would normally be found in cities.

Community development is an integral part of the demonstration project. All too often people equate the activities of the project solely with that of operating an elementary school. Our entire community development building, built of adobe with local labor, is a service to our total population, as well as to our school and our students. For example, the postal facilities serve the entire community with mail service that was not available before the demonstration project began. The personnel office serves the entire community as well as the school. The community recreation office, office of community development director, office of special services, all serve the entire community. The funds expended for these largely non-school related functions cannot justifiably be considered legitimate expenses in the education of children. The old bureaucratic accountancy method of figuring cost per pupil for education cannot be utilized at Rough Rock.

Our adult education program has been functioning since the first day that Rough Rock Demonstation School began operation. The courses stress basic English, as well as Navajo. Basic Navajo is also taught to the non-Indians employed at the school. Also taught are health, home economics, tribal and national government, and dealing with governmental agencies. This past fall, the Adult Basic Education Center was established, serving our more traditional Navajo people, as well as our youth who have had some elementary and secondary education but who dropped out. Dormitory parent aides and classroom parent aides receive regular instruction in the Adult Basic Education Center as part of their work at the school.

An extensive arts and crafts program was conducted during the first years at the school. However, as the types of skills multiplied and the number of practitiners increased, it was possible to phase out this aspect of activity. Now such work is pursued largely in the homes of various persons trained in 1966-68. Our emphasis is now upon the development of marketing.

Navajo people will not abandon their traditional cultural ways, and devote themselves to living by non-Indian standards. Thus, the role of the medicine man in Navajo life has received new respect from conventional physicians. Most people felt, when we went looking for help, that the medicine man is the Navajo religion. They know nothing about Navajo religion, and less about Navajo healing ceremonies. Finally, we went to the people in the National Institute of Mental Health. All the doctors sort of smiled at each other. Pretty soon, though, after a couple of meetings, they said, well, let's go out to Rough Rock. They spent a little time there, and they contacted about everyone who had anything to do with medicine men. They finally processed a proposal, which received favorable action. The program was funded for a three-year period. Now it is beginning to make sense that it is a viable program, and it does help in the area of mental health. The Navajo medicine man is very effective with people who talk Navajo and understand the culture. Right now about 95% or more of the Navajo people who go to Vietnam, or into the service, receive ritual help from the Navajo medicine man so that they are safe and sound, healthy, mentally capable of going into the various services. It makes them happy.

There was a time when indigenous medical practice was condemned by culturally egocentric non-Indians, who could not bring themselves to admit that any way of living could possibly contain merit, if it differed from their own lifeways. Now the trend has been reversed, as non-Indian medicine learns more about the incredibly complex mechanism, the human mind. Many public health physicians have come to realize that the traditional medicine man has the key to the healing of many types of maladies which can afflict Navajo people. Thus a feeling of mutual respect is arising as a result of cooperation between the two types of medical practitioners. The school's medicine man training program provides for apprenticeships on a one-to-two basis, with prominent medicine men relaying to their students the intricacies of their healing arts.

The preservation of our ancient and effective healing arts is one of the remarkable results of this program . . . one might say a bonus in educational achievement.

However, we feel that knowledge of the Navajo Way is, in one of itself, not enough. There should also be fundamental knowledge on the part of the medicine man of the types of maladies which will better respond to non-Indian medicine. Such patently organic ailments as broken bones, wounds, burns, etc. and the onset of such diseases as cancer, tuberculosis, etc., may well be referred by medicine men to Public Health physicians who are then able to bring their expertise into play. As a part of our medicine man training program there is in-service training by public health services, of both the medicine men and their apprentices, in basic physiology. It is another type of adult education, but one that brings together in mutual respect the different practices aimed at a single result: optimum health for the Navajo people.

The uses of existing leadership and the consistent training of new leadership is the keynote for the success of Rough Rock.

It is to be emphasized that the Rough Rock Community School Board controls policy and has the decision-making power. I could stand here and be fired right now, and may not know it, but the school board has that power. They hire and fire teachers. They make the policies of the school. Recently, they made the decision to make Rough Rock into a high school, so that we are working on this now.

Of particular interest in this discussion are the basic principles used:

(1) The work to be accomplished must be recognized by Indian people as being needed. Only after a realization of need for change by Indian people, can such change be effective.

(2) Indian people must be afforded recognition as competent human beings whose decisions (and rationale for them) merit the respect of all. An end to paternalism is demanded—though not to the services which were bought and paid for, hundreds of years ago. Here is a fine distinction that too often is completely overlooked by persons who would turn Indians into copies of non-Indian peoples. For example, on the Navajo reservation, the federal government is responsible for providing educational opportunities for our children. This is no largesse that has been handed down to us. It is part of the spoils of war which was written into the Treaty of 1868 between the United States government and the Navajo Nation.

(3) Indian people must be involved with the efforts their community is making to improve their lot. Such involvement can take many forms, such as participation on a Parents Advisory Committee, service on the school board, work as a dormitory aide, work as a classroom parent aide, helping supervise an off-reservation field trip, or addressing a convocation of scholars, as have several of our local leaders. Following these basic principles, Rough Rock has been an example.

The acceptance and consideration of objective criticism is a necessary part of an experiment, or any program. Indeed there have been evaluations of Rough Rock. We have one objective evaluation, however, which we think very highly of. It is in the best traditions of self-criticism in a positive and objective way—pointing out the weaknesses but also pointing out the strengths, and proposing such measures as will correct specific situations. The Navajo people themselves made the evaluation, and continue the process of evaluation. They go into a school system such as Rough Rock and spend a great deal of time talking to students, asking what they think of the curriculum, courses, subject matter, what they think of the people, the teachers. You don't have to interpret.

Finally, we at Rough Rock feel that this demonstration project has great significance for other areas and peoples. Concepts which were first put into practice at Rough Rock have been siezed upon as worthy of emulation by federal schools, and by state institutions as well. Noteworthy was the establishment of Navajo Community College, which is predicated upon the same principles as is Rough Rock Demonstration School, but serving an older clientele.

Emphasizing the need for Indian people to solve Indian education problems has been the Dine Biolta Association, a recently founded, non-profit corporation of Navajo educators and others interested in Indian education, which limits its voting membership to Navajo people. This dynamic group plans a summer workshop to train Navajo teachers for work in bilingual schools. Although college credit will be given, all instruction and administration will be handled by Indian people, for Indian people, to benefit Indian children.

In Ramah, New Mexico, the local people have formed their own corporation for operating a school. Rough Rock was studied before planning the Ramah program. The Bureau of Indian Affairs' project TRIBE is an outgrowth of the Rough Rock program. This could provide guidelines for a type of local control within the total federal school system. Thus far the results have been meager. There is one small school at Blackwater. However, the fact that this massive bureaucracy would move at all in an attempt to provide some way for greater local control is a tribute to the effectiveness of Rough Rock in proving that Indian people are ready NOW for such responsibilities.

Both bilingual and bicultural education have recently found much more favor and even entrance into formerly "Closed" curricula in Bureau and public schools. An example of the latter may be seen in the Navajo language programs at Gallup, New Mexico, public schools. The mere providing of educational opportunities for kindergarten age children (not to be confused with the long established beginners' classes) is a step long advocated but even to this day not implemented in the majority of public schools in our state.

This combination-extension of early childhood education to younger students along with instruction, heavily utilizing the Navajo language, produces a great forward step in raising the educational level of our Indian people on our reservation. A less tangible, but real benefit from the very existence of Rough Rock Demonstration School has been a spirit of competition engendered which cannot help but be beneficial.

While there is no point in the denigration of different school systems, the mere existence of this Demonstration School has served as a catalyst to other schools and has stirred them into action. Rough Rock stands as a symbol of *doing* rather than merely *talking*.

Indian people need to be doers, rather than objects to which things are done. They need to be masters of their own destinies, a dream that has been constant with American people ever since this nation was founded—a dream that Indian people, whose nationhood predates America itself, are now fulfilling for themselves, thus returning to their ancient and original rights as the first and only true Americans.

SAM BILLISON: Mr. Herschel Sahmount will comment on some questions in education.

HERSCHEL SAHMOUNT: Innovations in education for Indian people means having a chance to say what they themselves know are their educational needs, depending upon the area they're from, what they or you as scholars know are your problems and your solution. I think we refer to our idea of how we in our own way can bring education for Indian students to a parity of that which exists in other educational systems or even better. When we talk to people who are not Indians about education, they see it in the light of the formal education process as it functions today. We don't mean it in the same way. We don't mean "you shoot the facts to me and I will spout them out and I will recall as much as I can and you grade me on it." It goes much beyond this. It involves many services and systems that the present educational structure doesn't provide.

Two areas I would like to discuss are those that have been brought to the attention of our congress and president in Washington, through the Sub-Committee on Indian Education and the National Council on Indian Opportunity. I think as scholars you should be aware of what they mean when they talk about these things, because nine times out of ten if something develops it is going to come out of what these people in Washington know about Indian education. One of the things that NCAI has recommended is a National Comprehensive Indian Education Act, which will take all of the monies that come to Indian education and set it up on a title basis. In other words, they will have education funds and simply set it up to fight for different areas of education that Indian people say they want. I am not saying whether this is good or not, but I recommend that you look into that. This is also a recommendation of the Senate Sub-Committee that monies that go to Indian education be brought together and set up in a Title of Comprehensive Indian Education Act. What they have recommended is a National Indian Board of Education and the purpose of this or the structure of it is similar to that of a state.

A state has a state school board, and then local school boards, and the idea is that the assistant commissioner for education and the Bureau of Indian Affairs would be the director of the agency. It would allow him an opportunity to go around

140

to the area offices in the various areas. One of the hang-ups is that every time some effort is made in Washington to change education at the local level, it gets caught at the middle strata of the area offices and never is really implemented as it was designed to be in Washington. The same is true the other way, so these are two areas that I think you should be familiar with. The Indian Education School Board is to have the use of all of the offices of education, technical advisers, consultants, OEO, everybody that is available in Washington. They are to pretty well run the whole education system of the Bureau of Indian Affairs, and also to make recommendations for public schools, including the funds that come through that source. So it looks like if they follow up on these recommendations, Indian people should make themselves aware of it. If they don't think that is a good idea, fine, and if they do, I think they should get behind it and back it.

A SPEAKER: You might indicate that some of those recommendations came out in the Meriam report in 1928.

HERSCHEL SAHMOUNT: Right, but I think this is an Indian problem. We say that so and so had all of these in his recommendations forty years ago. But we have never said that is good or that is bad. Are we going to write our congressman and say, look, keep this thing going? We have got a bill to make our Commissioner of Indian Affairs an Under-Secretary to the Secretary of the Interior. We keep rapping about being under the Bureau of Land Management, but we have never as Indian people said to our congressman, in any kind of unified effort, that we think this is good or that is bad.

SAM BILLISON: Now we will have comments on education, from the standpoint of an Indian from California, Mr. Frank La Pena.

FRANK LA PENA: I am going to speak for myself as an educator and what I see as lacking in those California situations where we have had termination. You're dealing with the destruction of a whole people, and the white culture trying to either dominate and force an assimilation of the Indian or totally wipe them out. People say that the Indian and the black has an identification problem and I say no.

When I went to teach in my area, which is the Wintun, I proposed an Indian cultural course. They said, "There are no Indians here." It is a fact, that when the white culture came they pushed the Natives into an "underground" situation. The hidden Indian or this Indian who supposedly is not an Indian, must re-establish the value that he wants to see preserved. And so, in many areas the Indians who "were not," actually are the biggest minority population.

I went to Stewart Indian School in Nevada in '47. They

said, in five years you will learn everything that you need, to function in the white culture. It doesn't work. In California, when in recent years many tribes were terminated, they didn't even let the California Indian attend Sherman Institute which they set up for the Indian. In the schools of the white culture, you do not get the truth, you do not get the story of our ancient culture. You get, in a geography book, that these Indians either sold their land, or left them, when in fact they were just pushed out or killed. So two things are going on, the Indian must re-establish himself tribally and you have to somehow implement that into the educational system, and you can do it if you affirm yourself first.

In California we have problems that could be discussed like, when an Indian person comes into the educational system, they look at him and they give him a test. That test does not test his mentality, it does not test his value, it does not test his culture. And so they put him in an emotionally handicapped program, the mentally retarded program. He never has an opportunity to get out of there.

SAM BILLISON: Thank you, Mr. La Pena. Medicine men were mentioned in both reports, and it reminds me of the song which states, medicine man, Indian Chief and doctor. For over a hundred years by treaty the Navajo tribe has been under the BIA School System and for one hundred years we have no Navajo lawyers, we have no Navajo with a doctorate degree. This is a population of a hundred twenty thousand people, but we have only medical doctor, and I would like to introduce Doctor McKenzie—he is the only doctor. Would you like to stand up, Doctor. This is our only Navajo medical doctor. Mr. John Compton will comment on some aspect of the report that was given to you on Rough Rock Demonstration School.

JOHN COMPTON: I am very impressed with the Rough Rock Demonstration School. First of all I think it should be viewed as sort of a symbol not only to the Navajo Tribe but to all Indians, because here is a live attempt at demonstrating how you can bring back cultural values, beliefs, the feelings that we have been talking about at this conference. I want to comment about one program, and that is the medicine man program. I think it is beautiful because as a kid on the Sioux reservation this was one of the most impressive experiences I was exposed to; you had to go to a medicine man to get medication or have them perform a ceremony when you were sick. And yet it was called superstition. So many tribes have lost this.

Now, it's funny because I am a social worker by trade, a form of medicine man I guess. I work with psychiatrists and psychologists and in a mental health clinic. I will be damned if, you know, there isn't the same kind of belief system operat-

142

ing when people go to a psychiatrist. People got better because they believe that this person can do something for them. They have fancy terms when they do studies. They call one treatment the placebo effect. I found that even white people put a lot of stock in believing that if this person can do something for me, I don't give a damn whether it is scientifically sophisticated or not. The fact is that as a child it worked for me.

So I think this is a live demonstration and I see it as a symbol. Beyond that I think all tribes including my own, cannot at present implement something like this because of the nature of our own situation. Take my home reservation. It is what is known as a closed reservation, but white people can live on it. It's almost fifty-fifty now. However, there have been some innovations, some intended and others not intended, and controlled by Indians. One was a shift from BIA schools to public schools, which I personally felt was useful to a lot of students because many of them have aspirations to go on to college as I did. I had to go to a BIA school and I worked six weeks in a bakery half day, and studied reading, writing and arithmetic the other half day. Recently, however, on my home reservation, for the first time in history, the Indians have taken over control of the local school board and it's causing a lot of sweating on the part of the minority group, which is white. These Indians who have comprised the minority portion of the board find the world doesn't cave in when they use these methods, in saying that this is the kind of school system we want for both Indians and whites, knowing that there may be casualties among some of the white students. Do you know what I mean?

It may be changed in such ways that some white people may feel that they are getting shortchanged on their education. This may happen. If you will recall, for many years Indian kids have been shortchanged on education because of certain policies. I see this as an innovation and I see potential. A Catholic Mission School in South Dakota is wanting to abandon their plan and I have heard some proposals that this be turned into a similar kind of attempt as the demonstration school, so that this may flower. This is where we are in South Dakota.

SAM BILLISON: We would like to have some brief questions . . . and don't rattle off ten questions at one time. I think this way we could shift around as much as we wish and questions can be directed to any one of the panel members. Please state your name and where you're from.

WILFRED WASSON: I am from Washington State College. And I would like to speak to Mr. La Pena. At the conference of Federal Agencies in Portland, I was trying to get a center for the training of Indian teachers established, because one of the greatest deterents to Indian education is the lack of teachers.

Most nonIndian teachers don't know how to work with Indian kids. One of the Federal officials told me it wasn't needed because there was a really good school to each Indian children at Humboldt State. Denny Baker, who is an Indian working down there stood up and said, "don't tell me it's a real good one, I have been working there. It isn't worth a good God damn, he said. All they have down there is white people talking to other white people."

FRANK LA PENA: Yes, Humboldt State has a program just as most of the colleges are trying to get programs. Their program is funded through the state and federal government. I feel that it is good up to a point but it can be better if those programs can be looked at in the sense of what they are teaching that can make you work as an Indian. Indian education programs are now much in vogue, but will such programs survive the acid test and stand up when you want to go on to doctoral study or a masters degree. If these programs cannot do this then, the courses offered cannot be utilized as a transfer course either, if you want to continue in another college.

LEE BACON: I'm Mississippi Choctaw at Philadelphia, Mississippi, and I recently visited the Demonstration School. Mr. Platero, I would like to address this to you. I was most impressed with the information that there was a Navajo school because everywhere I looked I saw a Navajo. But I wondered about the bridging of the earlier education, when you go from the lower levels up to where you teach English from teaching them Navajo. What kind of a problem does it have in bridging Navajo and English?

DILLON PLATERO: I imagine that in any culture, you are going to have some difficulty; mainly, because of lack of material in this case. In many cases, there is a lack of Indian teachers, who may be far better in this type of situation than other teachers, simply because they do speak the language and know how to read and write it. When we were six years of age we went to a Bureau School. We talked Navajo until we were six and then shifted over, forced to forget Navajo and learn English. So we are saying this should be developed on the Navajo side and continued, and not treat our Indian language in such a way that it is not useful, and forgotten.

LEE BACON: What type of resistance did you get once you decided that you were going in this direction. Did you get resistance from your teachers and other people once you were going to involve a total Navajo community?

DILLON PLATERO: We had resistance from the parents saying that they thought our children were going to be taught in English. Well, they had been used to that, but you have to explain that you are using a different approach to ease the shock of going over from one to the other. And from the teachers, too. Of course you are going to get resistance because they have to be retrained to accept the idea. Now, from the Bureau of Indian Affairs, the program was an extreme shock.

A SPEAKER: This is a question and at the same time a comment. I think Mr. Sahmount mentioned the NCAI recommendations for a National Comprehensive Education Act and my ears perked up at this. Then he mentioned the American Indian Education Advisory Board. This is the same outfit that is the head of the Advisory Committee that went into Albuquerque—

HERSCHEL SAHMOUNT: The Indian Education School Board will be a permanent board made up of representatives from all over the country. They will have the authority to determine what people want in Indian education throughout the country. They will utilize all the services from OEO, and everywhere else in Washington, to break down some of the red tape that we have been experiencing in getting education funds that are available to the Indian people.

The Comprehensive Education Act is a combination of all the different funds that are available from the various governmental agencies making such funds available through one compact legislative act. In other words, it would be set up on a priority basis or title basis, available to all the different areas of Indian education.

SAM BILLISON: Before another question is asked, I may just make an additional observation. In the first year at Rough Rock, teaching is in Navajo and a small percentage in English. Then the second year you keep moving the use of English up and essentially it levels off, maybe in the fourth year you have teaching predominently in the English language.

A SPEAKER: I hear Dillon say, "culturally deprived," and I hate that term because to me it's a textbook term used by sociologists to describe maybe immigrants from foreign countries who have abandoned their culture or who have been denied their culture. Often they describe many of these students as culturally deprived and I don't know of very many southwestern kids who are culturally deprived. They have more culture than the dominant society. If we Indians use terms like that, we are wrong.

DILLON PLATERO: I don't think I used it with the Navajo, I think—if I used it, it was with another group, it wasn't the Navajo.

A SPEAKER: That word comes up in President Nixon's speech again and again.

FATHER BROWN: Father Brown for the Blackfeet. In Fort Belknap, some BIA "experts" decided that children in all the schools on the reservation were culturally deprived and so the school districts were entitled to funds to bus the children into Great Falls or to see a circus, to hear a symphony or one thing or another. What it meant was that they were deprived of the experiences of the middle class Anglo-Saxons. There was no question at all of their own cultural heritage or riches. They weren't talking about that at all.

We had a meeting in Denver a year or so ago and we were talking about the difference between education and schooling. The question had come up in which the BIA wanted to revise their curriculum and social studies and the problem was finding the textbooks and the content, but above all, the teachers who could teach this. Someone said, well, are we not begging the question, what you're proposing is to find some teachers who are not Indians to teach the Indians what they already know. So really you are not providing for having the Indian community teach its own children.

The Supreme Court has already decided that the teachers are just helpers. They are supposed to be professionally trained helpers to convey to the children what they need, to function in that community. And so these teachers will teach these Indian children now. They are going to be strangers to this heritage that our children have. They are taking the job because they are offered more pay for teaching Indian children.

And at Fort Belknap they introduced a headstart program and brought in teachers who had gone to take special training to be headstart teachers and then more special training because they were going to be headstart teachers among Indians. None of the teachers were from the neighborhood, but the longer they had this preliminary training, the more pay they would be getting when they came to work on the reservation. That was their main concern, this additional pay.

From all of the teachers in that training class there may have been some who were very dedicated, but they weren't the ones we got. Then, when they arrived on the scene, they found that the children just looked at them and smiled. They didn't run away, they didn't answer, they just stood there. So they decided to hire some of the parents as teachers' aides and the teachers observed the parents in operation. In one program a group would come in the morning and they would leave after lunch, the other group would come after lunch and leave at the end of the day. And the parents got very little pay for being teachers' aides but they were the ones carrying on all the work.

Right *now* the children knew them, and they were educating them and developing the potential of the child, rather than drilling into so many words or so many nouns, like Mr. Rodgers does. Rather, they were taking this particular child who lives in that community and his experiences, his heritage and everything else might be very different from the Apaches or Navajo or the people in Alaska. The parents knew that and the teachers now are getting this tremendous salary and all they're doing is "observing" the program.

So a group went back from the reservation to suggest that maybe they could split the difference, give the parents a little more of the pay and get rid of the observers. After a lot of discussion they agreed back in Washington to let the parents carry on this headstart program and give them a little more pay. On the other hand, they would not give them full pay because they said they had not been academically prepared. We thought: what would happen if the BIA did succeed in training a whole group of teachers to school Indian children. That would deprive the Indian community of passing on their native knowledge in the classroom. The problem is how to get more people involved in this work and also keep them in their own community, not for teaching *anywhere else* in the BIA service, whether Alaska, the Southwest, Carolina, or some other place, but in *this particular community.* They said, "No, no, we can't do it that way" if we can convey these academic concepts to the teachers aides, whether they are Inidans or not Indians, they will be able to function anywhere. And we said, "No, you can't, this education must be for our community."

WILLIAM DEMMERT: I would like to re-emphasize what was just said concerning teachers' aides. In my opinion we are missing a very important concept in education in getting the community involved in the school system. Right now in Klawock, Alaska, we are training five teachers' aides and the improvement in relationship between the community and the school has been tremendous. I would like to see more of our people consider becoming teachers' aides not only to help the teacher, bu to develop a closer working relationship between the teacher and the aide with the ultimate plan of giving that aide a teaching certificate after some years of training. Then, we will have a permanent resident teacher.

SAM BILLISON: There is a Federally funded program at Arizona State University. Maybe George Gill would comment on this Teachers' Aide Program.

GEORGE GILL: I am from Arizona State University. We have, through the special education services, received a grant last year from the Office of Education, to train forty-seven teachers' aides. I believe, Mr. Platero, you have some of them up there. They take their basic curriculum work at the University and then, depending upon their tribes and backgrounds, they are sent out to the various reservations in Arizona for practical training. I checked with the University recently and the program will be funded again next year for an additional sixty teachers' aides. This is an innovation in Indian education. It must be sponsored by the Office of Education.

SOLOMON COOK: There was one other thing that came to me. The mention that there are some Indians who are awakening to the fact that Indians should be considered in the educational program of Indian children. You probably heard of our reserve in New York State where we had a school boycott. Our Indian parents had no voice in the operation of Central School, and the parents were very unhappy. They had one teacher who abused our Indian children to the extent that they got broken collarbones or broken wrists. The children were so afraid of this phys-ed teacher they wouldn't report these injuries. They kept on with their tumbling exercises or gymnastics. So the Indian parents got together and demanded that this teacher be fired. He had been on the staff for twelve years, so the supervising principal said, "He has tenure, he cannot be fired." The second complaint was that the Indians had no representation on the Board of Education. They used that as a wedge to boycott. The boycott was successful and the school was closed for a week. The State Education Department finally said they wanted the school opened and that it was illegal for the parents to declare this boycott.

Well, there were over a hundred parents involved. We all faced the prospect of jail. But there wasn't any jail nearby that could take care of such a large group, so the Administration sat down and listened to the Indian Educational Committee. They wanted representation on the Board of Education. A week or so ago they won, and now two Indians are sitting on the Board of Education. They also got the phys-ed teacher out of that Indian school. Now they are trying to get Indian history taught in the regular social studies program; also the Mohawk language will be taught on the same level as other languages, such as French, Russian, and Spanish.

I might add one other thing. The school in this program is, I think, a very advanced school. We have a new wing added onto Central School, through Federal appropriation. It's a ninety thousand square foot addition with a playhouse, a planetarium, a "cluster-room," which is a large classroom that can be subdivided into four, by bringing the walls in, a rather modern concept. This will start functioning right after Easter vacation so I can't tell you how effective it is.

HENRIETTA BLUEYE: I would like to make a few comments, Doctor. I come from the same State. I think as long as people are talking about innovations, I might mention some things which are similar to what is going on in New York State. That is the Akron Central School District, a public school outside of the reservation where all the Tonawanda children go, and is this year offering for the first time on an experimental basis a course in the Seneca language which is being taught by a woman from Tonawanda. It is available to all children in the reservation in the fifth grade, and there has been a tremendous response.

The children have a choice, after consultation with their parents, to take the course, if they want it. All of them have done so and there has even been a response that nobody expected, from some of the white students in the secondary school, to take part in this plan. Mrs. Blue Eye who is my own aunt, is giving this course to Indians and whites in separate classes. Also at the Tonawanda Reservation, there is a Parents' Association which was formed last spring as a result of the student strike which did not originally have Indian issues in mind. But it came to light that each school district in New York was to receive a certain amount of tuition for each student and it became apparent at Tonawanda that it could be appropriated for Indian students.

It's also been the work of this association to aid students who are going away to college, once they have graduated. This is certainly helpful, because usually they don't have the needed money. They have rummage sales, concerts, anything you can think of to help kids pay for books and even maybe just bus fare. Something like this in trying to help support them, at least in a very small way, is being done.

SPARLIN NORWOOD: I am a western Cherokee from Oklahoma, and I would just like to shoot some comments at Mr. Platero and ask a question. We have a demonstration school in Oklahoma that very few people know about, it's called Chilocco. (Laughter) I knew everybody would get that.

But when I say "demonstration school," Chilocco is usually the students demonstrating against the BIA, because that is the kind of a "demonstration" school it is. We have for instance, been really making headway in Oklahoma. In the boarding schools we have just this past year outlawed capital punishment. Some of you laugh, but we have had a few deaths there that they are not too sure how they happened and keep happening each year. This is all leading to something so have patience.

I am interested in innovations in education, but we seem to be talking mainly about mechanical things, while I keep thinking of *children*. We touched on teachers a while back which is very vital. I teach in the public school and I listen to everybody everywhere I go. This includes Education Associations' Conventions, State conventions, the BIA educators' meetings, and so on. By the way do you know the BIA educators are united in a small way, in Arizona and New Mexico? They are affiliated with the National Education Association and as a result the teachers of Indian children number very high in the public schools because two-thirds of our children are in the public schools. My concern is with those Indian children who are almost unidentifiable in the public school. One of the aspects that I am concerned with is innovation with the teachers as well. We don't have adequate teaching and training centers for teachers of minority children. But that is not a surprise. We don't have any books to teach minority education either, and we don't have any books to teach minority history. We don't have a lot of things.

Now then, Mr. Platero, how do you handle discipline in your school? There must be a bad Navajo somewhere. Or there must be some bad Cherokees. I know that. What you are going to say is probably just as common to you as the sand that blows in Arizona, but to the other people this may be an innovation: How children are handled.

I know how Indian people in the past have handled their children without striking them. The reason I raise this is because we are thinking of putting a detention room in our junior high school. To me it is an unthinkable thing, like pushing the first button for the atomic bomb. It can set off things we don't want to happen. In the detention room the paddle is still used quite frequently. Here we have black students and white and brown, so it is quite indiscriminate. But I am wondering what your disciplinary innovation is.

DILLON PLATERO: From our standpoint I think it is very simple and yet very complicated in a way. Our students, in the first place, are free to go home whenever they want to. In other words, if they are in the boarding school situation on a day basis going to school and if they wish to go home and spend a little time to go over some things, why they do. They simply ask us.

SPARLIN NORWOOD: During the day?

DILLON PLATERO: During the day. And we *take* them home. Our fundamental policy is that the child belongs to the parents. We don't say that once you are in school here, you belong to us. We still feel that the child belongs to the parents. When for instance, we get a kid who runs away from our boarding school situation, we wonder why and we talk to them in Navajo and the first thing to remember is that we have a policy that we do not strike a kid, that no one in the school is allowed to do this.

This is the tribe's ruling, through the tribal council. Rough Rock is probably much more lenient with students. But some days we spend time with the parents who may come in, and we want to get at the root of the trouble with this particular student. In some cases it is just an urge on the part of the kid to

150

take off. Maybe school doesn't mean anything to him, or this isn't his day. We go after the child to the home and speak to the parents, and the child does get home if he wants to. If he is home we talk to him and then tomorrow might bring him back.

We have a full time counsellor who works directly with the child in such cases, with no administrative responsibility. We have parents who directly counsel with the children. Still we have these problems. In some cases two out of four hundred kids are all that we have this trouble with continuously, so we work at this. The counsellor makes many home visits. He goes home with the children and spends time with the parents, so that a great deal more of this is done at home on a one-to-one basis and very little on a group basis. But with the group it involves a person like myself and also includes a teacher every so often who gets to the group once a week at the minimum.

The people from the community speak to the children. Of course they have their own authority. So maybe they come to expect a little bit too much. We are beginning to find some of these things out. The response from some of these kids themselves are interesting: some say bluntly, I don't like school.

"Well, you don't like it," we answer. "Do you want to go home? Do you want to stay?" Some want to stay, some want to go home. We give them the privilege of making their own decision in most cases, but counseling with them and their parents brings them to some reconciliation and usually back to school again. We also have the student-teaching-student program which is very important in a program like this.

SPARLIN NORWOOD: Some of the things you talk about would be disastrous in our school, which is mainly white.

A SPEAKER: I have a question that I want to put before the panel and Mr. La Pena particularly. We hear a great deal about culture identity for Indian students and I am not quite certain just what the goal of this cultural identity is. Supposedly it is to get Indian students to do better in school and make something meaningful of their lives. I am not exactly certain of the dynamics that the educators would draw out on the board: Say, how cultural identity would eventually lead to success in life. I get the feeling from talking to my students who feel that they have failed because they come from a particular group of people, from a particular type of people.

Now and then I meet with other people who have done well, who have their PhDs, who have teaching positions, professional people who are recognized in their fields. I often get the feeling that perhaps we are putting the dynamics in the reverse situation. Are we putting the cart before the horse or the horse before the cart or what, because I see people who are eminently successful in their particular endeavor, Indian people . . . and to me many of these people don't seem to be either ashamed that they are Indian, or proud that they are Indian, and in a way this kind of enhances their Indianness, if you will. Then you have the student who has tried and failed. The dropout rate is tremendous. They look back and they say it's because I come from this particular group of people. I just wondered whether the dynamics that we talk about is something that has been worked out in emphasizing cultural identity. We have to be careful that we don't under-emphasize the quality education which which will permit the Indian student to excel in whatever field he chooses. It is not enough for an Indian student to barely succeed, you know. We feel he ought to excel.

FRANK LA PENA: Well, I probably didn't say it well. In Chester, California, a study was made of the so-called poor people there and they found out that 85% of the Indian population was on welfare. This is bad but it really doesn't present the problem in that area because we depend on lumber and timber and some farming and tourists. The season has been bad for lumber so that is reflected. But there is also 14% unemployment. Out of that 14%, 85% is Indian.

Now, what I want to emphasize is that quality education open to the Indian has not been evident, except in recent years. The history that the Indian student has studied in the twelve years before he is eligible for college mentions his own history in one sentence. I talk to fifth and sixth graders who visit the school on a special program, and I ask, "How many of you are Indian." Six hands came up and to four of them I said, "What is your tribe?" And they didn't know their tribe. These were the students who were dropouts in their class.

Now, I say don't put the entire emphasis on the values of tribal pride, but the idea that the natives have always had a sense of history and culture is most important. The emphasis is also whether or not the young Indian has an opportunity to get an education at all. That is why I say there are two sides to this question.

A SPEAKER: I hear a lot of white people saying, "I made it, I worked my way through, I got through by myself." Now, I don't want to put myself in that bag because there are different circumstances for different people. Besides, the schools are not designed for Indians. Schools are designed by white middle class people for white middle class students, to be taught by white middle class teachers. A lot of Indian kids can't fit themselves into this. So the schools are going to have to change a little bit and there will have to be a little more emphasis on Indianness, whatever that may be, to identify with so that he can feel he is a part of it instead of feeling he is sitting over here on the outside and he doesn't understand what is going on.

One more thing, Mr. Chairman. We are running out of time and I would like to continue this. If we can get a room over at the Inn, I might be tempted to buy the first drink.

HERSCHEL SAHMOUNT: You asked, to what extent do you emphasize culture and tradition over the education that we all indicate we want our students to have. I mean, have you balanced the two, and *how* do you balance the two, one against the other? I think probably in Oklahoma this is a tremendous problem because of the fact that we have no reservations. The State is responsible for the education of all of the citizens, including the Indians. We don't have any Indian schools as such, except for Bureau schools, and most of these are for out of state students. In the public school situation, this is a tremendous problem as to what to emphasize. I think, as an Indian people, we talk about culture and position, and I don't think we really mean that. If you stop and define culture, it's just not the same any more; it's changed.

Among the Kiowa tribes, for example, Christianity made significant inroads into our culture. It changed the way we practiced religion. Our religion came from a certain ancient way, to a Ghost Dance, to a Sun Dance, and eventually, as it is today. It's a little bit of everything: a lot of Christianity mixed with remnants of changing cultures. Peyote, for example has supporters today. But it still is the same thing: a lot of Christianity and the Jesus Christ concept. I really don't know where you start when you say you want to hang on to the "Indian culture and tradition." What exactly are you talking about? To me, in my own mind, it is a philosophy of life that each individual tribe is trying to discern. I guess you can call it culture, but I think, if someone stopped and really questioned us as to what within your culture are you trying to preserve, or what are we going to emphasize, which part of Indian culture are we going to emphasize, which part of Indian culture are we going to go back to and hang on to—the Ghost Dance part, or the Sun Dance part—or are you just going to hang on to the philosophy that is clearly present: that of maintaining our Indianness. If this is what you desire . . . then in what sense and in what way? These are important considerations.

SAM BILLISON: I think this is where I mentioned that each tribe differs. There are two extremes, in which the school will say: let's give them all culture and really emphasize it. Then, at the other extreme, there is the idea of the public school to completely assimilate Indians. I always have the feeling that a comfortable position for me would be to learn some of the very important things from the Anglo, and from the Indian, and try to utilize both cultures so to speak, and put myself in a comfortable position where I can compete in Anglo society, and compete in an Indian society. Like competing with the medicine man, which is, I think culture without any style. This is an individual position, and I will use it the best I can to fit certain conditions.

A SPEAKER: Well, I would like to describe a major situation which I will ask the people here to consider. I have recently been working in North Dakota on a program which is designed to do something about a particular problem that seems to be the major problem in education in this area. You have boarding schools in Navajo country, as I understand it, because you don't have enough roads to be able to maintain schools where the children live. But in our area the problem seems to be that 80 to 95% of our children who are in boarding schools are there because their parents have in some way defaulted. The home situation is so impossible for the child that the parents send him out. Either there isn' enough food, or there isn't enough room in the homes to be able to accommodate the child. Often the problem is with alcoholism. This is something that nobody has brought up.

By and large, they are described as being in a boarding school, for what they call emotional and social reasons. I don't think any of us would have any of our children in boarding schools run by the Bureau if it were possible to do anything else. I would like to see education entirely in Indian hands, when it comes to Indian children. But the situation that we are faced with in my area is that there is no way we can pull the children immediately out of boarding school. So we have been coming up with a few programs to try to improve the boarding school situation. I mean, as Indians we have been putting this together, and we have asked the Bureau of Indian Affairs to cooperate with us in the program. One of our problems is that in what they call the dormitory aid program, at night there is a one-to-seventy ratio of children to a dormitory. During the day it drops down to perhaps one to thirty-seven.

The attitude of the people in the dorm is generally described as poor. The situation as far as the classroom in the schools, is, from all the children I have talked to, (say at Le Sabre School) that the teacher expectation for children is low. The Indian children feel that even if they put forth their best efforts, the teacher will say, "Well, we don't expect very much from Indian children anyway."

We have so many of the children in these boarding schools that we are not talking about a "small segment" of the Indian population. We are talking about a fairly large number of children from tribes of the Northwest who are in these boarding schools. We are trying to have a small demonstration program

154

with the United Tribes of North Dakota, who are sponsoring this. As I say, the Bureau has agreed to hire Indian people whom we will train, in child care. We are trying to develop a program in which we will use traditional Indian approaches to discipline. We have had some pretty bad cases in my area, just as you have had in Chilocco, but it does seem to be getting better. We have been overrun with white people. Over two-thirds of the people are white. Half of the people in the dorms are white, and our problem is simply to get Indian people in there. Then the thing is that often those who have gone through boarding schools themselves are hardest on the children when they get back in there to give help.

It's a combination of problems; it's really tough. We are looking for help from Indian people all over the country who might have some ideas in terms of finding remedies. Unfortunately we are forced to deal with the Bureau. We don't like it. There are some good people we talk to in the Bureau, but by and large we have to fight the system, as well as having to deal with all the other factors. So what I am doing, is reviewing the situation for you, because from time to time you might hear from other tribes. We will train twenty-five Indian people. We will give in-service training to people already there. We are going to try to revise attitudes and rebuild a new team so that after the training period, they will be able to go into the schools. While they are in the schools, we will still be counseling and working with them, with what we hope will be a permanent counseling team which will be all Indian, and this, so far, is the beginning of our solution.

DOROTHY DAVIDS: I am wondering if anyone heard anything about the formation of a National Indian Education Board, and who is going to form this Board. I think you will have to be Republican to serve on it.

A SPEAKER: I went to a meeting of the current National Indian Education Advisory Board Committee. All I see in Washington is one group after another being formed. They all have similar names. They are all told to do similar things and it is really confusing as to who is representing the Indian people, because they are all Indians on these things, and yet who chooses the Indians? It is really the Bureau of Indian Affairs, and what I want to know is how are you going to select this other Indian Advisory Board?

HERSCHEL SAHMOUNT: According to the recommendations, the tribes would be asked to submit names and selection would be made from these names. Or, if it was the desire of the tribes, an election for those positions would take place.

JOHN WINCHESTER: I am from Michigan. That was the same question I was going to ask: What has happened to the proposed National Indian Education Board?

I have been sitting tight on a proposal that I was asked to put together. I don't want to get messed up in a power struggle, and I don't want to be involved with this thing any more than Navajo or Cherokees. But there seems to be a certain select few who end up with this kind of choice thing, and we are missing some grass roots Indians, so to speak, in these programs.

DILLON PLATERO: I think it has come up very plainly in this Convocation, that each one has a peculiarly different problem. Situations differ, and I think we all know this, so it brings up the question as to how then should something like this be organized so that the responses to the needs of these particular people will come forth? We Navajo have a great deal at stake, with about fifty thousand Navajo children in various schools. We feel the same as you do, our people should be represented.

A SPEAKER: I am a student here at Princeton University. I had the opportunity to teach at Rough Rock last summer and found myself after six weeks, in a real dilemma. I felt that no matter how high my ideals were, I was always imposing my Anglo values on the Navajo children. It's an unavoidable thing. I had anthropology thrown in my face. The bearded people and the Vista workers were asked to leave. I would ask you gentlemen point blank: What is the role of white students or even teachers, in general Indian education? If there is a role at all, what should it be?

DILLON PLATERO: Let me answer. I think, on the Navajo Reservation, there is so much work, that even the Navajo people will not be able to fill it for some time. We are utilizing others to a greater degree than we expected at this time. We have quite a few Indians from other parts of the United States also, so we thing this is a problem that is going to be around for some time. At Rough Rock we don't feel that there will be a hundred per cent Navajo staff. One reason is simply because there is inter-marriage.

A SPEAKER: I think you are not really as free to dispose of such matters as you think, as long as the school board can fire you.

A SPEAKER: All the teachers try to help, but you people are middle class and white, and it's hard to get out of that bag.

A SPEAKER: But you are also an experience for Navajo children, and you're removable by the people.

A SPEAKER: Then, I think if people feel that we weren't helping in their education, we should indeed be fired and replaced.

SAM BILLISON: Maybe to some extent, you answered your own question.

A SPEAKER: We were discussing this thing at one time at a meeting like this. You see, the Anglo is a minority among the Navajo in their own land. A comparison is the role of the extension agent of the State colleges, with the farmer. He comes out not to dig his ditches for him but he advises with him as an expert to someone who is learning.

SAM BILLISON: I would like to comment on one question that was on the floor, the National Education Board. Mr. Platero's report mentioned something about the fact that Indians need to be doers instead of objects to which things are done. I don't like the idea of this Board coming to us from Washington, or anywhere else. I would like this to come from the Indians themselves, and that we get together on it some way, so that we have equal representation. I also don't like the idea of partisanship—the elephant and the donkey. I am against anything being dictated to us, or somebody else calling the shots for us, saying that this or that is good for the Indian.

JOHN WINCHESTER: To come back to Mr. Venters. I think you should consider yourself and other students in this respect, as a servant—a highly sophisticated servant, and not as an educator. I am not trying to put you down. I am trying to do this in a frame of mind to serve our people.

A SPEAKER: Well, I thought that since most of the students were only a year or two older than some of the kids we were teaching, we were practically peers. In no sense were we educators, but since we were so close to their age, we could deal with them in a very straightforward manner, almost as age equals and also cultural equals. There were things that could be shared in that sense and we tried to feel neither as educators or as servants, but people who had experiences which we thought we could share with some of the kids and certainly I think they shared with us more than we could share with them.

A SPEAKER: Just the fact that you have a Princeton label, you are an educator to them. Even if you don't have the sheepskin the fact remains that you identify. You talk about cultural equality. No.

A SPEAKER: What is it then?

A SPEAKER: You definitely are not equal in that sense. There are two different values. We each have a different culture, so you are not equal to the Indian in that sense. I am not trying to put you down, believe me.

A SPEAKER: I think I see what you are driving at, but right now I am working in anthropology and when an Indian says to me, "No, we don't want any anthropologists," that is a question I have to consider. It is the same kind of thing, that if what I am doing is actually detrimental to the Indian people, then I want to know about it and I want to know about it now and I want to change.

A SPEAKER: I think a crisis is coming. A lot of people are going to have to turn to something else. It may be that the Anglos look to the Indians and say we have got ourselves in a fix, and you must get us out of it. I can almost see that happening. Because of that, I have an interest in what anthropology is, in that I want to know how Indians live because it may be the only way we can survive.

A SPEAKER: I can understand your point about being a "servant," but I am hoping to go to the Navajo Reservation this summer as a student and work. The way I look at it, our role should be more or less to learn, because we don't know what Indians are, what their way of life is, and our role is to learn more about it and come back and try to teach white people, so we can also find our own identity in knowing we came after the Indians. Do you see what I mean?

A SPEAKER: You are willing to compare to find out if there is any truth between the two.

A SPEAKER: No, just to let the white people know the Indians were here before we were, and to make people aware of the Indian situation and what we, our forefathers, whatever, have forced on Indian people, which many people are very sensitive to right now.

A SPEAKER: One of the best ways to learn about Americans and the way that it is, is to go to Europe and see how they view it. Anglos or whites are now beginning to look at the Indian culture. The Indian culture is very inferior, according to the whites. But now if you are willing to look at it and say, these people are human, they have all the things we have. They have had superior institutions in the past, then you can draw comparisons which can give you the type of sensitivity that can help you be a teacher.

A SPEAKER: Let me read you a quotation:

> "In our intercourse with the Indians it must always be borne in mind that we are the more powerful party, we claim the right to occupy the soil, we assume it is our duty to coerce them into the duties and habits and customs."

That was the Director of Indian Affairs in 1872. Now, he set up certain policies aimed in that direction, and part of that policy was boarding schools. I think I can probably find another quotation which will say we must get them away from the influence of their family and we cannot teach them in their own barbaric tongue. Think of all the concentrated effort through a hundred and some years now, and you haven't yet touched or felt Indian culture, so I think you are a little conceited in considering you are going to affect Indians.

A SPEAKER: I can see the dilemma of young people today who want to be anthropologists, maybe they should study the evolving world. Maybe they should study suburban man or middle class man, or some of the other tribes which have come into being in the country that have got some rather strange customs.

SAM BILLISON: I think it is good to speak our minds, to make confrontations, and I enjoy it when there is an exchange of opinions. Thank you. This panel is now adjourned.

Between sessions at Princeton University in the Woodrow Wilson School. Participants took their "breaks" in the lobby, where the Convocation art exhibit was displayed.

At the panel on Native American Studies Programs, these two participants, above (unidentified), Chris McNeil, of Stanford, (below), who said: "I'm just setting up a recruitment program . . . One of the questions asked of me by every Indian student is: Are there any other Indians there? . . . you will find that what attracts Indian students in the first place is familiarity, and any kind of a sense of unity that has developed there."

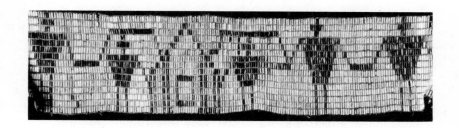

7

Review and Evaluation
Native American
Studies Programs:

W. ROGER BUFFALOHEAD

THE idea of establishing an American Indian or Native American Studies Program at the university level has a history. Contrary to what many Indians and nonIndians alike believe, the idea predates the recent proliferation of Indian Studies programs. As long ago as 1914, Senator Robert Owens of Oklahoma, at the urging of a number of Oklahoma Indians, introduced a resolution in the United States Congress calling for the establishment of an Indian Studies Department at the University of Oklahoma.

Nothing came of that resolution, as nothing comes of most resolutions. Again, in 1937, under different sponsorship, the idea was broached with University of Oklahoma officials, and fell on deaf ears. Almost every year since then, the topic has been discussed and tabled, down to the present time, despite the large population of Indian people in Oklahoma, and the recent national trends to the contrary with respect to the Indian Studies Programs. Let me make one thing quite clear. It takes change, basic and fundamental change in attitudes and viewpoints for some ideas to take root. While in Oklahoma, unfortunately, such change is yet to come, it has occurred in other parts of the nation and received the blessing of the academic world.

Another consideration raised by this glimpse into the past, one which I think Indian students in particular should ponder, is why the spiritual and intellectual source for the current Indian

Studies Program came from the movement of Black and Mexican American studies, rather than from the precedent set by Oklahoma Indians earlier in the century. But the answer of course, is that Indian students as well as most other people did not know about the earlier program. I can think of nothing which could more effectively state the case for Indian studies. Now there are a number of ways you can go about reviewing these programs. I sat for about a month trying to figure out if I could find any kind of a criteria which would be important or significant, as I worked through several of the programs. I could never come up with anything that I thought could be used as a model for evaluating the programs as to testing and hypothesizing about their particular courses or their aims and philosophies.

So, I thought rather than trying to set myself up as some kind of a judge of what are obviously experimental programs, I would simply report my experiences with the two programs that I am most familiar with. That is, the American Indian Culture Program at UCLA, and the Indian Studies Department at the University of Minnesota. I think there are some general remarks that can be made about Indian Studies Programs. First of all, you could call one kind of a program the type that has evolved in the last couple of years, and by and large most of them have been carved out of a larger and more encompassing program called Ethnic Studies. Some of these programs are mere collections of courses and nothing more. Others are programs as independent as programs can be within the present organizational framework of colleges and universities. At least one, the American Indian Studies Department at the University of Minnesota, seems to have a high status academically. I think you can also say that the present programs in Indian studies are in large measure, the work of Indian students. Indian students have done the spade work, sat on the committees, rounded up the people and faculty, and chased down the funds for most of these programs. In many ways you can also say that the mood, the temper, and the intellectual ferment among Indian students, is more encouraging and significant than the programs themselves.

As for content: almost all of these Indian studies programs have set up a type of curriculum in which they have evolved. They have a series of courses related to Indian history or culture. They have the general Anthropology courses, general Sociology courses, general Education courses, in which Indians themselves are supposed to receive an airing, and an intellectual discussion. I think probably too, you can make some generalizations about the students who have become involved in these many programs. Most of them have at one time or another been involved in a series of workshops. By and large most of them have attended some of these workshops held in Denver or by the National Indian Youth Council. Almost all of them carry over some of the things that they learned in those workshops, into the current programs at their institutions of learning.

You will also find lots of people in these programs, particularly in the urban settings, like the one at UCLA, who suddenly discover that there is opportunity and honor in being Indian. Then you can run down and get into an Indian program rather easily, and have your education paid for. This has happened in many cases. In terms of the program itself, I would like to talk about UCLA, dividing it into two categories, those that I think were external and those I thought were internal. Briefly, the UCLA American Indian Program began as an idea of several students who were going to school there. There were only seven in 1969, and in coalition with a number of Black, Mexican American, and Oriental students they presented demands to the University of California, for a separate program for Indian students. Originally, the University of California, like most institutions, had set up what was called an American Cultures Institute, in which Indians, Black, Oriental, etc., were each to constitute a segment of this American Cultures Institute.

As time went by, the coalition succeeded in getting this institute broken down into separate programs. Eventually, each of the groups got their own program. It was so structured that they have a Director. The emphasis would be on whatever the Steering Committee for the particular program wished to carry through. In the beginning, the Steering Committee was supposed to be composed of people not necessarily with qualifications in the normal academic sense. That is, they didn't want anybody but what are generally known as "community people," working on the Steering Committee from the Indian side.

As the committee was being set up in the summer of 1969, there was a great struggle for power among the various Indian organizations in Southern California, to take over the UCLA program, and the National Indian Youth Council got in on the act too. The California Indian Education Association got involved. Eventually it did come through as a UCLA-based kind of organization which had representatives from the Southeastern part of California, particularly from the reservations, from the ranch areas, and from the urban communities.

This briefly, is the background of the program. The original proposal was written by a conference of the Steering Committee which also had academic people on it, but they acted in an advisory capacity. The proposal called for setting up a program, with a director, who would develop among other things, curriculum, action, and research, and various ways in which the program overall could interact with the Indian people in the state of California, as well as throughout the country.

Now the external problem, as I saw it, might be divided up in a number of ways, and I think that what really is involved first of all, is the old coalition that had set up the original programs in the first place—between Blacks, Mexican Americans, Oriental, and Indian students. The coalition was fine so long as everybody was confronted with the common enemy, that is the white administration. But once you got problems going, such as who was going to get space in a particular building, and how much space, the coalition fell apart. One of the more serious, specific problems was how many students each part of the program in the Ethnic Studies framework were going to be allocated to each section or to each ethnic group. This was a question of finding money, and those who were pressuring more strongly, naturally got the most slots for students.

In almost every case, the Indians came in last in each of these specific problems. The Indian got the least number of students, the least money, the least amount of attention from faculty, administration, and in all other areas. Indeed, this was one of the major problems. I felt that it was a real problem, for anyone to try to work under these conditions, and to try to work yourself out from under those conditions. Secondly, it was my belief that the administration was the next bugaboo in the program, largely because university administrations are set up in certain ways for the programs within them to operate as all the programs operate, with certain kinds of criteria, and certain kinds of procedures. It was impossible to set up an American Indian Studies program within that type of framework, with that kind of content, and still keep within the guidelines that the Steering Committee and the students wanted.

For instance, when I took over the directorship of the program, they couldn't appoint me as a director. I was appointed as an *interim* director, because of a university ruling which states that no person without a Ph.D. could become a director of any program. At that time I didn't have my Ph.D. as yet, so I couldn't become the director officially. I became acting director, and that of course, limited my effectiveness and authority. Also, I didn't receive an appointment in any faculty department on the campus. Rather, I was appointed "Research Historian" for the University, whatever that was supposed to mean. Now these are examples of the sort of things that interfere with working relationships and the effectiveness of any individual who is supposedly heading up a program. There were numerous problems of this type, which acted as barriers to the carrying out of the work.

Here is another example. The committee would decide that the program should have a library. The university would decide that the committee couldn't decide that there should be a library. A university Review Board would have to decide this. And this would throw the whole thing back to the community people, and the community people would say fine, we want somebody on that committee. And then the university would maintain they didn't have the right to put somebody who was a non-academic person on the Review committee. I would be the person who would have to sit on it. Everything was covered by certain kinds of administrative rules and regulations as they exist in the university system. You just couldn't jump over these obstacle courses.

Another matter of considerable concern was one of an external nature. This was the relationship between the program in the university, and the Indian communities in Los Angeles. In the beginning, there was a very fine relationship with the Indian communities, largely because the Indian students went after the community to recruit people to sit on the Steering Committee. This honeymoon ended very soon, when the ideas of the Indian students changed. Red Power came up, and immediately you were confronted with a community-based kind of factionalism arising out of the program, and this brings me around to what was a major internal problem of the program that was and still is, factionalism.

The factionalsim that developed at UCLA, in the Indian Studies program, and in relationship with the Indian communities, was in my opinion, of the very worst kind. It had to do with the aims and the philosophies that were in conflict with one another in this particular setting. What happened was a play for power on the part of both students and the community people, because there were different kinds of concepts about what the program should become.

When we tried to develop curriculum for this program, there were those who argued the curriculum should be of a remedial nature. This, they argued, was because the Indian students didn't have the proper educational backgrounds for university work, and the program should concentrate on such subjects as English skills, mathematics, communication, writing, etc. There were others who emphasized that what should be expressed in the program is Indian nationalism, and Red Power, etc. So what you've got then, was whether or not there was to be remedial or revolutionary material. I don't know how you can get those two things working together in a program. We tried very hard at UCLA, but I think we failed, as in most other programs. I think that any program which comes up against this type of situation, will probably fail because you cannot get the students together. There are so many people arguing, but when it gets right down to developing even a curriculum, a kind of focus in adopting a good program, it is going to take a lot of work. Certainly you can't get agreement when people are arguing that if you give Indian students remedial work you are dealing in racism. Or, if your aim is to build revolutionaries, then why do it through university channels; there are other ways to do it than through the classroom, it was stated. In other words, the university is not the setting for development of revolutionary action required to offset some of the problems faced by the American Indian. These were the conflicting opinions.

To sum up, some of the many problems were curriculum development, factionalism, and the differing philosophies and aims of the various peoples involved, the question of whether or not the program should be remedial or revolutionary in concept. The University of Minnesota, on the other hand, appears to be set up in a different fashion. However, Minnesota is using the same logic that the people at UCLA used, through which they succeeded in obtaining an Indian Studies Department with its own faculty. So perhaps, it is within this kind of context that results may be obtained.

If you are constantly, as we were at UCLA, in a battle royal with the administration and with various people fighting with one another as to what will be the focus of the program, you cannot get anything accomplished. But, if you have a department setup which has prestige behind it and dynamic leadership, then there is a lot of opportunity for faculty members to be appointed and to actually succeed in developing curriculum in conjunction with these contrasting beliefs as to what should go into the program. Perhaps also there is a better chance, if the program could be constituted as an official department, to get things operating in the university in your favor. On program studies at UCLA all you could really do was to plead with other departmental members to incorporate Indian curriculum into their departments. But in Minnesota, if the curriculum is developed, it will have its own location within the Indian Studies Department and you won't have to go through all this mess of trying to get historians at UCLA to offer a course in American Indian History. It can be offered directly through the program itself. I think it is these types of obstructional things that tend to emphasize and bring out the kinds of factionalsim that exist in many of these programs and especially, the one at UCLA. I think that what should be asked of you in this panel, is that you explain what your particular program is about. All I can really do is to tell you about the things we experienced at UCLA in attempting to set up an Indian Studies program, and how these things have not worked, and how as a result, the program at UCLA is in serious trouble today. Now it doesn't make a hell of a lot of sense to be sitting there as a director of an

American Indian Culture program, when you have nothing to direct. That is what happened at UCLA. The Blacks knew it and the Mexican Americans knew it, and the Indians knew it. The whole point of the entire program was to attract funds to the university for research in certain areas. Some of these areas were for more minority studies. I think it's these kinds of things that have to be eventually settled by Indian people as to what role they wish to play at the universities. If they want to be tucked away in a convenient little building somewhere, really without power, but with a lot of verbiage that explains how you are going to be allowed to do nothing except busy-busy work. That is what I think happened at UCLA. I think it probably is happening in other universities.

I certainly don't want to close on a note of pessimism. I think that even under the circumstances which we were first forced to work in at UCLA, we were able to accomplish a number of significant gains; and I believe one of these was an awakening of the Indian community, if you can call it that, in response towards this program. Whether they carried it out or not, I don't know.

We were also able to get enough students together so that they could interact with one another and learn from one another what it was that they were seeking. For instance, the students there held sessions every Friday in which they would discuss current issues on the American Indian scene. Often times it turned into the kind of a situation in which students were actually, for the first time groping with some really serious problems. This happened, I think, because they were with Indian people in a session of this type and didn't feel afraid to speak their thoughts or be shot down in the classroom. I think that those little things we were able to do in bringing a number of issues to light, having an open exchange about them, and so on, were good, but overall, I don't think we accomplished very much.

DISCUSSION

Native American Studies Programs

CHRIS McNEIL: I am presently going to school, and what I wish is a point of information. Let me ask you, how long has the University of Minnesota Program or Department been in existence?

ROSEMARY CHRISTIANSEN: Last winter quarter, and fall.

CHRIS McNEIL: I'm interested in how it achieved this kind of prestige that you are talking about.

THE CHAIRMAN: In Minnesota, the situation is different than most other places in the country. This is because the Indian population in Minnesota exceeds the Black population. Or, there are at least as many Indians. At Minnesota, the Indian leaders set up an Indian Studies Department rather than to go to the other route with an institute or a program.

ROSEMARY CHRISTIANSEN: We didn't accept anything less than a Department.

THE CHAIRMAN: I think that is the position that should have been taken very early in the game before a lot of these things came up.

LIONEL deMONTIGNY: On the basis of your experience at UCLA, how would you define the objectives of an Indian Studies program? I mean, you pose some broad and conflicting objectives when you talk about remedial versus revolutionary programs. There must be something that lies between.

THE CHAIRMAN: There are lots of things that lie between. I think that what happens in the initial phases of developing a program like this, is that you cannot develop a curriculum as easily as you thought you could. Because, when you first get into it, it is pretty easy to say you are going to develop an American Indian History course, but unless you want it to be something different than what has passed for American Indian History, in college textbooks or in a lot of other writings, then you have to get down to the serious work of how you are going to incorporate all history, for example, into the program. How are you going to emphasize oral histories sufficiently? You are actually supposedly telling the Indian student like it is, for him, from the Indian point of view of history, rather than saying or concentrating solely on written materials, etc.

I also think what is really needed by Indian students is the kind of curriculum that is flexible enough for them to have experience at the university and take this experience out somewhere among the urban Indians or reservation Indians, or among whites, whatever they want to do with it, and to have time for them to think through a lot of things that have been bubbling inside of them. You can't really get this kind of curriculum developed, unless you have a very flexible arrangement, and you must use this as most of these students do and say that you are going to develop an American Indian Philosophy, an American Indian Literature, an American Indian History, an American Indian Anthropology, but I think it is easier to say these things than it is to develop them. I mean what in the hell is an American Indian Anthropology course? What is an American Indian Law course?

You know of course, but how are you going to develop it? What focus are you going to put on the materials, and what kind of materials are you going to use? There are so many kinds of things that could be raised in terms of curriculum development that I don't think you would want to blunder into developing a course that is going to be as terrible and insipid as many of the courses are today.

DICK WILSON: I am the Director of the American Native Studies program at the University of Oregon. I would offer one criticism that I think goes along with what Roger said. Early in the game the distinction has to be drawn very clearly as to the difference between the supportive services for Native American students, and Native American studies as an academic venture. One is likely to be favored and given a lot of lip service, and the other is much less glamorous and much more work.

THE CHAIRMAN: One of the really critical issues at UCLA was getting Indian students through all the bureaucratic and routine processes to get them in.

DICK WILSON: You will find, that unless you've got a real abundance of warm bodies at your school, it will eat up or it will occupy all of your time.

THE CHAIRMAN: What it got down to at UCLA was this: A number of us made the point that Indian students need more money in order to go to school because of their economic situation, simply because they couldn't go home to Mom and say, I need an extra $100 for this weekend party or whatever. We tried to point out that the current federal loan program simply put students on the basis of their income, and sometimes you couldn't depend upon that income, because your parents make $2,000 a year, for example, and that income might be distributed between three or four Indian families living together as opposed to $2,000 income for some other ethnic grouping. I think as an academic venture, you are right, these two kinds of things have to be separated.

DICK WILSON: Let me finish the last part of my statement. At the University of Oregon, when we started our program in 1967, there were five Native Americans in the school, and four from out of state. At that stage, we felt our first job was to get as many of our people into school and then, to fight the battles with course content, and what should be done to get teachers. This is the phase in which we are now. Once we get some momentum on campus, then we can go on to a Department of American Native Studies, and this may be different than other communities, but that is our situation. This is the battle we are fighting now. My own view is that we must be concerned with the Native American students, and what they get out of school. We have got a great abiding feeling that the white student is going to take care of himself in some way. There is no trouble in getting up courses for white students. They are going to take advantage of whatever is available. Our first responsibility is to our own students.

A SPEAKER: One other thing, we felt at Minnesota, that we educate all the white students on campus and the forty-four Indian students can find out by being an Indian, and by participating in Indian affairs. White people have got to be educated too, if we are going to get anywhere. That is one of our major premises.

ALFONSO ORTIZ: I would like to expand on Dick Wilson's comments. The real issue is whether you are dealing with hard money or soft money. All the ones except Minnesota are obviously dealing with very hard money, meaning that when you are a permanent part of the Legislative budget, you rely on the Legislature for funds. That is the real battle, which is one of money and simple economics.

DICK WILSON: That is the one we are fighting, but it is felt that in the Legislature it is being said that we are already giving the Indians an Ethnic Studies Program, and "why should we give them any more money for supportive services?"

THE CHAIRMAN: What happened in California was that the State Legislature passed a resolution calling for the creation of two Indian Studies Departments, one at a southeastern school and one in a northeastern school, with financing. What happened then was that everybody got into the act and everybody set up an Indian Studies Program. That is why you have Indian Studies Programs proliferating in the state of California. I don't know that any one of them will succeed in getting the kind of financing needed.

There was an incident in California with regard to a specific fund at UCLA. I believe they had $9,000 left in the Doris Duke money, and the History Department claimed they had turned that money over to the administration for the Indian Studies Program. The administration claimed they had never received that money. Mysteriously, our budget was to come out of somewhere—but nobody knew where. That is the kind of a shoestring operation there was at UCLA.

BUD MASON: There are well over a hundred students at Black Hills College. In watching other people in the development of Indian Studies we really wonder if this is the thing we should do. Our concern isn't really what we are going to teach our students, but in trying to keep them in school. Last semester we had an 80% dropout rate in college. I think we are dealing with two different types of students. Now I wouldn't want to classify the students in the urban areas in any special way, because I feel that they are not in the cities by choice, but because of actions of the federal government in deporting them to industrial areas.

I find in talking to different students, it seems as if the people who attend the large universities are more articulate than those in our local state colleges. All our people who come to the college are from one of the seven reservations that surround Black Hills. These people aren't as forward as the people you find in large universities. The attitudes of the people at the schools are not the same as those in the large universities. The attitudes of the people in the communities are not the same. What we are trying to do is to find ways in which we can help the student as far as his studies are concerned, because he comes to the college with very little preparation, and a very low concept of himself. He probably picked Black Hills State College because he figured it's the easiest college to get into.

One Oklahoma student had the same problem, and it's a small college too. There was total apathy towards the Indians in his area. I would like to hear from some of the people here, as to whether or not they have any ideas, how we could take care of this situation. Do we really need Indian studies? Should we concentrate on trying to help our people off the reservation? Or should we just help the people who are already in school?

THE CHAIRMAN: I don't think you have much of a choice. At least at UCLA, most of our efforts were concentrated on supprotive arrangements in spite of the fact that we had a lot of rhetoric about course development and that sort of thing. This is in terms of finances for tutorial work, and for preparation of courses that would give the student better concepts of themselves and to develop some skills at the same time. We tried to blend those two together into what was called the Indian High Potential Program. The theory was that you could use Indian materials to teach Indian students the skills they need. For instance, to consider English skills they would need to succeed in the regular curriculum at UCLA in this subject. But what you really need is the people who have the ability to do that kind of teaching, and the kind of teachers that we had at UCLA were inadequate to this task. Often they had the desire to do it, but they needed support, and they needed training themselves. One course that was set up that I thought was probably the most successful, was one taught by Karen Jakobson, on Indian Community Development. She would simply take all she knew about community development and put it into a training format, in which the student would have to prepare a paper or a study of a community; an Indian community, or a white community, or what have you, using all the techniques such as making them aware of political concepts in the community, or social concepts in the community. At the same time, she would emphasize, as much as she could, pride in being Indian and in Indian culture. What also occurred at UCLA was that we got the students very much involved indeed, as you probably know. The students all departed for Alcatraz. Here then another question was raised.

171

If you are going to teach students to be involved and to be activists, as was done at California, can you then draw a line and say to them: You've got to come back from Alcatraz and learn your lessons? Those of us who had approved this involvement at Alcatraz were caught in a fix. What could we say? The only argument that we could make when the administration told us to get the students off of Alcatraz, was that the administration would then have to call in ALL of it's activists in their involvements with the white world. We would just have to approach it on the theory that you couldn't have a double standard with respect to us. I don't know whether you can be both an activist and a good student. As an Indian student you are particularly pushed towards becoming an activist because you realize there is so much that needs to be done for your people. Often times it seems more important to do the things that need to be done, than to sit there in a classroom, presumably getting knowledge which is supposed to help you more cleverly do your work with skill and intelligence when you get out of school.

I don't have a ready answer. I think that this is exactly what happened at a lot of schools, because of a nationalism which gets carried away. I couldn't really say to them, after I had insisted that it was good to be involved in such activities as Alcatraz, "Well you know this is not really education." It is education indeed, and it was education to go to Alcatraz.

LIONEL deMONTIGNY: I am still confused. I still can't get what the real objectives of the Indian Studies Programs are. I follow you that they develop because you've got Black studies programs and therefore, you should have Indian studies programs. But I am still confused in this respect: If you are going to evaluate the success of an Indian Studies program, then surely you must have some overall objectives. I hear about remedial education, and keeping Indians in school, and revolutionary movements, and activist movements, and I mean, does this stuff all hang together? I don't really see what the objective of an Indian Studies Program is. I mean is it something like this: "Urban Indians, come on in and get processed through this Indian Studies Program. Maybe what we are creating is an instant Indian just like instant cake mix and maybe that is what we need.

BEATRICE MEDICINE: The whole movement was part of the Third World Movement, in which the colored minorities in the United States would have more relevant education. So indeed, in many of the California universitites and colleges, there was a deliberate effort to recruit Indians for directorships, and then have them work with students. But as you know, it's very hard thing to get qualified professors to go into such programs. This was the original objective, to make education more relevant for Chicanos, Blacks and Indians. The Indians just came in sort of as a red backlash.

LIONEL deMONTIGNY: You want to get these Indians through school?

BEATRICE MEDICINE: You want to make the curriculum more significant for the Indian?

LIONEL deMONTIGNY: There must be some general objective behind this. I mean, just your saying the Indians should go to school doesn't mean much. I want to know why. I'm not saying they shouldn't. I just want to know why. I just want to know the purpose. And I think the student also needs to be clear as to his purpose.

THE CHAIRMAN: One of the things I've thought of as a criteria, but never used, is that many of us who went through school in the Pre-Indian Studies Period, came out under the same conditions as any other scholars. Many of us emerged with some loss of our Indian values. One of the things that we hope to be able to do with Indian Studies is to get an Indian student through a university and still not remove him psychologically from his own people. I don't know whether that could be developed, but I believe what you are dealing with is the transformation of an individual from what he was in the reservation to what he is going to become developmentally speaking, on a university level. I don't know whether you have a right in the first place, to tell him that or not. Maybe that is a decision he has to make for himself.

DICK WILSON: Again I would like to answer that, and say that our objective starts here with supportive services. We feel that the Native American Indian in general needs a corps of trained people, trained in all fields; technical, legal, medical and so on. They also need to know how to protect their land base, to improve their conditions. This is going to require a lot of work and a lot of attention to the individual Indian student on the campus, because he suffers from the academic shock which almost all students suffer from. And especially does he suffer from it, coming from high school to college and being confronted with the cultural shock of a reservation Indian arriving on a campus where life is on an entirely different level. It is easy to get stamped and wiped out as a human being. The problem is one which I feel is too big for me or anyone else to cope with on an individual basis. I would certainly not beg the question as to what is relevant in education, but the question of keeping all people in school is first of all our primary consideration.

I don't think there is such a thing as Black calculus or Indian physics. I think it boils down to the idea of getting somebody in school and into something he can make use of and then hopefully help his community with. Certainly a supportive service program doesn't ignore the problems, but what is studied is necessary to what he wants to make out of his life and so I say again that the supportive service program is what we must concentrate on first of all. As to the academic side of the question, it's most difficult for me to cope with, struggling as we have a deep feeling that the young Indian student is about to be dropped out of school—or, at the end of his four years of college education, he will have no place to go. If you have to rely on four years for the Indian, then you have lost the battle, because if you rely on those four years alone, and you cannot check the first twelve years of his education you cannot redeem him in the last four.

HENRIETTA BLUEYE: If I may make a comment, I go to Radcliffe. I think it is important to consider something that Miss Christiansen said. Many are at odds about where to place emphasis in connection with the Native Studies Program. I don't know how many of you were at the Red Power discussion yesterday. But one of the phrases that was thrown around very much and which to me had a lot of meaning is the idea of cultural self respect and cultural dignity on a truly academic basis. The academic side of Native American Studies Programs is quite important and what is still more important is for the students themselves to have resources and courses, tutorial services or whatever may be available to them, so that it is possible for them not merely to be enrolled but to be aware that something is there for them, and that part of their heritage is what is there for them. On the other side of the coin, it is something also which is going to educate the white man. To me this is imperative in this country.

The American Indian Studies programs are probably more important in this respect, just as the Black studies are, at Harvard. However, what has happened is that Black studies was pushed through last year after the April strike. It has been a dismal failure because, in fact, the faculty buckled under failure from militants who wanted Black studies, so that they could go out and proliferate about their bitterness in connection with the white society. This is not what this type of program is supposed to do. I think you have to consider the idea of cultural dignity and Indian identity, working both from the student's viewpoint from what is going to gotten out of it, and what the white man is going to get out of it. I disagree slightly with what has been said regarding four years of college education as being unable to counteract twelve years of high school education. I went to a public school off the reservation and it was integrated as all the Indian students in New York State are. When I went to Radcliffe College the first year, I had some memorable experiences. I haven't thought about my identity and this is something entirely different. When I hit Radcliffe, people there were amazed at what they did not know and they made me say what it meant to me to be an Indian. I think that the Native American Studies Program has to be geared partially to the students and partially to the majority of the white people who are obviously going to be involved and going to be taking the courses, whether you think they are or not.

A SPEAKER: I would like to discuss this from a different point of view, that of an Elementary School Administrator. I think you will find that you will continue losing many students and you will continue having people who question their background. You will continue having people affected psychologically and wondering about their identity until we can start in the first grade or even in kindergarten. We must let these students know that there is a college available that will take them when they finish high school. We must get their parents geared for it as well as the student, and prepare them psychologically, academically, and financially. Until we do that, we're going to continue to lose them.

THE CHAIRMAN: I think you're right, and Mr. Wilson is also right in saying probably that four years of college experience is not going to make that difference. But I operated on the theory that you had to start somewhere. You have to operate at the university level. One of the things we tried to do at UCLA—and one of the more difficult things to do, is to introduce a curriculum change in the elementary school level with respect to minority peoples. If you think that university administrations are bureaucratic, full of red tape and slow to change, then try to take on a school board about curriculum in the elementary schools. I'm sure you're going to find it as difficult if not more difficult, to find people who are really receptive about change.

We have people come in, and I know Jay Silverheels was involved somewhat with our Programs, and he was very much concerned that he had played Tonto. He was so concerned about it that the poor man suffered all the time about it and tried to do all kinds of things that would erase that image. One of his primary concerns was to get curriculum change on the elementary level and also to get change for the Indian Actors Guild. He even offered to go and present Indian plays and that sort of thing at the elementary school, free; the schools refused it, simply saying, that it didn't have any relevance to the youngsters and they would misinterpret or misunderstand. You're really getting into a can of worms when you get down to the local level.

A SPEAKER: If I may, I have been in elementary education for many years and we still have problems determining what kind of teacher we need, and what kind of curriculum to teach, and how to teach it at the elementary school level. If you think your problems are great at the University level, I think it will take work from the kindergarten level all the way through the University before we can eventually come up with an effective way of doing things.

A SPEAKER: I go along with this: I go along with the idea of having to start from the kindergarten. In the meantime we have to take care of these thousands of kids who are becoming available, right now. I go to Eastern Washington, and we call ourselves an Eastern Washington Indian Education program. It's almost a remedial thing (going along with what you said). We had about seventy to eighty per cent drop out, especially in the treshman year. So, we concentrate on retaining these kids through various counseling and tutoring methods, and almost baby sitting services in so far as it depends upon the students. They are not all alike, but they all have basic problems.

GEORGE ABRAMS: I'm from the University of Arizona. I would like to inquire about these Indian Studies Programs as far as staffing is concerned. How do you staff? For instance, at UCLA, did you staff whites mainly, or try to recruit Indians, or what?

THE CHAIRMAN: We recruited Indians. There were lots of politics involved. But one of the demands insisted upon by the Steering Committee, was that all personnel be Indian, and we managed, miraculously, to round up four Indian teachers to handle four courses being offered to the High Potential students at UCLA. Two Indian instructors were teaching American Indian Literature and another was teaching Community Development. Still another was teaching American Indian History. Then, in terms of the Program itself, we had a Director and two Research Assistants, and a Secretary. All of these were Indians. The task of the Research Assistants was the ordinary kind: compiling bibliographies and preparing proposals, working on various plans. I think what is really needed, if we're going to have this kind of occupation such as Curriculum Specialist, is to get someone who knows something about developing curriculum.

Really, it was very difficult to get anybody to come in, say from the elementary schools. We contacted schools particularly in an area of L.A. with large Indian population, and brought them in. We tried to get some innovations in terms of Indian programs on the elementary school level, but that is as far as it went. If we had had someone there who could have presented them with a well developed plan for curriculum, maybe they would have been more responsive than they were to the rather few things that we did have in mind.

THELMA STIFFARM: We have a program at my University, also in Indian Studies, but I'm not in a position to explain it. However, I would like to warn all the other college students that are thinking of fighting for their own programs, that our biggest problem has been in finding a Director. It took us over a year. There aren't that many interested Indian people walking around. All we wanted was an educated Indian who was interested in the program and would not use his position as a stepping stone to something bigger and better. We had to settle the first year for an Indian Advisory Council, which we have this year. We have someone who will come to us in June, but for all you students who are thinking of fighting for your own program at the same time, have some thoughts in your head of who you're going to ask to apply.

We had a lot of people who applied. They were not familiar with the northwest region, which we thought was definitely one of the qualifications in our area. There aren't that many people walking around in our area who are Indians and qualified for the job. There are three openings right at the moment in the State of Washington.

A SPEAKER: With regard to Indian Directors, Instructors and Programs, I don't know where we're going to find them. I've got $1,000 a month for one.

HARVEY McCUE: I'm from Trent University in Peterboro, Ontario. I would like to describe what we're doing at Trent, in terms of Indian Studies. But before I do that, I want to make a comment. I will use the term Indian Studies because I want to include the developments encountered in Canada as well as those in the States. There is a dichotomy between them providing the Program is in a University for Indian Students. There are quite a few of them. On the other hand, there is adequate and justifiable concern for an Indian Studies Program which is concerned with the non-Indian educating the non-Indian about Indians. I think it's not enough just to say one Program or one Department is doing this or one Department is doing that in terms of these two concerns because we're going to really get bogged down.

For instance, if you have a Program, say at Minnesota—a Department, rather, which is justifiably and necessarily concerned with providing instruction in education for nonIndians, then I think in five, maybe even in less than five years you may have a great deal of difficulty in attracting Indian professors or Indian instructors, because I think it would be safe to say that as an Indian instructor, seeking a position in an Indian Studies Department, personally, I would prefer to deal primarily with a majority of Indian students.

ROSEMARY CHRISTIANSEN: Minnesota offers tenure to its professors.

HARVEY McCUE: On the other hand, in the programs that are dealing primarily with Native Studies, there is going to be one hell of a job convincing the administration (and we have heard from Mr. Buffalohead, already), that the administration is going to have to relent in certain areas to permit enough Indian students into the University, simply to make it valuable and simply to have the Indian students to work with. So, I think theoretically, the whole idea of American or Canadian Indian Studies is a good one, but I think before we sort of go off in a tangent and say every University is trying to set up a Program and attract people—(I mean already, we have heard people say that we can't get staff and there is some sort of concern given), we might better co-ordinate things. I hate to see an understructure involved, but at the same time, I hate to see a proliferation of universitites get bogged down with their wooden Indians.

TRAVIS KINSLEY: I'm from Dartmouth College. Currently we're trying to work with the college administration, in regard to Indian Studies Programs for the next year. As it stands now, we're working with the experimental college, which is a community-class type thing. We're trying to educate the white community and the non-Indian also. However, once we get this Indian Studies Program through at Dartmouth, and instruction organized around the idea that it will be based upon the Indian students, our primary concern would come whenever other students wished to participate in the programs.

We have funds available right now to employ a Director of the Indian program. We have the funds from the BIA, but the BIA would like to have one of their people to build it and we don't want it. I gather that something is being considered about trying to structure a program so you can have perhaps a pool of available scholars and if you can't find somebody likely, you could have a list of all the scholars. I must admit that a lot of the scholars who are here now, are new to me because I can't find them when I try to look for them.

ROSEMARY CHRISTIANSEN: At Minnesota, we're trying to attract people and trying to make them happy. The structure, I think, is highly important. We must have the proper qualifications in personnel. The Indians are demanding, say, that the people we hire are as highly paid as anyone at the University, and that we give them tenure, and that they are able to work their own discipline; I think we're getting all mixed up in what is a Department, and what is the American Indian Studies. We have been bluntly saying at Minnesota, "This is not a Welfare situation." We have the Department and we take care of the Indian students in other ways. Let me ask: What is a quality education? What goes into a quality education is that we're to learn about all the peoples, not just the white peoples. This is one of the things that we were driving at in Minnesota. I think too, that you've got to start talking about structure.

THE CHAIRMAN: I think the quality education factor has to be kept foremost in your mind. What could happen is that you may find some people involved in these Indian Studies Programs who sell out to the forces of ignorance. "Everything that isn't Indian isn't worth knowing," as an example of one concept. Or the only way it can be valuable is to have an Indian who has written it. You get involved in these things, and I am afraid that you could torture yourself for the next three hundred years on whether or not that particular viewpoint that you wanted is in that particular book. It seems to me that this is an awfully narrow conception of what learning and education is all about. In other words, somehow or another, it's going to be packaged into you on the basis of the books elected and so forth.

We've gotten into many arguments at UCLA which actually approach the censorship of books, or even phrases or passages. While I can whole-heartedly and sympathetically support censorship of certain kinds of things that have passed for American history, in the sense that you explain that this is the wrong approach, but I could never support the argument that these books ought to be removed completely from the library and burned as some of the students suggested. It seems to me this is a ridiculous approach to take if you're going to learn anything at all.

For example, I don't think you can really understand the American Indian without reading all this nonsense that has been written about him. Some students turn this whole Indian Studies Program into their own kind of bag, where this identity-seeking becomes all important to them at the expense of whatever else is going on in the program.

BEATRICE MEDICINE: This is what happened at San Francisco State and many of the people who went to Alcatraz didn't keep up their studies. Others stayed on campus and made the Dean's List. You have to set your limits as to what you want to do. I was very fortunate because I wasn't tied in with the Ethnic Studies Department as such; I was in anthropology independently. I volunteered to work there for that one semester and we have had a terrible time recruiting people who are qualified because they don't want to lower the standards for that Department. On the other hand, we have had the revolutionaries, who really aren't doing much in terms of intellectual growth or in social movement either.

DICK WILSON: What is emerging here, is the realization, that not only is the dichotomy drawn between supportive services of Ethnic Studies, but what was real for the University of Minnesota and real for us at the University of Oregon. We are dealing with Reservation Indians who have no trouble knowing what their background is. They are not the slightest bit evangelistic about the Indian culture, and there is a course that I'd like to throw at the Indian students and not one of them wants it. I mean our students wouldn't function in that course. There is another in Native Literature, which our students do very well in and they wouldn't if the whites started to invade the course, right now at this stage of development.

This is not racism; it's not segregation, but it's group dynamics of our kids expressing themselves around themselves. Maybe your approach to Ethnic Studies is the best thing for you. Maybe the only danger I see in this whole thing, is that at some school like Black Hills State or the University of Oregon, students might take off on this trip and just find it a diverting kind of situation—and ignore the less glamorous work of coming up with a valuable supportive service program. But we're going to have sixty-five per cent of our kids surviving their first year. Now, the main proof of the pudding is how many of these kids make it by their second year? Actually, we're going to have half of them surviving. This to me, is what our reality is.

A SPEAKER: Arizona State is trying to meet the need of both the Indian students and the non-Indians by setting up a center of Indian education. There are many Arizonians who will indicate that the Program started in 1959 as a center for Indian education. We teach sixteen courses in Indian education and we have an Indian reaction project. We have a head-start project and Indian Programs and Clubs; we have all these services and that of a Master Degree in Indian education. All I'm saying to those of you from different institutions—if you're having problems in your program, perhaps you ought to come down to the University of Arizona, or at least write to us, and we will try to offer you what our successes have been and our pitfalls have been and so forth, because we haven't run into this problem. Possibly, the reason is because the program has been accepted. Several people here have worked at the University and we have a graduate assistant here working at the University. We have the staff of nine; six of these are American Indians. We have the financial support of the University and perhaps this is the basis of the whole success.

A SPEAKER: You also have students.

A SPEAKER: We have a hundred and fifty Indian students. That is a great difference between what we used to have, which was five.

A SPEAKER: This is true. I came to the University in 1957 and we had fifteen Indian students. This has grown and the important thing now, is to have our program work with the Indian clubs and with the Research Services at the University. Our mortality rate for Indian students is about seven per cent per year, which isn't too bad. I just want to re-emphasize a point that Dick Wilson made. At one point it seemed as if we were trying to produce a universal model of some kind of Native American Studies Program and I don't think there is such a model.

A SPEAKER: I think it's become fairly clear now, that depending upon where you're trying to set up the particular students in that area, might have a great deal to do with shaping the program. I think that might also explain the comments that Henrietta Blueye made. The very fact that she is from Radcliffe, shows she is quite capable of surviving under almost any circumstances. That is not true, however, at the University of Oregon, or at Black Hills State.

CHRIS McNEIL: There are very similar factors affecting all programs. One is that of keeping Indians in school. I have been at Stanford University. We're just setting up a recruitment program, but nothing about the Indian Studies Program as yet. One of the questions asked of me by every Indian student is: Are there any other Indians there? When you talk about private institutions like Stanford, you're talking, of course, in different terms, but still you find that what attracts Indian students in the first place is familarity, and any kind of sense of unity that has developed there. This is what is apparent in trying to teach students who are not willing to be in these other schools. Sometimes they have been successful and sometimes they have not been.

I would like to comment about the whole question of setting up the studies program itself, because at Stanford, the Blacks and Chicanos have raised their population in the University substantially. In the past few years the Blacks have raised their student population from around fifty to three hundred. In just a couple of years the Chicanos have been raised from twenty to two hundred and they didn't have programs set up when they first came there at all. What occurred was, that there were several students who came into the university and were successful there. They were able to attract greater numbers of students, whereas before, they simply weren't encouraging it or considering the university, because they thought it just was too difficult, and they wouldn't be able to get in.

In other words, the students themselves, after a while, set these things up out of their own coalition and they are strong programs academically. The structure of the public university and the private school is somewhat different. The successes of the students and the success of their program was very much due to the fact that the students wanted it.

THE CHAIRMAN: On that same topic, there is a certain amount of "stepping-down" process that goes on in some of these programs which I think I didn't mention. You can only live off Red Power for so long, and then you have to get down to the basic assumption of what you're going to do in the Institution. A lot of times if you let the students run their course, (at least it's been happening in Black Studies and in Mexican-American Studies, and I will assume it will happen in Indian Studies) after a while they come up with a kind of self disciplinary thing about what they want to get out of the University and it may be that is what colleges, (at least with Indians from the urban scene and the Reservation scene), have to develop. They haven't yet reached the point where they will decide on their own; that is more important. It has to do with getting communications skills and mathematics, accomplishing on their own terms and on their own standards, rather than flying off somewhere to get involved with activities.

THE CHAIRMAN: Before the coffee break, we were getting a number of significant criticisms and viewpoints about Native American Studies. If you want to continue talking about your particular program, let's do so.

A SPEAKER: I'm the co-ordinator of the Indian Program at University of Washington. We have about 157 Indian students now, and I've been taking notes as each one of the people here has been speaking. I thought I'd stop, because I'm going to have enough for a deck of cards pretty soon. I think Dick and Miss Christiansen are altogether correct about their statements in connection with their Indian programs in their context and in their area. But each has different needs. I think there are two basic philosophies upon which to build an Indian program. One, as was pointed out, might be to help reinforce your Indian identity, because granted you may be very Indian once you get out of high school. But you think of spending four years in an institution or a college whose primary purpose is to instill values in you which are predominately white middle class! That may be a form of assimilation, and it would be difficult to get it out of your system after four years. An aspect of the program might be to educate the public as Miss Christiansen said. You know the American people are naive about the Indian people. They don't know about our culture and you know we don't have an Indian problem; we have a white problem.

The reason we have a white man problem is because the white man is naive about our cultures, our values. Today institutions of higher learning carry a mandate into the Indian community which says they must, "Make over the Indian for his own good." This, I think, is a basic philosophy of colleges today. Therefore, I'm saying that Indian Studies can instill, in the academic world, respect for our cultural values or the Indian student's background. As for the first suggestion, as you know, "reinforcing our Indian values once you get to high school or to college," I don't particularly care for this, because it just wouldn't work too well. I figure that Indian student organization outside of the University can very well help us retain our Indian heritage. It's necessary, in formulating any kind of Indian Studies, to have Indian people as instructors, because we do have a different philosophy.

Someone mentioned the coalition at UCLA between Indian people and other ethnic groups. In the initial stages of constructing any kind of a program a coalition is very beneficial because with a coalition, you have power to gain what each individual ethnic group needs.

Once that is done, I think each group should separate, because each has different values and different objectives. Therefore, a coalition continuing from that point would serve to weaken the Indian Studies Program. If the primary purpose of Indian Studies is to keep Indian students in college, because you know, we have a very high attrition rate of Indian college students and I don't think this would be very effective. Like Dick said, there is a distinction between supportive services and academic Indian Studies. We've got to make that distinction.

As far as keeping students in college, I think the place to work is in the elementary and secondary schools. One way might be to have Indian college students recruit Indian high school students and talk to the Indian high school students about college life. This serves as a means of identifying with an Indian student in college and it's very effective. For instance, we're recruiting out of Chemawa Indian School. We have been there three times now, and we have twenty-five per cent of their students who are going to the University of Washington. This self-identification with another Indian individual is very necessary.

Miss Christiansen mentioned forming Indian Studies as a department. I don't feel this is very effective, because you're studying social, political, economic aspects of Indian life. To do any justice to these subjects, you have to have an interdepartmental situation. I'd like to make two suggestions. One is to set up a National Indian Studies Information Bureau with research and material in these programs throughout the nation. Things are being done haphazardly and we lose our effectiveness. We should have a national pool of educators.

A SPEAKER: I'm from the University of Arizona. I'm thinking of a Native Studies Program, but taking it out of the university and placing it within the community. You could work side by side with a central program in a university. This would have a lot of repercussion in our work with the communities, with the high school students, and with elementary schools. In the Southwest, what is developing is a lot of what are called Cultural Centers. No one really knows what they are going to do with them. At the university we have a seminar in which three tribes are represented and we go over these problems and suggest what our university should do.

THE CHAIRMAN: What you have said brings to mind what some urban Indians are doing. I don't know that any of you are familiar with the Indian Welcome House in California, but they have a tutorial program for Indian students in the school system, and they bring them in on weekends for sessions in different subjects in English and nonIndian themes, for example.

HARVEY McCUE: I'd like to describe the program being developed at Trent University in Canada. We're more or less maintaining a status quo, primarily because we're not sure whether we want to move in the direction of an Institute or a Department. Right now we haven't settled the restrictions and disadvantages of either. There are certain disadvantages as well as advantages in both. We require a certain flexibility at this time. We're developing a three-pronged type of Indian Studies Program. The academic program leads to a three-year art degree in Indian studies. That is well under way.

We have the students enrolled in the first year of the three-year program. However, we feel this is important because it's an academic program and it merely perpetuates the White-Indian relationship, because maintaining university requirements for admission into an academic program prevents many students from enrolling. This sort of relationship serves the necessary requirement of educating the nonIndian as well, but we feel the main responsibility is to the Indian people. To do this, we are proposing to the administration that a non-credit program be opened, taking the shape of a year or two-year degree diploma course, consisting of six to eight week semesters or semester courses, to be developed within the framework of the university studies program. The diploma courses would be determined primarily by consultation with the Native communities and the Native personnel who would be responsible. There are many Native people employed by various agencies, who are unable to become full time faculty members because of other commitments. However, we would encourage a part-time appointment to offer the faculty instruction that would take place in this non-credit or diploma course. Frankly, the instruction in this new development won't be remedial nor would it be vocational because we feel there are other institutions in the Provinces of Canada to facilitate this type of program.

The third area is to make strenuous attempts to recruit the students or adults who graduate, for example, from the diploma course, to go back to the communities and establish some sort of learning program on the Reservation. They would be retained on a part-time basis by the university. The Indian studies program would provide the resources and the curriculum assistance for these people, to enable them to set this up. They would be utilizing the experiences received in the non-credit program on the Reservation. The interesting facet of this non-credit program is that a certain number of six-week semesters would actually qualify younger people who aspire to a full time program, upon completion of a three to six-week semester, who could be elevated to the full time program. That would be without the necessary high school graduate requirements. This is basically what we are doing at Trent.

THE CHAIRMAN: One of the points to consider is, to what extent the universities are hiding behind academic requirements in setting up Indian Studies Programs. I maintain, that in dishing out the criteria to you, they are getting you hung up on the kind of criteria that prevents development of a program. They have never maintained such criteria, and have certainly made exceptions in establishing other types of programs. For example, if you are told that the Director must have a Ph.D., then you can go over (at UCLA for example) and find that the man who is teaching courses in Architectural Design and Research doesn't hold a degree at all. It's experience that brought him there. This is true in other departments as well. I think you've got to be very careful when setting up such requirements not to get fooled into thinking that the universities are always interested from the standpoint of the Degree, as to the quality of the program being set up. A lot of times it's a way of shoving a program into incubation and "deliberation" which is done to avoid giving you the needed funds.

A SPEAKER: I'd like to make a comment on that. Dartmouth College was founded as an Indian school 200 years ago, and has done very little if anything for the Indians. It has realized its faults now and is trying to make amends, and lookint for a person to fill the position of Director. They will accept any person capable of functioning in such positions, but it need not necessarily be a Ph.D. Another idea is that those students coming in have a basic problem with English because so many of them have English as a second language. What we propose to the college is that perhaps those entering freshman year will be given special status so that they can have English as a second, or foreign language and get credit for their own Native tongue, instead of having to hassle through a third language such as French or German which wouldn't benefit them because they will go back to their tribes or Reservations anyhow.

A SPEAKER: I'd like to elaborate on the question of requirements. All colleges and universities have made exceptions on this matter. It's up to the students to find out everything they can and uncover these exceptions. Also, write down everything the administration tells you, because we have had this problem too. A white person in certain cases will say something. Then, a month later will say, well, "I didn't really say that." You have to write it down so they can't renege on you. Many are trying to please the Indians right now. When it comes time to perform, they claim, "I didn't say I would do that." I don't think anyone here can say there are no problems, because there are. You have to learn to fight just as hard as the administration will probably fight, even though they are so nice to your face. When you turn around, they aren't so nice.

A SPEAKER: I want to get up here where I can see you people when I talk. Let me talk about one problem we have that hasn't been discussed. That is, the structure of the schools, which must change, because the entire educational system as presently set up, is not educational. It's a system of acculturating people. Take history courses. They are set up to reinforce a cultural background. Literature courses are set up to reinforce a cultural background. But you can be sure it isn't Indian cultural background, and an awful lot of Indian students, when they come into college or grade school, are immediately hit with somebody else's values and standards to which they must conform. One of the big problems is culture-pressure, the pressure to conform when they get into college.

I had one student who made straight "A's" but dropped out because he couldn't stand the pressure to conform. By the way, I am from Western Washington State College. I am Director of Indian Studies in the College of Ethnic Studies. The college has a unique situation. They have a cluster of colleges within the school on the basis of the school's growth. To maintain the advantages of a small school, while retaining the advantages and facilities of a larger school, they form cluster colleges within the main complex. Right now we have Fair Haven College, a social science oriented college; and Hutley College, in environmental sciences, and a College of Ethnic Studies, which was formed this year. It isn't as good as it sounds, but I am finding more and more in the last three schools I've been at, that Indian programs do not work well in conjunction with other programs. Last year, we were setting up an orientation of Indian educators and somebody wanted to know if we were going to let white people in. The students said, we don't want white people in, because then we will end up being dominated. They will dominate the whole thing and the Indians will be sitting off to the side again. This is what happens when you have programs running in conjunction with others.

At the moment, we are dominated by the Black people. This idea was originally conceived by the Black Students Union, which wanted to set up a Black Studies Program at the college. There are very few Black people around Northwestern Washington, but there are an awful lot of Indians. The Blacks didn't want this to go all Indian, so they set up this Ethnic Studies Program with the Black, Indian, and Chicano. The Dean of the college is Black and the Director of Black Studies is Black and we don't have a Director of Mexican Studies full time yet. I'm the only Indian and I'm feeling like an up-front Indian because I'm there all alone. We started out with complete control; we could do anything we wanted; the school wasn't forcing any structure on us. We were wide open for any innovations in education. I'm finding out that most Black people in higher education are very white middle class oriented, especially those who have made it. They've gone through the system and made it according to the rules of the system and they don't want anybody changing the rules no matter how irrelevant the education might be.

I refer particularly to the motions you have to go through to get a Degree. They are still going right along with the system. We were going to do away with grades. We wanted to eliminate the time system. We wanted one grade and that grade to be pass-fail. A student would study under an instructor and he would go to lectures and classes. When he reached a certain level of competence, he could receive a grade of pass, which entitles him to go on to the next higher level in the same subject-area. In this way a student would progress through school. But all of a sudden we have to have time limits. These were decisions made without consulting me, because they knew I wasn't going to go along with it. All of a sudden we have the regular grading system so that you have students working strictly for grades and not for knowledge.

The one big innovation was that the Black people thought everyone should respond to a single theme and they wanted to do away with courses. I've never had any argument with courses, because they are easy to handle as subdivisions of a larger discipline. So the three areas, Black, Chicano and Indian, now have one massive course in which you respond to the central theme. I never can remember what that central theme is. I teach my course the way I want to, anyhow, and the hell with them. I don't know how long I'll last there though. The main thing is that even when you get away from the regular administration of a college, you still have people who are trying to maintain that same system. I don't know about the rest of you, but I had a real tough time getting through that system. It took me 19 years to get a Bachelor's degree because I couldn't stand it for more than a couple of terms at a time. I would go to school for awhile and then get out. I always found an excuse: to go to work, or have something else to do in the spring. I could always find an excuse. I see a lot of kids doing the same thing.

On academic programs and support programs, if you have an academic program which changes some of the regular structures, and some of this curriculum, it is going to be a big help to your support program because it will be a lot easier for kids to get through. If you get a good Indian history class that will be acceptable to the schools, and carries the same credit for graduation as Western European history, this student is going to respond because it will reinforce, or be reinforced with his own cultural background. If we can start teaching coyote stories in class—and I don't know if you people know any good coyote stories—but there are many in the literature, that would be an advance. I have had more kids who just didn't understand Greek literature. They tell me the white kids don't either. These are our problems. I haven't yet figured out how to solve them. Maybe I can get some help here.

A SPEAKER: I'd like to return for a moment to the question of resources. We ought to come up with some practical proposal. We should have available resources such as books, courses and programs that have been done in other universities. I would like to see us doing programs with the American Indian Historical Society, with outlines of the course programs. At Harvard we have been making no pretensions about setting up a Native Studies program, because there are only 10 Indians in the university. But we have set up a standing committee on American Indian Affairs which will be after the model of Latin American Affairs, to research all other projects as well as all of the departments, to find out what has been done, what there is in some of the library facilities, and what there is in Harvard's charter, which I believe originally had precepts for Indian education. From that point, we will be building a foundation and adding courses within the various departments to build a foundation. Perhaps in the future it will develop into a degree program. But what I would really like to see from all of this, is to have people who are professional scholars, historians and social scientists, sociologists and whatever, to look and see what is at Arizona, Harvard, or Montana; and what there is at some of these other schools. That would be helpful to the people.

RUPERT COSTO: We believe that with proper training, starting right at the elementary level, directing them all the way through high school, preparing them for college, we can have something in the future to benefit everybody. Not only Indians. I can assure you that the white people who are teaching Indians

188

about white culture are worse off than the Indians who are teaching Indians, because niether one of them knows much about themselves. Those of our people who are talking about ethnic studies . . . sometimes I wonder if they know what they are talking about, because 80% of our young people know nothing about their cultural background or history. What do we do about that?

BEATRICE MEDICINE: We discussed the fact that there is a vast difference in the kind of people from the rural reservation areas, as opposed to the children of relocated Indians in cities. I think there are many Indian educators in North America who know quite a bit about their cultural backgrounds.

RUPERT COSTO: I agree with Bea, but so many of our educators have left us, we hope we can get them back where they can be helping their own people. There are some very fine people at this Convocation and many of us didn't know about them. They are scholars in their own right, but they have not been working with their people. We hope they will come back.

DICK WILSON: I think what Mr. Costo refers to was the comment made on the University of Oregon. Obviously, I don't oppose ethnic studies as such, but I feel that in so many cases education can equal alienation. Many Indian people send their kids to college. It means they won't see them again. We would love to have an integrated program, to guarantee financial aid and give them something relevant. But so many programs start like this, and then go the same way. We have looked at a lot of Black programs; they turn into rap sessions for the first half dozen meetings. The students themselves get bored. They have no academic value or merit.

The Associated Students Union asked for $17,000 to research ethnic studies. We have all the standard concessions from the administration, whatever this means or doesn't mean. What we were trying to do was to come up with what Mr. Costo voiced: thoughtful, deliberate, valuable programs to take all facts into consideration that are long on content and short on air, so that when it does go into effect, it will endure. Then we can be proud of it. If we come up with something like that, we will be right in the saddle pushing it. But until we see it, we're going to stay off and look very skeptically at what is being done. I would like to see more people in the program, because I think it might be quite a lonely line. I would love that kind of help.

THE CHAIRMAN: To summarize this session, we might say we haven't decided whether we're planting ivy or poison at the universities, I'm not sure, at this point, that we should be making judgments, or throwing cold water on new ideas. New programs have to go through some kind of sophistication. I don't think we can throw it completely out, because Indian students, despite the fact that they may not know about their past, are asking why in the hell did I not know about my past. I think we educators have to give them an answer. It's one thing to condemn them for not knowing and getting involved in what we may think is a lot of foolishness. It's another thing to answer the really hard questions they are asking, and hopefully will continue to ask, as we try to work out what kind of Indian studies programs will have to be put on the university level.

The Panel now stands adjourned. Thank you all.

LOUISE DESCHEENY, student participant.

CHARLES LOLOMA, Hopi participant, at the panel on Native American Arts.

8

Native Arts in America

FRITZ SCHOLDER

W E are very fortunate indeed to have a professional panel
on the subject of *Native Arts in America,* comprised of
practicing Indian artists who have already become part of the art
world—not only in what is called Indian art (for want of a better
term), but of America generally, and of the world.

I would like to introduce Yeffe Kimball. Yeffe is Osage.
She has exhibited all over the world. Miss Kimball is a noted
space painter and received the NASA Commission space artist
assignment for participating in that program. Next is Charles
Loloma, Hopi, jeweler, sculptor and painter. He too is known
internationally. He is a member of the Kachina Society and the
Snake Society—significant honors shown him by his own Hopi
people. Also on our panel is Frank La Pena from California, a
Wintun. He is a painter and photographer.

We would like to make this session a working one. We
would like you to give us your ideas because it seems to me that
the Indian has a very positive power, expressed most certainly
and first of all, in the arts. I have been asked by the American
Indian Historical Society to deliver a formal paper, and will
introduce the panel subject. Some of you may not realize that
we are embarking on a whole new era in the arts, an era which
has come about in the past few years. I refer to all arts in
which our people are engaged now: painters, sculptors, dancers,
musicians, writers, artists in pottery, artists in wood, artists in

whatever field they may choose to express their creative ideas. My paper is entitled

THE NEW INDIAN ART IN AMERICA

There has always been a common link for all North American Indians; a well-developed aesthetic sense. No tribe had a word for "art," that self-conscious Anglo-Saxon term. Art was a most important part of the Indian's daily existence. Whether it was painting, or tattooing one's body, carving a fetish, decorating a pot, painting a tepee or parfleche, weaving a basket or rug, singing or chanting, dancing or meditating, story-telling or reciting the latest coup, the Indian did it with ease and beauty.

The nonIndian attacked and tried to alter almost everything beautiful that the Native had. The missionaries tried to change the Indian's religion and his dances. The anthropologists tried to analyze his non-literal mysticism. The teachers tried to cancel out the language and alter the art forms. The Bureau of Indian Affairs, through ignorance, apathy, frustration and often hate, tried to make the Indian white. They all failed. One cannot destroy a Native group spirit. One cannot change the need for creating with one's hands, feet, and voice a thing of beauty. Today, new art forms are emerging for the new Indian. But to understand the validity of these, one must briefly survey the many-faceted aesthetic tradition of the numerous tribes which have been collectively called the American Indian. The early history of the tribes and their art forms is far from complete. We know that the Mound Builders did very sophisticated sculpture, banner stones and bird stones. The Snake Mound of Ohio must truly be the first example of the current "earth works" movement we now have in contemporary art.

It is known that in the late Ninth Century, the influence of the Hohokam in Southern Arizona had drifted Eastward to the Mimbres tribes and that the result was some of the finest abstract pottery design in the western hemisphere. Around the same time, the art of the petroglyph, pictograph, and mural painting was developing in the Southwest and the West Coast. Meanwhile, in the Northwest Coast, one finds the emergence of cultures completely dominated by visual design. The totems, long houses, boats, clothing, and numerous objects were masterpieces of craftsmanship and design. Today in the auction houses of New York, London and Paris, a Tlingit rattle sells at prices up to $9,000. The old Eskimo ivory objects also share in this prestigious market which has just recently been discovered.

When one contemplates the enormous range of beautiful objects which were part of the life of the American Indian, it is truly impressive. The Indian made and painted hundreds of items including rattles, drums, flutes, rasps, hides, shields, utensils, totems, houses, tepees and the parfleches. Often the most beautiful items were ceremonial and esoteric in nature, such as masks, altars, wands, screens, kachina dolls, yei figures, coup sticks, feather bundles, medicine bundles, effigy pots, prayer sticks, bow guards, costumes. Certainly we must mention the great basketry of the Apache and California Indians; the blankets, rugs, silver and brass work, jewelry and bridles of the Navajo, the turquoise work of the Zuni, the beadwork of the Plains, the carving of the Eskimo and Northwest Coast, and the sandpainting of the Navajo, Apache, and Luiseño.

Today a Zuni War God would not look out of place at the Museum of Modern Art, and a shield design can certainly compete with the best non-objective painting. The universal power of these objects is undeniable. Yes, the Indian Before Columbus was his own man, and the freedom of his spirit was a natural ingredient for his art forms. When the white man came upon the scene, many of these forms slowly disappeared. Some Indians started to use the media of the non-Indian. One of the earliest known examples of this was a sketchbook by an unknown Cheyenne artist, done between 1870-1890.

Probably one of the most unusual ledgers is the "Book from Wounded Knee Battlefield painted and written by Red Hawk," which contains 116 drawings in pen, ink and crayon and is a history of the Ghost Dance and the shirts worn by the Indians in the Ghost Dance. The book was captured by Captain R. Miller on Wounded Knee Creek, South Dakota, January 8, 1891. In 1898, the first exhibition of Indian Art was assembled by the Smithsonian Institution and the Bureau of Indian Affairs, for the Trans-Mississippi Exposition in Omaha. It was a "presentation of arts and ceremonies in the first gathering ever attempted of our swiftly passing forerunners in our continental area." It is true, that by 1880 the buffalo were almost completely exterminated, and the ceremonial objects were becoming things of the past. However, no one had really been aware of the tenacity of the Indian and his arts.

At the turn of the century, the Indian was still around. Indian artists continued to amaze the nonIndian with their vitality. A number of Anglos became patrons of Indian art. Some gave a great deal of help; many however, hindered progress and imposed their own cliches on the Indian. In 1919 Susie Peters, a service worker, persuaded the mayor of Anadarko, Oklahoma, to provide a studio for young Kiowa painters. After that, many nonIndians discovered the great potential of Indian artists. Dr. Oscar Jacobson, Rene d'Harnoncourt, Oliver La Farge, Dr. Kenneth Chapman, Olive Rush, Dr. Edgar Hewett and John Sloan were a few of the many Indian supporters. By 1920, Maria and Julian Martinez of San Ildefonso were becoming known for their excellent pottery. Southwest painters, as well as Plains artists, were being encouraged by private individuals. Eleven years later, an Exposition of Indian Tribal Arts was introduced by the American painter, John Sloan, at the Grand Central Galleries in New York City, for a period of three months. it toured the United States in 1933.

A year before the touring exposition ended, a nonIndian "art researcher and guide" arrived at the Santa Fe Indian School, after completion of her studies in the Art Institute of Chicago. Thus started "The Studio," which has been called the most artificial art movement in the United States. The "guide" of The Studio literally dictated the style of painting produced under her direction, according to one former student. The so-called "Traditional" flat-style of watercolor painting was certainly decorative and very popular with collectors and tourists. Work even sold, and exhibits were organized. The Studio was termed a success. Years later, at a conference held at the University of Arizona on "Directions of Indian Art," Robert M. Quinn, Associate Professor of Art History, gave this evaluation of The Studio:

> Mention was made of the past success of special schools, and a call was made for the re-establishment of special schools. The primary example is the Santa Fe School, which I deplore. The Sant Fe School was one which, in the process of producing an Indian artist, actually taught him a style of painting derived from the Persian miniatures. At best this style is an unwarranted electicism and at the worst it is a fraud.

Let there be no misunderstanding however. Out of The Studio came a number of excellent artists, who were able to transcend the style inflicted upon them. Today's traditional artists such as Oscar Howe, Dick West, Blackbear Bosin, Fred Beaver, Solomon McCombs, Robert Chee, Allan Houser, Fred Kabotie, Al Momaday, Pablita Velarde, and Jose Ray Toledo are greatly respected. However, the style which has been referred to as the "Bambi syndrome" gradually became an easy cliche.

> . . . blue rabbits and yellow procupines, purple mesas and cookie cutter clouds. It is this kind of Indian art that sells like hotcakes today in trading posts throughout the Southwest . . . Such work is inevitably a copy of a copy.

For years the young Indian artist labored under the fallacy that if one were Indian, one must paint in the "flat-style." Finally the Bureau of Indian Affairs, after years of trying to stamp out Indian arts and crafts in their schools, recognized the Indian artist by organizing the Arts and Crafts Board in 1933.

This agency has had periods of activity and inactivity ever since. It is yet to be directed by Indian artists, or to have Indian direction of any kind.

Six years later the Indian Art Exhibit at the Golden Gate Exposition in San Francisco attracted great attention. And by 1941 "Indian art" was at the Museum of Modern Art in New York City. The exhibition, organized by Rene d'Harnoncourt and Frederick H. Douglas, was a milestone in Indian art.

The Philbrook Art Center in Tulsa, Oklahoma, initiated the first annual national competitive exhibition for Indian painting and sculpture in 1946. Jeanne Snodgrass, as curator of Indian Art, was a vital force behind the program. Through the years, other Indian shows came into existence, including those at the Denver Art Museum, Heard Museum at Phoenix, the Inter-Tribal Ceremonials in Gallup, and All-American Indian Days at Sheridan. Then in 1960, the Rockefeller Foundation funded the Southwest Indian Art Project at the University of Arizona. The project and the results were a turning point for the American Indian artist and craftsman. This is where the "New Indian Art" began. For it was here that the question was asked: Does and Indian artist have to work in a certain style or with certain subject matter? The answer was *No*.

Up to this time only a few individual Indian artists were working in a non-traditional style. People like R. C. Gorman, Patrick Swazo Hinds and Joan Hill were not influenced by The Studio. In a similar manner, the Southwest Indian Art Project reproduced outstanding work in painting, sculpture, ceramics, fabrics, jewelry, and printmaking, by young Indian artists who were introduced not only to their own rich heritage, but to the whole range of art possibilities. The product was Indian, for no artist can deny who he is when given the freedom, but more than that, it was fresh and creative. The work was both Indian and contemporary. All artists must reflect or react with the times in which they are living, whether they be Indian or nonIndian. The project lasted for three summers, and at the end, the Indian artists, both faculty and students, continued the concepts of the new Indian art. Lloyd Kiva New, along with Charles and Otellie Loloma, went to Santa Fe to help establish a new government-directed art institute. For Fritz Scholder, it was the beginning of a new period of painting, merging traditional Indian subject matter in a contemporary idiom. Younger artists like George Burdeau, Jimmie C. Fife, Jim Red Corn, and Roger Tsabetsaye began to see their traditions in a new light.

In 1962 the first annual national Scottsdale Indian Art Exhibition opened. in Santa Fe, the Institute of American Indian Arts also came into being. In the beginning, the Institute was fresh and vital. The arts staff consisted mostly of Indian artists, and the students were greatly motivated. The best materials were available, and the new national art school was the pride of the Bureau of Indian Affairs. A large touring exhibition to Europe and South America began in 1966, marking the beginning of the end of vital productivity. The marriage of Indian Art and the government began to go downhill.

Again it was the same old story of bureaucracy and inefficiency in the government, resulting in disenchantment of the Indian people. Today, at the Institute of American Indian Arts, there are only three Indian instructors on an arts faculty of 16 members. The students are rebellious, in face of the apathetic nonIndian faculty. The work emanating from the Institute has become progressively weaker. The Institute is going down the road of all BIA Indian schools. However, a purpose was served. In the first years a number of young artists came out of the Institute in Santa Fe, and now have joined the ranks of the New Indian Art. T. C. Cannon, Larry Bird, Kevin Red Star, Hank Gobin, Clifford Suathojame, Earl Eder, B. J. Goodluck, and Bill Soza are some of the new names in Indian art. Today, the future of Indian Art is very bright. Unlike the Commissioner of Indian Affairs, who spoke on the subject for five minutes at a recent dinner at Scottsdale, Arizona, one could talk for days on the potential and future of the arts of the contemporary Native American. In the last few years, exhibitions like "Young American Indian Artists" at the Riverside Museum in New York City, and the "7+3=10 Indian Arts" Exhibit at the American Indian Historical Society's Museum of Indian Arts prove that the new Indian art is ready to take its place in the world of art today.

Yes, a new Indian art is emerging. It will take many forms and it will be vital, not faddish. A merging of the traditional with the contemporary in painting, sculpture, dance, music, writing, philosophy, and even fashion and life-styles has recently surprised an apathetic country. In the wake of seeming disaster, a number of the young generation is looking toward the North American Indian for help. Should this be so surprising? The qualities of the Indian are impressive. Take away the white man's ills and you have a reticent, generous, and subtle individualist with a true sense of life, time, and the elements of the earth. In a time when identity is a most sought-after ingredient, very few races can boast of such a recent rich heritage as the Indian.

This is a new time for the North American Indian. It is not often that the attention of the world has been focused on the Indian as it is today. The New Indian has a responsibility not only to his own ancestors and his people, but to all mankind. It may well be that the most dignified and universal approach to this new role be through the arts.

Now first of all, do you have any questions you wish to direct to me personally regarding what I have said?

A SPEAKER: Who are the major artists, if any, who influenced the new Indian artists' movement you spoke about? Are they influenced by any international trend?

FRITZ SCHOLDER: I would say that the new Indian arts is certainly influenced by what is happening today in contemporary art, if you consider the fact that for the first time Indian artists have realized that they do live in the whole world, not only the Indian world. Certainly they are influenced. For instance, I know many young Indian artists who dig Dillon, you know, the whole bit. There is one going at the Slade School of Arts in London right now, and I am sure he has been influenced by some of the English pop artists. This is natural. However, the young Indian artist probably is more strongly devoted and attached to his own artistic heritage than even his father and mother before him. They were often too close to the Indian thing and most of the New Indian Artists have been able to rediscover that through different eyes. So it is contemporary but it is very Indian.

A SPEAKER: Robert and I were talking about the contemporary Indian Artist working through the contemporary media. Do you know of anybody who is working in the area of films or film making, which is something quite new to everybody, but which can be used very effectively in projecting art to a very contemporary medium of understanding.

FRITZ SCHOLDER: Yes. Film is kind of the new media, and I know of Ron Dera here of the Northwest coast who is devoted fully to film now. Buffy, do you know of any?

BUFFY SAINTE MARIE: It seems like everybody in films, dress design, music and painting has all of a sudden begun to try to put on an Indian show. They just don't know how, even though they really want to do everything right. So I think that this seems to be the time that we should try to establish a Native American Theater for the Arts. I have proposed it to the City of New York. They seem to want their name attached to such a project. What I am talking about is a thing that would be entirely Indian, I mean the business end of it also run by Indians. If we need a lawyer, an Indian lawyer, and the publicity, the direction, scenery, art and library, a film library as well as some kind of school. I am talking about a building, something like this one. We would also have a gallery that would have perhaps something from ancient times, something from today, perhaps a mixture. It would give Indian people a place to preserve their arts and to develop because really if you're an Indian in the arts, in the performing arts anyway, for instance, if you are an actor or actress, sure as heck you're not going to get any chance to play a white guy, not for a long time anyway. As you might know, in Hollywood the concensus is that anybody can play an Indian, which is wrong, and we all suffer from it. So I am proposing this theater and what we are going to need is Indian people to staff it. If you are a performer, a student, a teacher, or a participant in any way, let me know and we will see if we can get it off the ground. What they have offered is to sponsor a summer festival. They will give us Central Park for a day.

About film makers, do you know if there is a list of films made about Indians and about Indian situations? I know Canada makes some pretty good ones but there are a lot of wildcat films around and nobody knows who makes them.

FRITZ SCHOLDER: I think there are many Indian films, some done by Indians and some not. I thought some of the Canadian things were excellent.

CHARLES LOLOMA: If you want to go on to anthropology which deals in the older form, then you can bring it up to date and re-interpret design, form, etc. Then on the other hand if you are going into present civilization or problems that we have, that's a different kind of approach in film.

FRITZ SCHOLDER: I would like to call upon members of the panel to give some of their ideas. First of all I ask Yeffe Kimball to take over for a while.

YEFFE KIMBALL: Well, I will just go back a little ways and discuss what was a very sad period, and that was the discovery of the new world at a time when art in Europe was in a rising period of great religious art. The art that existed at that time saw some of the greatest architecture, which is now at this late date being recognized and copied, in Expo '67 and so on. Frank Lloyd Wright and others took from the great architects the idea of the Indians, which they called adding rock to living rock. As you know, many of those structures still stand today. If the sonic booms don't tear them down, we may have them for a few years to come. Also at the time of the European contact with the new world, we have some of the greatest art of all time, the religious gold pieces, the mound pieces and so on. The new settlers, when they came in search of souls and gold and destroyed a great deal of both, a lot of it went down at sea with the pirates. Others wound up on the crowned heads of Europe. Very few of the artists of that time in the early part of the sixteenth century even took notice of it or mentioned it.

I came across a rare item by Durer who was called in to evaluate the gold art objects that was then going to the King of Belgium and he looked at it and said, in essence, "What great men they must be from this golden land to have produced art of this kind." We had at that time great architecture in the

High Andes around Lake Titicaca which possibly, (and there are different schools on this) may have been the origin of man on this continent. There were walls two feet thick, enormous doors, great architecture, and even toys for the children with wheels. So the wheel was not unknown to the Indian, as many people have said. He did not put it to use but we do not know why. In the great Kivas, the Southwest for example, where Coronado stabled his horses in the early part of the conquest, murals done in beautiful designs, painted fifteen, twenty feet long. Unless art is a part of your daily life, it has no reason for being. When art becomes merely decorative, that is the sign of its downfall, and Indian art never showed this tendency until recently.

The palettes on which they painted were sometimes painted and carved and some were painted on the inside as well as the outside. But this was to enhance his daily life and his sense of beauty. I believe it is emerging again with great strength. To copy what someone else has done is no other than a sense of technique or learning. To me you are failing as an artist. We live in a time of techniques, new emphasis, and new materials. In my opinion, you should know what your past is, the heritage of your people and all the things around you. I do not say that you necessarily have to limit that but I feel that if an artist doesn't make an attempt to understand and contribute to it, he is either a failure or a charlatan. I think this is becoming more and more evident today, when people overnight decide to become artists. In this hysterical world producing hysterical art, one must find his own place and figure out what that is, then set out to do it because in that way you can make a contribution. I chose space after I had been through some four or five different periods. I had a very academic background. I went down the long road of the academy. And I found out one day the thing I really could contribute something to, was the age in which I lived, and that was space.

A very important statement was made here, by my colleague and great artist here, Charles, in which he says the sun can no longer get through to the earth. Now, this is a part of our daily life and we should do something about it. If we cannot see the sun to paint it, and the clouds, then certainly it will affect art and man, and certainly space. Thus, you may find that in your canyons and valleys there are things that you haven't discovered and the method taught in the school today is a kind of brainwashing thing, but despite all of this, you find some five or six quite talented and very young people, kicking over the traces, doing their own thing very well. The technique, the knowledge, the search for something new, a new statement and using new materials, this is necessary.

The documentary kind of thing of the flat art that took

form around the turn of the century, when Indians were handed water colors, has given an awful lot of people the idea that this is Indian art. It has nothing to do with Indian art, except that Indians did it. In prehistoric times, when we had great architects and other magnificent art forms, we didn't have water colors. They made their own colors from the earth and found very beautiful different kinds of colors, and ground the rocks and pigments, even turquoise. That art is dead. We have had the great Quincy Tahoma, who was one of the finest draftsmen this country has produced, Fred Kaboti and others. Those people have done a very good job of documenting the ceremonies and the daily happenings of their times. Look for something new and you will find it.

FRITZ SCHOLDER: Thank you, Yeffe. Charles, what do you have to say?

CHARLES LOLOMA: It's very exciting to dream, and to imagine lots of wonderful things, when you come to think of the kind of areas that you can get into because of your heritage. I have realized more and more, and I know it is here and it is being felt, that being Indian today is a fad. I am very concerned about this, because of the public interest and the public is foolish today. I think that with films, you can do real things. You can *feel* through films—make other people excited. This is a period of commitment, when we are also getting scared away because people are now talking about "grass," and acid. This is not true imagination. I feel that it doesn't belong. I have gotten high coming over here, but in an airplane, TWA, I was above the clouds, I felt like a Kachina over the clouds and I could see that there were fields over there. I can get very high on some of the contributions that the fashions have made. I have gotten really high on mini skirts, what's left of it.

You can do things in a very wrong way, a stereotype sort of way. What are you going to do about it? Why do you begin to become an Indian? I don't know, because I was born an Indian. I attempted to solve it when I was on the staff of the Institute. I went there because I felt needed there. My interests were strong for them in the Institute. Now, I think you have to maintain the rules after you know the rules. And when I speak about rules, coming here is exciting. I think you have to formally know everything. The dominant culture of today came along and unbalanced nature. I feel that any culture has to be aware of a number of things in this day of the coming of truth. Let me go just a little bit further about films. If we are going to concern ourselves to project further on, there are people who are specialized in various fields and this is an age for specialists. The thing that scares me is that it may not last very long, because there are lots of forces that could upset this. One, to be an Indian probably is desirable, I am sure because there are examples of this. It takes work, it takes lots of understanding.

BUFFY SAINTE MARIE: I would like to ask, in your experience, where you have all studied and yet you have come from the kind of background that produced the art of centuries ago which may or may not have included any study at all, what do you think about study as opposed to just doing whatever you do, I mean not going to any schools?

CHARLES LOLOMA: I think anybody can study.

BUFFY SAINTE MARIE: Do you think it is necessary?

CHARLES LOLOMA: I said everybody can study. There is certainly a capacity in each individual, I feel. If this person has the capacity to *want* to learn more in *terms* of his capacity and fill it up, this is determined by your want, and if you have made up your mind that you are going to study for the purpose of getting to your objective, you will gain more from it, otherwise even if you went to the best schools, you will still not have learned anything. I live at Hotevilla, Arizona. In that village, the people have a system of teaching which is another area for our anthropologist friends. It has been going for centuries. They have grown a system of what their education should be about. I feel that these people are only Indian people who are doing things in such a way that they are not dominating. You can learn as much and perhaps more if your direction is one to learn sincerely for your goals, from your people, because it means there you have responsibilities.

FRITZ SCHOLDER: It seems to me that to be an artist, either you have to, or you shouldn't be. Some people come to me and say, should I be an artist? Students have asked this. And you really can't tell anyone. In fact probably the worst thing in the world is to become an artist, unless you have to. Yet there is somewhat of a paradox in this, because to me, personally, an artist must say something. A painter has a responsibility, just as much as a writer, or any other person who is doing something creative, and he must be able to say something. You can't say anything if you haven't looked into things and if you haven't studied— "studied" is a bad word but how can you react to something if you don't know about it? The world of painting, for instance, is a fantastic world right now. All kinds of things are happening, all kinds of new material has become available, and it just really blows your mind when you look into it and then from there you can personally do your own thing. So you have to study to be a good artist, however you choose to study. You can't really cancel it out.

FRANK LA PENA: I'm a sort of young guy who hasn't worked too long at it. But I have done it all my life and I check with what Charles says, that the culture gives you some awareness of your place in life. When you make an effort out of that and you end up with a painting, that painting is not Indian if you just throw feathers in or just throw an Indian figure in, and call it "Indian." I don't think that represents the Indian so-called art as much as an idea of your place in life which expresses an Indian concept. Another thing that comes to mind, is that the type of art we have talked about is generally alluded to in the modern sense, and that has been the Southwest, except for space. Now, who makes the distinction and what is this "modern art," if it is good? Who says it is Indian art and who says it will be included in this overall presentation of the Indian artist?

You see, the reason I ask this is because I think anyone starting in art as a painter would like to get into some shows maybe, would like to get recognition. How does he go about this as an Indian? This is what we are asking. How does he go about that, as an Indian? I am not going to say that I have a magic formula because I haven't. I paint how I feel as an Indian, and I am not quite sure what this is. I am just stating this and wanting a reaction, and can anyone answer it?

FRITZ SCHOLDER: I think Frank brought up a good point. Now, if you want to become known as an Indian artist, you almost have to start out in the national shows. However, one of the things that seems disappointing to me is that most Indian artists, after entering these shows, never go any further. They never enter, for instance, a nonIndian show, and this is changing because the new Indian artist is realizing that Indian art can no longer be isolated. They are entering the nonIndian shows, they are being recognized to a great extent, and this is the first time that this has ever happened.

A SPEAKER: Does it necessarily have to be that you have something to say, or may you say something, some experiences? You can work into some figure and it seems to hold in Charles' case, his work. He has put a lot of his heart into it, and people realize it. He doesn't have to promote it, they come to him. I wonder do you have to come and say you have to give this to people and this is the purpose? Can you just work around with your emotions, dabbling around with it?

FRITZ SCHOLDER: I may have oversimplified that. In using the word "statement," I didn't mean it as a literal thing. For instance I think that Charles' work has great depth, just as you say, the way he works. It is a real creation, not only because it is innovative. However, if an artist doesn't come across in some way, I would like to think about it as wave lengths, you know, some people are on the same wave length and this is nice. They catch what you are talking about or what you are doing. They really don't have to "communicate." Some people aren't on your wave length. This is fine, too. A lot of people get disturbed when they look at a painting and they say, gee, I don't like that, maybe I don't know about art. Art is a natural thing, and whatever reactions are yours, it is valid and you don't have to like every painting or every piece of jewelry. In fact, personally, about 85% of the people who see my work don't like it. This is great; this is fine. I am painting for myself first of all, and if somebody else happens to dig it too, great. I know Charles is the same way. Charles' clientele is very select, but it is so nice when you do meet somebody who is understanding of what you are doing.

CHARLES LOLOMA: Think of it this way. In making jewelry I am selling. The way I am doing it is that I am not selling my work as Indian work, I am selling my work as Charles Loloma.

YEFFE KIMBALL: If you produce good work, it will sell. If you have something to say and it comes out and you have made a very strong statement about it, you will have no problem. You don't have the problem today as you had when I was starting.

A SPEAKER: When you talk about Indian art, essentially what I heard you say is that it is not so much that there is one thing that is Indian art. You each are artists and your culture is Indian, and I am wondering, if the culture then produces the artist. The artist then produces what? I am wondering if there is any feeling of responsibility?

FRITZ SCHOLDER: As I mentioned before, there was just one skill of painting. Now there are many skills because Indian artists realize they must also function within this world, in 1970. As far as a conscious thing of putting down Indian art, here again you cannot limit the artist. However, a true artist can only work with whoever he is. All you can do is be yourself. If you aren't copying, if you're doing *you*, it will be you and so if you're Indian, fine.

CHARLES LOLOMA: The work which you do will show the strength of who you are. It will reflect out of the work that you do.

A SPEAKER: I can see that, I am wondering if it will also reflect the strength of who your people are?

CHARLES LOLOMA: Definitely yes.

FRANK LA PENA: You talk about the so-called primitive art in the sense that there is no perspective of pure colors and the like. I think there is room for just expression as an artist, which does not necessarily shout out and say, "look, this is done by an Indian," as much as this is done by an artist, and when I said the feathers things, that does not make it Indian art. So therefore what you are saying can exist, you know. It doesn't have to be that direction. On the other hand, there is the cultural basis that you are working from. It can be very much there, but I don't think you can come up to something and look at it and say, "that is done by an Indian artist." I think that when Mr. Scholder presents the idea about new art, why the heck is he using "new art" and do you have to have the thing that is so literal—well, I keep coming back to the feathers, but when I first mentioned the anthropological films, I was in essence leaving someone room to say as I said, you can go to that fine arts, not "new art" as you used it. What is your culture, how much culture does the Indian have today that he knows? There is not that much identity culturally as to the ancient way. The Southwest is fortunate in the sense that they have had an established cultural society, which has lasted. It has been used now in a number of different articles, by a number of different critics. It distinguishes the so-called flat style traditional painting that came out in the thirties and was developed by a nonIndian.

JACK REYNOLDS: Could I respond if I may? I am not sure what your background is, but I have been taught since I was three years old the dances of the Cheyenne. There is a part of the ceremony in a play I recently saw in which Cherokees were involved. Now, they had dancing that did not bear up their responsibility to their people.

FRANK LA PENA: I think what you are saying is that you are trying to reaffirm that these people with the cultural basis of Cheyenne, they are making a presentation that is not true Cheyenne?

A SPEAKER: No, that is not what I mean.

CHARLES LOLOMA: What specific thing are they doing?

JACK REYNOLDS: I am actually asking if there is such a thing as an Indian artist? In other words, you say my culture produced me. If I am a part of that culture, it will be reproduced in my work. But if that culture cannot be seen in your work, then in fact it is a work product of the culture which can't be called "Indian art." And I am not saying it should be or shouldn't be, I am just asking whether or not it is.

FRANK LA PENA: I think that is a good basis, because what you are talking about is the *idea* of the new Indian art. The idea of where did the arts fit specifically into Indian culture, and of those were mentioned. Now, the type of form and thinking that went into that, how is it translated into other than the artist being in Indian art. I will tell you about a painting of mine. I have gone back to my elders and I know a little bit of the language and I am re-learning it. I have re-established a contact. The picture that I am doing is the landscape of Mt. Shasta, which contains the whole idea of the gods. But I

204

went out and gathered the pigment in the area and if you have ever been in northern California you would know the different kinds. The idea is maybe that you're giving the connection one of ancestral worship, but you're worshipping an idea more than you are worshipping this northern California presentation of design, maybe the circle meaning of oneness, which is universal. I think this runs through all cultures and this is why I say you can justify it on that basis.

FRITZ SCHOLDER: In the first part of our session, we talked about Indian art, mostly about painting and sculpture. We touched briefly on films and the theater, and we will be happy to continue that. As I mentioned, we will want to get into other areas, including jewelry, fashion for instance, food, there may be some jokes. We have a lot to talk about. Also please start thinking if you have any really solid ideas about recommendations.

YEFFE KIMBALL: While you're thinking of a question, I would like to repeat a quotation from Einstein, whom I had the pleasure of meeting here in Princeton many years ago, and he said and it was later published, the most beautiful thing you can experience is the mysterious, it is the base of all true art and science. Coming from that great man it might be something, like the gentleman here who was talking about his emotions and his creative statement, might be something to think about.

A SPEAKER: Could we set up sort of an art structural program, throughout the United States and have some sort of communication? I mean this could be the basis for some thinking.

FRITZ SCHOLDER: Can you give us any details of what you're thinking of?

A SPEAKER: Well, I mean to have a listing of peoples, according to their accomplishments, professions and so forth.

FRITZ SCHOLDER: That is one of the things we were talking about. It could take many forms, one of them could be a book for instance. I would like to see a book on Indian art come out that takes off from where Dorothy Dunn's book left off. Some of you may know that Dorothy Dunn has a book that came out last year but her book leaves off at about 1930. There is so much that has been done in Indian art that nobody really knows about and certainly—now, several years ago Snodgrass came out with a book called "American Indian Painters," but by the time it came out it was out-dated. None of the addresses are right. The weird thing is the government has never kept addresses. Philbrook hasn't kept addresses. A lot of Indian artists are hiding, but it is certainly something to think about.

A SPEAKER: Is there a recognized Indian society or Indian art society of this sort, a professional type thing?

FRITZ SCHOLDER: No.

A SPEAKER: Have you contemplated establishing an association of Indian artists in the various Indian art fields, you know. You could have sub-sections within this so-called Indian art professionals?

YEFFE KIMBALL: No, I think that is one of the things this society could do, would be to bring forth, compile such a directory or whatever you want to call it, of the artists, and list their addresses and their areas, too.

FRITZ SCHOLDER: I think the time will come for a national Indian art conference and it would seem to me, it could be part of what this Society is doing.

A SPEAKER: I was going to say, not only a directory of the artists but also where people can purchase arts and especially crafts.

FRITZ SCHOLDER: Of course the best place is to search out the artist in his studio. This is where you can not only find the best selection but the best prices. I think that a list with addresses would be valuable, because there are Indian artists in the east as well as the southwest and the west coast.

BUFFY SAINTE MARIE: I think there is really a need for a gallery run by Indians, one in New York and one in California. There are enough Indian businessmen who could do this.

A SPEAKER: I just want to expand a little more on that. By forming this National Indian Art Association, whatever it may be, we can promote our own sales and by-pass a lot of these museums or what not that are putting on the Indian art shows. For example the Scottsdale Indian Art show takes a flat 20% right off the top. I think we should be getting the money, the whole bit. I think we can advance our arts as well as get the profits from it without going through these different museums and galleries, if you have a sharp association.

FRITZ SCHOLDER: Miss Kimball is going to write a report for instance on the Scottsdale show which is a show that has certainly helped the Indian artist a great deal, but as you say there is a big commission plus artists have to pay five dollars to get into their openings. No artist should have to pay to get in and see his own work and you know, it's weird because the whole jury is non-Indian that judges the show.

YEFFE KIMBALL: There aren't any Indians on the committee, which is something else that will come out in my report.

A SPEAKER: There is another thing, you said for people who had submitted written entries, was that the people there had full publishing say over what you submitted, and you know, you could either say I will publish or will not publish or something like that, but they had priority over this?

FRITZ SCHOLDER: I believe you're mistaken, I believe the

way it read was they would try to get publishing for the written things. We will look into that, too, because it is really weird the way these things happen.

FRANK LA PENA: I would like to get back into the earlier discussion. One thing you talked about was the woman (The Studio) starting this school. What did she base her structure on, what kind of form did she go back to and how did she justify it? If those forms had no meaning, how does that affect the southwest today?

FRITZ SCHOLDER: What I mentioned in my paper was the school called "The Studio" and the instructor of course was Dorothy Dunn, a non-Indian who came into the government school and showed the students different types of art, especially Persian art. There were many exhibitions and she showed them how to use water colors. But she became a dictator and as one former student said, for instance, he was doing the painting of a horse and he put some shadow in and she came over and said, we cannot have shadow on your horse because this isn't the flat style.

You see anybody who sets himself up as a dictator is just not valid, because the one thing the artist has is freedom. If he can't have that, of course it is what we are especially resentful of. This continued. In fact it is a truism that in the southwest, for instance, if you want to sell your paintings easy, you do the flat style. Tourists will buy them like mad, but the sad thing is the young artists find that this is so easy to do and often they lose their integrity in doing this. It is pitiful, it is too easy and I think almost any of us in this room who are artists know that sooner or later we realize what will sell. It's nice to sell but art is doing your personal thing. If you get trapped in a certain style or certain people say, "Oh, I like that, what you're doing," it's so easy to keep on and keep bringing in the money, but you're dead as an artist.

FRANK LA PENA: Here is what I was referring to. In her "Southwest Painting," Miss Dunn went back to the Kiva murals. She went back to artifacts and to the different stages of potteries, so in essence you say these have no value?

FRITZ SCHOLDER: It's not that, the bad thing is that she dictated.

FRANK LA PENA: This is why I wanted to clear it up, because if you want to say that, you're cutting down in essence the whole cultural value.

JACK REYNOLDS: Freedom to me, once again going back to responsibility, the degree of freedom you have is frequently the degree of responsibility you are willing to take. Going back to the example of dance form, it is almost easier in the sense you're disciplined to traditions of dress, traditions of step, although there is freedom allowed in certain war dances, solemn dances, etc. . . . It is restricted in the sense that you have to know the culture to do it. In other words, you have to know, if you're painting Cheyenne, how they dress, what their customs were, what the bonnet was. You have to know all those things and there is a certain responsibility to the culture, to represent that culture. Once again I am going back to the question of what an Indian artist is.

FRITZ SCHOLDER: In the thirties, when that particular school came about, it was also a parallel in that regionalism was in evidence in the rest of the country, and this was a very literal thing in showing the countryside, of being proud of America. This regionalism was evident throughout the thirties. It was the same type of lateral thing that this type school had. Certainly it had validity. We are not saying it had no validity because to have a background in the traditional form was a good thing at that time, but the style was imposed on—it wasn't a Cheyenne, it was that students were brought in from all over, Sioux artists, Apache artists, you know, you could go down the roster pretty much as to who was there. This person tried to dictate to them all, that they had to paint this way, when in fact they all have different traditions.

JACK REYNOLDS: I wasn't questioning the validity of that form, I'm questioning the validity of some of the forms today. In other words, the responsibility was apparent in that form and with this new freedom there is a need for a new responsibility.

FRITZ SCHOLDER: Then you get into the concept of contemporary modern art.

FRANK LA PENA: I'm wondering how we go about questioning the art as Indians, to really find if it is *us* or whether any person who knows about Indians can begin to be an Indian artist. You know, what is an Indian artist?

CHARLES LOLOMA: I cannot help but think what you may be getting into. Perhaps this might help to clarify as far as I'm concerned, and a number of other things come into my mind when you talk of freedom. There are a number of connections that have been made in terms of what we call religion. The present Chamber of Commerce now every year puts on a snake dance ceremony in the way the Chamber of Commerce thinks it should be done. They identify themselves with Smokey. This disturbed Hopi people, therefore they didn't want them to do it. They said they don't want this type of thing. Because of their inability of how to take it to court and then also their stand in terms of their laws, they didn't do anything about it.

All right, there are several more examples, but another good one is that not very long ago it happened to involve me. I think perhaps you should know this part of it. We term

Kachina as something that we worship, because it has value from the spiritual point of view. Well, a choreographer and a young musician worked on it for something of this nature. I mean this was to be a creative thing. And I was there at the Institute, I talked about it and I objected to the use of it in a public performance. After I resigned from the Institute, a couple of years later, I read in a Santa Fe paper that this performance had been going on for a long time and then performed in Washington, D.C., using the Kachina. Well, not only I, but a number of other people who are not Indians, protested against this. In the newspaper we argued back and forth, some of you people may be familiar with this, so as it turned out, somehow they quit.

But my feeling is, that this is a religious point of view, and I feel that since I respect other people's religion, why I think these people should respect mine. I put it this way, if you want to see something authentic in its own area, you should go to that area. For instance, I sometimes like to see a very good opera. So what do I do, I go to New York City perhaps to see good opera. If I want to see a stage play, I go to where they have a good stage play.

If you want to experience mask dances, which is a learning of people, of its philosophy tied with its spiritual value, if you want to see this, I feel you should come to Hopi, Arizona. We don't discriminate there, non-Indians could see it, they could go down into the Kiva and view this. Very recently we had a thing called Bean Dance, which is an initiation dance for young children to receive a grownup mind. In the final way of personal exposure between Kachina and human, this was portrayed and nonIndian people saw these things. This has been going on for a long time. They still can come. They have room; they can get in. I noticed this time it was crowded. It's not any larger than this room, but my point is this: you must be aware of these things in terms of respect, if you want to see this and there is something about it, you go there. You cannot interpret otherwise. How can you, the setting is not right, you cannot get the feeling the way you would if you came home.

DAWN RIEKER: I was wondering out of the general audience gathered here, how many are presently in the arts and hope to continue? Seven. I am wondering if possibly the limit of students that are involved in the arts and interested in it as a career and not just as an interest on the side, might possibly derive some benefit. Without the talent not only as an artist professionally, but in the areas of managing it, of being directors of museums, of galleries, we are not going to be able to support the arts. I am wondering what we can do possibly through this Convocation to be able to encourage people to move into this area.

FRITZ SCHOLDER: Hopefully some action will come out for, let's say, a large national Indian art show of the highest quality. Many other things can be done, like this book on American Indian Art, but you brought a very good point about people getting involved in the management of the arts because right now they are building all kinds of new art centers and museums, there's hardly anyone to staff them.

In fact, if any of you are so inclined, I would certainly start getting into that field, because it is wide open. The museums are dying for directors, for assistants, for people to hang shows, it's one of the best professional opportunities at the moment. And you mention the professional part of the arts. Truly we are interested in those who may become professional artists or those who are artists already. You don't have to be an artist to get involved with art. There are so many ways to enrich your own person by looking at the exhibits, by getting involved, seeing what is happening, because this is an area that is so alive. In fact, one could spend his whole life looking at art exhibits as they open continually in New York City alone, and you would never see all of them. The wild things that are coming out and not only wild, but they will just give you a whole new perspective of life in 1970, which is of course part of all the arts and I am not just talking about painting or sculpture. I am talking about everything. The Indian person especially has been reticent in getting out.

CHARLES LOLOMA: I think any professional person in any field for that matter is very anxious to help, which is very encouraging. You can possibly figure out some way to go to whoever might supply your immediate needs. This is the encouraging part, you can do this. Professional people will be ready and willing to help and sincere people will be ready to help.

FRITZ SCHOLDER: Yeffe Kimball a year ago wrote a book on Indian food, I would like to take a couple of minutes to talk about Indian food if she will.

YEFFE KIMBALL: I would be very happy to, but there is one thing that goes through my mind and that is the kind of thing that became known as Indian art which was foisted upon the Indians. At that time and even before, they did not consider this art. Whatever was being done in a very limited way was being depicted as a ceremonial "something." I am talking about this stuff that is plaguing us today, and is being turned out by the thousands and thousands, some of it very bad, some of it done quite skillfully.

Around the turn of the century, in fact about 1898, Doctor Chapman, who was then and later became the head of the laboratory of anthropology in Santa Fe, went into the area of the Navajos and the Zunis looking for people to help them dig and discover. Mostly Doctor Chapman's interest was pottery. He went out recruiting people to help them dig and also to help them identify some of the pieces. Some of the designs they did not know and they went out on the Navajo reservation. Looking around they would say, how about that guy over there and they said, well, he is busy with his crops. He is a farmer, and finally he looked around and saw a guy leaning up against the building, and he had a black crayon in his hands. His name was Abby Begay, and they came up and said that guy up there, what does he do? And they said, he doesn't do anything, he is an artist. And he just found an old black crayon and he was doing some very rough sketches of Kachinas and things and Doctor Chapman said I have got some colored crayons and things. They distributed these and they brought forth some of the earliest and nicest things in crayons. They started to draw their Kachinas and some other things and that was later published in a book by the Bureau of American Ethnology in Washington. It's in color and there are probably maybe a hundred and fifty, two hundred Kachina drawings of just simple pencil crayon, and they never thought about them as art till the water color movement. This one woman said, it's Indian art, it will sell. We got such a disease of that, that we haven't recovered yet.

FRANK LA PENA: Where do the so-called traditional arts and crafts of the Indians fall in, and where does the so-called ledgers—

YEFFE KIMBALL: The ledgers were done mostly during the time the Indians were in prison. There was great Indian art in prehistoric times in the Kivas which I mentioned at the earlier session, where there were great nine mile canyons. They found great pictographs and many of them had color which was dug out of the earth and probably some fifteen beautiful colors that they used and this was art. They were depicting their thoughts and their feelings of a religious or ceremonial statement.

Now, those exist today and they have been published in a number of books. That went on and they continued to do that. Then in some of it, when the missionaries came and established churches, you will find horses painted on the front of some of the churches, but they would continue to decorate the churches inside with bird forms and corn blossoms or whatever they wanted to do. Then when the Christian religion came in and the missions were set up, you will find they never mixed the Madonna skirt with corn blossoms. They managed to separate it. Later on, when the real conquest set in and Indians were put in prison, the only thing they had, that they could get their hands on and most of these were done in pencil and some were done with some colors, crayons and what not, they were ledgers that these Indians used, as they had nothing else to do. So they were forced to put down whatever they thought. Some of it depicted people, whatever they looked out of the window and saw. Some of it had to do with what went on in prison. These were ledgers that they got from the army in most cases. Today the Heye Foundation in New York has some, and I think there are some in Santa Fe of this kind of reporting art about what was going on. It was certainly not the highest expression, but it was depicting a pictorial statement about what was affecting their lives at that time.

FRANK LA PENA: Well, what is the difference then between the highest expression of art and this kind of art?

YEFFE KIMBALL: Because it was a creative thing and this was not. This was a pictorial statement about what was affecting their lives—

FRANK LA PENA: This is what I am trying to arrive at, whether that pictorial thing that you are talking about, versus the idea of crafts, maybe blanketry, jewelry, whatever it is, where do you make that distinction?

YEFFE KIMBALL: I think the only way you can judge any kind of art is through the aesthetic statement. A great piece of Charles is an aesthetic statement.

FRANK LA PENA: How about blankets?

YEFFE KIMBALL: Yes, indeed, blankets, too.

FRANK LA PENA: Okay, then I think you probably should explain about where the ideas of art and crafts fit in today's picture.

YEFFE KIMBALL: I think our craft level today is very high and this is one of the things I made in my rough draft of the Scottsdale Exhibition, that the Scottsdale level of the show was very soupish.

FRANK LA PENA: What kind of standard did you arrive at, to figure out if they were Indian and how that translated in the artistic sense as a standard?

YEFFE KIMBALL: Well, take this piece for example, and you look at it. The finest craftsmanship, a sense of beauty is in it. This is related to religion, and you look at it, it's a beautiful thing to look at. Had it been done crudely, had it been something you found in some souvenir store or something, and they do things about corn and then make dolls, and you look at it and you know the difference.

FRANK LA PENA: How can you know the difference?

YEFFE KIMBALL: Well, as an artist of fifty-five years I think I have some judgment about what is good and what is bad.

JACK REYNOLDS: In terms of the aesthetic sense, I am wondering if a man who is imprisoned, you know, and all he has got is a piece of paper and a pencil in his hand and he expresses himself. He says what he sees. Maybe he makes it ugly because that is what he sees. Now, I would have a hard time judging that that wasn't aesthetic to him, in comparison with one who sits in his studio producing art.

YEFFE KIMBALL: I am not saying it isn't. I said from the level of art of this period it did decline, if that's not what I said, that's what I meant to say. As a high example of this same sort of thing, an artist by the name of Amos Badwolf who depicted the Custer battle and the other battles and who did beautiful paintings of buffalo and animals on skins, there exist some portfolios of this and it shows for example the horses, and probably you have seen them, of the horses going in the river on one side and all you see is their behinds and coming out of the other side is their heads. Then you see the water flowing down and this is beautifully expressed, a beautiful expression of a very tragic affair. But the level and the manner, you know that it has been done by an artist, an artist's statement. I think what we are saying here is that there are a lot of people in the world who are not artists because what they are turning out is not art, it's junk.

FRITZ SCHOLDER: We have got into a very complicated thing, which is really down to the root of it, first of all because it is so complex. You're talking in terms that many people can't come together on, although most people would agree that there are universal reasons for the aesthetic and it doesn't matter if it is Egyptian, Hopi or what, but first of all it has to be a good piece of art. Now, how you can define "good" does become quite personal. The whole issue is clouded because today just as in Rembrandt's time, there is a lot of charlatan art, there are a lot of people running around saying, I am an artist. I mean this is a real "in thing" and they are producing junk. The poor public really does have a rough time because unless you devote your whole life to it and, believe it or not, if you do spend many, many years, you can tell an important painting a mile away, just like that.

When I first heard, for instance, that artists were bringing in dirt and putting it on the floors of the museums, I was a little shocked myself but in Amsterdam I walked into a museum where they have the dirt artists as they are called and it's really pretty nice and I can't tell you why but it made sense. So I think in the long run all we can say is "keep open."

CHARLES LOLOMA: What you are saying, Fritz, is that people can experience the most ugliest beautiful scene.

FRITZ SCHOLDER: Ugly and beautiful is almost the same.

BUFFY SAINTE MARIE: This calls for the need of an association. I strongly recommend that you form a non-profit corporation of some sort to promote and protect authentic Indian art and when you have this corporation formed, you can have some sub-corporations entered to sell Indian art to gain profits for the artists themselves and with this establishment, you can protect religious values like Charles was talking about. You can have a strong lobbying force. Say Pueblo tribes, their arts are inherently tied with religion. A group can protest, we can photograph or put out junk art.

FRITZ SCHOLDER: The sad thing is that some Indians find themselves in a very difficult position. For instance, in Santa Fe there are Pueblo people who are very poor and there is nothing in the winter for them. So what they have to do is to go out and find non-Indian made things and sell them on the plaza to tourists. It is very, very sad. I wish it was clear cut. It isn't. But I can see your point and I think that some type of society certainly is needed. I think some type of Indian gallery is needed, and some type of Indian theater, and these should all be resolutions along with a touring Indian show of the top work in 1970.

YEFFE KIMBALL: Let's examine the word, "authentic." The Philbrook Museum was the first museum to originate a national Indian exhibition in the early forties. They had this kind of a water color school and they had certain traditional northwest coast carvings and things. They set this up and they brought in juries who had a very closed mind about this. They determined that this kind of thing, including the water colors, was authentic Indian art. Well, we know everything changes and even the guy who is doing the same thing over and over, may slip a little and decide to do something else. He gets bored maybe and makes the tail longer or ears longer or makes the rabbit a different color and this comes in, so where are you going to draw the line?

As a matter of fact I was out there in those early days and participated in the show and was one of the Trustees. They had a number of things that were offbeat, according to them. They had the buffalo that didn't look like a buffalo. Their image was, and so on and so on and they said, well, this is not authentic and I went in and I said, "authentic, as of 1598, 1600, 1700, 1800 or when Amos Badwolf did the drawings of Custer's 1876?" Now, just where are we going to draw the line? The first thing they had to do was split the thing in two and they set up what they called the traditional and I don't know what they called the other, non-conformists. They had two exhibitions and then the new guy coming in took a look and said, "Well, I am tired of doing that horse, I am going to get in the other group." You found this transition taking place, the guys jumping over into the new group and the

214

buffalo was still a buffalo and it was done better in some cases than the traditional image that they had in mind as Indian art.

A SPEAKER: With a National Indian Art Foundation or something like this, you can have your spiritual, traditional Indians.

YEFFE KIMBALL: Right, I think you're saying "authentic." I think you mean that it should be on a Guild level. Now, the Navajos have a Guild, the Hopis have one. There is a standard which reaches a plateau of fine art, aesthetic statements, in craft or baskets or whatever it is.

A SPEAKER: How can already existing non-profit corporations or foundations in the arts be utilized to help implement Indian arts? I mean we may lose ourselves by the time we get established. Maybe there is a way to go through organized channels.

FRITZ SCHOLDER: As a matter of information, the Commissioner of Indian Affairs at Scottsdale mentioned a year of awareness, exhibitions at the end of the year. What he is talking about I have no idea and I have talked to other people and *they* have no idea. It seems there is so much interest. For instance the Director of Edinborough Art Center Festival was here and wants to make Indian art the main feature of the next Art Festival, and yet what is going to happen I don't know. This is why we almost would have to do it ourselves.

YEFFE KIMBALL: You represent them here, don't you?

A SPEAKER: Right, but I am not here as an official representative, I am not speaking on their behalf. You see the Arts and Crafts Board might be interested in an idea like this but they could never propose it themselves. Because you would say, my God, here are the white men trying to come in and take over our arts again. You see you're the one who would have to produce an idea like that.

A SPEAKER: Could I just drop all this and say what I am really concerned about is what I have been having problems with doing various things in art which I guess Mr. Loloma had made it clear for me this afternoon: you as artists have made a separation from religion.

FRITZ SCHOLDER: I think of course and as most people realize there are only a few tribes that have that conflict and they are in the southwest mainly. Some of us don't have that type of conflict.

CHARLES LOLOMA: I think we could title this under identity for youth. Most of the time it's a youth or young man who cannot make up his mind what he wants. The forces that go to make up your mind are concerned with identity, who you are and what is your background. This means cultural appreciation, and therefore these are the forces that will do it.

BEN BARNEY: There is a significance that does exist about the religious thing. I remember very distinctly, and I believe him because I love him, I mean my uncle. When I went through the ceremony of acquiring the mind of an adult, he told me never to say certain things, never to tell certain things, never to tell especially a white man. Yet in that ceremony there were so many beautiful things, the essence of human life. He related the history and religious essence of our lives and yet he limited me to only relating this among my specific tribal groups and other Indians but especially never to a white man. This kind of limitation has proven also a strength. So therefore, on that basis because of my uncle, my father and my mother, I must never tell certain specific beautiful things and it's all right with me because I still work well. I still write well, I still express the essentials or at least make an attempt to express the essential quality, the goodness and the beauty of not only human life but the lives around us, the whole circumstance that we find ourselves in.

As long as we find ourselves, as long as the artist finds himself strong and tries to remain strong in whatever context that he happens to be in, even with the limitations imposed upon him by say his elders or by the religious procedures of his community, of his tribalism, I think a person can still operate and express himself well and work well, without the conflicts that could destroy or distort his work.

CHARLES LOLOMA: I belong to other societies at home and I look at it this way, I thought about this a lot of times. When a mind is limited to the way you put it, it always puts forth an unlimited quantity of other things. If that makes any sense or not, I don't know, because it means that you don't need to share it with the world or share it with anybody else. You should be the force on your own to live this, to be true to share it with the world or share it with anybody else. You should be the force on your own to live this, to be true to it, to worship this because by doing so, you are gaining a grown-up attitude, an unlimited amount of thinking forces to penetrate future imagination because people have predicted things a long time ago, later life will be this way and eventually this will happen.

BUFFY SAINTE MARIE: Talking about this, not that we need any more trouble, I think eventually we should consider the role of the museums in Indian arts because I don't think except for a few exceptions, the museums have title to most of what they have. Not that I am against them displaying certain objects and things, but I think that eventually we should as Indians and as artists make a claim on things that really don't belong to the museums, whether they continue to be displayed there or not. I think this should be up to us and I think that it should be stated that these objects are on loan from the tribes that either takes them back or allows them to continue to be displayed, and there are ways of doing this. For instance if it is acknowledged by a museum that this is a genuine Hopi article, then it has to be admitted that it still belongs to the Hopi people.

FRITZ SCHOLDER: That's a good point, but I doubt if museums are going to do that. In Paris, it was so sad to see the best Sioux headdresses in Europe because they ran over and grabbed all sorts of things the Europeans and the Russians. They have the best Eskimo things. They gathered everything up and it is really sad because the top Indian things are not even in this country. I think this is a very good point because these should be national treasures. In Japan they have the national treasures set up where they will never leave the country.

A SPEAKER: Bring a suit in the world court.

CHARLES LOLOMA: Maybe that's good. Maybe somebody who wants to see that bad enough could go over there and see it. Meantime, they could meet other people from other countries and talk their language, and that might be great.

YEFFE KIMBALL: I promised to talk a little while ago about food, and I will touch on that briefly now. Together with Jean Anderson of Cornell, I wrote "The Art of American Indian Cooking," by Doubleday publishers. It has a history of foods, instructions, the main introduction, and deals with the subject in five or six areas. We start with the Vikings and what they discovered when they came here. They found what they described as enormous wheat fields. We now know these were corn fields. They described acres of vineyards, and that is how Vinland got its name.

Then we describe the Conquistadores, then also Columbus and their ilk. They found other products growing in the West Indies and other places. Actually, more than half the world's food was a direct contribution of the American Indian. I wonder what they ate before they got here, because they had no peppers, corn, pumpkins, squash, artichokes, avocado, pears, fruits of the vines, beans. Our so-called "Boston" beans was cooked in heavy earthenware pots, placing fire all around the pots. They cooked the beans for days. The so-called American clambake, is an American Indian custom. A hole was dug in the ground and rocks were put down, grass was put down, a layer of lobster, clams, oysters were laid on the rocks and grass. Then they went off to get the meat, came home and dug up their dinner. That became the "clambake" and peppers, chilies were all products originating here. Many fruits existed here; wild grapes, some type of crabapple. Among the things that were brought

here were the peaches, and the Indians loved peaches and before the land was settled, ahead of them were great peach orchards and they loved to grow things and produce all of this
great food and they sent other people. An Englishman went
around and spent two years learning about foods of the new
world and herbs, medicinal herbs which we have more than
fifty per cent that is used by the medical profession today. I
think that if you're interested, I am not trying to sell the book,
it doesn't cost very much, it has the history of the foods and it
has over two hundred recipes that I personally tested and cooking along with my co-author that you might find interesting.

Doctor Dockstadter wrote the introduction for it and it was
pretty well screened. I find the book limited. I wanted more time
to work on it. I also illustrated it. I don't know whether I will
ever add more to it. It certainly should be but it has got a lot
of things like last week at the school we got to talking about
cooking and I found myself in the kitchen cooking sunny green
chili for fifty people. There was an art in the cooking and they
thought nothing of barbecuing a whole buffalo, but they did this
for food and not for sport.

They knew how to dry things. They knew how to cure them.
They had great cellars under their houses and kept them during
the winter from freezing. We knew an awful lot about the art
of growing and preserving beautiful food. What is Indian food?
Everything that you eat practically is Indian food.

A SPEAKER: What about soul food?

YEFFE KIMBALL: Why don't you define what you think
is soul food.

A SPEAKER: I think it was the American Indian cooking
that was taught to the black people who were brought over.

YEFFE KIMBALL: Thank you, I agree with you.

The Panel was then adjourned.

9

The American Indian Case:
Modern Psychology and Child Development

LIONEL DEMONTIGNY

EW if any discussions have been held by Indian scholars on the subject of psychology and child rearing. Mainly, this subject has been the exclusive property of the Anglos. We have only a few of our own people specializing in this field, and this perhaps betrays our weakness. My contribution to our panel, such as it may be, is derived entirely from my own experiences, which include the rearing of white children, and the rearing of Indian children in a nonIndian setting. Certainly I will not try to play the part of an expert, because I am not an expert. My presentation is a critique of the historical rearing of children in the Anglo-European community.

First of all, it is my opinion, that the field of psychology and child psychiatry in the present era of American thinking is very immature, and functions on a very small knowledge base. I think you know this comes out in contrast to American Indian forms of thinking about this topic, which are centuries old, and are in fact as old, or older, than that of China. The mode of thinking of our modern psychologists and psychiatrists are really six decades old, or less. So we start by taking a look at what type of material is really pertinent. We find that most of the work done by psychologists and psychiatrists, has been done by the psychoanalytic people in the 1930's and 1940's. This, as you know, is the "id" and the "ego" and the sexual trauma, and so forth. In my opinion, that has not a great deal to offer, largely because the people who developed this philosophy did so from a biased viewpoint. Assuming now that at the top of the scale of civilization, they then draw these evolutionary scales and put man at the top of the evolutionary scale, where he didn't belong anyway, at least not from a scientific, reasoning standpoint.

The behavioral scientists developed another one of these evolutionary scales for society, and they progressed in approximately this way: Food gathering, then hunting, and fishing, then agricultural, then finally industrial. I have forgotten all the stages now, but at any rate, it's not particularly significant, because it starts off with the premise that an American industrial-type society is superior, and that is not good judgment. Our theologians have essentially done the same thing, and again our criterion people are saying that they draw an evolutionary scale, and that *they* are at the top of this scale. I would contend that this is not scientific reasoning. I say that it borders on racism, and was developed as part of an ideology in American society towards conquering, controlling, and exploiting.

The other thing which I think is important is that the American system has developed one of the most complete systems of denial of any group of people in human history. Such a system of denial, is one in which the people deny actual truth, reality, emotional behavior, reaction and inter-reaction. Essentially, we have two types of denial systems upon which Americans operate. No. 1 is the apathetic type of denial and the other is an aggressive type of denial. The apathetic type is the kind of denial Americans are most frequently exposed to, but you talk with the people in a local school for example, and they will say, "Oh, well, you know, that is the way Indians are, and nothing can be done about it." That would be an apathetic type of denial system; whereas an aggressive denial system would be: "Boy, those Indians are getting hopped up over there, we better do something about it." I don't want to relate all the jargon here; I talk from a gut level. I'm just a country boy myself, and each time I start reading all this high-powered jargon, I find out that whenever someone develops a new field, they usually formulate new words with the same old ideas, and so I just talk from the same old country vernacular that I'm used to.

Let me say that behavioral science then utilizes an apathetic denial in development of work. The American Indians, in developing this new knowledge base, as it's termed (and as I'm sure you're aware), are taught to believe, that when the Europeans came to the shores of America, after revolting against the noble classes, they rejected what the noble classes stood for, including their intellectual development. When they came here, they developed their own knowledge systems. You see, this is where you get all this social science bit from. I mentioned the denial system as far as denying that the American Indians have any kind of civilization. There are people in the social sciences who have studied the Native Americans on the premise of trying to find out why the American Indian people do not civilize. This is an apathetic denial system, which states that the Indians are not civilized, therefore, you never really have to recognize this particular group as having a civilization. Some other examples are usually the white children who are denied any knowledge of sex or the birth process until the late teens. The American educational system denies that anyone without a degree can be expert in a given field. When the Negro demanded equality, the response of white Americans was to deny that differences exist between Black and White Americans. You have heard this business about people being basically the same. In doing so, you really are denying that a valid issue exists.

Your criterion relies on services which are held in a very rigid word-by-word fashion. Say you've got a person who has a lot of problems and he's exposed to a disorderly kind of system, and maybe his wife runs off with another man and the finance companies foreclose the mortgage and he loses his job and his daughter is pregnant or something that is important to him. So what he does is he goes into this church and it has a big thick wall in it and he goes through his rosary word by word by word. In effect, then, in going through this rigid orderly process, he actually denies that all these disorderly things that are disrupting his life exist, and he is all sealed off. This is important whenever you think about our Indian religion and how reality is dealt with. The American Indian is even denied *existence*. He is depicted as a mystical fellow—a wary, gun-toting, dancing, horse-riding and whooping being who once resided on the North American continent. It is actually denied that the American Indians are real today, and are human and have problems. Even in the '50's when the Indian people brought some of their problems before the Congress of the United States, those people were surprised that there were a few Indians left.

Programs were quickly implemented to assimilate, integrate, or relocate these unfortunate few who remained, thus denying that Indians should exist and have real problems. It was denied that denial systems are substituted not only for intelligence, but are substituted for culture, ethics and morals. Recently, I witnessed a debate between a Canadian and an American. The Canadian stated that Americans really have no culture. The American responded with an aggressive denial statement and said, "Then why are we the richest and most powerful nation in the world?" You know, you try to piece that together, as to what that has to do with what the Canadian said, and it doesn't make much sense, because in fact he is denying that the guy even said it. Our educational institutions, with a small knowledge base supported by systems of denial, have been built to suit the needs of an industrial society oriented for conquering and controlling. Little knowledge is needed to achieve these goals. Obtaining a degree does not guarantee income and power, but is necessary before one can *begin to proceed*. Thus, American youngsters do what they must to obtain a degree in whatever field they need to use it.

They are taught, whether by example or implication, whatever you do is all right, as long as you don't get caught doing it. The emphasis is not upon the wrong act but upon being caught doing it. But American students are becoming a lot more well informed. They are getting tired of these denial systems. They are present in all the educational institutions which are set up in an industrial society fashion: through the educating machines, they all come out like cans of peas. They are all stamped and made of ticky-tacky. But for some reason they are not all coming out the same. Something is happening now and the students may be all made of ticky-tack, but they are not all coming out the same, and so, we have a lot of turmoil in our educational system.

The American Indian child comes from a society possessing a cultural, ethnic and moral maturity. He's raised in the world of reality. Suddenly he's exposed to society, through the school system first of all, where his very existence is denied. If he is accepted at all, it's on a partial basis as a sub-human species, or he exists only as a mystical being. You take an Indian child who is born into a real world, and he is taught to deal with reality from the time he is born. Our psychologists and psychiatrists term this "normal development." I would not accept that idea, but I would rather support the idea that Indians look upon these things the way they really are. I mean, like a little child is born and he gets an idea and he sees his little brothers and his little sisters around and he is not denied any knowledge of sex. He sees dogs having intercourse; he sees them born; he sees chickens born, and I mean there is no big mystery to him in all this.

He sees all this. He understands it. He's exposed, you know, as to how leaves come out every year and die in the fall and he knows pretty much about the cycles of life. He sees birth and death and he sees nature in life every single day. He is not sealed off from the world like another child might be. As a result of this, the Indian child develops a lot quicker and at an earlier age. That is the reason I want the Hopi gentleman to hear this, because I wanted to compare some other tribal traditional child-rearing techniques, with Hopi techniques. I'm not familiar with the child-rearing practices of all tribes, but pretty much familiar with my own. In this setting, the Indian child receives a great deal of attention. We don't have a nucleus family to start out with: My brother's children are my children and also my wife's sister's children, are also my children. In our normal setting, a woman is permitted to have a child only every six years, to insure proper upbringing of the child, because when the children come too close together this deprives the child.

The father teaches the child how to make a good living. The child learns a lot of skills, and the grandparents primarily teach these children about philosophy and religion, and how to live a good life, and the meaning of things in the world. If a child should misbehave, the parent or the father does not punish him. He becomes very disturbed about the kid misbehaving, but he will generally go to a cross-uncle and say, "The child has misbehaved and it's your responsiblity to do something about it," because if the father were to punish the child, this would destroy that teaching relationship. You see, that teaching relationship, it is thought, cannot really exist in a place where the child is experiencing physical punishment. Our children are taught to go through what is termed four "eyes," and by "eyes" we mean ways of viewing things. At an early age it's believed that a child generally thinks of himself only, and he cries and he gets bad and he needs his diapers changed and all those things. The adults hover around the child, and gradually the child becomes aware that there are other people in the world, until he reaches a point when he takes a mate and gets married. Then he enters into the second "eye," where he now must have concern for two people.

The third is whenever he has children. The fourth is when the person gets old and you're not full of sparks and flames anymore. But rather the sparks are now turned to all kinds of glowing embers and are always filled with warmth. When you see older persons in a village, they talk to the youngsters. They talk to all those children as grandchildren, and refer to them as grandhildren. In other words, now they see over their entire world, and this is generally considered the height of maturity, when the individual reaches the fourth "eye." Each stage along the way, a person has a particular role to play. Each goes through this gradual stage of development.

Well, I've thrown in quite a few ideas here and there and I don't pretend to say that they are all completely developed. In fact, they are deliberately not developed completely, so that we can have some discussion. Panel members, do you have some comments to make? Are there any questions from the floor? Just what do we mean by child-rearing? Do we mean that the natural parents are bringing up the child? Might there be, in the case of the Indian, extended family members who have this responsibility by custom and tradition? Or might there be some type of foster home, child-care arrangement?

DISCUSSION

Modern Psychology & Child Development

DOROTHY DAVIDS: I'm from the Stockbridge Munsee Tribe in Wisconsin, and I work at the University of Wisconsin. It seems to me there is a great relationship between child-rearing and the theory of learning. It doesn't matter who you are. One of the first things I think of, is the consideration of a human being who is supposedly a little different from the animals—and I get a little hung up by it because I don't know if we are human beings, which assumes that we are born human, or whether we are beings, or whether we simply exist and we are learning to be human. We have these two things here: whether or not you know which is the noun and which is the adjective. If we are learning to be human, and we have got to define something as to what it means to be human, what does a human being do that other beings do not do?

A SPEAKER: Supposedly think.

A SPEAKER: Language.

DOROTHY DAVIDS: Language? Yes.

DR. deMONTIGNY: Do you mean communicate?

A SPEAKER: I don't mean communication. I mean the use of grammatical language.

A SPEAKER: To create and to make, that is another one.

DOROTHY DAVIDS: Before you go any further, the lower species do all those things, too.

A SPEAKER: Animals speak and lower species do not have a language.

A SPEAKER: I'm from Indiana University. Lower species communicate a little, but they have no well organized speech, even vaguely approaching language. This has been proven by study.

DR. deMONTIGNY: Do animals see, hear, and feel, other ways than human?

DOROTHY DAVIDS: What makes this human being different from others, and then, just thinking in terms of the learning process. I will come back to what I think here.

EMERSON ECKIWARDY: Another characteristic which can be considered, is physical mobility and dexterity as it's carried out in comparison with other types of situations.

DR. deMONTIGNY: It seems to me that horses and dogs

get around pretty well.

A SPEAKER: How about spiritual being?

DOROTHY DAVIDS: Like inventiveness to make a car or aeroplane or rocket?

DR. deMONTIGNY: Would you go along, that animals don't seem to do that, in other words, the extension of our senses— animals don't seem to have the ability to do that?

MARIGOLD LINTON: I would like to comment on the language question, because one of the very interesting things that has been studied, I guess for 20 or 30 years, is the whole question of whether the ape talks. A very interesting study was done in the fifties where certain people would take a chimp in the home and try to teach it to talk. They could get it to say "mama" and "papa" with great difficulty. After many, many years, the people learned to love the ape and the ape learned to love the people. At the end of this series of studies, everybody decided that it really wasn't possible. Very recently—a clever group of people said, "What is it that is essential about language? And they said it may be possible that you don't have the voice box, but is it necessary, you have language and you have a voice box in order to have language. They took a chimpanzee and a group of deaf mutes and they started teaching them sign language and it was proven that in fact apes can talk providing you give them the symbols. They now have an ape with a 200-word vocabulary. He has been learning at an accelerated rate.

Every month we get reports about the number of words that the ape has learned. They have taught him all the colors. They can ask him questions like "What is your favorite color, what color is the grass, what do you want to do," and the ape replies, "want to go out, want to go out," and that is it. It understands relationships between the symbols and it will try standing at the door with its coat in its hand and jump up and down and say "want to go out, want to go out," and you ignore it and it says "go out, want to go out." "Washo wants to go out," which is the name of the chimp. Finally you let the ape go out and the ape is, you know, quite delighted.

One of the things that is somewhat amusing is that this chimpanzee is a black chimpanzee, and they ask the chimpanzee "Washo, what color are you," and it can discriminate between colors and it replies, "I am red, I am red," and they say what color is this, and this is black, and what color are you and it keeps saying, "I am red," and she perceives herself as being red. In other words, there is something much more complicated going on than her having learned a set of responses.

DOROTHY DAVIDS: As you were talking, I jotted down some things and let me say that when we work with animals, maybe we think in terms of training and conditioning. I think you condition animals to distinguish between shapes and colors. When you work with humans you call it education, don't we? I want to have my say and then I want to sit down. Humans are able to stop and reflect upon their own behavior, not only backward but forward and sideways, and we can step outside ourselves and look at ourselves. In connection with that, is not the training delayed response, but the educated trained response —I mean delayed response—in other words, we can behave differently from each other, and think, because we have the ability to care and to think we care about other people. I think in that realm of the delayed response is where our "learning theory," all of our teaching for humans where humans exist, and this is what makes us human.

For example, you can train a dog not to grab for food until you give him the signal, but the human can have a certain amount of food and a person might say, "Oh, you're hungry," and he stops, because he cares enough about another human to respond. He might delay his action for the sake of another. When it comes to learning, I suppose, in tribal societies, children are born into the tribes and they learn who they are in relationship to others. In other words, when you find out that this man over here is your uncle and you are the nephew, somehow the behavior is built into the tribal society. It isn't quite so clear in the non-tribal places what this type of behavior is, but if you're born into a tribe and if the behavior or the meanings are pretty much intact, (and of course it isn't in a good many of our tribes anymore). In my own tribe, for example, we don't know particularly what it means to be a Stockbridge Munsee and we certainly don't know particularly how an uncle is supposed to relate to his nephew.

This has been Christianized and civilized out of us. However, we learn very soon, and we get this as we're coming along, that we do belong to a group known as the Stockbridge Munsee, and we have different behaviors to each other because we are tribal members, but we are not very clearcut about it. I want to go back just a little with regard to this question of child development and child rearing practices, and see what you can throw in about what you feel Indian parents do, whatever tribe is, that creates or develops better humans than in the urbanized world. Are these the kind of children that we want to still have into this world?

BEN BARNEY: I'm from Arizona. Are you making the distinction between say the civilized or what you would call the urbanized world and the Indian world, whatever tribe you're from—and the distinction between that as a difference expressed on a human level?

226

DOROTHY DAVIDS: Let's just take the typically urbanized honest people who live in cities, but living close together with all kinds of other people in a relatively small group. They live in a different time world in the city. It's necessary that you have control of the time; we do it with clocks, and of course the clocks come out of the urbanized people and street cars going on time, and things have got to run on time. The child born in either one of those worlds, relatively speaking, learns a different kind of time system. Of course, built right in with time is the urbanized world, and they tell the kids what are you going to be when you grow up, as if you aren't anybody now. In this world, it's pretty much known what you're going to be, you're going to be a member of a particular group and behave like they do, considering that in speaking about it, it isn't lost in this world. They are going to be much more individualized, and by that I mean selfish—"I take care of me and my own little family, and my family's family and my whole extended family." It may be that this is more human, I don't know, but this is just a framework.

A SPEAKER: I'm from New Mexico. Isn't that your own reaction to that situation, because I don't feel that way. I don't think I'm in an urbanized world. I don't feel that people are selfish. I live in a big city, but I find people who care and I think we react to that world and we may have an unpleasant experience and so we say they don't care about me as in the other world they do, which is your own experience. I get all confused; isn't it your own reaction, or is it reality?

DOROTHY DAVIDS: I found that the tribe, when I lived in the city, doesn't exclude the fact that other "tribes" exist, and sometimes they name them the Beetles Club and the Lions Club and they form different little groups. They relate to each other and maybe this is why Indians would like to try to live some place together in the urbanized world, and with all these individuals they can find some sense of unity by being selfish, and I don't necessarily mean in the extreme sense.

MARIE CORWIN: I'm from the Seneca Reservation. You talk about people caring for you in urban society, and yet the thing about people in the urban society, they care about you as long as you can take care of yourself and I don't think this is true with tribal society.

DOROTHY DAVIDS: If you run out of money, you got no friends, is that what you're saying?

DR. deMONTIGNY: I think on a very low gut level. You've got to put it in simple language for me. Many times people start throwing around these big words, and I want to break them down to something that has meaning to me.

KAREN PETERSON: I am from the Eastern Cherokee

Tribe. I think that when you speak about both tribal and urban living, you've got to speak of materialistic values, because again, as pointed out, you have your poor, your medium class, and your high class range. These, again, would differentiate the people. In the poor they will click and the medium will click and you would still not have the same thing or same type of tribal living, but you will have the closeness and the idea of being together. You can't say you get that when you mix with the richer people. That is just my idea.

DOROTHY DAVIDS: There are two categories here and most of us fall someplace between, you know, fairly urbanized. I mean I'm a fairly urbanized Indian myself. As an example, when I am teaching school in the city I'm a drop-out teacher, and they tell me "Dorothy, you don't have any problems, you're so calm and relaxed." But I'm nervous all over on the inside. When I go home to see my mother, she says, "Settle down, what are you rushing for?"

I mean it's enough to make me wonder who I am. I realize these are two worlds—this is rural and the tribe. We have two different situations. When I'm roaming around between them, I might be the same, but different in relation to this dizzy world of the city. The other thing that might happen in our educating process, and as built into the English language becomes specialized, is like this: You ask someone who he is, and he says: I am an anthropologist, or I am a box-maker or a something. Hardly ever do you hear him say I am a human being, who happens to make boxes. So we objectify ourselves in the city. One time I met Gordon McCrae, the anthropologist, and I was talking to Betsey Morgan, and I said, who is Gordon McCrae, so she sid, "Who the hell is anybody?" and she was telling me, well he is a human being, and you don't have to know what he is doing to know who he is. We did that right here when we came and everybody asked what do you do, and what is your first name, and, of course, you're a human being. I'm just wondering when we are talking about the children born into this world now, who are going to think in terms of population and some of the values that may be here, for example, among these individuals, there might be the value of choosing to be kind, but just in the point of view of learning to be human. I think we've got to decide what kind of human do we want in this world, and to choose from our tribal backgrounds or from what we have learned in the urbanizing process, as to what we're going to teach and what we're going to train for and what we're going to do.

DR. deMONTIGNY: We have touched on a lot of topics. A lot of people have been doing a lot of writing about it. I'm not sure I understand what I'm talking about myself. The more

I read about them, the more I wonder if they know what they are talking about. I wonder if some of the other panel members have some opinions.

WILLIAM DEMMERT: I'm from Alaska and I'm in the field of education. I'm very interested in concepts that clash in white versus Indian development— or psychology, and its relationship in educating one or the other. Or why one method of training or teaching appears to work better for one group and not the other, or works as well.

MARIGOLD LINTON: May I respond to that? I'm very much interested in learning . . . learning in general. One of the most important concepts that one should consider is the concept of what you intend to teach and what you intend someone to learn. There was a very interesting study that was done (and I hope I can recapture it briefly)— that some of you who are in education may have read, and that is the study by Rosenthal called "Pygmalion in the Classroom." Rosenthal said that there are some problems to study, but probably the major finding holds. He went to a school in San Francisco with a large number of students. There was considerable prejudice and they were interested in what kind of an effect the prejudice could have upon the varying capacity of the students. So they gave an IQ test, and then they chose randomly from among these kids— that means they took some of the kids who were smart and some who were not smart or did not measure high on the tests, and they said, "As an example, Mrs. Jones, you're so very fortunate. Do you realize you have in your class some very bright little children!" Well, okay now, the only thing that has happened is something that is happening in the mind of the teacher, and she has to look at this little dirty and despised member and say, "Golly, that is smart." They measured the IQ again six months later and discovered that those children they had pointed out in fact tended to score higher than they did before. They had a number of interactions, which means that some things were true of one group and not of another group. They found that the more Mexican looking you were, the more likely your IQ will rise, so apparently the teachers were doing something quite different to the ones who looked very Mexican.

The question is what are these children learning in school? What is anybody who is being looked at as a sub-human or an undesirable, what is he learning about himself in school? I think that we're being taught a lot of nice things about ourselves. I think it's probably possible that in the last three to eight years, to take some pride in the redmen, but I think that there is some hope at least among some people. But where you have a teacher who still has a problem— that teacher is teaching the child to despise himself, his culture and his relatives.

The second problem that I will only mention is the whole question of the intelligence test which has been devised by psychologists, probably the most valuable psychological tool that has ever been developed. There are enormous problems in measuring Indians, Blacks, Brown, and minority groups of any sort. So you take the test, and they ask you all sorts of goofy questions, and, of course, we didn't grow up learning the things you have to know. The assumption now is that no intelligent person uses the tests as they have been used. They have certainly been used to discriminate against the Indian.

DR. deMONTIGNY: You're talking about Rosenthal's terms and expectancy levels, and what some educators have termed prejudice of low expectancy as far as kids are concerned? You don't have to tell kids, I think, that they're dumb. Like you say, well, gee, you spelled "cat" just like Jane over here, a white girl, can spell "cat," and I mean he essentially is saying: You're doing pretty good for an Indian. You get the message pretty darn quick, and people behave pretty much in ways calculated to fulfill the prophecy of the way they are treated.

WILLIAM DEMMERT: I'm not looking for the surface reasons, I'm looking for the underlying factors or causes of these things. I know we have a tremendous drop-out rate. We have many problems in school that the Native student and the Negro student has to put up with, because of the way we're taught and what we're taught. I mean you have a reaction that starts to develop in Grades 6, 7, and 8, which is part of what causes many of our students to drop out.

What I'm asking you is, what is the feeling of this group concerning underlying factors that cause some of these things, like, for example, under the Tlingit culture, the aunt or the uncle always taught the children. When Alaska became a territory, the missionary schools and the Bureau of Indian Affairs Schools came in. Later the state operated schools came in and eventually the public schools came in. Well, the aunt or the uncle who did the teaching kept falling further and further into the background because we had to tell them that they were no longer considered important to the educational system that was brought in by the dominant society. Here we have one example of the parents turning against the school because they are no longer involved. You have some important underlying factors here, so some of the students reflect upon this. When they begin to understand it, their later grades reflect the way they have been taught and what they have been taught.

DR. deMONTIGNY: That is interesting because just before I came here I was out at Coulee Dam and we were talking about some of the issues present there. One of the school teachers, who is very interested in Indian people, very intelligent and mature, said that we have a lot of problems with our Indian kids dropping out. "Our brightest young girl suddenly decided to drop out." I said, "Well, why did she decide to drop out, did you talk to her?" He said, "Yes, and she said that she didn't see any point in going to school because there was nothing there that would benefit her whatsoever. I kept telling her, you have to complete high school and college, if you're going to go out and make a good living. She replied, 'Well, I plan on marrying and the man I marry will make a good living. I will just be a mother and I don't need to go to school any more.'" They cited several cases like this. You know, they use the word "cases." Gradually we got around to what the white kids are saying, and this is very interesting. One of the things that fascinated me about this conversation was that one of the math teachers came in and said, "You know, my daughter doesn't want to go to college and I have saved up all this money for years and years to send her to college . . . and she doesn't want to go!"

"What am I going to do about it?" he asked. "Well, how come your daughter doesn't want to go to college?" I asked him. And he said, "She wants to study what she wants to study, and she didn't even want to complete high school. She told the teacher that the only reason she is completing high school is to please her mother." Then another teacher spoke up and gave me essentially the same story. Finally I summarized it by saying, "Well, as I get this question, the problem you are presenting to me is how can we get the Indian kids to sit in the class tuned out like the white kids. I mean that is the problem you're presenting to me, isn't it?" The teachers thought about this and after awhile they said, "I guess that's what it is, and what are we going to do about it?"

I said, "Well, are you reaching these kids and teaching them anything that is particularly relevant?" They said then, "We can't, because the school board won't let us." The point I'm trying to make is that maybe what we're seeing with Indian kids is just a little bit different symptomology—maybe just a little bit different—of the way things are expressed, and I'm just wondering if a lot of the stuff that the white kids are experiencing is not the same, only they express things in a little different fashion.

DR. McKENZIE: I'm from Shiprock, New Mexico, and I am a Navajo. I'm a physician and general surgeon. I grew up as an Indian child and I am now working among the Indian people myself. Perhaps I can see some of these things first hand, apart from reading all the esoteric material. I think that child-rearing is a long-term project. The Navajo, in order to survive, have had to rely on cooperation among themselves. Therefore we get this phenomenon in which the small tribe or the individual has the obligation to take care of the extended family. That is what the Indian is looking forward to, and it's a survival mechanism, so that the final things that are expressed in the Indian culture is cooperation, honor, respect for one another, and respect for the elders. This is the ideology toward the parent, or the extended family, or whoever is bringing up the child, is looking forward to. So we have in our society a situation in which as one doctor suggested, the child is pampered and hovered over. From that moment on he is considered an individual and he rarely sees the whip, if ever. I know that I received the whip only once. I think that this has some bearing again on your drop-out rate.

I have a small family, and children, and this happened to be true in my own family. I think that when my father wanted to get at me for something I had done, all he had to do was speak in some sort of a derogatory tone and that was it. That hurt more than the whip. Nowadays, within my own family, I can see that when I say something, it seems to carry more weight with the children, and I can get them to stop doing this or that if I say it in a certain way. Whereas, if I were to take the rod to them, in that instant when I do that, or even with words (you can be violent with words as well), at that instant they have a rebellion started and it will carry on.

The Indian family is bringing up the child in a sort of permissive atmosphere, if you will. The extended family is talking about honor and cooperation, respect for the elders. These are the things that are stressed. Rarely if ever is there any physical harm for something that is done or not done. So then the child is taken out of that context and put into a school system where there is punishment. At that instant there is rebellion, and the Indian child is not used to that. I think that accounts probably for some of the dropouts. Therefore, I don't know how to resolve this whole thing, but in one instance some Indian cultures, or some Indian tribes will completely go back to the original cultures that they had, which stress honor and cooperation, which may be better. Of course, many tribal people argue that those are the better traits. So then you have young people who are geared towards this sort of thing, who are thrown into a mechanized society. There is a reaction and a rebellion to this; then we see a situation which is not compatible. The youth are in there trying to decide for themselves what should be done. So we come to the situation that we are faced with today.

There is a great deal of emphasis nowadays on the resurgence of tribal cultures. On the other hand, some of our people say that tribal cultures should be abandoned; we should become completely acculturated and assimilated. I think the truth, or the important things, lie somewhere in between. I believe it is important that we retain a culture, but it should be a sort of dynamic, pulsating culture geared to the times. For instance, you have a culture that is based on religion and superstition. The white man has his problem far in the past. As scientific truth emerged, some of the old superstitions had to be abandoned, and the culture had to be renovated to fit present day knowledge. I'm thinking now in particular of the Jewish culture still being distinctly Jewish, but moving ahead. This is the type of thing the Indian people will have to do. I think this is part of the answer, at least to the drop-out rate that we have, apart from the usual excuses that kids give you now: no money, or I want to get married, or the draft, and so on. A culture that should emerge would be distinctly Indian, yet geared to the modern world so that it has meaning for the young people of today. I think this is probably where the answer lies. I'm certainly not an expert, and I deal mostly with physical illnesses. This is kind of a homespun philosophy.

A SPEAKER: Could I add to this, and I only speak from experience, as to how I was brought up, by grandmothers who were philosophers and religious types. I think the main thing that I became aware of in my upbringing, because I am a Navajo too, was that through the whole development, there were greatly stressed relationships. The family was really structured on that basis. I think this is based on what you might call respect for elders, and what they have developed is not so much respect for their elders alone, but it's some sort of harmony situation between two individuals. It's not so much that a child respects anyone, or that the youngster respects the elder, but it's the responsibility involved. It seems almost that the elder must also respect the child, in which the child has no choice but to return that kind of respect and it is that kind of balance that you know they are adapted to.

DR. McKENZIE: Whatever the name for it, it's essentially the relationship between the young and the old that I'm talking about, yes.

WILLIAM DEMMERT: This is what I'm looking for, just what you presented. Since you presented the survival mechanism and you brought up the permissive atmosphere in the home and moving into the school where we have a structured atmosphere, this question of the return of culture and the development of cultural values.

DR. deMONTIGNY: I think you missed it. The atmosphere in which the Navajo child is raised, is very structured, but it's not a domineering type of atmosphere. In other words, we mentioned earlier that American type of society is oriented to where it can be controlled and it can be controlled by an economic system. Religion, for example, is a way of controlling people and the criterions are subject to religious power, whereas Indians regard religion as a source of power. This is why in white society you have the bureaucratic structures, like the Public Health Service, in which there is a chain of command, and you're saying that the Indian child is raised in a highly structured society, but it's not on the basis of authority as such, according to the way the Anglo system is set up.

If you take a look at the child with our groups, they gain a certain amount of linguistic ability, and they begin to learn. Then, when they begin learning, they become courageous and obviously then it is the responsibility of a whole series of people to begin teaching this child. Usually the teaching sessions are initiated by the student, or initiated by the child. He goes to an adult and asks him questions, and then begins getting some answers, receives some information, and then finally, the child begins to get a little bit confused, so the teaching sessions are stopped. They say, well, go sit on the hill and think about it for awhile. After you think it over, maybe you will come back with some other questions or issues, and they will think it over maybe for a couple of days. Then they will come on back. And when he is ready to go through with some more discussion, they will go through with more discussion. When the adult finally runs out of answers, then the child takes them to somebody else who knows more about what the topic is and quite obviously, whatever a child is going to do or be is determined at any early age. It's very rare, obviously, that two siblings will go into the same thing or become the same thing, in that tribal structure.

In the Anglo system, there is not that situation. In fact, in the Anglo situation sibling is pitted against sibling. It is said, well, your older sister is good at art and how come you're not good at art. This kind of thing is a traumatic situation. I'm referring now to the man from Alaska. I think he might have misunderstood that concept, or didn't understand what I was saying in the first place. The other point brought up in connection with three concepts discussed previously, is what can we do to bridge that gap. I have my own ideas, but I would like to hear yours.

DR. McKENZIE: It's very difficult to say, and I have thought about the matter, but in an amateur way. I think that probably on our reservation an attempt is being made to do this sort of thing, to teach the culture to these young children. The young people are taught the things that have led to the type of approach that the older people have with respect to child rearing. It is a family responsibility. A cliche goes that the Bureau of Indian Affairs is paternalistic, the bringing up of the child is taken over by the BIA Schools. In other words, the BIA is supposedly a substitute parent, and this is an undesirable thing because there isn't the relationship of child and elder in that sort of a system. The relationship traditionally is between the child and parent, or the child and the elders, so that the teaching of culture traditions and language should take place in the home rather than in the school. The answer to the Navajo problem is to return to the old method. The family should realize that the Navajo culture means something. They should practice it and live it, but it should mean enough to them so that they can pass it on to the younger children within the home setting.

A SPEAKER: I would like to add something to what Dr. McKenzie said. I think true learning is only when you live it. If you have to teach something, I don't think you're going to learn as well if you haven't lived it. I think that is one of the problems in our educational system today. We take a child when he comes to school and we say, "Okay, you come to school to learn," and the child already knows how to learn when he comes to school. I don't think any of us could say that we taught our child to speak. This is probably the most difficult thing that we, as humans, have to do. I think by contrast of what we're talking about here, the only way that we are going to learn, is if we have to do it in schools. We haven't yet learned how to teach children. Of course, we know how to obstruct their growth in most cases to the point where they eventually drop out.

DR. deMONTIGNY: I think you have brought out some very good points. The child is taught in the Indian traditional learning process, as an enjoyable process. You go to school and you know you go there to learn something, but that is not what the educational system is set up to do. It is set up to process you so that you can fit into the industrial type of society and come up like cans of peas.

A SPEAKER: I'm from the Sioux tribe and at this point I am sort of confused. At times we say, in this discussion, that what should be done is to use certain types of Native values and inculcate the children with these values. I get confused because I am familiar only with the Sioux. Other influences operate among my people. It is not such a simple thing. On the Sioux reservations in South Dakota the child is surrounded by the TV . . . and you also see a greater trend of inter-marriage. These are factors that may influence what we are talking about. The third thing is this: I don't know what it is that we should capture and try to promote in our present educational setup. I feel uncomfortable when we say Black and White. That—in other words—"their" educational system is all bad, and there must be something that we can retain and build on with both cultures, because it's going to be enough of a job for us, in promoting certain parts of our current programs.

DR. deMONTIGNY: There are other factors that are operating, certainly, and they are also an influence.

CARL DOWNING: I'm from Oklahoma. What it breaks down to, to me, is the fact that we have one subculture that is being absorbed into a major culture . . . and the effort is to prevent our complete absorption . . . to remain a subculture, yet to live within the main culture. It seems to me there is only one way to do this educationally. That is, to let the subculture be responsible for choosing the part of the major culture it wants in its education. In other words, let Indians be responsible for what Indian children learn and let them decide what part of our subculture remains a part of their life, and what part of the major culture becomes a part of their life.

DR. deMONTIGNY: How do you propose to do this?

CARL DOWNING: Like get with it.

DR. deMONTIGNY: How do you mean?

CARL DOWNING: Like right now go back to where you came from and determine what happens to your own children.

DR. deMONTIGNY: Let me try this on you then: My reservation is going for a community-based school system.

CARL DOWNING: Is the community going for this, and are you and the people like you going for this . . . or is this something that has come from someone else?

DR. deMONTIGNY: It came from members of that group, and there were a whole series of factors involved that resulted in it.

CARL DOWNING: If it comes from within that group, and you are the determining force as to what is included, then . . .

DR. deMONTIGNY: I am not the determining force.

CARL DOWNING: You're not lining up to what I said.

DR. deMONTIGNY: I am not the determining force. I mean, the people decided they want to do this. They decided they were going to put this in effect, with or without me. The direction that we are going to take did not hinge upon me. Certainly, I did what I could . . . but whether I took action or did not take action, it still would have happened.

DR. McKENZIE: On the Navajo reservation there is a move to have the Navajo people control the schools through their own local school boards. These school boards will determine who shall work there and what sort of a curriculum will be taught. They will also determine what kind of relationship the school will have to the community. I think the Rough Rock Demonstration School has shown that Indians are capable of running their own schools. However, don't forget you have some children growing up, and we would like to think that these are young people who have the right to make up their own minds as to what they want.

If they want to remain within the culture, fine. If they want to become completely acculturated and assimilated, fine. If they want to live somewhere in between, that is fine too. This is the type of system that should be established. Therefore, we should be extremely careful that these community school boards, or county-run school systems do not forget the academic aspects of a school system, so that somebody will be able to say that the young person who has been materially deprived comes up through the school system and has the wit and the knowledge about him, with which the school may have helped to equip him, to accomplish something. For instance, he might want to be a lawyer or a physicist, or an M.D. and I wish there were another one among the Navajo. But I would say that they should be put in that kind of an environment which would help them develop to the best of their ability within the Indian culture. The school board will have to get together with the academic community and establish excellent schools instead of just Indian schools. We have enough of those.

A SPEAKER: It seems to me that the Indian people develop child rearing practices, and these differ in some way from tribe to tribe, so that it would be very difficult to form an institutional capability to study the Indian child-rearing process, because the Navajo may want to do it one way and the Chippewa tribe another. The notion that seems to be central through all of this discussion is that the reasons for doing things a certain way over centuries ago, are no longer consciously being thought about today. The Navajo used to raise their children a certain way, but they aren't consciously thinking about WHY those ways were developed at one time. The human being has certain supportive elements necessary for maturation mentally and emotionally and if so, what are these elements and can we list them?

DR. deMONTIGNY: I think we ought to be getting down to some specific questions . . . We have thrown out an awful lot of topics. It seems we have touched upon nearly all the problems of the world. I would like to summarize a couple of things that we might develop.

I mentioned, for example, that our people in the behavioral sciences and social sciences really hadn't done us much good . . . a case which is really irrelevant so far as Indians are concerned. No one seems to challenge that, so I assume that that is a truism and there is no point in discussing it further. We talked about the school systems, and we have talked about some aspects of child rearing. We haven't really isolated out the specific factors involved, however. Also brought out was the question of expectancy levels and some of the fulfilling prophecies, and this was not completely developed. I don't know if it needs to be. We terminated our discussion with the suggestion that we put our brains together and come up with some basic things such as: What are the supportive elements that a child needs to mature emotionally and mentally? Supportive elements, that is what we are looking for, elements that are necessary for a child to mature. Is it necessary to have a society with some kind of maturity? This morning, I said that Indians have a cultural, ethnic, and moral maturity, whereas the American society does not. Everyone seemed to accept that pretty well, and it went completely unchallenged. Right?

HURLEY PARKHURST: This may sound like I'm going afield, but I'm trying to bring in an analogy, and then see if there is a connection or not. I read a study on nutrition, and since we have some doctors here, I will throw that in. They examined the fact that genetics is not applicable in terms of a program time table for development in bio-chemical maturation of the human being, unless within that environment the necessary nutrients or nutritional elements are present. There are other elements which we must have in our environment in order to grow. A study was done with a number of babies . . . in which they were deprived of any handling for the first two years of their lives, and at the end of two years they were all dead. What was proved in this experiment was that humans need physical contact and to be touched at least in those first two years. This is what I mean by maturation, that we do have an in-built time-table and there is a goal built into us. Maybe it keeps going as a matter of fact; it doesn't really stop from birth till death.

DR. deMONTIGNY: I think you mentioned three common things that can hardly be challenged. Certainly you have to have some kind of genetic structure. There are some good studies on nutrition done in South America. They show that a child's mental capacity is really developed to about half the degree they are going to develop, in four to six years of age. If an individual is deprived of the proper proteins plus building blocks of the other elements necessary to utilize these proteins, the brain does not develop normally. Would you say that would be pretty much correct? I mean, this is a well proven fact. Fevers and illnesses will often hamper development of the normal brain also. Of course, there is a lot of junk in the literature with regard to this, as well as some valuable material.

DOROTHY DAVIDS: I am thinking that you can have these things and exist, but it does not necessarily mean you are in the living-learning stage of being. I mean, you can be a vegetable. There are certain other supportive elements that we need. You can affect a child by thrashing him daily. It is going to produce a different child than the one who is loved and caressed.

KAREN PETERSON: You can also have the opposite— the over-loving . . .

DR. deMONTIGNY: Do you want to qualify this?

KAREN PETERSON: Well, perhaps the child learns better if we praise him, and he also learns when we punish him. Probably the worst thing we can do is neglect him entirely.

DR. deMONTIGNY: We can add the word "loving," to "attention."

DOROTHY DAVIDS: The nurturing elements must also be present.

KAREN PETERSON: You could, but I don't think that is a supportive element.

DOROTHY DAVIDS: TLC covers it, if you have the right amount that we need to be exposed to.

DR. deMONTIGNY: It sounds like a lot of work for undeveloped people, because they have never gone to school. So when the child cries, what do you do, give her a pop, or maybe get money from the social worker to buy it, and at the time when they're doing so, the Headstart people take them away at six years of age. Now actually, it's a wonder we have a nutrition problem, isn't it, because the money isn't there. How is it that there are so many people who have succeeded. That is a real good point, and we might spend a lot more time on it if you wish, with regard to proper nutrition.

A SPEAKER: My point is that, well, what do I want to be, and where am I going? Do I want to become part of the society that is now dominant, and live in that society? Do I want to be that type of person, and do I invite that type of situation? There is a lot in the newspapers about the Viet Nam situation, and about air pollution. In Arizona we don't have that problem as yet. Do I want to become a banker, or open a shop every day and go back home every night? What I must do is to go way up on an elevator and go up lots of floors and heights, to be this kind of person.

DR. deMONTIGNY: You're talking about personal goals?

A SPEAKER: I'm talking about identity and how I would like to be identified.

DR. deMONTIGNY: You have to be somebody.

A SPEAKER: In this business of identity, do I want to still maintain and use Indian elements? Is this the kind of power I would like to use? I think we have to make up our minds as to the direction we should be going.

A SPEAKER: That is not such a small thing as it seems to be right at the moment. I'm an old man. I'm 67 years of age and when I was a boy, I had lots of uncles, and when I went to their house, over in the corner there was always a big wooden box full of jerky. They expected you to take some when you went home. The reason for this is you can take a full pocket and walk all day, or run all day. Most of the old Indians ran all day. You never stop in order to eat. You were chewing this stuff all day, and you stopped to take a drink of water in a stream which you could then do without getting polluted. If you are an old codger like I am, you can remember very, very graphically examples of this kind of diet differential. We used to do that back in the Cherokee hills in Oklahoma. Now, at 67, I notice I don't have anything like the good teeth, or good health, my father had. He lived to be 102 and he had all his teeth. After these many years, I have lived pretty much like a white man. I have good jobs, I pay my taxes, and I have raised a family. I'm very well integrated, so I am beginning to wonder whether it's wise or it's good, or it's anything, as an example, to eat the kind of diet that we eat now, when we're talking about diet. You've got a whole subject there about nutrition. My father was an old-style country Cherokee and he didn't know what the word diet meant. I don't remember him ever being sick and for that matter I haven't been either. Obviously there was a certain amount of nutritional wisdom Indians had. Of course, the jerky was not the only thing they ate.

I don't know how many Indians nowadays think that the white diet is better. But I have come to the conclusion that it's not. I may actually choose to live the rest of my life among the Cherokee. I think I would be better off for it.

DR. McKENZIE: Perhaps I sould say one thing about nutrition. I think it has a very important bearing upon our discussion. It becomes one of the most urgent problems. The main development of a child occurs within the first year, and this is where the Indian people are having their greatest problem: that of feeding their children properly both before birth and after. If you talk about the denial approach, this can be an easy mechanism in regard to nutrition. We talk about germ warfare and gas warfare, and, to carry an analogy to a rather ludicrous extreme, if you stop to think about it, a great many people—particularly among the Navajo—(the average income is said to be about $1500 per annum) you can't very well feed the child properly on that kind of income.

The problem is, when you have an income of this sort, and you have six or eight children, you are feeding them on a below-subsistence level. So then you are influencing the development of that child's brain. If the great majority of the young are developing with this kind of nutrition, you are indirectly influencing a type of mentality—their own and that of their society. The logical conclusion is that the problem of nutrition assumes an extremely important aspect with regard to feeding the children while they are in school, so that they can learn properly, and attack the problem right from birth so that by the time the child gets to school, his brain is at an ultimate functioning level in order to learn. I think nutrition is an important element that needs to be discussed. What I'm saying is that it's not something that is just to be mentioned in passing. It is a very important and crucial question. It is said that once you have deprived the Indian child of proper development within the first year of his life, you have retarded his mental growth. In the ensuing years, he will never make it up.

HURLEY PARKHURST: I'm an Oneida. What do you feel are the foods lacking in diet among your people for the first year of their lives?

DR. McKENZIE: I'm not a nutritional expert. I'm not a pediatrician either. I think we should not forget the dietary traditions of the people. We shouldn't impose upon them a diet which is completely foreign to them, because they may not take to it. Rather should we improve on and enhance the diet they already have, so that they can use it and get the proper nutrition.

DR. deMONTIGNY: Would you say it's primarily a protein deficiency?

DR. McKENZIE: Both types of deficiencies exist—protein and carbohydrates. We have a condition known as quash core disease, which everybody thought was a foreign disease, usually related to the African dietary modes. It has been amply pointed out, on the Navajo reservation, that there were about 15 cases of quash core disease and an additional number, something like 29 more on the order of carbohydrate deficiency—a bone type of deficiency existing in a country said to be the richest nation in the world. I was even surprised to learn directly that in my own backyard there were many cases.

A SPEAKER: With regard to these nutritional deficiencies, I think they are fairly current among the white population as well. In other words, this is a question of knowing what basically good foods are to be fed to children as well as being able to buy them, which Indians are not able to, even if they did know. But knowing is something also, that lots of white people lack.

DR. McKENZIE: I think you have to make some continual evaluation. Quash core is not generally found in the dominant cultures among the whites. In fact, it has been found among some of the Blacks, but quash core is an extreme condition and could damage a child's brain. You don't have to go that far, all you have to do is approach the point, and it may not even be obvious, but you can look at a child and the child appears to be healthy. You have to be a physician to see the telltale signs on the skin if this child is in fact in nutritional trouble. Yet sometimes even physicians can't tell by looking, so you are talking about a situation in which, if there are 29 cases of serious illness, there is perhaps 20% of the whole population sitting right next to that point, which is in enough trouble to retard mental development. Also, different populations have different susceptibility to serious deficiencies. The amount of vitamin usage of a certain type might be able to tolerate that deficiency and not show damage.

DR. deMONTIGNY: You have brought up some topics that can be debated.

DR. McKENZIE: What we are saying is that to produce one case of that particular disease, requires a pool of so many kids suffering from severe malnutrition, and can produce cases of quash core. How many children are there who are suffering from malnutrition to yield this known one? I think it has been suggested that within a city as big as Philadelphia, there may be one case of quash core, and this is a kind of medical curiosity. So, when discovered, the child is made to go all the rounds of the physicians, so they can refresh their memory, perhaps for the first time see a case of quash core, out of a pool of many children in that particular city.

DR. deMONTIGNY: This is what is often termed an epidemological pyramid. You get the whole population in a given location and there exists a certain number of the population who might be exposed in some manner to a specific disease. There are some people who produce some subclinical symptoms, and they don't get sick enough to see a physician, or get tied down in the practical matters of life. You get some clinical cases, and of course, there are some deaths, and what we are trying to say here is that in a certain case we have a diagnosed death from it. But what we should really be dealing with is this whole "bottom" part of this pyramid. What we have is the iceberg of the pyramid. You have got somebody hospitalized for quash core, and that is the top of the iceberg. For every case serious enough for hospitalization, or serious enough for death, you have a whole series of lesser degrees of the specific illness, undetected.

HURLEY PARKHURST: If this is as big a problem as it seems, we should do something in regards to agricultural production. We should find out what these deficiencies are, and we ought to work on the crops that would be acceptable and what can be raised in a certain area, and explore the use of possible edible wild plants that might supplement the diet. This then, would be a partial solution to the problem that we are discussing. That is what I wanted to find out: What are the deficiencies, and what food supplies are missing so far as nutritional problems go.

242

DR. McKENZIE: If you will recall, at the White House Conference on Food, Health and Nutrition, these things were brought up and discussed. Recommendations were made. These have been sent to the White House. We are beginning to see initial signs that something may come out of this, so that now in our hospital in New Mexico, we have vitamins and food supplements that are available for mothers in the pre-natal stage. Now we have a provision whereby families can apply for food supplements, and food for younger children who are in the first year of life. These people can come to the hospital and sign their name, and it is given to them without charge. The next step is to educate them to the fact that these things are available. I think something is being done along that line.

A SPEAKER: I would like to discuss the problem of genetics.

DR. deMONTIGNY: Not only must we consider genetics, but you must of course have normal senses. A pretty high percentage of people on reservations can't hear because of ailments of various kinds. If the child is going to develop and he can't hear, he will have problems of course.

DAVID REDFOX: I would like to ask a question with regard to identity. How does this affect the child in its early years? I don't think it does myself.

DR. deMONTIGNY: What do you mean by early years, what age group are you referring to?

DAVID REDFOX: The first year, and I am inclined to think he doesn't need "identity" to develop until his later years.

CARL DOWNING: I think the identity of an individual, or to use the term self-concept, or self-image, has its initial stages in the first year. Equally important too, is his physical development. It's during the first year that you can do the most damage to an individual emotionally, and sometimes irreparable damage.

DR. deMONTIGNY: Well, it is generally believed the age is approximately 18 months. If I follow you correctly, you think that identity is a lot more important later on, when the person is verbalizing and comes in contact with a whole series of other people. I believe that what he is saying, is that this communication, from the time a child is first born, is carried out on a non-verbal level. The individual has to be recognized as an individual of some importance at an early age in order to develop. Therefore, they do have an identity, even though it is not expressed in verbal ways. Does that summarize it pretty well?

CARL DOWNING: To verify what I have said, the Harlow studies, with the chimpanzee, where the hard and soft mothers were utilized—one terry cloth and one chicken wire. In that experiment, those that had the "chicken wire mothers" grew up and didn't produce. I think these were only done in studies for about two years.

DOROTHY DAVIDS: I'm thinking about discipline and about sisters and brothers, interpersonal relationships, and maybe that it is some place in the whole sum total environment in relationship to other people.

DR. deMONTIGNY: What do you mean, interpersonal relationships?

DOROTHY DAVIDS: Psychological needs. The other thing that strikes me is that we sometimes divide these needs into physical needs, social needs and intellectual needs. In the urban needs, we take in the urban world; we take care of the spiritual needs on Sundays, which is consigned to the child, and the intellectual needs five days a week at school, and the physical needs during the recreational program in the homes. Well, perhaps we need an integrated environment, whereby the spiritual is not necessarily separated from the physical.

WILLIAM DEMMERT: This will refer to your original statement concerning what, if anything, we could receive from the behaviorist or the experimentalist of today. I think I would disagree with you that we haven't received any good from them. In order to exist in this modern world, we need to know not only our own culture and background. We need to understand the dominant culture. Until we do, we will have a problem with ourselves. So, if nothing else, there is one point that we can learn from modern psychological concepts.

DR. deMONTIGNY: Maybe I missed something. We have to learn to understand this, or learn to understand what our psychologists are saying?

WILLIAM DEMMERT: We have to understand the make-up of the dominant society, as well as the make-up of our own minor culture in order to have a wholesome and total environment that we are talking about. At the beginning, I think you made the statement that (and correct me if I am wrong) . . . we haven't received anything good from the behaviorists or from the experimentalists of today. I didn't challenge you on that, because I wanted to get on with the rest of these things, and I felt we might get bogged down on that one question.

DR. deMONTIGNY: What I dealt with was the approach and use of psychology which is for supporting the dominant society's status quo.

MARIGOLD LINTON: The word "identify" is used in many different ways, to answer a question raised earlier. It's clear that if a child doesn't have somebody that he can see as another person, because of some peculiar handling of the child by parents, in which the child grows up not to be able to identify, he can't tell where he ends and the world begins. Clearly, there has to be some model. There is some very good evidence, that if you don't have some kind of model, a child isn't going to be a child. I think the kind of model that is necessary depends upon what you want your children to grow up to be. I think it should be stated that you need siblings and discipline, and the answer is which is the one of the things that we want, or more, in a time when we can decide what we want to do. You can answer all of the other things in terms of what your end-product is.

A SPEAKER: Are these things matters that Indians need to be so much concerned with?

MARIGOLD LINTON: Are what things?

A SPEAKER: Children with the first year, for instance. I had always assumed that Indian mothers were good mothers.

MARIGOLD LINTON: I don't think that is the question. I think that Indian mothers are very, very varied and that is another thing we have been assuming, a generalization of the way that Indian mothers are. As an example, both of my brothers have married white women. How well my brother's children are being brought up by a lower class white mother, is a question . . . and I have very little faith in what they are doing to my brother's Indian children.

A SPEAKER: What I have been trying to say is that being born to be brought up by Indian mothers, wouldn't be of much concern.

MARIGOLD LINTON: I look around here, and the thing that strikes me is that I thought I would be a freak here because I am so white. It's very clear that I'm not the only one who has a nonIndian parent, and a lot of us have nonIndian parents. If you ask whether we need to be concerned about this . . . of course, we need to be concerned about it because none of us is the Indian that we're talking about who existed somewhere in our past, and our children aren't being reared by those people, either.

STEVE McLEMORE: I'm Cherokee and the Cherokee is supposed to be the most intermixed of all tribes. I remember when I was a boy there was a kid in school and we used to call him "Spec" and he was red-headed and freckle-faced. But he was on the rolls as a Cherokee Indian. I suspect he was about one-eighth, so he was, to all intents and purposes, white. But spiritually he wasn't. His mother wasn't white, obviously, because he was one of the most stubborn Cherokees and he wouldn't speak anything but Cherokee and this was a curious thing. This was in a deep backwoods Oklahoma Indian school, where almost nobody but Indians were students. This boy was accepted by the whole run of the school as a Cherokee. To be accepted legally, they had to be at least one-quarter blood quantum. But this mother had raised a red-headed, freckle-faced kid . . . an INDIAN kid. So it's the culture rather than the blood quantum. I think there are cases in history where white women have been captured, and after a few years of this "captivity" they have simply refused to go back to the white world from which they came. The woman wasn't kicked, nor was she hollered at, and she didn't want to go back, that was it.

DR. deMONTIGNY: Well, we are running overtime. I want to thank all of you for attending and giving so much to the discussion. We will adjourn this panel now on "Modern Psychology: The Case of the American Indian."

Said Alfonso Ortiz: "We anthropologists cannot continue year after year mindlessly reciting in the classrooms our litany of Indian exotica and assorted trivia. Speaking as an anthropologist, the Indian people will no longer permit us to get away with it. Speaking as an Indian, the students will no longer permit anthropologists to get away with it."

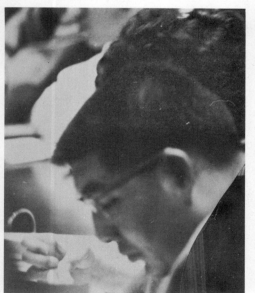

Early arrivals at morning session. The presentation subject: American Indian Philosophy and Its Relation to the Modern World.

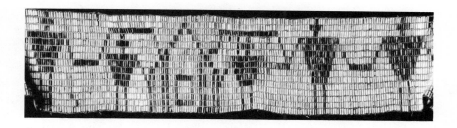

10

Indian Land Development: Good or Bad Economics?

ROBERT BENNETT

THE Chairman opened with these words: The panel on *Indian Land Development: Good or Bad Economics?* is now in session. I would like to start by reviewing what most of you may know already, but in terms of the orientation to the discussion, it is important we understand that we are talking about two different types of land: Tribal land, and Allotted land. In the case of tribal land, this is set aside by Treaties, Executive Orders, or Acts of Congress. There are certain types of authority these tribes have in relation to their land. Most tribes, of course, are prohibited from the sale of tribal land, except where some special legislation has been passed which authorizes the sale. Most tribes have authority to lease lands for 25 years, with an option for a 25-year renewal, except that some specific tribes have received authority from Congress for longer leases, as long as 99 years.

There is a basic disagreement between the Senate Committee and the House Committee with reference to authority to lease land for long periods of time. The Senate would like to pass a general bill authorizing the lease of land for a period of 60 years. The House, however, prefers that each tribe come to Congress for special authority for long-term leases. At the present time the Senate general bill has not been taken up by the House Committee, but there have been several Acts of Congress authorizing certain tribes to lease lands for long periods of time.

In connection with the Allotted land, the authority is primarily with the owners of these allotments with certain exceptions. Exceptions exist in reservations where there is considerable grazing land, which is in extremely complicated heirship status, in which Powers of Attorney have been granted. So that the BIA might lease land on behalf of owners. Any development involving allotted lands, is always complicated by the heirship status of that allotment. One reason why I believe that the heirship problem, with reference to allotted lands, has not been solved, is because it is the one problem that has many solutions and we can never get anybody to agree on one particular solution acceptable to all the heirs of any particular allotment.

My preference has always been to have a general authority to tribes and landowners, with several options. Each tribe can then determine the option under which it wishes to solve their heirship problem. Most of the political opposition comes from the initial "Church Bill" which did not give tribes the option they wanted—which was to purchase heirship land when it came up for sale. In carrying out the authority now existing, tribes are beginning to move away from the standard type of lease, which surrendered the land for a long period of time to a developer, made his money, and the tribe received only some small return in the way of annual rental. Tribes are now beginning to develop an interest in "getting a piece of the action." Most leases now, since tribes are beginning to develop such economic interests, make provisions for this. In such cases there is more or less of a partnership or joint venture, with the tribe putting up the land and the developer putting up the capital under a working arrangement which eventually provides that the tribe will own the particular development. In connection with the development of land owned by tribes, particularly near urban areas, there is an impact on the tribes. This was established as Congressional policy in connection with the long term leases of the Papago Tribe and the Salt River Tribe north of Mesa in Tempe, Arizona, and the Papago lands on the reservation just west of Tucson.

Here several conditions were put into the law, which require that the tribe conform to the zoning laws of the urban community, and the impact of urban community attitudes also is felt in the development of land, even where it is not a legal requirement. A case illustrating this was the attempt of a paper mill to be constructed on one of the Pueblos near the city of Albuquerque. There was so much pressure on the Pueblo because of the dangers of pollution, that the Pueblo people turned down the application of the paper company for constructing a mill on the Rio Grande River. In this case, both the tribe, the community, and the Indian people as a whole objected to the mill.

One of the policies of the government with respect to Indian land has been the economic view which the government takes of this resource. As trustee, the government attempts to get as much return from the resource as possible. This has run into conflict with some Indian owners of the property, who would like to see the land remain in its natural state. So here, I think, is the question of the conflict between maximizing the return from these resources, as against other views held in relation to pollution and the views held by the Indian people themselves with respect to the land. One case where such a reaction has been experienced, is that of the UTE Tribe in Utah, where for several years the members have approved a big game hunting program. This is a package deal, in which sportsmen have Indian guides, camps are set up, and a considerable amount of money is paid for this arrangement. A strict count has been kept on deer population in this area, which is not hunted too much by the Indians themselves. The kill under this program has been less than the allowable kill, but so much opposition has been developed by the tribe, that after this year the program will be discontinued. They are willing to forego the $40,000 a year profit, plus employment of several members, to maintain what they see as the balance of nature.

These are some of the areas that are giving concern to the tribes. One is that they not surrender this valuable resource for long periods of time, for a mere rental fee, preferring either to own the businesses themselves, or at least not having the capital to engage in joint ventures with developers of their property, they may in time participate as a partner at the outset of any program and eventually become sole owners of the project. I believe this latter is a coming trend. Again, inhibitions upon such development will be brought out in many areas by the tribal members, as they begin to see any kind of interference with the balance of nature, or how they might view their natural resources. The protection of their natural resources, and maintaining a balance of nature is being insisted upon, even to the extent of foregoing income which might come from certain developments. This is just a brief orientation to the subject. I will call upon each of the discussants for their comments. Then we can begin general discussion. Mr. Vincent Knight.

VINCENT KNIGHT: I go to A & M in New Mexico. Here the Chicanos have received some technical help, and have set up a non-profit corporation, which is eligible for grants. I'm trying to work out a plan for Indian reservations. The Chicanos don't have any BIA or federal laws controlling their lives. We Indians have to work through or around the BIA and the federal laws. For the sake of discussion, I'd like to throw this idea out. The first problem I'm running into is this: Can Indians as people, just band together and incorporate into non-profit corporations, like everybody else can? I've been researching BIA regulations, and so far as I see, they can. However, I'm not certain. Once they form a corporation, the next step would be to find the money, and ways they can develop their lands and economic status. I am referring to my own reservation. Let me do this on the blackboard. This is the Ponca reservation in Oklahoma. It's under the General Allotment Act. These people have lost their lands.

If there is a tribal corporation, I'd like to know if such corporations are eligible for federal funds or grants, such as are not coming from the BIA, HEW, or anywhere else. I'd like to conceive of this: There is mostly farm and grazing land. I want to find some money so that we can buy tractors, cattle, and so on. Hiring Indian people, mechanics who are Indian . . . preferably from the tribe itself, the economists also. Everything to come from right here (indicating Indian basis on board). What is generally termed "Indian Land Development" seems to me to look like this: There's a big company out there in New York City. They will put a little plant right here (indicating reservation). That's okay, I suppose, but I don't like that, because they just take our labor force, and the money goes back here (indicating area of New York City)—I want the money to stay here on Indian land and reproduce itself for the benefit of the people. We would consolidate the land as one big farming corporation and pay the people salaries, their share. We have to run a socio-economic survey of the area and will need to take into consideration the human resources available, natural resources, educational, availability of manpower, and the feasibility of the program under the existing laws, despite the BIA and the state and the federal laws.

The basic thing, is a private sector, using non-governmental agencies. You do it yourself . . . form your own organization independently. You don't need a BIA to tell you this is good or bad, or how to do it. It would be good to work with a tribal governing body, but that might cause some legal questions.

ROBERT BENNETT: We will ask Mr. Echohawk what views he has on the subject.

JOHN ECHOHAWK: As you are aware, the Indian is about the most poverty-ridden minority group in this country. Yet, we don't fit into the usual stereotype of a poor people. This is that they are poor and landless. We have fifty million acres in Indian land. In a country where land is the basis of wealth, the fact of our poverty is hard to realize. We ask "Why?" When you ask this, you find that there are really competing interests here. One of the basic considerations, is that we gain a livelihood from our land. But we have another consideration that most other Americans don't have to contend with. That is, we really have a crucial interest in maintaining our land base, because it's the basis of our whole culture. Once the reservations are broken up, as they have been through the Allotment Act, it weakens your tribe, your cultural ties. We've got these two interests, and if we want to develop these places we have to make them produce a good livelihood for our people. But we don't want it to slip away from us, because when it does we will be losing something that is a part of ourselves.

On the specific question of reservation development: the basic question is, what kind of an economy are we going to have on the reservation. What do we need? Right now, it's pretty well government financing and outside companies are brought in to provide jobs. But they take all the profits back to New York City, and we can't call that a self-sustaining economy. The tribal authorities have a great opportunity in this area, if we can get the people to do it, get the business "know-how," so that we can set up our own companies and keep our economy going. We can keep the money with our own people. The problem is an immediate one, and it brings out the trust status of the land. If we are going to develop as tribes, we must have some capital. How do you get loans? Well, you mortgage your property, lease it or some other way. Restrictions are seen right there. We can't go to a bank and say, lend me some money, and as collateral I'll put up my land. Our land is restricted. Therefore, we have to find a way to the private sector of the economy for financing. It looks like our only way out, again, is to try to negotiate with the private sector. Then you have difficulties immediately. On the one hand, we don't want to break down our land base, or to gamble with it either. That's what we will be doing if we mortgage our land, even if the federal laws allowed us to do it. We would endanger the status of the reservation. You might make a bad investment, and if we do we will lose a lot more than our land, because we wouldn't be allowed to make up the loss, say in some years of special contractual arrangements. We would lose everything. We will lose a part of ourselves.

What we can do is look to Congress. Part of the Omnibus Bill, presented in 1967, considered the question: Congress was to increase the availability of capital to the tribes. What was involved was a revolving fund. This fund now has some millions of dollars in it. Many people in Washington are fairly well satisfied with it. But, it's not enough. These proposals called for authorized expenditures of 500 million dollars to be placed in the revolving fund, payable to Indian tribes on terms they could meet. We've got to get this financing, the business know-how. As reflected in this group, we have Indians now who can handle some of these things. Some of our tribal authorities are a little skeptical about it, but I think if they look around they can bring in some of these people who major in business. Instead of working for the BIA, they can come back to the reservations and run these businesses. That's the kind of economy we need.

ROBERT BENNET: Thank you, Mr. Echohawk. Let's hear from Mr. Parkhurst now.

HURLEY PARKHURST: After attending many conferences, I find we have many problems. Some of our people are in pretty bad shape. I ask myself: What can I do to help? My field is horticulture, and I will discuss what can be done in this area. I'm not familiar with government, law, or other related matters. I'm looking at people, and what I can do to help them. What they can do to help themselves. First, a little history.

Indians have been industrial farmers. Most of the food we consume today are Indian foods: corn, popcorn, potatoes, sweet potatoes, tomatoes, field beans, lima beans, pumpkins, squash, peanuts, peppers, among many other foods. These are commonly known foods, raised by the American Indians a long time before the white man came. Corn is an example of crop adaptation. It grows from forty degrees south latitude to sixty degrees north latitude, from sea level to about 10,000 feet in altitude. It has a growing season from a hundred to 190 days, depending upon the variety. This was part of the economy before Columbus came. Our forefathers knew how to farm. I am discussing this to bring up some of our success in this area for those who believe Indians are not natural farmers.

As to commercial farming. This, I think, is the answer where we have agricultural land, where we can gain a profitable return. We have heard some talk about this in Oklahoma and other states, where they do have fairly level land, close transportation to market and possible sources of financing. A lot of Indian land isn't good for farming, or not good enough. Some of the land out west in mountainous area is too rough, too dry, too salty, too something . . . to be useful as a profitable commercial agricultural land base. Still, there are people living in those areas. Those people have to eat. They can do like Indians do in some places; go out and buy their food, and buy it under governmental commercial programs subsidized by various sources. My area of particular interest is in these particular people, the average Indian who doesn't have a lot of money to buy the food he needs. Perhaps the land is such that he can't raise what he needs. We have two answers here. One is to go out and show these people how to raise this food, in greater quantities than they have done, to help them from this point of view. Another is to utilize wild plants. First, I'll deal with the raising of the crop yield. We are dealing with farm technology here. During the last few decades science has been applied to agriculture to the point where they can get a crop yield undreamed of a few years ago. Taking this scientific knowledge into the backwoods places on the reservations, maybe we can apply some of it to help people who are farming for subsistence, farming to eat, to raise their crop yield. A great deal can be learned from these people. They have learned a lot that hasn't been done by our scientists, commercial farmers, because they have an entirely different situation. We can help through soil tests, moisture content of the soil, as an example. Testing this, and telling them how to use and find a better crop variety, and perhaps limit the use of fertilizer to their means.

The answers we have to find are such that they can be used with the existing finances available, and their land. Plant breeding is another area to be considered. There are ways of plant breeding which can be used to bring up better adapted plants for specific areas. I could use some of the technical jargon, and tell you the various types of plant breeding schemes, but I think this could be easily taught to people. Farming is not such a complicated thing that it requires a degree. I suspect most farmers don't have one and they are better farmers than I am, degree or not.

So those of us who have some knowledge can help others in raising their crop production yield. We should go out there. I feel that this is what I want to do, go out and help with what knowledge I can, to get something better for our Indian people.

In other words, what is needed is the teaching of practical agriculture. Finding ways that they can use what they have right there, to raise their crop yields, so that they eat a little better. Perhaps freeing some money for education and medicine or whatever they wish to spend it on. Yesterday, I heard a doctor talk about nutritional problems on the Navajo reservation. I don't know much about this, but I'm sure there are some crops that they can raise which are acceptable for them to eat, which would help them to solve the problem of nutritional deficiency. Perhaps we could find some edible wild plants that they can utilize in this area. As I look back, our forefathers used these, and I don't think there is any doubt that each tribe had its own knowledge about wild plants used for medicine, food and fiber.

I've done a little checking on this in my spare time, and I found more than eleven hundred species of wild plants throughout the United States, Canada, and North America in general. I look back when I was a kid back home. We ate wild plants, not always because we were hungry, but we ate them because we enjoyed them. Some wild plants taste pretty good. I'll just give you a few examples. I think of the springtime when we used to go out and gather leeks. We went out and gathered a washtub full of these at a time, and boiled them all day long, then fried them in butter. This is really a treat. There was only one drawback. It has a garlic smell and you have to cook it outdoors. The school that we attended in those days asked us Indians to please eat this food all during one week and the teacher wouldn't be feeling too badly about it.

Wild strawberries, I think you all know about these. We used to go out and gather wild strawberries. They are about the size of peas, and the way we used to use them, was to make them into our bread. What they call wild strawberry bread. This is very tasty and it's a utilization of a wild food source. I'm trying to think of other things we used. Lamb's quarters that's a weed that grows around damp places. In our area it grew around manure piles. This weed is kind of like spinach. We would go out and gather this all summer long and we'd boil it and serve it with hard-boiled sliced eggs and vinegar. I still like this better than spinach.

I found this plant throughout most of the United States where most green plants grow. Now I'm going to describe a few uncommon plants that people wouldn't think were edible. Bul-rushes, burdock, most cactii, cattails, pigweed. Some people call pigweed "redwood." Kwakrats . . . in the past these have been ground up and used for a kind of meal or flour. Stinging nettles. You wonder about this, because they are not much fun to handle. But when they are cooked, all the hairs that give you so much trouble are no longer any trouble. You can safely eat boiled nettles.

Now, I'll give you the vitamin content of some of these wild plants a bit later. But let's continue with some of these little-known plants. Thistles, who would have thought thistles were edible. I didn't know this. I have gone into this area somewhat, and I'm beginning to find out many interesting commonly nuisance-type weeds and plants that could be eaten, could be used. The best way to get rid of your enemies is to eat them.

Let us discuss vitamins and minerals. This may be a problem where there are nutritional deficiencies. Vitamin A: dande-lion, lamb's quarters, pigweed. These are edible plants that are high in vitamin A, and these are very widespread. Vitamin C: lamb's quarters, pigweed, rose hips. That's the little bulbous part beneath the flower on rose hips. Stinging nettles and wild strawberries. Now I don't know about wild strawberries. They don't grow very well in the desert country. But we have roses out there, and nettles in some of the same areas. These are high in Vitamin C. This could be a food supplement. Some of these things won't taste all that good. It depends. You have to become suited to it, I suppose. Develop a taste for it. I think roses would taste good because they smell so nice.

In connection with one of the wild plants, there is one caution I have. There are some poisonous plants that look like edible plants. Therefore, it's not a matter of going out and grabbing any wild plant you see. You have to be a little cautious in what you are doing. You've got to know if a plant is edible before you eat it. But if you want to experiment a bit, then the way to do it is to eat a little bit and wait for results. If you feel sick after half an hour or so, then don't continue. If you don't get sick, try a little more of it. Just don't go out there and eat a whole lot all at once, if you aren't sure of the plants you are gathering. What I am describing here is something you don't hear much about. One of the possible answers for people who have a food supply problem is to use our weeds for food.

A lot of Indians are moving into cities, like the place where I'm going to school. It has been said that there are ten thousand Indians there now. Of course, agriculture is not really going to be handy for these people living in town. They could use some of these wild plants. I saw a number of these growing right along the sidewalk, in cracks of sidewalks, and if you're not too proud to bend down and take some of these, I think this would help. There are miniature varieties of food crops, too. They came out with miniature corn, tomatoes, cucumbers, musk melon, lettuce, radishes, and so on. What we've been doing, experimentally, is to see what kind of a yield you can get with such miniature varieties. We grow these in tin cans and stick them in the window. There are some growing now, and I would like to see if something happens, if we can get something useful out of this. It might be an answer to city dwellers who don't have the money to buy vegetables.

I just want to throw these ideas out at you. Mainly, my point is that there are two or three ways we can help out commercial agriculture. Great. Let's get in there and do what we can, in such practical directions. Still, for people who don't have good land we can try to help them raise what it is possible, so that they can help themselves. I'd like to do what I can to make people self-sufficient. What's acceptable to them, to make them independent of help. I know we have been getting government food supplements and vitamins and so on. But how long will the government be giving us the things we need in the way of food and supplements? And how good are these? We have to find some solution we can manage ourselves independently, to make us free of such aid.

My personal plans are, when I get through graduate school, to go into Agricultural Extension Service, and bring aid from that organization to fellow Indians, to bring in knowledge and experience from this organization directly to the people.

I know I don't have any great and glorious plans in connection with dealing with the government, because I personally don't have much faith in anything to do with big organizations. It doesn't lead to much immediate action.

ROBERT BENNETT: Mr. Knight raised the question about Indian people who own land and the possibility of forming corporations to receive grants and other financing, to economically develop their own property. He also expressed a concern that from some kinds of industrial development no secondary benefits accrued to the tribe or tribal members. The primary benefits they are able to receive are the wages they get. But the economy does not get any secondary benefits from such programs. He also raised some question as to whether the group of Indian people could incorporate into such a corporation and whether they could receive grants, whether or not such a proposal was feasible.

Mr. Echohawk raised the question that you have Indian people owning so much of the land in the United States, yet they are classed as poverty people, and that this is quite distinctive from most of the other people in poverty, because most of them are not land based, or do not own land to the extent the Indian people do. He pointed out the Indian interest in land as more basic to the Indian than this economic interest, because it is the basis for their culture. He recommended very strongly that Indian owned companies and Indian owned businesses develop these resources, but there were handicaps because there were restrictions on financing, and the desire of the Indian people to maintain the trust status of their property must be considered as paramount. He felt revision of the proposed Omnibus Bill, which increased the revolving fund to some five hundred million dollars, was desirable because of the fact that capital was needed in order to develop resources.

Mr. Parkhurst pretty well summarized his own statements, so the meeting is now open to questions, comments, or discussion.

DISCUSSION

Indian Land Development: Good or Bad Economics?

MICHAEL MISIASZEK: I thought the second speaker, Mr. Echohawk, had a very good idea. On our reservation, one of the main problems in economic development is to get the educated people, with a degree of some kind, back on the reservation, to help the people who live there, and who don't themselves have the education or ability to better themselves without such help. I think that once we can get an organization started on our reservation, it wouldn't be so much farming as it would be timber. We are in a mountainous area, and timber is the primary way of making a living there. If we can get some kind of industry going there, owned and operated by the Indians themselves, that would be a great incentive for the educated Indians to come home and help develop their own land. Instead of going off the reservation to make a living, without really making any effort to help the others, there's the incentive to draw them back to the reservation, where they have an opportunity not only to better themselves but to help those that don't have the ability to do so.

A SPEAKER: I want to address this to Mr. Knight. Let's take the problem of financing a particular situation like that of the Poncas, where the tribal area has non-tribal people interspersed. It seems to me that one of the problems of financing is the inability of the tribes to alienate by mortgage or any other means, certain rights for a period of time. But it comes to my mind that a thing to be used, and something that I have been using, is the concept of tribal property in this sense. I think things can be worked out with the BIA. I think financing can be had from private financial institutions, in the sense that whatever the land is worth, only wages are paid out. This, to me . . . a job for a tribal member, is the profit motive. Their children are eating. They are being educated. They are being clothed, fed, entertained. This, to me, is a profit. And you could use whatever remaining profits until you got to a point where you could be independent. You could also cut your prices. You can undercut any other corporation in the country, even the Japanese corporations, by not insisting on shareholder profits, because the shareholders are the tribal members. So long as the tribal members have a job, and you don't have heavy management expenses, this can be done. You do have investments in equipment, and in land. But the thing of it is, this is for the benefit of the tribe and you're also profiting in a way. You're gaining title to the other land. I think this might defeat the idea of a non-profit organization, but in this case, you wouldn't need a non-profit organization.

VINCENT KNIGHT: The reason I used the non-profit idea is because most federal agencies, when they do grant monies, require you to be non-profit, and most private sectors like the Ford Foundation also have the same requirement. The Chicano organization I was talking about is a conglomerate. The basic grant is here, it's both governmental and private contributions. Underneath the initial lending agencies you have profit making corporations. I mean, they can make money, but in other words, this lower structure can make money, this other structure cannot

JACK RIDLEY (left) and WILLIAM THACKER, during a Panel recess. In background, facing camera, DONALD ROSS, and MARY NELSON.

make money in the form of profit. I understand also that the new income tax law passed by Congress put a limitation on this kind of thing. We have a non-profit grantee controlling all the stock or some of the stock in a profit-making corporation. I ran across this from one of my professors and he did not know the extent of it and nobody does, because it has just been passed. It is a direct change from existing law.

I'd like to respond to the question put to me by the previous speaker. You say the educated people leave the tribe and reservation, and there are no educational facilities. You made a very good point. We have all these scholars around somewhere who are Indians. I would like to see people like Mr. Parkhurst, who is an agricultural economist, set up a business as the head man, and we'll hire him to come down and do the socio-economic survey. The law students here can form some sort of an organization, and we'll hire them—you know, keep the money within the Indian people. I mean, not just here, and on my own reservation, but nationally as well.

JACK RIDLEY: I'm in the department of planning and science at University of Idaho, and I function with the agriculture department in the state of Idaho. As such, I'm also responsible, not only for research and graduate work in this connection, but to the farmers in the area. It's rather interesting that there are some other problems that have come about. One is that Fort Hall is being left open for intensive agriculture. This reservation does not support its people right now. Yet we have a problem in concept here, that the Indian won't get off his horse to look at farming. They would rather work from the back of a horse. you have the break in concept here: what is good and noble? I feel that farming is good and noble. They don't. I'm also involved with the Nez Perce. My wife has land on that reservation, and I've asked her what do you know about it. She knows nothing. It's being handled by the BIA. So I've taken it upon myself. I've got her relatives who are on this land, who agree with me and I go back to the person who wants to lease the land then say, "Look, this is what we will do." Often I wonder why these tribes don't go outside the BIA . . . have somebody else take a look at it. I offer my services to the tribes and take official time off in the name of agriculture to do these things. I'm glad to see that I have a fellow friend here who is also going into agriculture.

PETER LITTLE: I'm a student at New Mexico majoring in social welfare. This is directed to Mr. Knight. Corporations are not new to our tribe We have had a Cattle Growers' corporation for several years now and we have some five or six thousand head of cattle. It's run on corporation status. We have our Cattleman's board and the Indians are shareholders. The first five years it was planned on a non-dividend basis, and after five years they were able to start paying dividends. So far it has worked well. The point I'm trying to get across is that this is not new.

VINCENT KNIGHT: Could you relate to us how you got around the BIA. Did you manage to do this on your own?

PETER LITTLE: It involved quite a bit of work. Originally, the association was set up on what they call a multiple brand system, in which various members had cattle run on the reservation with their individual brands. This got out of hand through heirship incumbrances and the complexity of that problem. So they incorporated where they had a one-brand system, like a regular outside corporation. They also resorted to outside financing. They borrowed from various banks to carry on the corporation. But to begin with, they had the cattle, which was an asset to them. They still use the BIA, but on a consultative basis. They have been very successful without the BIA.

RUPERT COSTO: I happen to know that there was considerable opposition from the white cattlemen, in the first instance, opposing you in organizing this corporation. There was a great deal of difficulty. I'm a cattleman too, and I know many of your people in this venture. What I am interested in is this: We are talking about agriculture per se. Now, as was stated here, there is, on various reservations, a great quantity of grazing land. In the plains country, much of it is rented to white people. Most of it has even been sold to white people . . . *sold*. I noticed in one of the newspapers from Pine Ridge, where they offered for sale some fifty or sixty parcels of Indian land. Why is this being done? There are plenty of young people from these tribes who want land; they are not getting it.

From my investigation, and experience of many years, on these leases that the Bureau has with the white cattlemen, the grazing land is leased at a ridiculously low price. In other areas, where land is being used by industry, with leases of 99 years, hiring perhaps 15 to 20 people to start with, and taking over the leadership and direction of the tribes, they are destroying the initiative of the young people. Certainly Indians have no decision-making powers. In other areas, like the Coachella Valley, in California, one of the most famous areas for growing winter crops, the Indians there still have thousands of acres of land. The All American Canal came down through there, but not one piece of Indian land got any water out of it. The white farmers got water. The Indian farmers got no water. The Bureau did not supply them with water either, and there was no way in the world of getting it.

I know many people, and I'm talking about Indian people, who have had to sell their lands because they couldn't utilize it without water. They didn't have the money to install pipe lines, or irrigation lines to bring water into the property. This has certainly resulted in loss of land, the finest land in the country, and still to this day, these Indian people don't have water. The reason for this may be a squeeze play to get the Indians to dispose of their land, since they cannot support any economy, or grow any crops, or in short do anything without water. I know that cooperatives have been successful on many reservations. Such as the Cattlemen's Association mentioned here. I believe the Flatheads have organizations too, and are doing well. But there must be some initiative among the Indians, so that some of these things can be done. I don't know where it's going to start, but I think it has got to start from the tribal groups themselves. On the other hand, we have our tribal leadership, most of which is practically under the dierection of the Bureau of Indian Affairs. They are, in many places, merely rubber stamps for the Bureau. It is only quite recently that some of the younger people are getting on the governing boards, tribal committees and councils.

Let me note also, the Owyhee Reservation in Nevada. I believe they have a Cattlemen's organization there, and they are doing very well. How they have been financed, I don't know. But I do know they are doing well there with their herd of cattle. Some individual Indian farmers are doing well too. We have a young gentleman here, who incidentally, was the Farmer of the Year in 1969. Here is Bill Thacker, sitting right in front of me. He is a Paiute of Nevada. There are indeed possibilities among our people and we do indeed have the expertise to do these things. But we don't have the financing in order to do it. Many times our own tribal organizations are the obstacles holding us back.

WILLIAM THACKER: Mr. Costo has a good point there. As he stated, I was just selected in Nevada as outstanding farmer of the year. This is sponsored by the National J.C. and I have competed for it the last four years. I worked real hard, and got financially in debt for it. I know that each of you have your problems. Well, we all do, just like Jack Ridley was saying. Jack is from Nevada too. He was at the University of Nevada when I was there, and like Mr. Echohawk said, this financing is quite a problem. On our reservation, we have a revolving credit fund and we give loans to individuals. For housing loans, there is a 4% interest rate. Agricultural loans, 5% interest. For those who have animals, say 15 or 20 head, we could mortgage, we refer them to the Farmer's Home Administration, and they carry them for five or six years to the point where they can let them go. They have an FHA loan for 5 or 6 years, and if they're financially able to carry themselves, the Farmers Home Administration will let them go and refer them to the bank at higher interest.

It's a step by step process. If you want to stand it all your life, you can move right up and as you move up you can get bigger if you want to. On our reservation, we just took it kind of on our own. On the Farmer of the Year award, 50% is counted on progress in agriculture; 25% on soil and water conservation; 25% on your contribution to your community. This soil and water conservation is something I had an awful hard time with. I rated very low in this, during the first two years, because we have this land and water problem on our reservation. Our reservation developed through the BIA special program in land for the Indians. I just happen to fall in the wrong end of the valley. So I didn't qualify. I don't think I will for another ten years. So I took it upon myself to do it alone. There was no farm machinery available for us through the Bureau. We would ask for it, but we couldn't get it. When we did get some, we had to repair it before it could be used. What I and most of the duys did, is to work through the Soil Conservation District in Apple County. This has worked real good for us. They will pay 50% of our seeding, and 50% of our cost for land development. Our seeding and land preparation, they pay 50%, which makes it nice, because it would cost you two or three thousand dollars to develop a piece of land, and they come through with fifteen hundred. This is one way we found to develop ourselves, through the Soil Conservation District. There are many problems we have to overcome on our reservation. The Indians have taken it upon themselves to go ahead and do it. Things are different on most other reservations.

A SPEAKER: One of the problems we have now, as Mr. Costo said, is getting any type of land development program through the tribal council. Right now, our tribal council in Colville is for termination. If they want to terminate, any type of land development program is vetoed. They don't want this development program to happen, because if the majority of the people found out in the long run they would be money ahead by developing the land they've got—as against termination—they would be opposed to termination. Right now they're trying to keep things hushed up. They don't want any type of help, or any group of people who could explain the progress and economic stability they could have in developing their own land. We have great potential—terrific! There's timber, minerals, just idle now. There's nothing we can do unless we can get it through the council.

JESSE GREEN: How do we get around Title 25 (Indians), which is utilized by the BIA as a Constitution for Indians? We have a land lease enterprise, supported by tribal money. We have a lease sub-committee within the governing board, created two and a half years ago, to try to increase the rental on tribal lands. There are individual leases and tribal lands. The governing body controls the tribal lands, but individual leases are controlled by the tribal member. We try not to dictate, but if they want to ask questions or help, we give it to them. In most cases, they will not ask. Of course, that lease goes into the land lease enterprise and then they have the expertise from the BIA. On the development of tribal lands, the governing board of our tribe, by the constitution, controls all tribal lands and reserves.

The question I want to pose is this: Taking illustration #2 on the board, where you have blocks. Some are crossed in and some are left open. We will assume the ones that are crossed in are tribal lands and the others we'll say are individual lands or agricultural lands. We will also say that the crossed ones are timber. (I started this in 1965, when I was elected to the governing board.) Why couldn't we develop these tribal lands? They are not cleared, the timber was taken off already. It will be another fifty years before the timber will be ripe enough to cut. Most of it will probably not be cut, because the stand is what you call too thick and it can't grow. Now, we'll say in those sections there, we have approximately 2,200 acres of land that in some cases is nothing but scrub pine, and is sparsely covered with timber. Up to now we couldn't get the okay. The BIA will not let us clear that 2,200 acres and this is what they rely on: Title 25. How do we get around Title 25, so that we can clear that land. Or, how does anyone in that situation?

ROBERT BENNETT: It all depends on whether Title 25, in that case, is an administrative regulation or is based on an Act of Congress. If it's an Act of Congress, you can appeal to have the regulation modified, if you don't feel it's important to the particular Act of Congress. Or, you can seek an amendment to that Act. I think, the first thing Title 25 will indicate is whether it's based on an Act of Congress or not. There is always a tendency in government, when you have a broad general authority, that the regulations are more restrictive than the law itself. Quite often, even under the same Act of Congress, you can probably get it re-written, if you think it's too restrictive. On the other hand, if it quite clearly follows the Act of Congress itself, you have to get the Act amended.

RUPERT COSTO: Here is something I think many tribes are overlooking. We ran into it down in our country several years ago, when it first came into effect. This is the payment for agricultural practices, like letting land lie fallow for a year or two or putting in some sort of conservation project, like contour farming or control of flood waters. When this first came into effect, all the white farmers who were our neighbors were making use of these laws. Of course, the Indians were talking about them, but the white farmers said we were not entitled to get any monies for this. But we got them just the same, like any other citizen. We obtained payment for letting the land lie fallow and using contour farming and for various other practices approved by the Conservation District.

We were entitled to it. Every Indian is entitled to it, if they are ranchers or farmers. Another thing we did, was to establish a Conservation District and a great deal of the planning and advice was done in cooperation with them, such as surveying, supplying of caterpillars and other equipment, at very nominal cost. These things can be done, but you have to know what you are doing. Another thing we did on our reservation, which benefitted the whole country, white and Indian both, was to establish a Rural Electrification Administration District. I think there were probably only four Indians including myself who wanted this. But immediately upon the power lines being established, everyone on the reservation blossomed out with a radio, a television, refrigerators, appliances, and farm equipment. You can do these things if you have the proper leadership, and it isn't necessary to go through the BIA. You can get these things by practicing conservation. I'm sure they are still in effect.

These are available to Indian people, but you have to ask for them and go through proper channels. In most instances you can get what you want and I hope that a lot of you people request these things because they are practical and benefit you and the reservation as a whole. As for these cooperatives, they can be worked out to great advantage for the people. It has to be done with everyone cooperating and everyone wanting them. With you young fellows coming along who are doing the things I spoke of, you can help to solve many of our problems. I think you should take more active part in your tribal governments. Both men and women. If you do this you will progress more rapidly than we have in the last hundred years, because now is the time. We have you young men and women, who are our greatest asset.

A SPEAKER: Could you give us a brief rundown on the history of this revolving loan fund?

ROBERT BENNETT: The revolving fund was set up by the Indian Reorganization Act of 1934, and was continued for Oklahoma, the Oklahoma Welfare Act, the Navajo-Hopi Act, and the Alaska Welfare Act. Initially these funds were used for financing industries with relatively short repayment schedules. Like the loans would be out for five years or ten years at the most. This fund went up to several million dollars and was loaned out and paid back. There was a continual source of funding for such things. However, in the last few years the big tribal drive to buy land began. Where formerly you would get a $50,000 loan repayable in 5 or 10 years in support of some industry like cattle, now you are loaning $50,000 for thirty years.

So, as more and more funds were loaned out for land on thiryt-year loans, that takes three times as long for the money to come in, and this is actually what happened to the fund. Of course, there were also other increased demands for small loans What stopped this quick turnover of the money was the millions of dollars put out to buy land and the money coming back very, very slowly; a thirty-year loan as distinguished from a five- or ten-year loan, and this exhausted the amount of available funds.

A SPEAKER: How much money was available?

ROBERT BENNETT: I think it's been added to time and

*BEN HANLEY, participant at panel In-
novations in Education.*

time again. I think it's around twenty-five or thirty million dollars.

A SPEAKER: But it never achieved the half billion?

ROBERT BENNETT: That half billion has never been authorized.

A SPEAKER: It's still in committee?

ROBERT BENNETT: Every time we get the bill recorded
out of committee, the committee in the Senate ties the Heirship
Bill to it, which the Indians politically don't want. So we are
caught in the position of not being able to push the revolving
loan increase or increasing the authorization for further lending
because if you do that then you buy the Heirship Bill with it,
which the Indians reject. This is a problem. Also incorporated
with this bill to increase the authorization for the revolving
fund were two other features. One authorizing the Secretary of
the Interior to insure loans from private financing and also authorizing the Secretary to guarantee loans made from private
financing. But the minute the Senate attaches this Heirship Bill
to it then the Indian people back away from it.

A SPEAKER: Well, is there any particular Senate that
continues to attach this particular Heirship Bill or do they just
run it around the bush or what?

ROBERT BENNETT: I think it's done in the committee.

A SPEAKER: Can anybody point a particular finger at a
particular Senator?

ROBERT BENNETT: There's so much going on in the Senate right now that there's a great dependency on committees, staff. So if you have a man on the committee staff you know very well Mr. James Gamble is the one that attacks this Heirship Bill every time it comes up.

A SPEAKER: Where a tribe has a large land base, and I'm talking now about a tribal corporation, where they are driving lease money, is it possible for them to use their future lease receipts as futures to float loans?

ROBERT BENNETT: So far they have been accepted by the government for security, but I don't know of any case where it's accepted by private financing institutions. I believe this is going to change, because there are now several million dollars of tribal funds that are out on deposit in private financial institutions. So, I think, that this is going to pave the way for more transactions between tribes and private financial institutions.

The reason this step was taken was to take advantage of the high interest rate because the Treasury of the United States only pays four per cent simple interest on the principal. And whenever an interest payment is made it is put into a separate account and not added to the principal.

But if you have this money in private lending institutions you're getting up to seven and three quarter per cent and you're getting compounded interest on certificates of deposit, short certificates of deposit, that is. Thirty, sixty, ninety, six months, twelve months. I believe, this is going to create a very favorable climate for the entry of Indian businessmen into the private money market.

A SPEAKER: Maybe you covered this, but I didn't hear it. For instance, at Rosebud, the tribal land enterprise, how was that incorporated? Was that incorporated by the tribal council or is that a separate corporation or the tribes corporate charter, or IRA Charter or what?

ROBERT BENNETT: The tribal land enterprise at Rosebud is a separate tribal corporation.

A SPEAKER: But it's chartered by the tribe?

ROBERT BENNETT: Yes. It's approved by the government and has its own board of directors. The tribal land enterprise at Rosebud is one which is a stock corporation wherein they issue redeemable stock certificates to owners of land and the corporation takes title to the land. These certificates are redeemable on presentation to the tribe for cash and dividends are paid on these certificates, if you keep them— so much a year depending on the appraisal value of the land and the income from it. So the certificates, where you have a certificate that represents a certain interest in this corporation twenty years ago and has kept it's value has grown with the value of the land.

The only problem that has arisen in connection with it is that sometimes the tribes don't have the ready cash to redeem the certificates at the time you may want the money, but they are gradually improving on that.

HURLEY PARKHURST: Now, the Indians, the young men that are veterans, has anyone gone through the Veterans Administration for loans for business?

ROBERT BENNETT: Yes. There have been several loans made to veterans, but I think the number of veterans' loans for agricultural oriented economic enterprises is in a very small percentage compared to the loans made to veterans for other kinds of business or uses. You know, like housing or automobiles and things of this kind. You always run into this predicament in general legislation, because the solicitors of these various agencies get into various kinds of legal arguments whether or not Indians are eligible.

In order to get around that I doubt that the policy of having tribes specifically in place of Indianss so that when they say that the juvenile delinquency program, the enforcement assistance administration, the law specifically states that these grants, and so forth can be made to states, counties, cities and Indian tribes. And that's right in the legislation and you don't need to get into all the arguments like we had with the general housing bill, which the Indians were denied for so long. By having Indian tribes right in the legislation, then there is no argument. They have Indians declared as eligible right in the law, rather than these long legal arguments afterwards.

A SPEAKER: How can you make the BIA more responsible and more responsive to the people they govern?

ROBERT BENNETT: This is a bureaucratic disease. It's not limited to the Bureau of Indian Affairs. It has its origin in many things. First of all, you get a law, and then it says the law shall be administered under the regulations of the Secretary of the Interior. In most cases, these regulations are more restrictive than the law itself is. This is true of most national programs. The problem arises in the administration of these regulations, because under the regulations you have a commissioner who has considerable latitude. He will operate in this area and then he passes his duties on to the next guy and so within the Commissioner's direction, he has a latitude in which he can operate in carrying out such regulations.

You get a broad authority, and while delegation of authority is practiced and acceptable in administration, as long as there are people in these jobs, this is the way it happens. So you take your broad law, with restrictive regulations, and by the time it gets down to lower levels where the action is, it is even more restrictive. This happens in all bureaucracies.

A SPEAKER: Does the Indian Act apply to what we are discussing here, or does this act only cover services which were taken over by tribes? Could an individual here, who wants to become an entrepreneur, get some of this action, or does it apply at all?

ROBERT BENNETT: It applies. It's an act of 1910, that the Secretary of the Interior can acquire goods and services from Indians and it has been interpreted to mean tribes and individuals. So that there are several types of contracts under the Indian Act, which are available to individuals, groups of individuals or tribes.

BEN HANLEY: I believe that Indian land development can best be accomplished through a corporation. I want to comment more on that. A non-profit corporation, I don't think it necessarily has to be non-profit. It could be a very profitable venture. These corporations can be set up with an Indian board of directors controlling and this can operate on a tribal basis or a group of individual Indians. I think we have the managerial skills to incorporate. Once they incorporate you get to the funding program. I think that comes easy when you're a corporation. One of the good points of being a corporation is you reduce the risk of loss. You have a limited liability, which is good to consider.

As to the funding problem, you can contract government services. The government is always coming out with some research program. You can go into agriculture and say, we'll do a research program on the reservation. Contract them, get the funds for this. This will be independent of BIA or any other governmental agencies. The funds will be there, but we will be doing the work for ourselves. We will be pumping the economy back into the reservations themselves. The Indians themselves will be taking the money back among themselves. This is a very reasonable approach, to bypass the BIA, which hasn't done much. We've got to take the initiative.

VINCENT KNIGHT: A while ago, when I drew my conglomerate, the head structure was non-profit, and the sub-corporations were profit making. The reason I set it up this way is because the non-profit corporations have a lot less taxes to pay if any. These people here can make profits, and this goes back to the non-profit education (for example).

BEN HANLEY: I realize this. But what I'm saying is the corporation can be tailored to your needs. Our lawyers presently know these and we will point them out for you and develop corporations and take the Indians with us.

(Whereupon there was a 30-minute recess)

ROBERT BENNETT: We will reconvene our panel. When we recessed, the discussion was around the concept of developing corporations owned and managed by Indian people, who would engage in economic enterprises using the resources of the tribe as probably a better way than the continual leasing of these resources to other developers, with only a small rental return to the tribes. This was the last comment we had, and we were getting into the advantages of using corporations in terms of tax benefits and freedom from liability and so forth. Do we have any other comments?

A SPEAKER: If you hire strictly Indian help and no white people working in such a corporation, is there any tax benefit to be derived?

ROBERT BENNET: The tax you avoid is the income from trust land. Whether it's for crops or whatever. A corporation also has certain tax advantages the ordinary person working on a salary does not have. Under the law, however, you would be required to pay social security income tax deductions.

JOHN ECHOHAWK: Depending upon where your reservation is, and your jurisdictional situation, there may be some question as to whether the state could impose their income tax on wages of Indian employees. There are some suits occurring right now in the southwest where the same question is being litigated. It's essentially a question of jurisdiction. So far, it looks like the state of Arizona will start taxing the Indian employees working on the reservation.

A SPEAKER: Would that depend upon whether or not the state has jurisdiction on the reservation? On our reservation, they voted for state jurisdiction. That would be a vital factor. If we hadn't done that, they would have had no jurisdiction. Is that right?

JOHN ECHOHAWK: You would have the same problem as the Navajos. You would be litigating the same thing.

A SPEAKER: I'd like to pursue this Indian Act a little more. From my interpretation, it looks like, an individual who wants to start his own business by contracting services from the BIA could utilize this act. It also looks like tribal development through contracting services, now being performed by the BIA, could be contracted by the tribe, which means this might be an avenue where the tribe could set itself up in a better financial position. Also they would be taking some services away from the Bureau. How does a tribe or an individual use this Act? Who funds it and for how long?

ROBERT BENNETT: The BIA Indian Act is being used increasingly for goods and services. Under the authority it has, it can be acquired from individuals, groups of Indians, or tribes. The kinds of contracts that are in existence today are the rental of bureau Agency space in a tribal building. This is taking place at Winnebago and Fort Peck. Within 8 to 10 years, the tribe will have the loan paid off on the building, financed by HUD or EDA, from rent the BIA pays. In addition, they have the use of the building for their own tribal activities. Another area is busing. The BIA has a contract on the Cherokee reservation, with a Cherokee Boys' Club. They operate the whole bus system for the schools. In Alaska we had a catering contract. In other words, we contract with the local communities, and they perform the services. There are road construction and maintenance contracts with the Apaches. This has opened opportunities with other federal agencies, particularly because of the isolated areas where most of the Indian reservations are. Other federal agencies like the Forest and Parks Service are also entering into contracts with Indian people.

The Zuni tribe has a contract with the Forest Service. There must be between 15 and 20 tribes now that contract with the Bureau to operate the General Assistance Program. Administration of this program requires work on tribal projects. It's usually in the wintertime. One consideration is that the minute you pay federal funds for services, the individual becomes a federal employee. But by making the grant to the tribe, they can acquire these services, so our contract is with the tribe. This variety of contracts are now being undertaken between Indians and BIA under the BIA-Indian Act.

We were having some difficulties . . . rumblings . . . from the Solicitor's office on this. I hope they don't come out with any restrictive ruling on it, because this Bi-Indian contract is a good tool for eliminating the agency town. You have an agency town, and in the center of it you have the agency compound, which was inherited from the military. When the military left, the civil government moved in. They had all capabilities for community services, construction of public buildings, operation of all kinds of programs, utilities, water systems. Then there were the Indian families in this town. In terms of their participation in the community and having any voice, they might as well have lived 50 or 100 miles away. More recently, the tribe and individual Indians have been given the capability for public buildings, public utilities, and so on. This means, that through the BIA-Indian Act, individuals and tribes can begin by contract to take over the providing of all these services and the position is that we have authority to sell these utilities to a tribe or a group, and they will furnish the services. The Winnebago and Fort Peck groups did; they got money and erected public buildings.

All of these controls, which the federal establishment had, the community could get through the Bi-Indian Act, and can be transferred over to the Indian community. Care of the children in boarding schools, feeding in the schools, operation of utilities, eventually becoming landlords for all the governmental activities, including operation of the school bus routes and everything. This begins to put the economy, as was discussed earlier, in the hands of the local people, as distinguished from a transient group, which most federal employees' groups are, who are transferred in and out after three or four years. Eventually, this becomes entirely a community-controlled and owned operation, with the federal government as the tenant. I think this can be used in tribes. Some tribes are taking a good look at this, and intend to move in this direction. Some tribes will wait and see. Others are not a bit interested.

A SPEAKER: I might add that this Bi-Indian Act has provided the threshold of contracting all the BIA services and at least some of the tribes are taking a good hard look at it.

ROBERT BENNETT: Through this process, you get a reduction of federal employees; we estimate at least 50%.

A SPEAKER: Would there also be a corresponding reduction of the fund allocation to the tribes?

ROBERT BENNETT: No, because the government is still responsible for the services, and as long as they are responsible they have to appropriate the money. This is nothing new. The government has already made substantial sums of money available to other communities for building of hospitals and all kinds of public facilities.

A SPEAKER: What about residential patterns in the town?

ROBERT BENNETT: Well, this again can serve to break up the outworn residential patterns, because once the tribes get control over housing they make assignments of housing.

A SPEAKER: At the same time the public buildings are turned over to the tribe, the ownership of all these homes would be too.

ROBERT BENNETT: Yes. The first step, of course, is contractual. Then next is leasing, and then the lease back. The third is legislation to transfer the title. Once you get control over employee housing, you will have as a total community a mixed pattern with an Indian resident, maybe a teacher and a soil conservationist, or whatever.

BEN HANLEY: Then the tribe takes over the BIA services?

ROBERT BENNETT: Actually, yes. It's going to be difficult if the BIA cannot get any money for housing. As housing becomes old, then the tribe has the capability of rental housing. Eventually all of this governmental housing will be gone. It will be entirely tribal housing. They will have control over it and rent it as they see fit. I don't have any concerns about some of the key staff that will be required, because, like any community they will have housing for key staff. But it does away with one of the vices of the administrative community. You get a community just like any other community.

A SPEAKER: I see what you're driving at, a bureacracy replaced by a bureaucracy . . . No . . . I was kidding about that.

ROBERT BENNETT: The community would gain control over its own affairs, which it doesn't have now.

A SPEAKER: My question has two parts. First, do you have any idea how much submarginal land is within the boundaries of reservations, and two, can you suggest a strategy for accelerating the transfer of submarginal lands back to the tribe?

ROBERT BENNETT: This varies considerably. The economy of some tribes is dependent upon the submarginal land. These lands were bought by the Department of Agriculture and they were then turned over to the Secretary of the Interior because they were within Indian reservations. They are to be administered by the Secretary of the Interior as long as they are needed by Indian people. There have been several attempts made to have legislation enacted to give the ownership of these lands back to the tribes, but the Cattleman's Association lobby has prevented the legislation from being enacted.

I believe that an opportunity to set a precedent might be in connection with the submarginal land of the Stockbridge Munsee in Wisconsin, because here you have a case where the entire community even for the location of their community in housing is dependent on tribal lands. This is the one group I know of where this is all the land that the community has, this submarginal land. They have located on there, built homes on there and have a federal housing project. I think, that this might be a good key case because we have this added human element which might be successful in breaking the log jam and getting the submarginal land to the tribe. . . . Mr. Thacker, how many acres do you operate and farm and what kind of crops do you raise?

WILLIAM THACKER: I raise alfalfa hay and I have about one hundred sixty, one hundred seventy acres of lease land that I lease from the tribe. I lease quite a bit of land from each individual Indian. Some of them aren't in the cattle business and they lease their land to individuals on the reservation. We don't have any outsiders come into the reservation, they won't let them in. This is one good thing because we are surrounded by two big cattle outfits. One is the Butan Company, which run, I believe, ten thousand head of breeding cows and on the other side we have Butan Company's son and he runs about ten thousand head of cows.

So, if we go to this process of leasing out to outsiders we know that they will just come right in and take the whole thing over. They have talked about it, but because of the tribal council we have kept them out. But they are just waiting for the opportunity to come in. But as we talked before on this corporation, I think, this would work real good on this land development. Now, for the Indians and for individuals that would like to have more land it would be good, and it would stimulate work for Indians on the reservation, I think, this corporation would work real well, if we could get the Indians to work together to do this, because all over the United States we are facing the problem now of existence, especially in the cattle industry, the small operator. It's either stay small and go out of business or get big and stay in business. That's the problem we are running into now.

So, I think, by going into a coop operation, getting the Indian people to work together on this, which could develop a real good program and get big, and have a big income for the individual. That's the only way I can see, because if we don't do this and try to stay on our own eventually we are going to get pushed out, because I know there are a lot of small operations on the reservation and off the reservation that are in the cattle business, that can't compete with the big cattle operators.

Therefore, they are selling out. You take an outfit with ten thousand head of cows and say, they'll sell five thousand head of steer calves—and that's a pretty good income at the going price now of forty dollars a hundred. So, a small operator running only a hundred cows and selling only forty calves, there is quite a bit of difference. You just can't make it. So, I think, if we really think seriously about this coop, and working together in the cattle industry, and developing land, we'll be able to stay in there real good and the Indian people will be able to have a real good income.

ROBERT BENNETT: I guess, there is no question that this is a trend. The Congress is giving consideration to it. In the ownership of land, I guess, one of the biggest farmers in Arizona is the Goodyear Tire and Rubber Company. This is happening all over. Of course, this is what is going to take care of the sharecropper in the south. If you go through that country and you observe the small cotton farms in the south you see no young people there. Everybody that I've seen in any of these cotton farms, the one family operations, the one with the two mules, are sixty years of age or older.

Their sons and daughters are carpenters or plumbers or dentists or lawyers and they are not following around the cotton farm. These big corporations, the Goodyear Tire Company and large banks will be buying these up.

WILLIAM THACKER: Going into developing land and cattle it's not real easy to go into the cattle business unless you've got someone behind you to help and push you along.

ROBERT BENNETT: I'd like to illustrate. One reservation received a considerable sum of money on a settlement for land, which was taken by the Corps of Engineers, and in the discussion of the ways to use this land, between the government and the tribe, it was agreed that it would be used to put Indian people in the cattle business. The ostensible goal, self sufficiency.

Quite a bit of these range units were leased to non-Indians. as a consequence of this program to put Indians on this land they in course of time cancelled all of these leases and permits. Then all these units were taken up by Indians. Now, of course, it's obvious from what you have said, Mr. Thacker, that this fellow is locked in. There is no way he can go. He can't go any direction and expand. He will either get bigger or go out. That's the economic problem they face. But they have a more serious problem and that's the motivational problem. This is one of the restraints on economic development in any country. Because self sufficiency was the assumed motivation except for the Indian people. Here was their motivation: Get the non-Indians off the reservations.

Once they got them off the reservation they had accomplished what they wanted through this federal program. With this added handicap of having locked themselves in, you can see the very serious problem they are having. Eventually it will be a very expensive screening out process. The bad ones are the ones that can't cut it, will be losing out to the more progressive ones. So, with the increase in population you will end up again with a relatively large non-supported population. What gives a lot of concern is the motivations of the various land owners.

I have had land owners tell me they don't want anything done with their land. They want to leave it just like it is. On the other hand there's a requirement of the trustee by law for income producing and you always have to report on the acres of idle land you have. When you get before the Congressional Committee they jump down your throat. You're not carrying out your trusteeship because of all of this idle land.

A SPEAKER: There was an issue of scale that was raised by a guy at Pine Ridge and I would like to hear your reaction to this. According to him there were a number of people that he was familiar with, including himself. Not only of Pine Reidge, but on other reservations, who were interested in using their land, on a quite small scale, which was to them providing an adequate standard of living. According to him he couldn't get assistance to use his land and to purchase cattle and other things he needed, because the Bureau, he said, demanded that he enter the business on such a scale that would provide the standard of living they thought he should have. His position was that he was not interested in that standard of living, and he didn't feel he was equipped to run that kind of operation. Now, have you found this to be a problem? Are the issues properly framed in what this guy said and what's your reaction to it?

ROBERT BENNETT: Well, yes, they are. The reason for this family-plan concept was to allow this individual, assuming he needed one hundred fifty or two hundred breeding cows, to operate a program of fifty, which was the kind he felt he could manage. Of course, to all of the economists that's just like waving the red flag in front of them, but that's all he wanted. He was not interested in any more than fifty head of cattle. This will continue probably as long as he lives. Again, you have these motivational factors; he doesn't want to get big. Another place, particularly, where you lock yourself in, is in calling everybody a cattleman, because by that term of measurement you can only go down. Because, on any given reservation like this, where you have one hundred cattlemen today, you better be down to seventy-five in five years from now. Otherwise you're in trouble. So this means that if you're calling everybody "cattlemen" you get yourself locked in because your program is failing, you're having less and less cattle. So we try to make a distinction between commercial operators, who should pay the going rate on tribal land, as against what we would call the subsistence operator.

A SPEAKER: Or who at least eventually pays the going rate.

ROBERT BENNETT: Yes. Or eventually pays the going rate after so many years. They usually start out on a gradual basis and there should be room for this kind of operator, because that's all he wants, and he takes care of himself with that.

A SPEAKER: Do you think that it would be appropriate for someone to try to frame this whole discussion in a different way? I get the impression that the guy who only wants to run fifty head of cattle is considered some kind of dummy, or backward. Is there some way to expand people's minds so that this guy can be considered with some kind of dignity, as well as the guy who wants to run five hundred head? Do you think it's appropriate or possible? Because it seems to me that's the cultural problem, that there's something wrong with you if you don't want to constantly expand your resources.

ROBERT BENNETT: Well, you see, this is the problem, and what are the restraints on the good economic development on the reservation? The restraints are these motivational factors. It starts with the basic definition of what economics is. Indian definition of economics is completely different from what we generally understand as Indian economy. As a consequence we get into all kinds of difficulties and this is a case in point. As a matter of fact, the primary motivation wasn't an economic one to begin with. It was to get the non-Indian operator off the reservation. The only way you can do it is by using the land yourself. Now that they are in this position, they are caught in this economic trap, but the fact is that this was all parcelled out to these people, now he has to expand, and he has nowhere to go. So, this means eventually the poor operators are going to fall off by the wayside and these good operators are going to perform. It doesn't make any difference how you start an economic development program on a reservation, because it ends up the same way. It ends up with the economically motivated having less.

A SPEAKER: When a guy is forced out of business he has to be re-trained.

ROBERT BENNETT: If there is a training program, or if he is young enough. In the traditional economic system you have two divergent systems and they are in conflict with each other. The whole economic basis for this country makes it such. The traditional economic system of Indian people: subsistence. Many people are satisfied with this as an economic base. And this in other terminology is consumption economics.

A SPEAKER: Where does this become a problem, at what level is the person who wants a subsistence operation of what some people who conceptualize this as a problem, what level does this become a problem to his neighbor, or another person who could accept this idea, and where does it become a problem to him?

ROBERT BENNETT: Well, it becomes a problem because of his dependency upon someone else's land. In other words, very few original allottees are still alive; and people who inherited Indian land inherited it in many ways. The difficulty is if he is using some other individual's or the tribe's land for a subsistence kind of effort, when there are all kinds of demand for this land for those who are interested in such economic growth and development.

A SPEAKER: I was accused of being metaphysical yesterday and, of course, I will be again today. But I think there is a problem, at least we ought to think about in talking about this thing. That is, and I hope I will be corrected on my economic analysis. It seems to me that the whole ecological movement in the society is coming around to face the necessity for limited or no economic growth in general. At least abandoning the notion of unlimited growth. Abandoning the notion of unlimited "raising of the standard of living" for everybody, by trying to find some way to convince people in the culture to settle for less than an unlimited standard of living.

276

It seems to me that the dynamics you're talking about is going the other way, for the guy who is willing to settle for a standard of living that he's comfortable with, and is getting pushed out. He's still being defined as the dummy rather than the guy who is twenty-five years ahead of the rest of the society.

ROBERT BENNETT: Well, this is true in the present economic environment. Whether this changes or not only the future can tell. But, this is the way it is now. Then, of course, this same principle you're talking about also goes into other areas which are important to Indian life beyond the economic, and the whole basic orientation of this person is he's got enough for today and for his immediate future and that's all he's interested in.

This other guy, no matter how much he has, he never has enough. So, he has a drive forward. This subsistence fellow doesn't. He's satisfied. He's not going anyplace. He's going to have his fifty head of cattle and there isn't any amount of working with him that would get him up into another area.

If you begin to measure this in strictly economic terms, this person looks the way he does. But when you begin to consider all the factors, with trends which may possibly be developing in the future, maybe he's not so bad off. But, you see, when you measure it in terms of strict economic measures, then this subsistence fellow and the program as a result, look pretty bad.

A SPEAKER: The northern Cheyenne Tribe, I believe, tried to address this problem by limiting the amount of cattle or amount of acreages that any tribal member could lease from the tribe from tribal assets; more interested in providing a land or lease base for cattle operations of the fifty unit type. They were not interested in leasing to a few large Indian operators for them to get richer and grow, but instead to satisfy the needs of the largest number of people, which was along that lower line of the subsistence economy. Now, one of the things that they had to face (and, I think, this is where ideology is so important) was this: The tribe had somewhat of a difficult time working with the Bureau to accept this kind of concept of "it's all right" to work on a subsistence level. This is a decent kind of thing and it can be well not only for the individual but for the community as a whole.

ROBERT BENNETT: What is going to happen is that by the time these people get up here, then society is going to change. They would have been better off to stay where they were.

A SPEAKER: I think that's one danger, but also, I think, history might suggest also that many of the people who are there are going to stay right there no matter what happens to them. They may lose their land, but at least intellectually they are still going to feel that way about things and no amount of education or force is going to get them on that other line.

ROBERT BENNETT: There are many of these areas that I think are very important and are basic to this. Another thing, these people here are not motivated for equality. You can talk to them about equality for the next fifty years and they are not going to be motivated one bit. Whereas, other minorities, the thing that really turns them on is to mention the word equality. But not for these folks. Because right or wrong, inherently what they feel, what they have, is better than what this guy has. So, if they feel that way, what ways are you going to use to have them take advantage of an economic program? Because right here he feels he is better off than that guy. "I don't have to worry about him, I won't get as many gray hairs as he has." All that sort of stuff. "I'm happy where I am. I'm not interested in being equal with anybody because what I have is better than what anybody else has."

A SPEAKER: This would take you into a different direction if you respected the wishes of these individuals, then perhaps you'd have to go to attracting some type of industry to come in.

ROBERT BENNETT: Well, again you run into these same factors when you bring industry in. There is an assumption that if you have two hundred unemployed employable Indian men or people, and you bring a factory with two hundred people, your economic problem is solved. It isn't solved, and besides you don't solve the economic problem; you create a lot of other problems because of the industry. There are some Indian tribes that will not work underground. There have been many underground industries, mining and everything, close to Indians, but there are no Indians working there because they don't work underground. So, it has to do with their attitude about other things, and, the problem of an industry on an Indian reservation is considerably different than the problem of an industry in any industrial area for this reason.

Here's an example: When New England lost the garment industry, three and four generations had been working at these benches in the garment industry. They lost it and the electronics industry came in. These people are now the fifth and sixth generation, and they are going back to the same benches, same building, but are now working on electronics.

These Indian people haven't been working on anything like that. So, you bring in a garment industry or electronics plant, and this is their first entry into industrial economy. It's quite a bit of difference between taking two hundred people, who are

278

entering the industrial economy as against bringing an industry where they have been a part of it for three, four generations.

A SPEAKER: What kind of a balance do you strike here?

ROBERT BENNETT: Well, this has to be supplemented by all kinds of training programs. The training is not only in skill, but in the attitudes and what-not that make up a person who is willing to go to work five days a week, eight hours a day, for fifty weeks and two weeks vacation. That's considerably different than what he has been doing. So, it's not his skill, he's very trainable as far as skill is concerned, but it's all these other things that he has to get used to. Like going to town on Saturday and not Monday, Tuesday, Wednesday, Thursday, Friday. To cash his check in a bank instead of a bar. All these things are what make him a good employee, not especially the skill training. He doesn't need it, indeed very little.

A SPEAKER: Have there been some industries which try to accommodate in some way to Indian attitudes rather than the other way around?

ROBERT BENNETT: Well, I think, the fishhook plant at Pine Ridge accommodates them in terms of the premium they pay for production. I don't think they have gotten any place, you know, just on straight time, but they pay a premium on production.

As a consequence they put in a lot of time. However, when the minimum wage went up recently, it put the fishhook plant out of business; they went back to Mexico. They had about five or six hundred employees at one time in that operation. What they used here was production incentives. The more you produce the more money you get. But they did have these other problems to overcome. Going to town on Monday, Tuesday, or any day of the week. When they first started out, 80% of their pay checks were cashed in bars, because that's the only place they thought they were welcome. After they found they were welcome in banks, in a couple of years it changed and people began to have their checks cashed in banks, and they began to have bank accounts.

A SPEAKER: What about the Winston diamond cutting operation?

ROBERT BENNETT: Well, I understand it's a very limited group. The problem there too, I guess, is the long years of training it takes to be an expert diamond cutter.

A SPEAKER: But there is also another problem on incentive, and that is if you assume there are people who are satisfied with a limited standard of living, those incentives don't really mean anything. The fishhook people said that at least one guy was such an overproducer that, to make an example of him they gave him two weeks' bonus pay. So, he quit and said I'll come back in two weeks. They tried to get him to put it in the bank or buy a car, and he said, no, I work for money to support my family and you guys just gave me two weeks' work. So, in two weeks he was back.

A SPEAKER: That's fine, isn't it?

A SPEAKER: It's fine, but it raised hell with the factory, and in this particular case their complaint was that when they missed a day of work it was such a high degree of muscle skill involved that it took them a day or so to get back to peak production, because all the movements got rusty or something. So, when a guy would miss that, when he did come back it would take a couple of days for him to get back up. That's what they are complaining about, and they had to pay him the minimum wage while he was getting back in shape.

A SPEAKER: I guess, idealistically what we are really saying is, maybe Indians can teach whites that a five day week isn't all that necessary.

ROBERT BENNETT: Well, again this kind of orientation in the whole economic structure is in relation to his immediate needs. It's not in relation to a need which might develop two or three months down the road. When that need develops he will meet it when it comes. Again, this is an orientation to what is presently needed. There are other things that have impacts on this problem, in terms of their motivation, and again it looks like they might be coming around. Another fundamental difference when you relate to using an economic resource of this orientation to living and harmony with nature and leaving things as they are is as against changing. But it looks like now, with all the pollution and everything, this might be coming, this might be beginning to bend in this direction.

This has an effect on what you do to natural resources, and this fellow back here he doesn't want anything done with it. He just wants it left the way it is. Then you have a directive from Congress saying to get as much money off it as you can. He doesn't want any money; he just wants it left the way it is.

A SPEAKER: Did I understand you to say when we were talking about cooperative cattle, a cattle co-op?

WILLIAM THACKER: I was thinking more of land development, but I was going to say to Mr. Bennett, that, I think, what we are trying to do here is we are hitting on the point of everything. What I think we are trying to do is advise and direct some of the Indians to do what they want to do. In other words, like on our reservation there are quite a few in the cattle business, who only have fifty or sixty head. They have graduated from school and come back to the reservation and gotten in the cattle business. They had no other place to go, so they had to do something, so they got in the cattle business. It actually boils down to the fact that they didn't want to go in the cattle business, but that's the only thing that they could do. This just relates back to the lack of education.

We've got some of them doing things that they don't want to do. I think that's where our problem is with some of the Indian people, why they are not doing well in certain things, because we've got them doing things that they don't want to do. It all comes around to a point that we all need to teach each individual in the field that they are interested in. Like, we can't all be ranchers; we have to have someone in the law business, extension service, and different things.

ROBERT BENNETT: Well, there's no question that in the past history of the Indians their operations have been limited. These operations have been limited by the actual manufacturers' isolation and actual resources available to them, and also by the failure of society in general to recognize their capabilities in other areas.

Of course, the basic wrong assumption was made during the allotment system, but that's history now. I think this has an affect on attitudes to Indian people, because in the northern tier of the state the tribes lost their land. When your whole system, not only economic, but the social and religion system is based upon the land, when you lose this, of course, it pretty well fractures your society.

But they didn't have this kind of traumatic experience in the western and southwestern parts among the Papago, Pueblo, Apaches and others. They retained in tribal ownership all of their land or the majority of it. So they have a good starting place in this respect. I think, when you speak about Indian economic development these are some other factors that need to be taken into consideration as to what happened to the various tribes in this country to start with.

Does anyone else have any questions? If not, thank you very much. The panel is adjourned.

Participants leaving the Woodrow Wilson School for lunch
which was served in another building on campus. In forefront
LEW BARTON, Lumbee of Pembroke, North Carolina.

11

Forms and Uses
of Tribal Government

RUPERT COSTO

This panel is an innovation in discussion. Many conferences have been held in the past concerning tribal and reservation economic development, the uses of reservation land, the leasing of land to developers and what the tribes could gain or lose as a result of such leasing. But to my knowledge, at no time have the Native tribes discussed the entire question of their own tribal government—whether this form of government is suited to the problems of the tribe as a whole in connection with the life of the people, and as to the uses of such government in improving the life of the people and the strength of the tribe as a politcal, social and economic entity. I have always wondered at this: why such a basic—such a fundamental question does not come up for serious discussion and consideration. I can only believe that the Bureau of Indian Affairs, which sets up and actually controls our tribal governing bodies, does not wish to entertain the possibility of profound change in this respect, and would rather maintain the tribe in a position of subservience to the Department of the Interior and the United States of America. Because it is clear to me, and to many other tribal activists, that the present forms of tribal government do not meet the requirements of our modern situation, nor do they serve to preserve the best of our philosophy of human values. What exists today is a very poor carbon copy of a white man's society, based on the European concept of government and with the principal purpose of either assimilating the Indian or controlling the Indian and his remaining lands for purposes other than the good of the Indian people themselves.

To take only one example of the resulting impoverishment of our people: the policy of long-term leasing, with the leases being approved by the Secretary of the Interior and usually foisted upon the tribes by the BIA agency, is clearly one of guaranteed unemployment and poverty. Yet, these leases continue to be made, and the tribal governing bodies continue to entertain them. I ask these questions: Should the Bureau of Indian Affairs have the power to negotiate them? Or, should not the whole question of independent tribal economic development be considered from the long range point of view. And, should not all the people of the tribe have an equal voice in such an important determination. I say that there is strong evidence the people of the tribes have little or nothing to say about this question and all others in connection with the tribe's economy. I say there is strong evidence that the tribal governing bodies are the creatures of the Bureau, and do not dare to run counter to the policies and instructions of the Bureau—or they will soon be disposed of. I also say to you that the present structure of tribal government is directly in opposition to the needs and the requirements of the people themselves.

We did not plan this panel as a discussion of the historical basis for the subject itself. We planned it as a discussion among ourselves as Indian tribal people, and we know what this history is, very well. We did plan the panel in order to raise some very profound questions in the minds of the Indian scholars and tribal activists who are present at this Convocation . . . so that some consideration of needed changes shall begin to occupy the minds of our people.

At the same time, I wish to make some general observations on the subject of this panel, by way of setting the background of the question in our minds. . . . It would be wrong to say that the same form of tribal government existed in every tribe of the land before white, or European contact. Just as religious forms and philosophies varied, so too did the forms of tribal government vary from region to region, tribe to tribe. However, the uses of tribal government were largely the same in all the tribes. These uses were: to govern as little as necessary; to make it possible for life to go on in close relationship with Mother Earth, and to utilize the land, waters and wildlife for the common good. I am saying *utilization*, as opposed to *exploitation*. The unrestrained exploitation of this earth is the cause of the present corruption and depletion of our land, air, and waters.

Upon contact with the Europeans, tribal governments changed everywhere so quickly and so severely, that the disruption which took place nearly destroyed the tribes and the people, even more quickly than did the diseases of the white man or his guns.

Reasons for tribal disruption were twofold: economic and social. On the one hand, the economy of the tribes was destroyed. And, on the other hand, the social structure of tribal society was destroyed. Both processes took place quite rapidly, as historic events are measured . . . but much more slowly in the form of man's conscious knowledge of himself and his world are concerned.

The basic and most important change that took place was economic. Tribal economy was based on the uses of the land, and the uses of the products of the land. This varied from tribe to tribe and from region to region. But the variation was only in form and complexity, based generally upon the geographical situation, climate, and environment. There was little variety in the nature of the economy itself. Variety existed also in the degree and complexity of development economically, depending upon the natural resources and technological evolution. Production was for use instead of for exchange for the sake of exchange as a profit motive. No power superstructure existed whose function was entirely to police and enforce government. The economy was based on small enclaves of human beings, either in families, or in clans, or in a combination of clans and families. Another aspect of the economy existed which was entirely at variance with that introduced with the coming of the Europeans. Food and food supplies were not hoarded for future exchange for profit, or for gain. Food and food supplies were *stored* for the use of the family, the clan, or the common good. The storing of food and supplies was a vital part of the economic function, and attested to the strong organization of the tribes. Without such organized living, organized production of foods through the use of agriculture in some areas and the use of gathering in others, and organized care of the natural resources, life would have ceased long before the coming of the white man. With the entrance of the European entrepreneur, who brought a knowledge of an economy based upon profit from land and commodities, a conflict took place almost at once.

The use and exportation of animal hides for profit and monetary gain was probably among the first to herald this conflict. Immediately, the Native was placed in a position of competition with himself, with his people, and with his land. He began to sell his hides, and his life took on the acitivity of hunting for gain rather than for use. The European, with his need for expansion and particularly for expansion of his land holdings, understood the matter of sale and purchase of land. The Native did not. To buy and sell land was entirely foreign to his philosophy of life, to his economy, and to his social structure. Thus did another aspect of this economic competition steal upon the Native, and the beginning of the end was in sight.

There was, then, an economic war between the two forms of society—the European and the Native, long before this war became a political and military one. The destruction of Native economy was the basic fact of white-Indian conflict. The injustices that followed, the treaties that were made and then broken, the effects upon Native society, were secondary . . . although they were just as severe and just as destructive.

The Europeans brought with them an economy best suited to the production of goods; the uses of money as a common means of exchange, and a form of political government best suited to the oppression of peoples rather than the consulting and advising with them for the common good. Our Native tribal economy was based on respect for the land, use of the land in conformity with the dictates of nature, the use of exchange of products themselves rather than the use of money as a medium of exchange. Money then later emerged as a product in its own right for the purposes of speculation, hoarding, and oppression, and finally a form of government unsuited to the maximum participation of the people themselves.

It would be a serious mistake to generalize, however. Because the Native peoples of this land were already beginning to develop more complex forms of economy. Even before the European arrivals, many tribes had developed the use of certain articles as a means of exchange, tokens of exchange. Wampum, shell money, and less sophisticated articles were already in use as money, gradually displacing the system of barter of goods in kind. My point is this: that the Native peoples were already on the way to a unique and quite different, but complex form of economy before the European arrivals.

After the Revolutionary war, the new federal American government attempted to deal with the problem of this economic war with the Native peoples, and failed at every step of the way, for two reasons. One reason was because the problem was dealt with at best as a social problem filled with humanitarian considerations. Another was the inherent greed and need for further colonial expansion on the part of the European class of entrepreneurs and dominant political leaders. Generally, it was not understood that what had happened was a war of economic systems. At worst, the indescribable greed of the European whites got the best of them and a centuries-long series of gross injustices and genocides followed.

Much later when the Indian Reorganization Bill was enacted, it was hailed as the one great, democratic event in the life of the tribes. The Indian Reorganization Act (also known as the Wheeler-Howard Act) provided for a ''reorganization of tribal government" purportedly giving more political rights to the tribes, with an organizational structure based on European systems of economy, and a tribal superstructure presumably "elected" by the people, but subject to the approval of the Secretary of the Interior. We Cahuilla Indians, in the Southern part of California, did not accept the Wheeler-Howard Act, and we fought against Commissioner Collier and his army of enforcers every step of the way. We knew that the Bureau of Indian Affairs, through the Indian Reorganization Act, would destroy the last remnants of our tribal lives, and would only help the United States to get more of our land, and would finally result in a degradation of our leadership, the corruption of our people. I think we were right, because democracy as the Europeans know it, is not democracy at all so far as we are concerned.

All this is history, and with my brothers present in this panel, I don't find it necessary to present more details. What is important, however, is the situation today.

The results of the Indian Reorganization Act included the end of the tribes in many cases, and the rotting of tribal life in all cases. Those tribes which have survived have a peculiar combination of European governing forms, and a remaining social philosophy of our own Native beliefs. In California, the tribes are a pitiful caricature of the real thing. In Fort Hall, Pine Ridge, Rosebud, and many other areas of the Plains, the tribal governments are usually puppets of the Bureau of Indian Affairs, and much as the people try, they are unable to cope with the corruption, the lack of understanding, and the moral degradation of the tribal leadership. Of late, among some tribes, there are serious and desperate efforts to change this condition.

Indeed it is mandatory upon us to explore ways of changing this condition. I think we should have a complete evaluation of the forms and uses of tribal government, to be done by the people themselves. What has happened, really, is that we don't have a European democracy, and we don't have a Native democracy. We have neither fish, fowl, or good red herring. Our tribal forms of government are stifling us. And our uses of government are continually at war with the people and their needs, with the tribal leadership, with the forms of government themselves, and with the success of any undertaking. In fact, our weaknesses in governing ourselves are making it possible for the Bureau of Indian Affairs to defraud us, for the federal agencies to trick us, for the whites to steal us blind, and even for our own people to become criminals against their people.

No one can set a uniform pattern for change. No one should try to tell the tribes what to do, or how to do it. Because no situation is like another. We can only explore possibilities, and then leave it to the people and their *accepted* leaders to find the way. We can only discuss possibilities, examples, ideas, and then make the deliberations and discussion available to all the people.

Let us take an example. In some Indian societies, even today, tribal representation is by family. Each family selects its headman, who is their representative in general council. The uses of such a form of government are clearly to fit in with a number of small landholders. If this is your situation, then this this should be your form of government, altered to suit your own specific conditions.

Other tribes are cattle-raising people, like mine. In our group, we have no government other than the simple meeting of a few elected people. We don't accept federal aid; we don't have OEO funding, and generally we don't allow anybody to tell us what to do. There is a case in which the County of Riverside owes us $6,000 for cattle guards, which they agreed to give us when we granted them a right of way for a road. By the time they got around to fulfilling this part of the contract, which was like twenty years later, cattle guards were no longer being used and in fact were illegal. So now they owe us this money, the estimated cost of the two cattle guards if installed. Then the Bureau of Indian Affairs stepped in, and they informed the County that the money must go to the U. S. Treasury "to be used for the benefit of the Cahuilla tribe." We decided to let that $6,000 rot in hell but we are not going to take it if it means being deposited "for" us in the United States Treasury. We are perfectly capable of handling our own affairs, and have done so from time immemorial, and we refuse to have our own funds doled out to us as though we are beggars. That money is still sitting in the County Treasurer's office, making the book-keepers mad—but to date our position remains unchanged. We can and we will handle our own resources, including our own money.

It is not so easy with other tribes, like the Navajo, or the Hopi, or Sioux.

I can only make a few suggestions to point out a direction leading to change, and the discussion that follows must deal with the subject in the same way.

Our first task must be to let the young people into the leadership of the tribe. We must bring them back to tribal life and involvement in tribal government. We must learn to listen, as well as to speak, and when we listen our minds must be open— open so that we may *hear* what they say and think, so that their ideas and suggestions may be considered as part of our efforts to improve our internal condition. We have the sharpest young people, the most intelligent and inventive in this country.

We are not using their genius and talents. I am convinced that this question is crucial to our welfare, and even crucial to our endurance as a race. We had better think about this, because if we don't our young people will disappear into the general population and will be lost to us.

Second, I believe some way must be found to involve ALL the people in the actual governing of our affairs, and make certain that important decisions are not reached without consultation and decision by the people. This does not exist today in most tribes. It may take longer, but it will guard us against such situations as misuse of funds, fraud on all sides, and it will bring the talents of the people to bear upon our problems.

I am opposed to long-term leases. This has degraded our people, and deformed our government. Because we cannot cope with this, and we are tied hand and foot if we permit this situation to continue.

I am for the strongest possible measures to stop misrepresentation of Indian people, who claim to be chiefs as soon as they get to the city. They immediately purport to represent their people. I think the strongest action ought to be taken against this. To stop it, we need a closer contact with the urban Indian people, offering our help, accepting theirs. If we have a stronger contact with the urban Indian people, our support will help them in their situation whenever they need it. In our own way, as small as we are today in population, we can accomplish more than those who go around screaming and demonstrating. The Indian has always had his traitors, from the beginning of white contact. It is what has been the greatest difficulty with us. In former times, we had a way of dealing with traitors and treachery, even though in many cases this was too late, as in the case of Elias Boudinot. Today, we must also be aware of the fact that there are traitors in our midst, white-livered Indians who betray their people for a buck, who want to be leaders without anybody to lead, chiefs without any chieftainship, generals without an army. The whites dote upon such people. I say to you, they are the poison in the Indian world, and we must point them out mercilessly and make it known to everyone who they are. I hear, by the old Indian moccasin trail line, that the Bureau of Indian Affairs will engage more Indians in ''policy-making'' positions. This BIA is a monster. Nobody can withstand its structure. No individual can stand up against its bureaucratic entanglements which are choking the very life out of our people. What shall we do, for example, if the BIA suddenly begins to have a majority of INDIANS as leaders . . . Indians who are working against their own people, even with the best of intentions. Do you think for one moment that we will be able to utilize their support, even if we get it? Do you think we will be any better off? I say no! I say that we can have INDIANS in government who are just as rotten, just as corrupt, just as ineffective and just as treacherous as any white man. Making leaders out of acceptable Indians will change nothing. What we have proposed has some chance of changing conditions, however. And that is, that Indian tribes, Indian organized groups, gradually supplant BIA facilities and services, and that these tribes and groups be given complete independence of direction, policy-making, and leadership.

Changing the personnel of the bureaucracy will not change the corrupt influence of the bureaucracy which has had a couple of hundreds of years of experience in making slaves out of people—our people.

The forms of tribal government must be changed. We have no right to dictate such changes to the tribes, however. That is up to the tribes, and to you as members of your various tribes. But the uses of tribal government are clear: to get the best and the most for our people.

DISCUSSION
The Forms and Uses of Tribal Government

(No reporter was present at this panel, because two other panels were taking place at the same time. Consequently, the following discussion has been placed in the form of a report and a digest.)

D'ARCY MCNICKLE: Dr. McNickle described the Lone Wolf case. This case was the first frontal assault on the tribes' right to govern themselves. (Lone Wolf v. Hitchcock, 187 U.S. 553, 1903.) Congress proceeded to adopt laws which brought more and more federal jurisdiction over the tribes. Dr. McNickle felt, however, that there was an area of control left to the tribes. Unless an Act refers to a tribe or right of action, the tribe is left a large area of control over internal mechanism as to the tribe's domestic affairs. He described how the local Bureau of Indian Affairs superintendents usurped many of the tribal rights. This individual had complete control over the tribal court system and law enforcement personnel. The superintendent had all powers of decision prior to 1934. The Indian Reorganization Act attempted to correct this situation with regard to the rights of the tribe. He discussed the Code of Federal Regulations—Title 25 (Indians), and explained how the tribe could set up a government of their own choosing. The Bureau of Indian Affairs did select tribal representatives, and they could remove those who would not "cooperate" with them.

Describing the way the Bureau operates today, Dr. McNickle said that a question of time is involved, in which the Bureau must spend the money budgeted for its use, or at the end of the fiscal year the unspent funds must be returned to the Congress. If funds are returned, the Bureau of the Budget assumes this Agency doesn't need as much the next fiscal year. This forces the BIA to spend, and this approach negates good program planning.

To implement the Indian Reorganization Act, an anthropological unit was created to help tribes prepare themselves for "self" government. The intent of the program was good. It provided for economic rehabilitation of the Indians, principally on the land. Organization of Indian tribes for managing their own affairs, and civil and cultural freedom and opportunity for the Indians was provided.

This social science approach lost its momentum when Bureau programs were thrown into the hands of the oldtime BIA hacks who had no respect for the Indian people. These people who made the decisions ignored the wishes of the people. Against this background the tribes have attempted to change to fit their own needs. One of the great problems the tribes face today is that they do not understand their relationship to the federal government. What can they do? They could change Title 25. The big question is: Can they . . . Will they? The land should be preserved for the people. Tribal councils do not communicate to their people.

CHARLES POITRAS, JR.: In essence, Mr. Poitras stated that the tribes say they want responsibility in managing programs, but not always are they willing to push, and prepare themselves for control of some of these programs. A hard look needs to be taken at the Buy Indian Act, and the Johnson-O'Malley Act, which is not only for purposes of education, as so many believe. Also, the Johnson-O'Malley Act can be amended. Mr. Poitras asked certain questions of the panel members. He asked: Are tribal governments responsive to the people? If not, how can they be made to be more responsive to individual needs? One may be by the process of election. Second, by voter registration. Third, by confrontation? As younger members of the tribe become more concerned and involved with the community problems on their reservations, will the tribal councils invite them to participate as part of the tribal government?

Are tribal governments capable, as they are now constituted, of providing the direction, the innovation, now needed to develop the reservations? Will social change be effectuated through the traditional channels, or will change be brought about through deviant members of the tribes ("deviant" not to mean psychopathic), but those who are innovators, implementers, etc. Will these individuals be allowed to surface by the existing tribal councils, the Bureau of Indian Affairs? These young people are not ''house'' Indians, but independent and thoughtful and concerned Indian people.

The core values of the tribe must be maintained. Women must become more involved in tribal and council affairs. There is no need for a generation gap in council affairs, or on reservations. Communication must be made to flow through all layers of tribal society. This brings about understanding instead of misunderstanding.

A SPEAKER: I would like to know how to get rid of corupt and ineffective tribal councils? These people are not really elected by the people themselves, many of whom have given up hope and don't even bother to vote. They are hand picked by the BIA. Some of us are young and anxious to change things. We cannot change things with these people on the councils. How do we go about getting rid of them? You might think this is an easy matter, but it isn't. How do we do it?

A SPEAKER: I feel sure that at least one of the old council members could be convinced to work with you. Find him, or her. Convince them. Work with them. Find some of the old-timers. Get them to work with you. Choose from among yourselves one person upon whom you can depend. Support him, or her. See to it they are reliable. Campaign for him, and get him elected. It's a long struggle, but worth it. There is no shortcut.

D'ARCY MCNICKLE: It seems to me you would certainly have to work through some of the older people. You would have to discuss tribal affairs with them. Get one or two on the tribal council from among the younger people. Mainly, get the younger people active.

A SPEAKER: How do you go about getting some land on the reservation? We young people have no land. The land is allotted to the oldtimers, and then through the heirship regulations, it becomes fractionated and we have no chance to get a foothold on the reservation. How do we go about getting some land on the reservation?

D'ARCY MCNICKLE: I believe there are statutes on the books, in which even the Bureau of Indian Affairs can be compelled to agree to certain distribution of land. Look into it. Get legal advice. But proceed with it systematically.

A SPEAKER: What is the best way to utilize land, if we ever can get it? The land on our reservation is mostly taken up by long-term leases. What chance do we have to break these leases, or to get some use out of our own land?

A SPEAKER: The trouble is that most of the reservation people have no training in agriculture, or land management. Nor is there any program in effect that would give them that training. There are plenty of ways that good training can be made available, and right on the reservation. If you are aware of the fact that training is needed, you can find a way to get it. But serious attention must be paid to finding out what the best use of a particular piece of land is, and to find out how to go about it, as to its use. In this Convocation, there are people who can help in this respect.

A SPEAKER: How can we get rid of these long-term leases?

A SPEAKER: That is one of the toughest questions to solve. The leases are matters of legal contract between the tribes through their councils, approved by the Bureau of Indian Affairs, and without mutual consent, through the legal channels, it is a most difficult matter to dispose of. I think perhaps the only certain way to get rid of such a long-term lease is by congressional action, and you know how long that takes. However, there may be some actions that can be taken of a public or tribal pressure nature, by which the holder of a long-term lease may be convinced he ought to voluntarily surrender his option and his contract. Certainly it is very unwise for any operator to work in an unfriendly atmosphere, under general pressure, and at the very least, most uncomfortable. I think, that you should see to it that no more long-term leases are made, and that would be protection for the future.

A SPEAKER: On the Colville reservation, the younger people don't want termination. It's the older people who want it. How can we fight this out, so that our land is protected. We don't want termination, but we may get it if the oldtimers on the tribal council have their way.

A SPEAKER: I think you have a hard job ahead of you. But the younger people can have an effect on the tribal council, if they would get together and act together, and bring up some sort of a program in land use . . . in reservation use.

A SPEAKER: The business and industries coming into the reservations are unsuccessful, many of them. They are coming into reservations with their industry, using it as a tax dodge. Pretty soon they leave, and we are left with nothing again. They work for a short time, and then they skip. They are unproductive, make many promises, and in the end the whole thing has been used as a tax dodge and nothing else. I think we should make plans to have our own businesses and industries, if we want them at all.

A SPEAKER: I'm from St. Ignacio, Utah. We are people who *want* the younger ones to come into activity. How do we get them to agree to act with us on committees for tribal development? We need them, and we want them.

RUPERT COSTO: It's a two-fold problem. On the one hand, you have to convince the younger people to run for office, that

it is worthwhile to run for office, and that they can accomplish
something for their people in such a way. But, it takes a whole
it is worthwile to run for office, and that they can accomplish
something for their people in such a way. But, it takes a whole
lot of patience to work in this way—and this is the Indian way.
Young people are not noted for patience. And the older people
know this. So it's a long-term program, and you won't do it in
one day. And you won't succeed in doing it in any other way.

A SPEAKER: There is no communication between the
tribes, and I think this is one of the worst situations we have
to face. We don't know about the experiences of other tribes,
other reservations. The Bureau of Indian Affairs certainly does
nothing to develop such communication. It looks to me that we
have to do it somehow. I wish we knew what other tribes were
doing, and what their experiences are. It's as if we are all working in different directions and we don't know what the other
people sre doing. They don't know what we are doing.

RUPERT COSTO: For seven years, we of the American
Indian Historical Society have raised this question. We have considered it one of the simplest-sounding, but one of the most
complicated questions we have in the Native American affairs
today. It seems to us that there is a deliberate effort NOT to
have communication between our people, between our tribes.
We went to Washington, D.C., and demanded that a listing be
made of all tribal council members, all school administration
and teachers. And they gave us the "Governing Bodies List,"
which is entirely worthless. If they don't have a listing, what
have they been doing these hundred years? We raised all kinds
of fuss, but nothing happened. And still we don't have such a
listing. We think such a listing should be accurately made, and
revised from year to year. I don't care how much time it takes,
or how much work is involved. If we don't know how to get in
touch with each other, we are dead ducks. And we can talk and
talk, and yet this is not forthcoming. It's the most frustrating
thing in the world—to ask for and demand such a simple thing—
and not to be able to get it. We need, and we must have,
independent communication between all the tribes. And we don't
have it. We never have had it. I am willing to take this issue
to court if necessary, because I think it is of crucial and critical
importance for all of us.

A SPEAKER: We have some real and important problems
concerning our hunting and fishing rights. How do we go about
protecting these rights?

D'ARCY MCNICKLE: That's a big question, and there is
plenty of experience already to show what must be done and
what can be done. I can only answer this part of the question:
The first thing you must do is to find out exactly what your

rights are. Study your treaty. Many Indian people don't know the provisions of their own treaties. Study Title 25. You will find some provisions there that can be used for your benefit. Generally speaking, you have to be sure of your ground legally, and according to your treaty.

The panel ended at this time, and no formal summation was made. However, the Panel Chairman has reconstructed, as well as he could, the gist of the discussion, and has these remarks to make in post-summation.

RUPERT COSTO: I would make this statement for the record. The time and place of this panel was changed from time to time, because many of the Convocation Participants wanted badly to take part. There were other panels, however, of equal importance, and in the end we arbitrarily took the time and had a very lively discussion. Our panel on *Forms and Uses of Tribal Government* had many young people participating. The questions raised were extremely serious, and showed great concern for the present situation on all or most reservations. The problems are of such a varied nature that each reservation needs to be considered in its own context, with its own problems, its own history, and the makeup of its own people.

I will say this: There is no easy route for us. It is a long and hard struggle. You have got to fight, and keep fighting. That's the hell of it. There is no end to it, because if you relax for one moment, you are into the fight all over again. Vigilance, constant acitivity and concern, constant study and constant involvement in every phase of reservation life—that's what is needed. And don't let anybody tell you there is a short cut. There are other ways too, for Indian people to keep up their struggle for their rights. And each must find his own way. In my experience with tribal affairs, we made many innovations as the occasion warranted it. There was one occasion when we wanted a road on the reservation so that we could bring our cattle to market. The oldtimers were opposed to it. I was then one of you young ones. We were stale-mated. Finally, we went to the tribal council and told them that the majority of the people wanted the road and if *they* didn't want it, they ought to resign. It was very uncomfortable. They resigned. We elected another tribal council immediately. And then we voted the road, reaffirming the decision of the people as they made it originally. That's just one instance of what can happen. We elected a tribal council made up almost entirely of young people.

I believe that one of the gravest problems we have is that the young people don't have any land on the reservations. The oldtimers have the land, and there is no re-distribution, nor any distribution going on. What they have, they don't usually use. And what they are doing, is leasing the land to the whites. Another thing: we must have an agreement and make it a part of tribal ordinance, that anybody who wants to sell an allotment, the tribe should have first choice in purchasing that allotment. And second choice should go to any Indian of the tribe. Under no conditions should whites be allowed to buy Indian land. I know of one tribe, some of the Blackfeet, who have been quietly buying land surrounding their reservation. They are investing their own money, tribal money, in land. Many are investing their own personal funds in land. It is all going into tribal land. This tribal land will be used for their own industry, cattle industry or any suitable industry which is natural to that type of land and to that type of people.

Soon these Blackfeet will have *bought back* great amounts of their own land. Sure, it's not fair. This was their land origi- nally, and it's not justice. But some day we have to come to the conclusion that the end in this case justifies the means, and if the "means" is only money, let's do it.

There are so many ways of getting around injustice, and your own creative intelligence will find it. We have a situation on our reservation where the hunting season brings out all the whites with their little shotguns and little families to shoot any game they can see or think they see. For a long time we toler- ated it, even though the reservation is fenced and they are not allowed to hunt on our reservation. There have been proposals that we should permit the whites to hunt, that there might be some income from this. I have always been opposed to it. Once we let them in, they have a foothold and might decide they have a *right* to hunt on our reservation. So we police the reservation at hunting season . . . from one end to the other. And we arrest any trespassers. You have certain rights as owners of property, in connection with trespass. You don't have to wait until you can get the sheriff or a policeman. There are certain property rights involved here. I will never understand why one Eastern tribe had to wait for a court ruling before they kicked out tres- passers who had set up trailer courts. Among us, among my own people, they would have been kicked out long ago. Just get together a small committee, and *put them out*. The moral of the story is: if you let them do it to you, they will do it.

Among my own people, we never had to suffer the prejudice that most other Indians suffer in other parts of the country. That's not because the whites are so great. It is because we won't let them do it to us. Again, if you let them do it to you, they will do it. I think that sometimes our Indian people are afraid of windmills. The time will come, if it hasn't come al- ready, when you have to stand up and fight. About the fishing rights struggle, now going on in Washington and other Northwest states. Very few people know that the trouble started a long time ago, when those tribes now involved in the fishing rights struggle, gave the State Fish and Game Commission the right to institute fishing regulations. They even allowed whites to fish in their treaty waters. Nobody could tell them this was foolish. Now they have to go to court, get arrested, and continue the fight. The point is, don't be such good guys. Don't allow the whites to fish and hunt on reservation property, or lands that are ours by treaty. Some of the people on the Hoopa reservation in Northwest California allowed some whites to build homes on tribal land. This was on lease, and they had the option to ask them to move at any time. But years went by, and the whites now refuse to move. They have "rights" on Indian land, *by adverse possession*, or so they say. So now it is a legal battle, all over again. I tell you, don't be such good guys. Protect your land, and your rights. Once the outsiders get in, you will have the time of your life to get them out.

There is only one thing I can tell you to take the pain out of all this . . . the pain that is involved in a whole lifetime of struggle, and fight, and court cases, litigation, and involvement in sheer protection of what is yours. There comes a time . . . and this is a law of nature, in which I believe implicitly, when quantity turns into quality . . . and when all of our struggles, all of our efforts will turn the tide in our favor. But for this to happen, patience and persistence is needed. Nothing else will do it.

I want to make another statement of equal importance. The young folks now fighting for "Indian rights" ought to be able to do it with intelligence, and they can only win by learning from the past. To listen to our young folks, they invented the fight for Indian rights. How foolish this is! We are giving up a whole history of honor and valor if we accept this position. There is much to be learned from the struggles of the past, and if we learn from the past we are so much further ahead, for then we are standing on the shoulders of some great men and women. We don't need to start from the dirt-bottom; we have their experiences and their sweat and blood to build on. Some of the young Indian people are relentlessly alienating the older folks, who would normally be their staunchest supporters and allies. This is a needless posture to take. Not everybody can picket. Some of us are fighting just as hard, on other fronts, in other ways, in directions equally important. We should support one another, and we can, if the proper measures are taken, and the decencies of Indian relations are observed.

D'ARCY MCNICKLE, participant from University of Saskatchewan, Canada, at the Princeton Inn, where breakfast and dinner was served throughout the Convocation.

12

Red Power:
Real or Potential?

BEATRICE MEDICINE

O RAL traditions, folklore and mythology have typically been instrumental in the cultures of the North American Indians. Thus, it is not surprising that the conception of "Red Power" is shrouded in fanciful and colorful "origin myths." One such tale from the "Moccasin Telegraph" relates the origin of the phrase. It seems that a group of *truly* Indian youth were driving around in an old Chevy at the meeting of the National Indian Youth Council in Oklahoma City (1966). Some bright, brash brave made a sign. He labeled it "Red Power" (with N.I.Y.C. beneath it), attached it to the side of the contemporary "speed steed" and Lo! a dynamic, vibrant force in Indian affairs was created. Still another creation myth states that as an outgrowth of a play on words of a name. "Mel Tse Thom," a logical conclusion resulted in the term, "Red Power." These are the flavors of indigenous folklore which are still persistent, and add spark to our existence.

If "Red Power" is indeed a factor in the present-day North American Indian scene, perhaps it might be examined in a meaningful manner. However, a comparative treatment with its counterpart "Black Power" is not the object of this presentation.

It is the writer's contention that many of the slogans such as "Red Power," or the standard conference opener referring to "Indian time" do indeed construe value orientations as native adjustment to another world view. Ubiquitous slogans on car bumpers both on reservations and urban centers are replete with phraseology such as "Eskimo Power," "Indian Power," "Think Indian," "Better Red than Dead," *ad infinitum*. Apparently, these proclaim an awareness of "nativeness" and might possibly portend a cultural resurgence of identity. Therefore, a closer, though somewhat superficial, examination of this nebulous phrase and its possible connotation seems appropriate at this time.

The first public exposure to the term "Red Power" occurred on the February 5, 1967 report of the Frank McGee Television newscast. This news item indicated that a coterie of American Indians advocated "Red Power" and, were spearheading a *movement* toward independence. This appearance was an outgrowth of the National Congress of American Indians' meeting in Denver. The then Executive Director of this national Indian organization apparently sanctioned the use of "Red Power" in these terms: "to run the reservations"; "to participate in American life on our terms"; "to withdraw from everything if the tribes so wished"; and claimed that "treaties give rights." He demonstrated the use of slogans—as "We shall over come" and "Custer died for your sins." Most importantly, it seems that this media presentation coalesced Indian sentiment to include these wants—"self-government," "not asking the bureaucrats," and "wanting larger revolving loan funds" (1). In short, the dominant theme centered upon self-determination by native enclaves.

The base line of the printed entry of "Red Power" into the life of Native Americans can possibly be attributed to Stan Steiner's ebullient book, *The New Indians*. (2). Statements provided by this nonIndian writer shall serve as a springboard to our presentation. This despite the fact that at the Governor's Interstate Indian Council (Wichita, November 1968), many of the Indians quoted in the book denied the authenticity of the quotations.

> Steiner writes: "In fact, the 'young educated Indians' who founded the National Congress of American Indians were mostly employees of the Bureau of Indian Affairs. The government in the traditional practice of colonial administration had sent them from post to post, from tribe to tribe. By this divide-and-conquer technique it had built the extra-tribal bonds that led to the new form of Indianness." (p. 273).

The observations simply express the fact that Pan-Indian forces which had been prevailing for some time had formed into feelings of 'inter-tribalness' in one organization on a national scale. Traditional indentities and separate tribal organizations point to the prevailing "*given*" that Americans did, and do,

BEA MEDICINE, "It is for us to determine how to use it, how we may wisely and intelligently utilize this growing capacity which offers so much potential."

indeed see ourselves as distinct from "Whites" and "Blacks." Our names for ourselves: "Dakota," "Lakota," "Nakota" mean "humans" or "allies." *Diné* in Navajo means "people," etc. The nomenclatures point to distinct tribal differences which form the basis for great ethnocentrism but establish clearly the boundaries of "in-group" versus "out-group." This idea of some movement transcending tribalness in existing organizations was really, in my estimation, a cornerstone for this movement.

Steiner quotes Vine Deloria, Jr. who says, "We are continually discovering groups of Indians in parts of the East." (p. 276). Steiner further says.

> "Many of the Red Nationalists come from such isolated or assimilated bands. The emergence of the new tribalism, or tribal nationalism, brought about the emergence into the light of hidden, forgotten bands of Indians who resided in the darkness of the cities. It was as if all these years they had been waiting. Waiting for the day." (p. 277)

Close examination of the native people in the forefront would reveal that the majority of them stemmed from tribal backgrounds. Many had been socialized on reservations. Possibly the stifling factor was embodied in the generations of administered human relationships and negating of decision-making of Indians in these social settings. These were the onerous conditions which had to be rectified, as seen by the people in the "Red Power" movement.

More significant, perhaps, is that the social climate in the 1960's was one of ferment by the darker-pigmented minorities in the United States. The "Red Power" movement might simply be seen as a backlash of the self-assertiveness of the activists in the "Black Power" and "Brown Power" components in modern American society. However, only one Indian stated, "in the future, we will work closely to bring our movement and the black movement together." (Steiner, p. 281.)

In general, Native Americans see their position as unique. The idea of power, or of a force transcending tribal aggregates and essentially controlling the destiny of Indians, obviously had great appeal to Indians. As this new social revolution appealed to the youth of all segments of the dominant society, so, too, its appeal was great for younger Native Americans. It thus served as a rallying cry for hitherto fractionated and isolated younger Indians. As a corollary, more Indian youth were attending institutions of higher learning. More personnel was available for involvement. Many of the younger people reflected the bumper sticker stance—"It's In to be Indian." Quite possibly, if the new, exciting "hippie" generation was so enthralled with Native Americans as to emulate them with beaded head bands, moccasins, and an interest in peyote, what, then, was wrong with being an Indian?

Whatever the speculation about the appeal of "Red Power," its implications centered in the connotations of its dynamic and manipulative qualities. The potential of control seemed powerful, indeed. However, its positive aspects have never been universal in the Indian world. Many Indian people consider it a misnomer; some consider it as action: picketing; destroying property; capturing islands. Some consider it stupid. The more common apellation of "Red" in the sense of *Communist* is a factor also considered by more conservative Indians. No matter what dimension provides the view, "Red Power" is a term of great emotional effect, and this is especially so among the youth of many isolated reservations.

According to Steiner, "self-determination and political independence are the source of the demand for Red Power," (p. 283). It seems evident that this new nationalism can be equated with power. It follows that the earlier Pan-Indian movement plus personal involvement and commitment to the effective use of social, political, economic and intellectual power can truly mean a cultural renaissance of the Native North American Indian.

"Red Power" as a diffuse concept has been seen and utilized differentially by each Indian-interest group. The *"modus operandi"* has been revamped to fit the immediate needs of the group. Early, the overt play of power began with strikes, fish-ins, which displayed a youthful inter-tribal character.

One avowedly militant group has followed the "black" pattern, with picketing, with signs, disrupting meetings, and using revolutionary rhetoric complete with four letter words. Some students of this description have not made the transition from confrontation politics to the exacting studies, which possibly are a better step to effective power.

Another group has organized to pressure the urban community, but has been aware of the community and its imagery of Indians. It appears to be aware also of particular and peculiar Native American "habits." Essentially this awareness has been accomplished by circumventing police arrests, by patrolling urban streets for inebriated "brothers" and "sisters." Apparently, it has also ventured into homes to insure that Native Americans hit the time clock train and get to work on time. One loosely organized group recruited Indians for the "March on Poverty" in Washington. All these groups present an inter-tribal group and they tend to be from all ages. The actualization of "Red Power" strikingly has caused splintering within some organizations. One youth group has devised an alternate to an either/or accommodation plan to an adjustment. It does dichotomize into reservation or assimilation polarities, which is usually the case.

This group suggests awareness of tradition and pride in Indianness as a third alternative. Additionally, the group is involved in direct social action on reservations. A further offshoot of this group is also enmeshed in reservation affairs and in "changing the community." Other splinter groups of youth have attacked the ceremonials, or the status quo, white-sponsored celebrations exploiting Indians.

If the type of anti-system approaches mentioned above are a measure of "Red Power," it can be seen as a strenuous force in social change. Congealing of social forces, i.e. power, has also been a factor in the numerous "Workshops to Train Indian Youth in Leadership." Very often, however, these workshops have sounded better in summary reports than in reality. Generally, but not always so, an earth mother cult in the leadership of the workshop has somewhat limited their effectiveness, because this adds further to the splintering of organizations.

There is great evidence of a lack of follow-through and continued concern with the student participants in these workshops. This is, essentially then, resulting in a dissipation of power and planned community change. Stringent evaluation and assessment of any program is sadly lacking in any of the action programs I have just described. Now, most of the previously designated social movement groups publish news sheets. Some have a familiar ring: *Warpath, Americans Before Columbus, Indian, Guts and Tripe,* and so forth. Writings in these publications vary from vociferous, clever, ridiculous to crude. However, they present articulations of awareness and an attempt to center upon contemporary Indian issues. Ideally, social cultural analyses of Indian communities and reservations result in specific actions. At present it's very difficult to assess the impact of "Red Power" on Indian reservations, communities, and enclaves of urban Indians.

It is also extremely difficult to obtain data about how power is diffused, utilized and channeled in these groupings. It can be postulated that all the aforementioned devices are utilized to change "The Establishment," and effectuate decision making on the part of the Native Americans, and to display a measure of control over our destinies. Recently, the reclaiming of non-utilized federal lands is the operational framework of militancy and radicalism, or to quote an elder of mixed tribal-hyphenated background, who is at one of these places, she says, "We want to be where the action is at." Insufficient planning and extreme struggles for power and control have seriously hampered events in this area. Still the reclamation project goes on. Thus far, all projections of power have been fragmented, and organizationally and egotistically controlled.

In some instances tribal chauvinism and "provincialism" has seeped much power from actions, which have captured the public imagination and, seemingly, at the outset, cemented tribal differences.

At present the cry for Indian unity as a prelude to power seems somewhat far fetched. Self-interest of tribal groupings have provided a stultifying effect. Insufficiently utilized, it seems, is power in the political realm. Involvement by Indians in this area is not as great as it could be. This arena presents great potential. Political savvy could procure Indian participation in local, state and national affairs. Power deriving from a legal stance, clearly articulated and understood by all Indians, presents the greatest and more realistic play for power in the dominant society.

The most critical and crucial component for Indian power might be termed, for lack of a better phrase, "intellectual" power. This does not necessarily equate intellectualism with academia and/or an advanced degree. We have only to look into the diverse tribal histories of our people to point out instances of wisdom and astuteness.

This portion of power would stem from wisdom and an awareness of the structure of power in the dominant society. Additionally, constant analysis, discussions, and weighing of the many fluctuating issues in the Indian world would seem essential. Hopefully, this level of power would not be built upon personalities, but upon resilience and the ability to retreat and turn certain issues over to others more capable of handling these issues.

In the days of treaty-making the creation of chiefs was standard practice. Contemporarily, this is seen in the "House" or "Task Force Indian," who appears on countless conference agenda and government committees.

None of the previous dichotomies of "Red Power" (Physical, mental, spiritual, intellectual), is mutually exclusive. However, it might appear that marching and mouthing militancy has not yielded great gains for the Native Americans. Indeed, the demand-and-reparations route might become obsolete for the Native Americans, as it seems to be doing for other minorities. Parenthetically, a complete understanding of treaties relevant to one's own tribe would provide a sounder footing for negotiations and Native decision-making and control. Underlying all of this, however, is a renewed pride of cultural heritage displayed by the contemporary Indian. A preoccupation with "identity quests" for tribal affiliation and feeling is paramount. This revitalization movement is seen in focused interest in "traditionality." Native dancing, music, art and costuming are as much a part of the reservation "pow-wow" circuit as the urban

Indian "pow-wows." Subtly, but with certainty, a recharged interest in Native belief systems is evident and has great potential for fulfilling spiritual needs. Conferences for Native Americans are saturated with "Indian values" panels. Many of these values have had to be ferreted out of books, some written by anthropologists. Others have come from memory cultures and knowledgeable tribal elders, and some traditional values have been construed fullblown from some modern Indian minds. However valid, these spiritual forces seemingly add to the fierce pride of being Indian and give strength to the movement. This is one aspect of power which somewhat resembles the traditional power. For example, *Orenda*, among the Iroquois, *Wakan*, among the Dakotas, which was thought to give a qualitative essence, and to bring a supreme awareness in being one of the "people." Being committed to the group and working for its welfare and benefit was part of the concept of the older power configuration of "power."

Spiritual power, which might impart wisdom, compassion, understanding and concerned involvement for all Indians might also serve to circumvent tribalism of the extreme vindictive sort, which is very damaging for Indians who are concerned and working for all tribes. The common plight of the Indian entrenched in poverty and despair might also foster commitment for the physical, mental and spiritual well-being of all of us. Common bonds of "Nativeness" and "Indianness" and a touch of tolerance may eventually cause us to rise above injurious punitiveness on all levels. I agree here with one of my previous speakers, but here I say it seems that factionalism appears to be endemic to Native American populations. I'm speaking in terms of how tribes break up and splinter and so on.

Intelligent dialogue and cooperation on important issues pertaining to Indian affairs is a goal worthy of exploration. "Built-in chieftainship" and a collection of power for personal "ego-trips" tear at the very fabric that many are trying to weave with multi-tribal wefts to produce a cloth of unity and concern, which is able to withstand the constant shredding inflicted upon it by the dominant society. Potential of power to Native Americans rests upon positive self-image and a strong identity and sense of worth. Subsuming this are long entrenched tribal heritages which have withstood the ravages of war, segregation, and deliberately planned destruction of indigenous cultural systems. We may not "overcome" but we confidently and with dignity shall find our destined place in the power structure of the dominant society.

Social anomie causing stagnation in our Native communities must be overcome by the diligence and wise use of "power" *by* the people. By the people I mean all the native enclaves in

North America. It is virtually impossible to secure closure on such a vigorous force as power, as it pertains to North American Indians. It is for us to determine how to use it, how we may wisely and intelligently utilize this growing capacity which offers so much potential. Or, stating this another way, how can we further make this latent and fragmented force manifest and functional? Certainly, the largest dimension of the power problem is the hard fact that we cannot achieve the goal of equal opportunity for all unless we can accept a significant redistribution of power in all aspects of our social, political, economic, and intellectual, as well as our legal existence.

Our discussants this afternoon are Mr. Ben Hanley, Mr. Bud Mason and Mr. Dick Wilson.

Mr. Hanley, would you care to comment?

DISCUSSION

Red Power: Real or Potential?

BEN HANLEY: My interest in "Red Power" is in trying to harness this power that apparently we have, this intellectual power. I find the Navajos exclusively have been able to harness this kind of power. College kids are coming back to the reservation. If they all have acquired this knowledge, what do they do with it? They keep asking us to go back and see the injustices done by the tribal government itself, the BIA, the bureaucracies.

So we formed the corporation to harness the power, and I think, we are harnessing it to the extent that they are advancing the cause. Do we want to harness it or go out and, say, take up arms, burn the streets, burn things; put on a fanfare over deprivations.

DICK WILSON: First, I think that the issue is this, in my own mind: Is the "Red Power" phrase meaningful? Really, is it something tangible, something we can touch, any number of ways we have to touch it? If there is such a thing really as "Red Power," then, I think, it must be something that binds both the urban and the collegiate with the reservation Indians. Because you have as a basis the reservation Indians, the Indians still steeped in the culture of the reservation. We may unite on pinpoints, perhaps, as we've said earlier, but we'll still remain the pinprick. But, with the reservations behind us, the pinpoint has a sledge hammer behind it that becomes lethal.

So, this to me is what "Red Power" should be. It's something that transcends these differences and factionalism, as has been said quite well. And talking about confrontation, the rhetoric of confrontation, as a basically urban Indian. (I was raised on the same basketball and bubble gum diet as any other urban person was.) It is said that a logical case before reasonable men of good will can bring results. I have discovered this isn't true. There is an old adage, "the screeching hinge gets the grease," and the point is you don't get any help unless you squeak.

Unfortunately, many administrators don't respond except to a threat. Now, there are several intelligent ways of using threats. Not necessarily do you have to make them yourself or direct them. Sometimes you can run a flat bluff, which we have frankly done. Some of our best gains at the University of Oregon have been achieved while running such a bluff.

Not highly publicized, yet there is an underlying veiled hint of some sort of unpleasantness that could occur. I don't think these things were posed in vain, nor were they concerned with trivia. The things we asked for were reasonable, not frivolities. I think the things we ask now, in retrospect, appear somewhat conservative: things concerning admission policies, financial aid for American Indians, our right to recruit and to form tutorial services for Indian students, as examples. These things, while making awfully good sense, always are presented with a thousand reasons in opposition, as to why they couldn't be implemented. Some Black people wearing panther buttons said, "If we can't go to this university, no one will," and for some reason money appeared. They got help.

So, it's unfortunate to have to use this kind of rhetoric and this kind of manipulation. Certainly, the people on the reservation do not understand, will not agree with it. This is not to say that we do not deplore the idea of having to threaten anyone. I find this repugnant. It's kind of like the idea of a volunteer army without the draft, would it work! I think probably the analogy is well taken, and I refer to the last point mentioned in Beatrice Medicine's talk, in connection with relying on treaty rights and guarantees. A government lawyer, in a rare moment of candor, told me that a treaty is only as valid as both signers are strong. In other words, can one signer force the other to keep the treaty? How are we going to do this? Because, frankly, who gives a damn in hell whether we burn the reservations. We don't live in the middle of cities, what kind of clout can we muster, what kind of impetus does the United States government feel to keep the treaty we signed? A moral right, a moral urging? These last only until the dollar sign appears.

So, I think, that as much as we'd like to play the game as peacefully and as quietly and in as orderly a way as we possibly can, if we're talking about any kind of power gain in which our interests are liable to come in conflict with the so-called mainstream, then we're facing the prospect of the need of using some sort of threat or force and this is something we're going to have to decide upon.

Frankly, if it's known that we are going to shy away from this, at any time, that there will be no such threat of any kind of an unpleasantness, (I don't mean necessarily physical violence or bopping someone over the head, or setting fire to a store), but if they know that no repercussions can possibly come of ignoring us or ignoring what we need or want, then, "Red Power" is simply an empty and hollow phrase.

So, I still have the question in my mind: Is it real and can it become real, because I see the reaction to the very phrase from reservation Indians in Oregon. I see reservation Indians in Oregon deploring some of the things that we've done and yet glad to send their kids to the school we fought for and to take advantage of the gains that we've got by these methods.

I'm not here to defend the means that we've used, I'm defending the things we've done with those means. That's my concept of "Red Power" and I'm willing to use it in conjunction with other minority groups or by ourselves, if we have to go that way. I think the term "Red Power" was coined by the American Indians four hundred years ago.

BUD MASON: My concept of "Red Power" is that of being an activist or a militant. I was born and raised on a reservation and went to the boarding schools and I know what the conditions are. I know what the conditions are around South Dakota. We have probably five thousand, six thousand Indians in the Rapid City area.

I went from being probably a conservative to a damn near radical here within the last year, because of the things that happened in Rapid City. There were a group of guys my age who were pushed into a corner and we had to come out fighting. There were incidents that happened in Rapid City where people were manhandled by white doctors of the Public Health Service.

I think a lot of you are familiar with the incident that happened up at Sioux San in Rapid City. This got us together; this united a bunch of guys and we became militant as hell. It wasn't until we were going to demonstrate, and finally decided to focus all our attentions against PHS in Aberdeen, that results came. We communicated with some Black organizations, and we communicated with some of the most radical Indian groups that existed. We were in touch with some of the national press. We had set our date to demonstrate at the area office in Aberdeen. We were told what they were saying. They were saying, "We'll just let them be and this thing will cool over."

It wasn't until we planned and went ahead with the demonstration against the area office that they decided to give in. Now, one of the things we were asking for, was an Indian

Service Unit Director. We wanted a voice in setting up our own health policies. We were talking about Indian involvement, we wanted an Indian Health Advisory Board, which they didn't want to have anything to do with. But it was because of these acts of militancy that we were able to get where we are now. We do have an Indian Service Health Unit Director now. We do have an all Indian health board. We do make recommendations to the service unit as to the health needs. And they do listen.

Some people are hung up when we start talking about militancy. I go back to my reservation and they have visions of me burning buildings. We organized students at Black Hills State. All of our students are people from the reservation. We have seven reservations within a two hundred and fifty mile area of Black Hills. And we have something like an eighty per cent drop-out rate. Neither the faculty nor the administration was doing anything about it. We had something like a hundred and eighty thousand dollars going to the college and yet they were doing nothing about it. It wasn't until we got organized and we marched on the administration building that they finally recognized us.

I think the big thing here is that there are so many organizations and that they are not flexible enough. They will just continue to tear down the establishment, but what we are doing, we opened through our militant acts. We opened up the doors, we established communications. Now, we're thinking about doing constructive things for our students. But, I think, really sometimes you're pushed into this position; sometimes you have to become militant. I think there really is a need for action. Pete mentioned a friend of mine, an associate of mine, Duane Bird Bear, who is in jail. Duane is a real great guy, and he demonstrated against the BIA at Littleton, Colorado.

Seventeen Indian BIA employees signed a formal complaint against the Bureau. Duane and a bunch of guys didn't want these Indian people to lose their jobs, so they demonstrated for them and took over the building. I was in support of this. I think it's great. I know what happens to BIA employees on my reservation where I come from: Probably every big promotion that comes along goes to the white man who sits in the office. I'm for what these guys are doing.

BEATRICE MEDICINE: I think we have a very good arrangement of involvement on various levels, as to how "Red Power" is conceived by individual Indians. Now, why don't we throw this open for questions. We're not going to come up with final well-planned answers, you know, to give you a blueprint to take home with you, but this will be a discussion open for questions.

BUD MASON: Since we have a group of students here, I think they should know that we're trying to set up a national student conference in Washington. We were talking about setting this up for Columbus Day of this year, so we could all be down there. Maybe we should talk about it.

A SPEAKER: There is one question I am interested in: When you talk about political action, I assume you mean action through traditional political means.

BEATRICE MEDICINE: No, I don't.

A SPEAKER: What do you mean?

BEATRICE MEDICINE: Any well conceived plan could fall in that category. But, I think, that if we had some very good Native politicians, and decision-making committees in Congress, it could help us. Also, I think, we could have a well planned action program to change attitudes in towns, but intelligently, and this could be only one of various possible directions.

A SPEAKER: The difficulty I have with that is this: If, as you say, (and I agree with you if you're talking about more traditional political channels like electing Congressmen or Senators, for example, if that's where the seat of power is in the scheme that you're talking about) what do you think the chances are of: 1) changing the way that those elections are run, and 2) of ever getting any significant number of Native Americans in those Congressional seats.

BEATRICE MEDICINE: I think the chances of getting Native Americans in those seats is increasing, but we do not have the economic power to really utilize the decision making power on all levels in Congress, because of various less interested groups in Congress. We are going to have to start somewhere, instead of this marching. You know, marching and planning these confrontations results in this: the minute they leave the meeting rooms the decisions are still made by people other than the Indians.

A SPEAKER: I want to bring this up. I think this will clarify the position of those students who are from Montana. Now, you raised the point that we can have economic power to make a change from the orthodox political system. We're working on such a concept right now in Montana. First, let me say that all these references to "Red Power" are applicable, but at different times, and at different places. For instance, protests would be the only reasonable form to use if for instance your reservation were being threatened with termination. I think if you simply barricaded reservations they'd have to contend with the fact that you may not want to leave. Now, for an example, the thing that we're doing in Montana to express Indian power through an orthodox channel is this: We've incorporated an organization called Voter Development, and Voter Development has this concept inherent in it, that we can start registering Indians. There are a great many people involved in this. There are people who are working in an environmental defense fund, there's a poet involved, there's an attorney, there are law students. We're working on a concept which involves basic reactions to this book called "The Emerging Republican Majority." Now, "The Emerging Republican Majority" says this: That Nixon will go after the south, he'll go after the west, and he'll go for the sunshine states in the midwest, this belt that runs through Kansas, Utah.

If you read the book I think this would be clear. He thinks he has the west tied up, so he can ignore us, and at this point he does, and maybe he can. But we in Montana feel that if there is any kind of voter registrations program the threat would be enough to give the Indians a sizeable amount of political power. If you look at the population statistics in Alaska, Arizona, New Mexico, Oklahoma, Montana, North Dakota, South Dakota, Idaho, California, Washington, you will see that in some places Indians, if they voted in a block, could control the elections.

Since the national elections are running so closely, if we had any kind of a sizeable vote in these states they could swing it one way or the other. Realistically they may not be able to, but the mere threat would give you more influence than what you have now. Now, our tactics are these, we are going to try to locate funds and use this as a clearing house outside the reservations. We're going to use volunteers from urban centers. We're trying to look into what we call the McCarthy Case. Our tactic is this, we're going to pick three or four different places in which there is a democratic underdog, and we're going to throw as much money and as many volunteers as we can into this area and get this guy elected. I think that it's a little bit like Napoleon's China. They should have left the Indian asleep because he is beginning to wake up and the whole west will shudder.

A SPEAKER: I don't actually have a comment or question, but what I would consider a dilemma. I think what was interesting were some of the comments made in this morning's presentation regarding American society, or North American society in general. As to the white society, that it's polluted in every describable fashion, and one would shudder to try to predict what the future is going to be for this country.

I think we all agree that this is true. We don't have to look too far to have it verified. This afternoon, so far, all the comments and presentations, have indicated that the only way we are going to improve our situation socially, politically, and economically is to become a part of that society that we deplored so badly this morning. This to me is very confusing. There seems to be some agreement that the mere election of, perhaps, Senators or Native Congressmen, or Indian school boards, or Indians to any organization that seems to manipulate power, and has influence over finances, will solve all our problems. I don't think we have to go far to find out what will happen. Surely, the Black situation is some indication of what we can expect by going this route. The Black Panthers are not part of Congress. They certainly don't get any support from Black Congressmen or Black Senators, or at least we are led to believe that. Who seems to be doing the most for the people? Not the Congressmen, not the Black Congressmen, not the Black Senators.

So, I think, in terms of "Red Power," if we are committed to some sort of improvement, and I'm not willing to say in what areas we should improve, but if we are committed to some type of improvement, then I think we have to reformulate and realign our definition in any sort of action, in terms of "Red Power" with the people, with the Indian people. Not with white structures, not with white organizations. Sure, they control the money, but simply by voting an Indian to a Foundation board, is he going to increase our chances? Money is available; there is no problem, anyhow. I think we have to realign along these lines, otherwise the structure, the system, is going to usurp these programs of our people.

DICK WILSON: I don't know if I can answer that, but I will try. I think it's a very well articulated statement and you might find it also from a large number of reservation-dwelling people. A statement very thoughtfully made and a point that I was alluding to during my remarks, is that we are compelled to use methods actually expounding a philosophy that's repugnant to the reservation-dwelling people. Yet what we say we do is trying to benefit these people.

However, my own view of this is: The Indian community on a reservation does not dwell in that kind of isolation. There is a certain amount of involvement already there which is not being used efficiently, and this is one item. The second thing, and this is a little more historical, I think if we fail to use effective tactics against the dominant society now, we are repeating history, we are repeating a mistake.

A SPEAKER: I don't really understand, because if we align only with Indians, then how are we going to economically feed ourselves if the white people are still out there destroying the atmosphere, and we don't have any power over them or any relationship with them. If their pollution can come over on our reservation and destroy the trees, how are we going to sustain ourselves?

A SPEAKER: Well, this is precisely the dilemma. We have to look for new solutions by putting an Indian on a pollution probe board or something, or having them on a board of directors of an industry. There is no guarantee whatsoever.

A SPEAKER: For one thing it's a contradiction of what you were saying a while ago. You said the last place you wanted to put an Indian was on the pollution board, but I think I see a real problem if we dismiss the economics of it by saying, "Sure they have the money." Two friends of mine who are Black Panthers are having a real problem because the white establishment has the capital, and until the Blacks get the capital they are in a lot of trouble.

I see a lot of validity in terms of where are we going to solve Indians' problems. It's not just a matter of getting the capital; it's not just a matter of getting the power, because if they aren't educated, if they aren't brought up to the standard where they can realize that they are living in a society in which now Indians are the smallest minority and that there does have to be some isolation. I can't see how we can avoid this. There does have to be isolation to a certain extent. As to which Indians can identify themselves, and prosper from their identity, but I don't think that you can work in complete isolation.

A SPEAKER: I'm not so sure we should worry about the environment as such. I think the Native Americans themselves have problems over and above this one. If we are going to concentrate ourselves on saving the enviornment, if we work for this benefit and in this direction, we work for the benefit of the whites, but it still will leave us in our same situation. So, I think, at least in my own mind, that we just want the same opportunities within the system as everybody else. We don't want to tear down and start over, nor do we want to isolate ourselves. I think all we want is the same opportunity and all the advantages that come our way within this system, and, so right now the question of environment, it is true, is becoming a problem, but that is very minor compared to some big problems that we have.

A SPEAKER: I'm talking about equal opportunity though. This was the exact rhetoric that was being spoken by Blacks ten years ago and look where it got them.

JEANNETTE HENRY: I think what we are all talking about is the fact that struggle is necessary, and you're not going to be able to get away from that. Some can squeeze through and get their doctorate, and buy a house, and bring up their kids, but a good many will have to take it on the chin. Now, if we take the premise that there will have to be struggle (and you don't have to make that premise because there is going to be struggle anyhow) then the forms of struggle should be understood. You look all around the country and you see our people split in all directions. A little organization springs up here, another there, mostly among our young people. There is a gap between the people whom our youth have a right to look to for leadership, and themselves. I'm not even questioning what the cause of this is. My point is that it has to be bridged, because by themselves the youth will not get very far.

The second point is this, I would think that the most important step that must be taken is to bring the whole of Indian society together including the adults and youth at some point in which they can work together and then develop a specific Indian form of struggle. You cannot utilize the Black form or the Chicano form or the White form. A specific Indian form of struggle must be developed. A creative intelligence must come together and develop such a form whereby a small group of people can make an impact and make changes in a nonviolent way.

BEATRICE MEDICINE: Now, what issues would coalesce all Indians in your present premise?

JEANNETTE HENRY: Well, there are so many issues that it would take a meeting of the minds to choose an issue. Nobody has the right to choose the issue. But that's what is happening. Some choose the issue, Ellis Island, which has no relation to what is happening on their reservation. Some choose the issue, Alcatraz, which immediately alienates aboriginal people still living, who own Alcatraz. It gets a lot of publicity; nobody is against it, but it does no good. To choose the issue requires the united effort and confrontation of all the Indian people, and it shouldn't be done by one group.

MARY NELSON: There is no doubt in my mind that there is going to have to be a struggle. The Indian people will be compelled by circumstances to unite and identify themselves as Indians. Once we attain this, we can pick our own issues. But, on the other hand, when you see a four year old Indian girl sitting in front of a television set watching a cowboy and Indian show and hoping the White hero is going to kill this Indian, you know we have lost something someplace. Those Indian people have lost the traditional value that Indians used to have, and some of the younger generation, especially on my reservation, which is Colville, right now are trying to push through a termination bill, and this is very dangerous. But a lot of the young kids would just as soon call themselves "not-Indians."

It's only when they get older and better educated that they begin to value their heritage. Education to me is one of the prime factors. There are a lot of institutions in the United States with programs going but they don't understand what the problem is. Why do Indians have such a big drop-out rate? The university that I go to started out with twelve, and before the semester was over with, two of them dropped out. They can't figure this out. For the Indians to unite or to get any type of education or any type of unity, it has to begin on the reservations, with education on the reservation where the people are. It's obvious that a lot of tribal councils are not doing the job and they are not going to do the job until people, Indians themselves, scholars like ourselves get in and actually do something.

BEATRICE MEDICINE: The Indian way has been brought up, and also the question of cultural background. How is this achievable? We're going to have a panel on Native American Studies programs and this might have some relevance. But we discuss these things, and what kind of a plan of action are we going to formulate in order to deal with these questions?

BUFFY SAINT-MARIE: If "Red Power" is going to be accepted at all it should be accepted on all levels. The Indian way of doing something is to do whatever you can the best way you can, which doesn't mean that we all have to become sociologists or lawyers or folksingers, or whatever. It seems like there's so much talent in so many fields among the Indian people that encouraging one another, like they were talking about this morning, is one of the best ways to do it. There are some of us who can operate on levels that others can't. Some of us can go back and forth between reservations and the white society and be effective in this way with nothing more than a blown mind now and then, and other people just can't do that. We should remain in contact as we are today with one another.

A SPEAKER: Well, it seems like we are all looking for the significant issue. There is always the one big issue. Are we going to keep the reservations? I don't think the question has come up here yet. I mean, I think it has but we let it go by. I know the big issue in my life is what am I going to do when they terminate the reservations? Until then you look for other things. Well, it may be here and it may be there, but I think you should express it. Now, when our people tried to take over Fort Lawton, I say, yes, give them help, because I think that's the way urban Indians from Seattle are going to express themselves. I think that those of us who don't live in the heart of Seattle have no right to say, "Don't pull off the job like that," because that's the way those Indians express themselves. I think that when the big issue comes we'll have a united front.

DICK WILSON: I think the issue has been touched on twice in Colville, which is the preservation of the land base, which I think is of paramount importance. I think the biggest reason for a generation gap, if you can say there is one (and I think there is) is the fact that at the time when the young people wanted the elders to stand up and be counted and say, "no, you go to hell, they are not going to terminate and liquidate the reservation," the elders didn't do it. The young ones who opposed it were made to look like young radicals, were not representative. I think if there is a generation gap, there is one developing in this area, and it's a failure of Indian adults active in the community to assume unpopular positions. Most of the time too many Indian leaders sound like somebody running for office on a law and order ticket, or someone trying for the Little-Brown-Brother award for that particular year. I think this is the reason for the gap. The present policies are not going to win anything. The adults on the reservation must take the lead in fighting for the people.

JOHN WINCHESTER: Educators, tribal leaders have discussed "Red Power." I've heard it at conferences and situations such as we are in today. I don't buy the term "Red Power." It's a connotation of communism. You have an individual like Steiner that comes along and writes a book in that area. A lot of ears are tuned into that and a lot of attitudes have developed.

In Michigan we have four reservations. They don't comprise many people. The people, the tribal leaders were kind of stunned by the book. However, it's selling well. The fact remains that "Red Power" has a connotation of interest, because of some activity that has been conducted in a militant way. I myself was involved five years in it. So I know what it is to be knocked around, slapped and pushed in the water and kicked by Washington State troopers. I know this means something to the youth and the people who are concerned about our life style. But to me I buy *Indian* Power . . . *Indian Power*, for the simple reason that you have tribes throughout the United States that will subscribe to that kind of terminology.

In Phoenix Saturday this was considered in a couple of workshops. The fact that Alcatraz has been prominent since the latter part of November and dating back into 1964, that it was a gimmick back in 1964, and that it was a gimmick the second trip around was discussed. This is fine, this is part of our total awareness, and I buy this too. But when somebody attaches "Red Power" to me, I don't appreciate it. Along with Ottawas, Pottowatami and Chippewas in the State of Michigan, and some Tewa people, spoke up at Phoenix Saturday. They can't quite agree with us. They say we are not Red-skins as such. The press takes care of this, they perpetrate these things. The New York Times just recently put this thing together along with a few other items. So if you want to describe yourself as believing in "Red Power" then you're alone. I'm not with you.

A SPEAKER: Let's identify who our enemies are and be honest about it. All the time we talk in these indirect ways, not telling honestly who is oppressing us. We imply, but yet we don't say who the real enemies are. I know who my enemies are. They are white people. Perhaps that is an expression out of paranoia, but perhaps we need paranoia power. Like last night all the white people at the dinner and the reception, I felt very much alone, scared. I think we should express ourselves honestly on such matters.

JOE SANDO: I'd like to try to identify one of our enemies. I work with college and high school students. I would like to identify the American school system as one of our major enemies, because they teach us to be white men. By the time a student begins to learn the English language, the teacher, usually a non-Indian, begins to prove his point. The students are frustrated; they are confused. This is the first stage and maybe then they begin to drop out. If they stay long enough, they begin to reject the Indian ways and begin to think that they can be white men, because if you're a white man you can get a color-TV, a big car, and other material things. This is the second stage, and I think we lose many of our Indians there in the American school system through their rejection of their Indian identity. They want to be a white man but they can't, because American people are very conscious of color. I don't care how much education you have. If your skin is brown or non-white you are never going to be a white man. You'll have to *find* yourself a place in society. But the whites go on, without such difficulties.

If the Indians get a good enough education they might reach the level that I identify as pseudo-acculturation. They begin to think, are my Indian ways all right, or are the white man's better? From there, I think they go on to a fourth stage and this is bi-acculturation, where they know that concerts are all right, operas are all right; if you understand these things and enjoy them go to them, but you also know that your Indian ways are all right and keep the two apart. Back home the Pueblo people have been getting ready for the past two or three weeks for a ceremony on Holy Thursday. They have these religious ceremonies, and every Indian who is around there who is a Pueblo is going to be involved in it, and they will find some sort of an identity. They don't have to go to a pow-wow in the city because they know they are Indians, but that is tribal. On a Sunday dictated by a Christian religious feast, Easter, all these Indians will be taking part in this pseudo-Christian activity again, but they find an identity there. They have made this observance in their own Indian way.

Unfortunately, I see in many other Indian areas, where it has been mentioned that the spirit of the tribes have been raped, you no longer have these things, so you are looking for identity. This is where I find some "Red Power." I could go on and

BUD MASON, ". . . what we are doing, we opened through our militant acts. We opened up the doors. . . . really sometimes you're pushed into this position; sometimes you have to become militant. I think there really is a need for action."

try to describe some of the relations of some of the young people who are no longer identified as Indians, but this is where
our enemy is, the American school system.

JESSE GREENE: I'm from the Nez Perces Tribe of Idaho.
I'm a member of the governing board of the tribe, the secretary
of the executive committee. I believe in Indian identity, and the
legal aspects of gaining "Red Power." Education, your own
self-determination, your self-respect, is involved here. I'd like to
give two illustrations of how it works. One is by an educational
process starting on a local level. There you have to go into the
school boards and set up your own policies in the schools. We
achieved this in the State of Idaho by going to the governor
and having him create by executive order the state advisory
board in education. We started in 1965. This year we have coun-
sellors in three different areas. But it takes a little time and a
little work. You could talk all day about it, but this is an idea
of how more or less your legal power works.

The other one I think was mentioned by the gentleman back
here about treaty rights. In one case this involved fishing rights
in the State of Washington. Now they chose a different type of
power, a demonstrating power. I looked into this when it actually happened. I decided that it was not what we the Nez
Perces wanted because we have a different situation. There are
four tribes which have rights on the Columbia: the Yakimas,
Warm Springs, Umatilla, and the Nez Perces. This Columbia
fishing area is completely off the reservation.

Well, back in 1962 when I became involved in this, (I came
there after I taught school in public schools off the reservation
in 1963) I decided that maybe something had to be done about
it. In 1965 they started arresting Indian fishermen. Of course,
what happened there was that in 1965 all four tribes were not
united. In 1966 they completely shut off Indian fishermen on
the Columbia River. There was only one group, the Cook's
Group, who demonstrated with rifles on the Columbia River.
They were a group of Yakima fishermen, approximately thirteen.
Finally in 1966, after this happened, the four tribes decided that
something should be done about it. So they started getting studies made of their culture, of the history, and how we acquired
our fishing rights.

Well, we acquired our fishing rights through the Treaty of
1855. This gave us hunting and fishing rights both on and off
reservations. Then in 1967 the Indians went back fishing again in
masses. The state did not bother them. Of course, it wound up
in federal court and the Indians have been fishing since, but
there is one thing wrong with this. The federal judge decided
that the state has regulatory powers. They have almost cut our
fishing areas in half, but we still have that one right; they still

can't take it away. We proved it through legal action.

BEATRICE MEDICINE: It's interesting to me that every group saw power differently and it's coming out completely in the discussion.

A SPEAKER: I agree with Mr. Sando on the four points that he brought out, even though I am still a student. I'm only acquainted with the southwest area, but I noted that a lot of these Indian leaders, whether they have a profession or not, forget about these young people that are still in colleges and universities struggling to get a degree themselves.

There are many of us wanting to do something for our fellow Indian people, but yet there are not that many Joe Sandos around to help us from day to day, from month to month, from school year to school year. We don't have that much contact with a lot of you older people who travel. I want to make one comment here, that we want to see you on college and university campuses talking about "Red Power" or Indian Power or whatever you like to call it, whatever you agree with, but give us something to follow. We will be ready to go, we will be ready to help you, but give us something to follow.

BUD MASON: Talking about leadership— I've been working with the Indian students. I'm an older student myself and still going to college, so I have more admiration for a younger student now because I have grown up. Some people on reservations who have become educated are more like white men, I think, than the Indian student is nowadays. Most of these people are geared toward the accumulation of wealth and hard work and concern themselves too damn much with making money. Somebody brought up the subject of where are we going to get our leaders? Our leadership is out there with these younger people, because most of these guys are interested in doing their own thing. I think if they were given the opportunity by their so-called older tribal "leaders" to help do something on the reservations, we would really make some advances towards bettering our situation on the reservation.

(A 15-minute Pause Was Called)

A SPEAKER: I wanted to talk to Mr. Sando on the point that he brought up about education. I thought this group was sort of a very good example of what he was saying, but the level of our discussion has gone from semantics to talking about various kinds of issues; talking about developing power when it seems to me that the power is going to be evident because there is a desperation that is growing among our people. That has been going on all through the fifties, and you all probably know this as well as I do.

Let's talk about the suicide rate; 15 to 20 per cent higher than the rest of the country, 25 per cent higher crime rate, arrest rate. All these things show we represent a certain kind of experience, but we cannot isolate ourselves from those things, because they are creating a desperation that's going to develop the same kind of power that the Blacks have had during the sixties and, in some cases, haven't known how to handle. So, here we are looking around for ways of acquiring power, and I think it's not going to be too long before power is going to be popping out all over. We better know what to do with it when it comes and stop talking about whether we are going to name it "Red Power" or "Indian Power" or anything else.

A SPEAKER: Talking about violence even in a black-white situation we have certain fears, a paranoia, about violent action. There are people who have termed rats eating their kids, as violence. They have defined a suicide rate as violent. And that kind of violence is going to bring about certain reaction. Because some Indians I know want to have the ceremony and the dress and the things that mean something to them, but right now that means the rats, the social situation, the economy and everything else. But it does not mean you can have your culture. You can have your pageantry and whatever, if that tribe has the cultural information and gives it to you. What that means in America, because of the majority of whites, in America you are losing out. It also means that as an Indian you're confined to all the rest of those statistics.

A SPEAKER: No, no, that's wrong.

A SPEAKER: You mean the statistic is wrong?

A SPEAKER: He didn't say the statistic is wrong, he said you're wrong.

A SPEAKER: When you go back just as I go back to my elders and ask them for information, they can give me information that you can apply to the white history and white information and it will be on the same subject. But when you dig a little further, that subject will emphasize the massacres, the slander, the put-downs that we don't see in our regular history. Now, if you can find correct information from different sources, then your Indian culture is of value to you. This is why some of the Indian cultures that exist with meaning have elders who are functioning and teaching their culture.

A SPEAKER: What does that have to do with violence of people who are Indian, and partially because they are Indian.

A SPEAKER: Because they don't have the information that gives them an affirmation for their culture. They have no way to identify—

BEATRICE MEDICINE: That's not quite so, because there are definite movements to get people of varying cultural backgrounds and views to try to better conditions, especially in urban areas, but that's what counts, for that particular level of social action. But we also have, on the other side of the coin, the result of the relocation programs in urban areas where they do not know their culture. We are getting these students in universities who are really not aware of their cultural backgrounds. Now, this poses a problem in terms of how do you help people like this find identities, develop involvement and so on. This whole idea of power, whatever it is, activization of attempts to control destinies, is on various levels.

LEW BARTON: I'm a Lumbee Indian from North Carolina. We're non-reservation, but don't be mistaken, we're Indian to the core and we always hve been. I wanted to say something first in regard to identification of our enemy. I think the greatest enemy the Indian people have is distance.

First of all, the federal government has moving control over us and I don't like what they do to the Indian people. Right now they are trying to force us to integrate our schools in North Carolina, which they themselves refused to help us build in the first place. We had to build them ourselves. They've already taken our college over and so I don't have very much respect for the BIA. The greatest enemy of the Indian people now, as always, has been distance. The old policy of divide and conquer still exists. You can be as scholarly about it as you want, you can justify it any way you want, but this is the main problem. And the problem has always been the problem of unity.

In the very beginning there were two minds among the Indian people. Some people said, "No, we see the handwriting on the wall. This culture is here to stay. Let us accept it, let us cooperate." This is the line my people took and we know that it doesn't work. The other people said, "No, let's fight." So, you had two minds from the very beginning. So much of what the enemy has done to us has been done through us and by us, because these groups were set at odds with each other.

The first need, it seems to me, is unity, and this is the foremost thing. In 1958 when the Klu Klux Klan came in and decided to warn the Lumbee Indians about some things, we had to devise our own strategy, in the light of the situation at the moment, and that was shoot up the place. But this doesn't always work. Sometimes quiet diplomacy works better. Believe me we have learned that too. I think some of the things that have already been done, have been gigantic steps in the right directions, you know, especially under the American Indian Historical Society. I think these are all good things and if these are good projects let us all support them. At least let us give them our moral support, let these people know.

When we got in trouble with the Klan we got telegrams

from tribes all over the country offering to send carbines, and men to use them. So we published this, and believe me, this helped. Now, this is a very extreme situation, but nothing takes the place of unity and it's so tragic for one little Indian group to be out here absolutely alone. The Negro stands off at a distance, he doesn't understand our problem. He may be sympathetic, but if it isn't in his interest he's not apt to get involved. And the same is true of all other ethnic groups.

A SPEAKER: I agree with you whole-heartedly and support that. All of us to some extent have been correct in our statements, in our assumptions, but let's get to the crux of the issue. The issue here is power, and *unity* means power. A lack of unity means factionalsim and factionalsim means weakness. So the crux of the issue is power. I think we all agree that self-determination of our people is our main goal, but what stimulates factionalism is in deciding what sort of tactics should be utilized to obtain these ends. Miss Medicine made a distinction between groups utilizing militancy and others utilizing wisdom, understanding. Now, these are two categories and to me I think this is manifested in the terms ''Indian Power'' and ''Red Power.''

We have two different philosophies here. One is ''Indian Power'' and one is ''Red Power.'' ''Red Power'' might possibly means militancy and ''Indian Power'' might possibly mean using the traditional ways. It's very important to reach understanding, because this lack of understanding is keeping us apart. This is bringing factionalism. I think this panel is a good example. We all have these different philosophies and we are not understanding one another. But at least we are talking.

FRITZ SCHOLDER: I'm from Santa Fe. I've been hearing about ''Red Power'' and ''Indian Power'' and it seems to me there may conceivably be another power and that is that the American Indian does have a common denominator and this is a well developed esthetic power, and maybe we should say pride power, a very positive power. Because the American Indian more than any group that I know has an esthetic sense. Whether it's been through painting, sculpture, or whatever. Writing is a new form, but it's coming in very quickly now. Through the dance, music, right on down the line of the humanities, this is our birthright. It seems to me, if this crazy world survives it will be partly through the humanities.

BEATRICE MEDICINE: Again, it's part of the heritage that I think many of the young people are not quite aware of.

HARVEY McCUE: This question of unity has plagued Indians not only in North America but Central America, and South America for hundreds of years. Although, to a certain extent historically, Indians in other parts of the western hemi-

324

sphere achieved a unity upon occasion which was never before realized and has never been realized since. But it seems to me that the whole question of unity seems to be a reverse process. Continual discussion is needed in unifying on political grounds. But before we can try to unify on political grounds I think we have to unify on a much more common, humanitarian, and more socially central ground. In Canada, hopefully, by this time next year there will be an organization under way to create and develop a national Indian culture festival which will try to bring together all of the cultural expressions and artifacts under one sort of common roof, hopefully to present to the Indians in Canada their differences along cultural grounds as well as their similarities. Once there is a common understanding and common recognition from the east coast to the west coast, from central Canada to the west, that as human beings we do share common things in terms of culture, we do share certain values, and at the same time that there are differences among us, then perhaps political unity will have an easier birth.

BEN HANLEY: No one can deny the Indians have been abused and most of the discussion so far pointed out the problems we have. But Indian Power is here—good grief, we have all these people here and that's power. Now, what I want to know is how are we going to use this power, how are we going to put it into operation? This can be a springboard for discussion. How can we make it operate? Let's make our battle plans and get out on the warpath and use this power.

A SPEAKER: I'd like to comment on the fact that I didn't know about the American Indian Historical Society until I was invited to attend this meeting. It seems to me here we have a very dynamic gentleman, Mr. Costo, and his organization, to unify us again along this line of unifying the scholars, the students. This is a way of putting this power together and I offer this as a suggestion. I know I'm using his name very liberally in this sense, but this is a start in trying to unify ourselves. Granted, I sometimes don't agree, but that still shouldn't have me fight it. I should lend my moral support anyway.

RUPERT COSTO: I wonder if I might say a little about this. I have been in this fight for forty years or more. Over the years I have been very much opposed to the Bureau of Indian Affairs. There is one thing that we could do at the present time. Some of you know about this and some of you do not. But there is a little black book called "Title 25, Indians." It is a directive of the Bureau of Indian Affairs that regulates everything the Indians do on the reservation; controls education, welfare, leasing of land and everything else. Now, it is my opinion this is unconstitutional. I think that would be a good beginning: to instigate some sort of action against the government to have this stricken from the books, because there are practically two constitutions, Title 25 for Indians, and the U. S. Constitution for everybody else.

If we can do something for the gentlemen in Lumbee county —we should indeed do it. We are glad that you are here and we have tried to bring in new people, young people, that you don't see going from one place to another all over the United States. You see the same faces, the same people, the same meetings, and nothing ever comes of it. We hope something will come out of this. We want it desperately.

One of the things we have touched upon is education. We have worked with the State of California for a long time in the correction of textbooks. We have formed a publishing company, the Indian Historian Press, the first Indian publishing house in the United States. We were organized in October and we have the first book out now. An evaluation of about three hundred and fifty textbooks used in the schools through the United States —has been made. Now, in our state we have laws enacted whereby any book that in any way demeans a minority may be taken off the shelves. We have helped the Minneapolis school district in their own program. In every one of these three hundred and fifty books the Indian is degraded in one way or another. In many places we are omitted altogether. There is no mention at all of federal relationship with the Indian tribes or the Indian people. These are areas we can work together in. As everyone has said, there must be some way for us to get together and we hope that this convocation will help.

A SPEAKER: I'd just like to make a few comments about what Mr. Costo just talked about. Last night one or two of us, as many of you did, sat up until all hours of the evening discussing what this conference is about, and what we thought we could do was to extend everything here that's going on, and this is a very broad area, in two regions where we could meet together periodically and right at that particular time we were only thinking of the inter-mountain group. But as I began to sense what is happening here . . . I think this is very aptly stated here in Mr. Costo's paragraph in his opening remarks. That is, "If the Convocation is successful, it will be continued. If not, then we must say that we Indians are not yet ready to unite for such purposes." So, I'm just throwing this out to you as a group as to what we could do when we leave here. Are we going to leave and forget what we talked about or are we going to continue what we're talking about? I'll leave it at that.

ARTHUR JUNALUSKA: I am a dramatist. I'm going to start by referring to some remarks—I hear one young gentleman make concerning the word communication. I think this is a field which is so much lacking among Indian people. I think there's a communication gap rather than whatever else you want to call it. I think this brings us power and again as the young gentleman said, there is power here, yes, there is. Everyone of us is part of that power whatever it may be. That's the unification of something because it covers every level of life that each one of us live in and work at. Through this medium we can help bring this unification about.

If we could think back hundreds of years ago, if we could just visualize these many tribes coming together on horseback to a big settlement (or convocation, is actually what it was). They came from many tribes. Even as enemies they came, but yet they were willing to hear even their enemies say what the tribe wanted, what their people wanted, what they were fighting for. This was discussed verbally. Each one had his chance to come before the council and say what he wanted to say, as we are doing here, and they arrived at some solutions to the problem.

I wanted to make one statement (even though many of our great leaders throughout the country made great statements, wonderful statements), this one time I'm going to the white man. I know Mr. Costo knows about this; he played football in his young days, I did too. I'm taking this quotation from the great coach Vince Lombardi in his retirement speech from Green Bay when he left the Packers. They asked him "What is your success due to?" He said, "I'm only the coach. I have so many players and each one is schooled and has a duty to perform. If he doesn't do it and come up to it we get rid of him and we get someone else." He said, "that is success." Here you have that unity of body.

This happens today in many parts of Indian leadership throughout the country. Some are chiefs, some are members of council, tribal chairmen, and many are officers even in the Bureau, or other agencies where there are Indian people. Many times we even have too many Indians who let our own people down. Sometimes we say, which happens too, we may hurt that person if we take him out, but actually if we are going to better ourselves we have to take such strict means and, as Lombardi says, "if they don't do the job we get rid of them and get someone else." There's too many who should be "taken out."

I worked with some young people last summer as a dramatist at Bacone and Santa Fe. We had a cross section of about six hundred young people and I feel that in my department of drama it was a successful program. I heard many young people from nearly a hundred tribes voice their opinions. Some of them said "Red Power," we are going to demonstrate; we want this power, or we're going to lose our culture. Some were schooled in government schools, some in public schools, and some in church schools.

So I do think I gained quite a bit concerning the young people. It isn't just their problem, it's so in every age group. That's why I say I don't think there is a generation gap; it's a communication gap. We are transferring our thoughts to the young, and gathering what they have in mind. This is unification of a representative kind in every field. I want to speak about my own Indian field just for a moment. I did work this summer with these young people and many of them came and told me that through this course they gained immeasurably. It helped them in school. This is my field: dramatic art. I've been in the professional theater as a playwright-director for the past twelve years. One of the very few Indian people in this field, and in every facet you can think of; production work, directing, scenic design, costume designing, every facet of it. I've seen so many in Hollywood who fail that it gives us a bad representation. They say that they can't get Indians to fill roles which call for Indian people. I say every role could be filled. I'm going to give an example of the drama in Cherokee, North Carolina. It's past the sixteenth year, a tremendous public success, about the Cherokee Indians. If you see it, which probably many of you have, eight of the main roles which call for American Indians are filled by white people and have been for the past sixteen years. According to the original contract, if the Indians were capable of filling these roles they would be filled and put in these positions. Those roles, after sixteen years are still unfilled by Indians. The producers say they can't find them. I went down there and challenged them. Even up to the Cherokee Tribe and Council. I stood up there, also I stood up to the Bureau people. I said I will come down here and run a dramatic workshop for six months and I will have every one of those roles filled by next season. I will guarantee it. There are so many of these things going on throughout the country. I'm fighting for the American Indian Repertoire Company to do these things.

I mentioned once to an organization, "How we can let people know about our own people and what we want." Select ten good Indian speakers and just let them absorb all the information we have and want and send them through the millions of television, radio and as public speakers throughout the country, and this is how we can do it.

A SPEAKER: I have an idea which won't save the world, but it might help us to implement this thing we are calling power, and I think of it as potency. It has to do with what somebody said about the American Indian Historical Society, which has obviously people, and not just the same old people. The Indian Historical Society is an organization that I know, and if you've ever seen their publication, which happens to be about the classiest publication happening in the whole country, you would agree.

It not only deals with history which has to be corrected, which many of us don't have the time to research for ourselves, but it provides a link between us, really. When I was on Alcatraz for a while—here were people all concerned with how to perpetuate Alcatraz from day to day but they didn't know about the Dos Rios Dam Project, which has been written up as well as most of the other current event things that are happening, in the Indian Historian. I think through a magazine of this kind and through our contributions to research and whatever else we have to contribute; licking stamps, whatever, we too can help.

I think that it's one way for us to keep in touch. The other thing that I want to say has to do with something else that would help us to communicate, not only between and among ourselves, but to the rest of the world.

GEORGE GILL: I think what we're talking about here is kind of hung up a little bit on "Indian Power," "Red Power." I don't care what you really call it. I think that what we need, if we want to perpetuate this convocation, perpetuate the Society so on and so forth in our Indian culture is to more or less dedicate ourselves to the particular thing that we can do.

I'm an educator at Arizona State University. Benjamin down there is going to be a lawyer and hopefully he will return to his tribe. I think we've all got to dedicate ourselves to the thing that we can do and if I can help any as an educator I'll be glad to and I think that's what we have to do.

BEATRICE MEDICINE: What about the pre-thirty generation?

A SPEAKER: One thing I'd like to suggest, because it hasn't been touched on, it's economics and one project that's going on through Oklahoma for Indian Opportunity in eastern Oklahoma is a buying club. I don't know how feasible it is for other people, particularly on the reservations, but for non-reservation Indians I think it's something that should be looked into and thought about and perhaps tried out in different places. Because what happens is you get a group of Indians together who are being oppressed by the white establishment through the whole country-store syndrome. Suddenly now they have a choice to buy the kinds of things that they want. They make the decision of what they buy and they're getting it cheaper because they are buying it wholesale as a group. You can bring in a lot of different people, like lawyers, because they can make sure everything is done within the legal structure, and businessmen who know how to get the best pieces. I think there is a whole field here that can be looked into and can be very important, for day to day living for Indian people; it also contributes to unity.

A SPEAKER: Now, I think that a good expression of Indian Power would be something like this. The Dean of Philosophy at Montana has developed a program called the Defender Program. He sends all of his senior class out each year to the reservations and this has a two-fold purpose. When an Indian is picked up and slapped with an indictment on a criminal charge he has the students research the case. In the past the Indians have been filling up the state penitentiary at the rate of one in four. Well, in the last year having the seniors research the cases, he found that seventeen out of twenty-one were innocent and he got seventeen of them off. In the years past, what would happen is this: They would slap the Indian with an indictment and the prosecuting attorney would say, "We have a great deal of evidence against you. We'll charge you with second-degree assault and if you plead guilty we'll get you off with a less amount of time." It was a wholesale railroad job. He's found out by sending his students out and researching these cases that he could stop this All of you who are associated with universities could push for your university law school to do something like this.

The second purpose of this Defender Program is of corrolary interest here. By getting the white lawyers out to the reservation it is believed a sense of involvement with Indian problems can be developed. Secondly, the law students go down to the penitentiary and they research the cases of the Indians who have already had sentence passed to see if he can get some of them out, and he has had a couple of successes. The Indian Club, with the law school, is pushing right now to get an Indian on its parole board because they find out the Indians get longer sentences and they spend more time in prison, and this is something we could all do; get an Indian on your parole board in your state.

A SPEAKER: I think a lot of you people here are thinking in terms of a national association of Indians. My question is, if such an organization was put together, where is the money going to come from to support the meetings and so forth? I don't think we can depend on a Ford Foundation grant two or three times a year.

BEATRICE MEDICINE: I don't know. We better get an Indian on the Board at Ford. I'd like to ask for a little statement from each of the discussants.

DICK WILSON: Well, I think this particular panel has tried to direct itself to the knottiest problem I think we've got, which is the problem of so called power development and use of it, which is also the development of unity. I don't think there is anyone here who will disagree that we do have tacit unity on specific issues. When you haven't got it you haven't got any power. So, it's most difficult and it's also the most needed; these two things are connected. Obviously if it weren't so difficult we'd have come up with a solution a long time ago, a lot of sharp people have been thinking about it.

BUD MASON: I'd like to comment again on what I said before. I think the greatest potential of power we have right now is the students we have present. I'd like to make a plea right now that they do get some recognition from their elders here. There are a lot of comments made on what we can do— a gentleman commented on the tactics. I know the tactics that I'm going to have to use in my area. If I'm going to have to demonstrate I'll demonstrate. If I have to go to more violent means, I'll go to them, but whatever is called for, for the betterment of my people in my area I'm going to make the sacrifice to do these things.

BEN HANLEY: I only can say that whatever solution or means you can conceive, put it in a proposal or resolution and submit it. Let's bring out the different ideas and get this on a concrete basis.

BEATRICE MEDICINE: I want to thank the discussants for their comments and the contributions made by the people in this panel. The panel is adjourned.

1. Field notes. Bea Medicine Garner. 5 February, 1967. East Lansing, Michigan.
2. Steiner, Sam. The New Indians. Harper and Row: New York, Evanston. 1968.

JOE SANDO, at panel in the subject of Innovations in Education.

"... activism is going to occur. We have sat down. We have professionalized. We have ambassadorshipped. We have done everything we could do like gentlemen and statesmen. It hasn't worked, and something has got to shake before it's going to give."

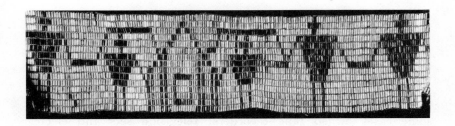

13

The Urban Scene
and the
American Indian

VINE DELORIA, JR.

THE subject for our panel involves a number of highly complex problems. When I was asked to chair this session, I
tried to find out what studies had been done on the question.
There are many studies, but these are predominately by non-
Indians, mainly the old statistics-type things such as the study
of the Indians in Denver, in which such questions are asked as
that of a Navajo housewife fresh off the Reservation: how she
figures her budget every week. I think the literature regarding
off-reservation Indians is incredibly bizarre. I think, too, that
it's time a few studies are done by Indians, not necessarily as
complex as those that have been done before in terms of complicated sociological and psychological factors, but a realistic analysis of what is the scene, in real life, in the urban area.

I hope that what comes out of this panel is that a lot of us
will begin to think about what literature and what studies should
be done regarding urban Indians. It seems to be the policy of
the Department of the Interior, during this administration, to
have nothing to do with off-reservation urban Indians. However,
I believe that the majority of the Indian population lives off the
reservation, so everything discussed at this Convocation relates
to our subject. I believe there is a desperate struggle to find
out what the contemporary Indian is doing, and I would like
to give you an example. Life Magazine is doing a study on the
alleged Red Power movement, which is just in Stan Steiner's

head, and only occasionally outside of that area. They came to Denver and we tried to show them around Denver. The reporters were really turned off at the fact that most of the Indian people in Denver dress fairly well and live in fairly nice homes, had cars that were not more than two or three years old, and in some cases owned tape recorders, television sets and electric typewriters. This didn't fit in with what Life magazine was looking for. So I took them up to Nevada to see Indians on the reservation. We went to see Mel Thom. He had a tape recorder and a television set. We were also on the Walker River Reservation. The reporters expected a conglomerate of Paiutes running around there. They found some very sophisticated tribal leaders having a conference. I think one of the leverages in defining what is going to be the urban Indian community is certainly to be found in the urban area where there are Indian people who have become used to white society and can deal with it.

This subject has relevance to development on the reservation, too, because I don't see that much difference in life between the two. When you go from one to another, there is really very little outward difference, and even little difference in economic problems. So the first person I would like to have address you is Herb Blatchford, who has been chairman of a Task Force on Urban areas. I really don't know much about him, except we were out Saturday and Herb tried to give a report, and something he said annoyed some of the Chippewas who were standing there, and they began carrying on and screaming. So I think that Herb has either something very important to say, or you are all going to be screaming like the Chippewas in about two seconds after he starts.

HERB BLATCHFORD: I'm really not prepared to take any screaming today. The essential thing we have to realize, is that the urban scene, as concerns the Indian, is really older than any one wants to admit. In going over the history, we found that there were some Indians transported from the East Coast to England, who lived there for a period of up to 30 years before returning home to their own country. A peculiar part of their existence over there was that they scattered themselves as much as the urban Indians scatter themselves on this side of the Ocean today in urban complexes. Now we have at one point, the first school erected for Indians. I think that was done by the Congregationalists. It lasted about two years because they had a peculiar way of returning to the Reservation, and they couldn't keep up the student body. So the Congregationalist school closed.

Then we run into the situation all across Canada and Montreal, and such areas. In these places there was a concentration of Indian populations more or less melted into the French element. They became known as French Canadians. In this country,

334

you still have this kind of a situation—Long Island and Wampanoag groups, for example. They more or less resided in the urban areas, and their whole life, it seems, in their whole tribal existence, is near an urban complex. A small part of the Indian population is still residing there, and when you get down to the present day scene, you find that a new majority is now on the urban scene. How did this come about? It dates back to migrations, when they were stepped up somewhat, and we can more or less check this right to the period of the allotment act of 1887, when the Indian land base was broken up into allotments, to dissipate land holdings or concentrations of populations. The idea for this was started around 1819, when Congress passed the first legislation setting up a Civilization Fund for the Indian through education, and education has gone through this process since then.

In 1824 Indian Affairs were under the Department of War, and the Removal idea flourished. This was an attempt at removal. Their idea was that concentrations of Indian population must be dispersed into areas unknown, to dilute the strength of Indian population. So essentially there would be no Indian problem, and eventually, as late as 1953, the House passed Concurrent Resolution 108, which essentially sets forth that these Indian people have to be terminated. According to federal planning, the Natives are mostly dispersed and now it's time to start chopping off federal services. These have been the plans in the past, verbalized or silent, but these plans were and still are very real.

Most of you know the battles in that connection. It was in this period when organizations began to appear, particularly on the college scene, and Indian clubs started to develop. They wanted to do something; they were not only moving into the colleges. These Indian youths were also attracting others on different levels. Certain factors are at work here. The first one is the coerciveness on the part of the government to push people into urban centers. Then there is a group of people who of their own free will went off the reservation into the cities and brought others with them. Of course this makes a strange combination of forces. A situation of more or less stagnant quality exists on the urban scene and the unrest that goes with it bubbles here and there all the time.

When you consider community development, or leadership development, you find a strange set of activities going on, in that the two comparative groups are not communicating together. They have a wave length all their own. They know where each resides. You can ask one family and eventually go the whole round of where they all live, if you have enough time. There is a great deal of migration within the city and without the city, back to the Reservation, away from the Reservation, and back and forth to the Reservation. All this activity is building up around almost every city, and of course in every city you find a powwow somewhere within the area where the Indians reside.

So it's something that has come alive in the urban group and the patterns are always more competitive and more defined. I'm finding out that it's a usable cycle coming off the Reservation to the urban scene and staying in the urban scene for awhile, getting some type of technology and returning to the Reservation. Recently I went around to several tribes to see who was the head officer and who is the administrator there. These were people who spent some time in the cities, who are now going back. We find out with our leadership workshops that those students who have spent some time off the Reservation are now willing to go back to the Reservation. They are much more capable of analyzing the Reservation scene than they would have been if they had remained there. A competitiveness is building up on some Reservations, where traditionally trained leaders and urban cycle leaders are forming a new type of brain trust.

This appears clearly within some of the National Indian Youth Councils, the things they have accomplished in vying for leadership and how they have filtered into the tribal offices, and how they have also filtered into the national offices. The curious thing about it was that something new was added. There was a new Indian as opposed to the old. The business of "off to boarding school and back to the Reservation" which went nowhere formerly, was really aiding and abetting the agencies that were in control— maybe church agencies, economic agencies, and maybe government or state agencies that always did the brainwork for the Reservation. This is being pulled away from them a little and these people are threatened by it. I don't mind very much threats, but now we finally get to the point in history, as late as three years ago, when we had a consultation about Indian centers in Seattle. Here we got together and suddenly this group of people who are running these Indian centers which grew up out of this bubbling activity on the Indian urban scene began to think in broader terms.

Most of these centers are poor day-to-day operations. They never have enough money or enough room, and have more Indians than services. But they continue to exist. There is no way of really stamping out an Indian center, so to speak. As soon as one dies another one crops up, perhaps in another place, and it's bubbling all the time. What is happening is that suddenly we have an administration that wants to ignore the whole problem again. We have shoved them into nowhere and let's leave it nowhere— this is their attitude. "Let's not turn our minds to the question of where we will put these people after sending them on relocation, boarding school trips, or vocational schools in the urban scene.'' This theme is being played, but this administration still doesn't want to look at what they have done with us in regard to this shuffling around of human beings.

In fact, in August, the Democrats did that. Now the Democrats will say that the Republicans started it, so what do you do about the present existing human being that is on the urban scene, who is trying to struggle up the ladder for some kind of livelihood and some kind of goal? You can almost guess that nothing will be done. We've gone through several discussions across the country, on urban affairs, and we find that the goal is to return to the Reservation, to something better than what we left it with. This seems to be an Indian philosophy that doesn't die out, as bad as things get. They have always got that one little bit of ambition, you see, that it's going to be better, and you know when we leave it behind, our young people are going to have something better than we had. That spirit doesn't seem to die and it doesn't die in the urban scene either. When we get the information that they are turning to drugs this is the ''new people.'' You have to reach out from this point, where many are not drunks, and in an Indian population in which I don't see there are that many drunks. The Indians are outdoor people and when they do get drunk, they like to get out in the open.

When they get drunk—they are shoved in a closet some place. Big deal, you know? Simply because someone goes outdoors and gets drunk, doesn't put all the rest of the people of like appearance in the same category. I think we put too much faith in the reporting of things, so we become an element of their salesmanship, and on a lot of stuff, they are packing the statistics more and more with regard to suicide rates for example. But this is what they are looking for and they are *out* looking for it and they find it, of course. Now the urban Indians have tape recorders, television sets, electric egg beaters, and I don't know what all. Back on the Reservation they have the same things, but nobody bothers to look at them. What these reporters are looking for is sensationalism, and you find it through all this reporting that is being done now. Somehow you have to live with the stigma, and I think the urban Indian is tearing down the stigma more and more. When you go into the development now, in spite of the administration saying we don't want to look at this problem, we really don't want to have any part of it, because, good-night, it's costing us all our money to keep them on the Reservation and why should we bother assisting them when they have gotten into the urban areas, they say.

Forrest Girard conceived the idea that we've got to do something about the Indian Center group. Within 15 years we went from two Indian Centers to over fifty. Then consider there are church type centers additionally. There are other types of centers growing up with the urban Indian. The cities and states are saying, "It's a federal responsibility," and the Federal Government is saying "It's not our responsibility." Whose responsibility is it? The Indians themselves are saying, "Well, let *us* be responsible, and we will have our own little nation in this myriad of activity. There would be one place we can be ourselves." Little by little it's come to four walls rather than being dispersed. I went to Albuquerque and asked: Do you know how many Indian people are in this town? They said "No, all our records show is mostly Spanish surnames" and most of the Indian people there have Spanish surnames. For instance, "Ortiz," does that sound Indian? These are Indian people who have melted into another population and been forgotten. This is dispersal; it's the same game all over again. You get a migration of 15,000 people every week and you have half a million people coming through this city every year. That is a big chunk of economy, and they say, "Let's do something about it," but also they say, "Oh, we can't believe those figures are correct!"

But we ask, "What are you doing with all that economic loot these people are bringing in? Business people have the right to the return of the product in some shape to the customer; and maybe this is tagged 'advertising funds,' or 'customer service,' but some of it normally goes back to the customer." In Albuquerque and other towns like that in which Indian people are spending money, there is a different standard, and nothing goes back in services, customer relations, or anything to serve the customer, in this case the Indian.

Here's the same old game and you start playing again. Of course the Indian and the Government funds seem to be married in some sort of process. Again, cities are lacking in responsibilities. The cry that goes up from these so-called city fathers is like this: "How do we put the burden on their back and keep it there long enough so they do their share of taxpaying, and purchasing, and keeping the community on its feet!" There's no end to this sort of irresponsibility. The Task Force considered this project: Let's take a few centers and demonstrate to the other cities what an Indian center can do for a community and to the community. So this is where the idea was conceived, and it was decided to do it through the American Indians United. The Task Force job was first of all to find out what activities went on at the Indian Centers. Item by item we listed them. We ended up with three boards full of services and activities. These centers, with a handful of people at staff, handle a bulk of up to a hundred thousand to two hundred thousand people a year who migrate through the cities, live there. The centers are of tremendous value to these people. But, since we don't have time or money for record-keeping, there is not data on the exact situation. Once we start listing the services we find a massive amount of activities going on. People on the Reservation take as commonplace many of the Bureau's and other services. But in the city there is no other support group, and of course you put it together and do it yourself. We select four centers for the project, and meantime the budget is creeping up, and finally you're talking about a million or so dollars that has to flow into this total demonstration program. We realize it's a selling job that has to be done for the urban Indian. So much on the monetary level.

On the moral level, they have created a problem which they now refuse to deal with, simply because if you step out of the Reservation it is considered you have stepped out of those roles in which the Indian finds himself. That this is not true, only the Indian himself knows. All kinds of internal struggles go on between tribes, among urban Indians as well as on Reservation and between Reservations. The centers deal with such problems in a kind of hand-method way. We just take a case at a time. For instance, take a tribe with three of its members in the city. They don't need a Reservation any more, as it happens. But they are holding on to the land base. They want to keep it all together. Most of them move off and manipulate the land base and disperse it. It seems like the urban Indian now sees a different value, but they still have the feeling of going back to some piece of land when they retire. They are getting crotchety and worn out and they want some way to restore their heads and souls when things get to where they are too heavy for them. But some promoter will get in there and sell off the land base and then most of the urban Indians feel it shouldn't be done, and policy should be to leave the Reservation intact. Some tribal members are going to work some promotion through. Invariably you find somebody else behind the scenes, and it's not an Indian. Maybe it's a politician or church, or any number of agencies that are presently instigating a promoter to do it. This is the old game that goes on, both on Reservation and the urban scene.

Something has to be done and some knowledge has to be gained out of all this. We don't know how many people are involved, and we're pressing the Department of Commerce to tell us, "Where are our Indians?" You know the first thing said was, "Well, in 1970 there will be a census and that should include the Indians, not only the Reservation Indians but urban Indians as well." We don't know how big a population we have, and we quote figures in each city. This sort of thing is only a thumb-nail sketch. We really don't know the number of Indians living in urban cities.

Fairbanks Indian Center was selected, a new center under OEO operation, but they have a peculiar employment problem, where the people from the interior drift into the city with only one thing in mind. They want to work on construction jobs and they will take nothing else. In the middle of the winter, when they start migrating into the city, when the snow is highest, *they want* construction jobs and that's all.

Take the Upper Midwest Center in Minneapolis. Here's another peculiar urban scene. There are two Indian groups . . . two youth groups and a couple of Indian centers, always in a kind of kettle of stew. They are never really fighting, yet they can throw a hell of an Indian educational conference in spite of their differences. Then came the Los Angeles Indian Center. Here again, there is an area of conflict with two centers which have been bubbling in two different corners, for years. What has grown up out of them is a coordinating council to do something for the Indian population of Los Angeles. This is probably the earliest Indian center movement in the country. It dates back to the 1920's and it happened during the war migrations that caused a great deal of shipbuilding in Los Angeles. Yet the Indian Center is a "survival" center. It hasn't been able to stand on its feet. I mean you get some volunteers for two weeks and then they burn out. There is a church-supported center there, and when you operate in that area, it goes back and forth also. Now it is, now it isn't. But the biggest urban population is probably in Los Angeles area. Still, it doesn't seem able to focus on anything. This is another demonstration project.

Lastly, there is an Indian center in Gallup, which is different again from the others because it's closer to the majority population in the country. Here there are a lot of borderline problems, drifting back from the other cities. Yet they are also drifting into the city from the Reservation scene. So you get hung up with 200 drunks on your doorstep and you've got to start babying them—or babysitting for them. You have got to do that. People become angered about Indians being all around town. But they live off the money that comes out of the pockets of these Indian people . . . like 75% of their income comes off these Indian people. The whole city lives off this Indian thing.

So now we have these four model demonstration centers, representative of different categories of services. Then we selected a negotiating team out of the Task Force members. They must go to these four centers and develop feasibility of what these centers could do. Then a proposal must be worked up, to go to the government. But in spite of the fact that the BIA doesn't want to worry about the urban Indian, HEW is now having a hard time working against a wealth of knowledge. It takes Indians to make a foothold into government activities. Also we have to negotiate this proposal into every Governmental agency we can think of, which might have further surplus funds at the end of the year. They will all lie to you and tell you there is no money. A few months later, suddenly they have big money for monumental activities, particularly with the Corps of Engineers.

We've got a lady working now trying to find all the funding possibilities in government agencies. It's a new approach. We will probably be running into plenty of flak before we finish. Yet, the Congress has given money to these people. I think none of us were really aware of the fact we were selected until last December, when we were told "You're on a Task Force." The group started to work immediately. They seemed to sense an understanding, and a different bond coming off the urban scene than you get from a Reservation. The other scene as part of this program is a training ground. This has a lot of potential, but we are just barely scratching the surface. One other workshop is going, which will develop Indian materials by a group of Indian students. They work in a council system. That is a different experiment entirely from any school system I know.

There are all kinds of potentials, to explore, to learn, to examine which has to go on in connection with group management. I served for a time as president of a Red Rock chapter, a traditional Navajo community. Their level of education is about third or fourth grade. It's mostly traditional people compared with development in the city. Of course, we can quickly outdistance the urban scene. They would go back to the city and send us more people. Even Reservations are now realizing that something is going on in the urban scene that can be used on the Reservation. In their thinking process, and in talking to their children, they're saying, "Well, go ahead and try it." And they are thinking, "Okay, live there for awhile, other people have done it and have come back better than they were when they left." Reservations are suddenly realizing there is another potential moving back on to the Reservation, but it's of their own choosing and maybe this is the process they need to decide for themselves.

This is again a new opportunity which isn't available on the Reservation, where people are beginning to look at this very curiously, thinking maybe there is something there, but still they call them outsiders. This is true even of the allotted lands people, who are also called outsiders. They are rural, not urban, but they are off-reservation, still at the end of the service line from BIA, or HEW or anybody else. Allotment is the first step into the urban areas. In other words, if you can think of the urban scene as urban boundaries, right next to that are the allotted lands people who have been fighting for their land base.

They have gone through all kinds of activity in trying to get their rental money, fees, leases. They have to be somewhat competitive to be able to do this. Then they go into the traditional Reservation scene. Some of these are Reservations which are building a little urban scene around themselves. These are agency places which are completely Indian-built, owned by Indians. So we are going to get an internal urban Indian Reservation. And so, these urban affairs are growing . . . with all the potential that is opening up and also with all the problems. We don't know the statistics; we don't have the staff to complete the data. But there is something miserable going on there, and I can't really put my finger on it. We talked about this on the Alcatraz thing, and where do we go from here? Let's have the government offices come up with the statistical work. Maybe in a couple of years we will know more about it, but at least we know now that we have our hands on something more human than judges, or being shuttered through pigeon-holes and our lives charted for us. We have something to say as to where we want to go and where we want to be and what we want to do. We will not be rubber stamps of the BIA.

THE CHAIRMAN: I think the Task Force has mapped out a lot of areas and will map out other areas that we need to know about.

A SPEAKER: These four centers, are they members of the American Indians United?

HERB BLATCHFORD: Some are and some are not.

A SPEAKER: Why was the AIU selected. I'm from New Mexico, and I have had experience with this organization. There is a stigma attached to them, of being incompetent. The people can't understand why HEW chose the AIU. On that account, the people would be opposing the project, that is the people in my area.

A SPEAKER: It was Forrest Girard's position that . . . well, where are you going to start and who are you going to go to, even though it may be a poor example of where to go.

A SPEAKER: I've got a question about this. I know Forrest Girard. One of the problems we have throughout our cities is that our people in the HEW don't respond to us, and we never respond to them. We have a program set up in Rapid City. We have one of the only health facilities in the urban areas, but we really have had no response from Forrest.

A SPEAKER: I talked to some people in Chicago this morning and this is what the urban people are doing. They are demonstrating against the practices of the BIA, also something happened yesterday. Twenty-one Indian people walked into the BIA office in Chicago and were arrested. Two of them were turned loose because they were juveniles and 19 had to post bond. This is a chain reaction. It's starting from San Francisco, Los Angeles, and Albuquerque. They are protesting the wrong-doings of the BIA, and here we are sitting, a bunch of activists, only talking about what we can do. These people are out there doing it. Why the hell can't we give them support. Let's talk about something that is happening right now.

THE CHAIRMAN: I would like to get to the other panel members. I think there is a real question of doing something, and also in knowing what you are doing. This leads me to Rosemary Christensen because over the last three years she has been one of the key people in developing concern in the HEW for the urban Indians.

A SPEAKER: Here again, we're talking about responsiblity. Now the Federal Government, in their appropriation of funds for 1970 . . . I think had something like 47 million dollars for vocational training and relocation, compared with 24 million the previous year, and 3 million dollars for higher education. What the Federal Government is trying to do is assimilation, to get rid of the Indians and get them off the Reservation. Even in appropriations for land development, there is hardly any money. What else can we do with the Indian people but send them out there and . . . okay . . . we can gripe about it and say this has really failed . . . we haven't gotten anywhere with the relocation program and what is it anyhow! But to the white man, this is a success, because he has half the Indian population off the Reservation now. All he has to do is lose them in masses and they become the responsibility of the state.

ROSEMARY CHRISTENSEN: The only thing I can relate is what I know about the Minneapolis urban scene. I'm certainly not taking any credit for any of the things going on in Minneapolis. I just think we happen to have some very active people in Minneapolis from many Indian tribes that don't usually get along. But still things get done. Maybe because the city is big enough so we each have our own area of work. Eventually we come together and everything is done by each little area already. So we really can't put each other down. We have sort of accepted what each person has done. We have two different groups in Minneapolis. I am chicken, I'm not going to say I belong to either, because I try to go between the two. That seems to be safest now. We have a very militant group and a so-called Establishment group. Whether I like it or not, I have been placed in the Establishment group. Bob Carr is director of the Upper Midwest American Indian Center, he is not even Chippewa, he is Pueblo. But he has done a great deal in getting things done. He has received funding from the local United fund . . . $70,000. They have a staff of four and various programs. The more militant group have a center. They also have programs.

So the people have a choice. Some don't like to go to the Establishment. Others don't like to go to the more militant group. We do have a choice, and everybody ought to have a choice.

The Upper Midwest has the Newcomer House, which is funded by another group in Minneapolis. This is for people coming off the Reservation to Minneapolis, who have nowhere else to go. They don't have a job and don't know where to get the rent. They've got like 10 kids, and that is bad in Minneapolis because you're supposed to have 2.4 and live in the suburbs, so where are you going to go when you can't get an apartment? So the Upper Midwest group has like three or four apartments where you can go and stay for two or three months until you get on your feet and get a job. We have a Guest House. We think Guest House sounds nicer than Halfway House. This is where the people go who have problems with alcohol. This is not funded out of the Upper Midwest funds, but from still another agency. These people have to promise to go into a work program. They can stay there and get on their feet again. We're trying to meet the problems and probably it's like a finger in the dam. But the Upper Midwest is really trying. I can't say too much about the other center, because I don't know enough about it. But they are also very active, and are getting money from within the community, and they are using it in a very good way. They have set up something like the Way Aid School, where the dropout student can go, if he doesn't like the public school scene. We're also trying to get the Urban Coalition to fund activities. Both Indian groups are constantly nagging at them, and they have such difficulty, of course, in deciding where to go at a particular moment.

I should mention the one militant group that has done something very important in the area of police relations. This is so difficult in the urban scene, to get along with the fuzz . . . (I've got to stop calling them that . . . that is what my kids call them). They have set up the "Indian Patrol." They do such a thing as keep track of the Indians who hang around Franklin Avenue. They take care of their own. If somebody gets out hand and starts making a big scene, they just hustle them right off, so they don't get arrested and they don't get mistreated, like Indians usually do by the police. I think this is a great service that many Indian groups could do. They are also recognized by the police force.

A SPEAKER: When I was working in Seattle I was with the Urban Coalition and we ran into competition for funds with the Negro people. The government had us in a bind. We had one project called Indian House, related to housing. It was an organization we sponsored, we needed another member on the staff badly, and we went to them and they said, "Sorry, you know, the funds are going to the Black capitalism projects." There was some resistance by the Negro people in the OEO organization. A lot of the Negro people didn't like it. But we were in a tough situation because we were competing one against the other. Did you find this situation in any other urban areas?

ROSEMARY CHRISTENSEN: It's true that in Minneapolis the Indians have to compete with the Negroes. The more militant group American Indian Movement has gotten together with the Negro organization. They have formed a coalition, the Poor Coalition. They are rapping together (that is where I picked up that term). What happens is the more Establishment-type Indians can kind of form a coalition with the other people. It kind of works out, but we still have problems.

A SPEAKER: Did you find much resistance from the Negro community on some of the projects you do, and in funding?

ROSEMARY CHRISTENSEN: This is only from my own experience, but it seems that when the Indians are doing something, they are in a different area and getting funded from different groups than the Negro people are. We work together in a lot of areas, such as education, on the high school level. Minneapolis has a big system of high schools. The Blacks and Indians have worked together to make demands on the school system so that now there is an Assistant Superintendent for Inter-cultural Affairs. A Black superintendent is there and there is an Indian consultant. If any problem arises, it goes through these people. They do make decisions. It's very refreshing to see. The Task Force could help solve many problems. We need living space where we can all fit in. That would be one building under one roof, and we could have activities there. No one seems to be getting money together for that sort of thing. There are no government services available. If you need more housing, renovating facilities, working facilities, you are in trouble.

THE CHAIRMAN: I would like to call on Mrs. Byler, because she lives in New York City, and knows the problems of Indians in such a high income area, where there are real difficulties in getting together.

MARY BYLER: The problems in the East, I have a feeling, are quite different from those in the West, for Indians. In New York City one of the problems is that as an Indian you fade into the rest of the population. To try to get any support for a center is virtually impossible. Nobody is really interested, or they are interested for a press conference or a television show, and that's it. I don't know that there are specific problems in finding jobs for Indians because once they are there, everybody wants the Indian on his staff or in the front office. I think one of the problems is the question of qualifications. They are not qualified for jobs very well. They don't know where to go. I think this is why Indian centers have grown up over the rest of the country. It's a place for people to go to get services. In New York City, I know the difficulty of getting a building. I know they have not been able to get one, although they have one in Brooklyn, but that is quite a distance for anyone coming to the city.

I'm interested in discussing the BIA. They have a relocation program, and are very active in recruiting people. It seems to me that the guidelines they use (if they have any guidelines), are not realistic as to what happens to the person once they decide they are going to go. I think it's up to the Indians in the cities to define what the responsibilities of the BIA are, in terms of who is going to come out and what they should do before they leave. A lot of people think Indians go to the city with money from the government and they live there with government money. If they don't get a job, the government still gives them money. That is not true. The question is, what happens after the BIA drops them; where do they go? How about health services? Do they terminate when you get off the Reservation, will the city provide them? I think people who run centers should discuss it, although my knowledge is very limited about such matters.

BUD MASON: One thing Rosemary pointed out is significant. There is a place for conservatives and a place for militants. My feeling is that this convocation is really aware of what is going on out there with these demonstrations. I think it's something starting, and should be supported, because of the injustices done by the BIA. What happened at Littleton, Colorado, is that there were 12 or 14 young Indian BIA employees who brought up some charges against the BIA in the area of promotions and job discrimination, mismanagement of funds and so on. But there was a group of young and older students, also some non-students who felt that if the employees were to protest, they might lose their jobs. So they protested for them, and they took over the building at Littleton, and tried to negotiate with Commissioner Bruce. They have got nothing but rhetoric from this individual. One charge involved the suspension of three supervisors, and the head of that area. Bruce suspended these three people, and 45 minutes later the Area Director signed a complaint against the protesting individuals and they were arrested. When the arresting officers came to the building, they presented them with a document Bruce had signed. So they called Bruce and Bruce's secretary who is also an assistant to Hickel, said that the Commissioner didn't have the power to sign the document. We have a Commissioner of Indian Affairs who doesn't have any powers. His signature doesn't mean a damned thing. A lot has happened since then, and people are beginning to demonstrate in other areas, in Los Angeles, Minneapolis, San Francisco . . . a total of 7 different areas. I think we should support this. I would like to hear some reaction from you.

A SPEAKER: I would like to address this to Rosemary. I also agree with Bud that the militant movements and other types of movements have their place. Some think that this conference is of secondary importance; that protests and demonstrations are primary. I think they feel, what is of major importance are the *actions* taking place.

THE CHAIRMAN: Well, I have talked about militancy too, and some people have told me it's all rhetoric. You have to take into account first, that there was excellent documentation of the militant situation at Littleton. I have seen the documents. There were 83 employees who are nonIndian. They are grouped in salaries of $6,000 and above. There are 17 Indian employees. They are grouped in salaries of $6,000 and below. There is evidence that there is job discrimination, and that the job descriptions have been changed from time to time to keep the Indian employees at a certain low level and to re-write job descriptions so that whites can come in at a higher salary level. We certainly have capable Indians who can run this Littleton area, more capable in many cases than the whites.

Part of the Littleton problem is that not all factors were taken into account. For example, to demand an immediate suspension from the Commissioner of Indian Affairs put him in conflict with the Civil Service agency. A letter of notification was required in this issue. The Commissioner doesn't have the authority to immediately suspend an employee, under the Civil Service Act. The papers Mr. Bruce signed were null and void immediately. A missing element was that there should have been someone in Washington, D.C., to serve notice on Bruce in person at the time the papers were filed, and demand immediate suspension of the employees involved, so that he could have written letters of suspension. When the demonstration started about 5 days later, a suffecent time gap would have elapsed so that when Bruce signed this suspension paper, notification to the Civil Service agency would have been fulfilled. In terms of demonstrations in other areas, I think people look at these primarily as support for the Littleton situation. Certainly that is a very valid type of demonstration. I don't know much about the people arrested in Chicago, but it would seem to me that if there was comparable research as to hiring practices, and with regard to the makeup of the office of BIA in Chicago, an addtional complaint could have been filed.

So the resolution on the question of employment practices

of the BIA in the city would not simply be a solution of the Littleton problem, but would also be a solution to the problems in cities where demonstrations are taking place. I think we have to look at what the Federal rules and regulations are in the example of the Black protest, to find out what we're *not* doing in our activism that the Blacks were, and are. In one case, the Blacks had legal grounds, the case of *Brown vs Topeka Board of Education*. They had a whole series of Supreme Court decisions when they went into the sit-ins. It was a Federal law already that they could sit at lunch counters and it was federal law that they could go to schools. They had massive support from elements in the white community. They had their own lawyers, and Martin Luther King to get thrown in jail, and he would be out on bail and in a northeastern city making fund-raising speeches immediately after his arrest. These Indian demonstrations have not shown an awareness of the very complex problems of an activist movement, so that now we are reduced to ourselves taking up contributions to make bail.

We have no group of young Indian speakers who can go out to where the money is, to sympathetic people, and raise the money for bail and additional money to continue. What we're doing is basically the reverse. We're beginning the basic research on discrimination and we do not yet have a ruling from the Federal government that discrimination exists in the BIA. It's an uphill fight for us, but the Blacks were starting from a Federally defined position that they have these rights. We're starting on the formally accepted fact that there is no discrimination, and we're trying to move it to the point where the Federal government admits discrimination exists. Consequently, I tell these young activitst that there are many more factors involved in activism if you're going to make it work. I don't think I'm talking rhetoric. We have been on Alcatraz since the middle of November. We're not raising funds in any orderly manner. We're not pushing the administration at the places where it can respond.

BUD MASON: Are you familiar with what happened at Rapid City last summer when we organized the Rapid City Steering Committee? A group of young guys that got together, most of us not even active in community work, probably all conservatives, began to consider the practices of the Public Health Services. What we found and were confronted with was outrageous. We opposed the service unit director and demanded his removal. We threatened a demonstration. The PHS said they would talk to us, and brought out all these civil service rules. We said we didn't care about civil service rules; we want that guy out of there. We broke this down and said, it is no longer our problem at Sioux San (sanitarium) but it's up to the Aberdeen area office. We planned a mass demonstration at

Aberdeen. We gave them a deadline and prepared to bring in all the minority groups. We were ready. We notified the President by radio and television what we were prepared to do. At 5 pm they called and said, "Look, call off your forces. The guy is going." And they put him out. As a result we got our Indian Unit Service Director in. Also we got a health advisory board of Indians in all policy-making positions. We plan the programs for the Indian people in the urban area. What I'm saying is that I think as a result, even if these people don't get suspended because of the civil service laws, it's possible to move them.

THE CHAIRMAN: At Littleton the thing was written up in terms of suspension, and I think, Bud, as far as planning these other demonstrations, they are spontaneous. I don't think there is going to be much planning as to what is going on in other places.

A SPEAKER: I'd like to bring up a point. When the Negro formulated his doctrine of "separate or equal," in 1954, they had a huge intellectual backing. The groundwork was laid for years. Now the issues we are facing are rising rapidly, and as we mentioned, we just don't have enough time to do the homework. What do we do about that situation?

THE CHAIRMAN: We've got the time to do the homework; that is why we're here.

A SPEAKER: I'm not sure if we do, because in this situation, Indian law is extremely complex. Sometimes to figure out the thin threads of this myriad of complexity would take a long time, but the issues are coming up from day to day.

THE CHAIRMAN: That is what we have to clarify. You can go in on water rights or on activist movements. It is going to do you no good on water rights because it's got to be litigated in court. But I am stating unequivocally my opinion that an active demonstration is one of the only ways to fight discrimination in hiring, and I stand behind these guys 100%. The only thing I am saying is that we're putting in a lot of energy and not getting much back out, in terms of accomplishments.

HERB BLATCHFORD: We tried to make a model very early in the game when we came out with certain problems in Washington. This we knew was a question of litigation. The court wouldn't take any more briefs on the issues, so the problem was getting the tribes organized where we could reopen those areas. In this planning, we went on for 30 months before the demonstration itself. Every tribe was contacted, and we got their particular viewpoints on how and where they wanted to push that particular issue. In all this, we were working together. At that time, of course, Alcatraz was being planned and many of you people possibly don't know, but Alcatraz had just gone on the surplus lists at the time the fishing situation cropped up. Now, 5 or 6 years later, Alcatraz gave us a model. We got communications higher and higher as we went along. What we're talking about is strategy and approach. The strategy the Indians have is a hell of a lot better than other groups have, but you've got to use it. We have several cases now in connection with the Gallup Ceremonial Association. We've had a civil rights suit against the city of Gallup and we have the warehousemen in the same situation at Littleton. There was negotiation but it's a very quiet agency and advisory group. It's very traditional. Most of them would never have done anything until one fellow came out of the Red Rock Chapter who knew how to strategize these things, and went in and got hired and within six months he had these people to the point of saying, "Let's do something about hiring and employment practices." Together with the lawyer they laid the strategy of how to approach the whole thing, and this was the forerunner of Littleton. This is the first major battle with the BIA, but it's so quiet that you don't even hear about it. However, the strategy with which it's done is far more important than the noise you can create.

JESSE GREEN: In the fishing situation on the Columbia river, we took the legal route. We won it. It took a lot of years. I am in sympathy with the activist group, but there is one thing I would like to know. What or who gave the initial money to start these movements? I have never received an answer to this question.

A SPEAKER: The fishing matter we did totally on credit, because we didn't have any money.

JESSE GREEN: What about this group here? As a member of the governing body of my Tribe, I'd like to say that we have been fighting for about five years since I've been on the committee.

A SPEAKER: I was interested in some of the answers Mr. Deloria was given a few moments ago. You're analyzing as a civil rights movement, for example. I'm in law school, and I would hope there is some kind of valuable alternative in going through the legal process, to work some kind of change. Unfortunately, as I go through law school, I end up being more skeptical about what change can be brought about through the legal process. A couple of things Mr. Deloria said by analogy to the civil rights movement I really question. Maybe you can provide some good responses. For example, you were talking about the existence of some kind of a federal court precedent . . . some federal laws that the civil rights movement can fall back on except for *Brown vs Board of Education*. It seems to me that the law in this area was constantly unfolding *during* the civil rights movement, and how far this case went, or the legality of so citing this with regard to protest movements, is questionable. The other difficulty I have with your reference to the Brown case, is simply that I'm not quite sure how you're using it. If you're saying that by laying this kind of groundwork and having a Supreme Court decision behind you, you necessarily have some kind of change, then I can't help but disagree with you. It seems to me that the actual change which came about because of this decision in the Brown case, in terms of integration in the southeastern schools, has been minimal at best. However, if on the other hand, you're saying that if we get this kind of groundwork such as the Supreme Court decision, it may not necessarily bring about actual change in and of itself, but that it somehow gives us the stamp of legal approval and gets us funds and this type of thing, I think I might agree with that.

THE CHAIRMAN: What I'm trying to say is, had the situation legally been nebulous as to "separate but equal," (it was still a valid contention), then the people opposing the demonstrators would have been able to go into court and would have been able to justify their arrest and put them in jail on grounds other than disturbing the peace. In other words, they would have said it still is federal law that we can have two school systems separate and equal. I was trying to draw a quick analogy because it seems to me that we have the documents in the Littleton case to show. I have seen them and I think it's conclusive that discrimination exists. I think the only way to bring that issue up is by activities and sit-ins at Littleton. The question is, have we examined the proper processes by which the BIA makes decisions, so that they have to change them in the way we want them to change. You know I really question whether there is sufficient groundwork.

A SPEAKER: I have a basic objection to this. We're improperly comparing what happened at Littleton. What I see happened in Santa Fe, Oakland, and Alcatraz is a very spontaneous gesture of unity and solidarity for one group of Indians who don't know another group of Indians, who are yet willing to back them. This is unity, Indian power. I'm sure you can find some kind of difference in the way they did it, but you can back it up and hope to play it for all it's worth. I would like to get back to the Supreme Court. I'm not familiar with the law, but I remember there was a Chief Justice by the name of John Marshall who made a ruling, and a President by the name of Andrew Jackson who said: It's Marshall's decision. Let him carry it out. So some of us haven't got that much faith in the courts, and we do have faith in actions. I can only repeat what Bud said, I think the conference would do well to endorse what the Littleton people did and say for whatever they did or whatever homework they didn't do, we're proud of them as Indians.

THE CHAIRMAN: I have no objection to that, the only question I would raise is in regard to the Bureau on Littleton. What is going to happen in Chicago and in these other cities, is it going to change there? Do we have to go city by city? Maybe we do. If we do, okay, let's commit ourselves to it, and do it.

A SPEAKER: I would like to respond to what you said before in terms of the fact that often activism takes place without prior consideration. The point is, you know it's happening now, should we stand behind this group? Even though we feel they could have done it better, and we would like to change how it was done. But it's happened, and the point is how do we respond to that and do we respond to it by discussing it to death, or do we respond by beginning to show some kind of support for it?

THE CHAIRMAN: Let's do some determining to see if you will support. Then let's go into these other cities and create the same kind of documentation as Littleton. Don't interpret me as saying the Supreme Court is the final answer for everything, because I think the answer lies with the Supreme Court in only about three areas, which leaves most of the issues in Indian affairs to be solved in some other manner. But unless we prove discrimination with regard to hiring in Chicago, I think the Littleton victory is minor.

A SPEAKER: About a week ago, a number of Indians wanted to occupy Ellis Island in New York. The government put a 24-hour ban on small craft going to the island, and some Indians wanted to set up the same idea as the Indian at Alcatraz.

A SPEAKER: In taking over the island, I guess they all ran the boat one way. People were supposed to call the newspapers early in the morning, but we didn't get on the island, so they called the press anyway and got it into the papers. The Coast Guard then put some big boats there, and had them go around the island. On the shore, police were on guard. We couldn't send a boat off. Some of the group went to the Statue of Liberty on Liberty Island, and they were followed around all over the place by agents.

A SPEAKER: They had helicopters following them.

THE CHAIRMAN: Let me give you a practical problem, you activists who say we need a revolution. The Aberdeen area offers a directorship which is open. It's my understanding that North Dakota and South Dakota have a candidate. Nebraska has a candidate and all three areas have candidates. No concessions can be arrived at. They are thinking of putting a white man in, the reason being that the administration is having a problem filling these upper slots because Indians have been kept at the GS-12 level forever, and you can't jump from a GS-12 to a 16 and 17. If the young people would work on the Reservation councils so that one Indian candidate can be put in the Aberdeen office, this would be a real gain. Otherwise, the fight will be among the Indian people. You will have whites filling the Director spots all over again.

A SPEAKER: A federal lawyer in Portland, in a fit of candor told me a treaty is only as good as the two signers are powerful, and that one signer can force the other to hold to the treaty. He said the Federal government doesn't fear the Indians. Therefore, "Your treaties pretty much aren't worth the paper they are written on." I would like to hear some people trained in law respond to this because I was flabbergasted by it. It makes me think of when my grandfather carried a gun.

A SPEAKER: I think there is probably one way in which he is right. Another way, I question him. A great deal depends on the makeup of a particular court in the final decision. I don't think there's any question as to constitutional law, that a treaty like this should be respected. If this lawyer was saying that as a matter of constitutional law a treaty is only as you describe it, he is probably wrong. Most courts would probably rule he is wrong. However, if he means it as a practical matter, whether treaties can be gutted, if one of the parties is more powerful, I assume he is probably right. Now, do you know what makes up the present Supreme Court, before Nixon gets too many appointments on it?

A SPEAKER: I happen to dig what the minority opinion is. It's a question, I feel, of whether they want what you have badly enough. If so, they can find any number of loopholes.

A SPEAKER: I'm not disputing that, and I'm not familiar with this particular treaty. I would have to see the language before I could state an opinion.

THE CHAIRMAN: Well, I think there are a number of ways to do these things. The BIA doesn't know what to do and they've got 31 spots above GS-12, 7 spots in reorganization, a total of 38 spots. Yet I don't think any of us have enough knowledge of Indian affairs to put good Indians into those spots, or move Indians who are good and have been discriminated against in the civil service on up in the structure. I'm certainly not saying don't be activists. I don't think the courts have the solution to many questions except taxation, sovereignty and water rights. All I'm saying, for God's sake let's just not get in jail for the sake of Indian unity alone. Let's accomplish something.

JESSE GREEN: Back to that treaty, I think he had a good point about treaty rights. We have to look at what's happening and the reason why this Convocation was conceived. There are some very important issues to be resolved here. I mean there is a handful of us trying to push, in our own little corner. It's the ability to handle the nationwide situation which is so important when a group of brains get together who can see the entire length and breadth of the field. This is one reason why, because of the lawyer's specialization in that area, he will see it from that viewpoint. But those of us who know, realize that the law can only function in response to a social condition, and that the social condition has its counterpart. But if both are on a reasonable and prudent scale, then something can be accomplished. But, if in one case this is being done for personal gain and not the principal of the issue, then what good is it? It dissipates. So we've got to look at the point where there is some technique . . . and the others who have gone through this are trying to back up what this technique is. I mean, if you are college-educated and usefully so, you must put that to its best use, and there are those who are living on the Reservation and in conditions of discrimination who just *want* to respond.

We have to take this knowledge and work it through a brain trust of some kind to know where the pressure points are. This is really why this conference has been brought about, because we're looking for that element. We have to come out, not with a lot of commotion, but with some definite direction, a reasonable approach will somehow predominate if you get in a tight spot. I've got the feeling that the guerrila-warfare knowledge of Indians is going to materialize while all of us study and cogitate. It's true . . . activism is going to occur. We have sat down. We have professionalized. We have ambassadorshipped. We have done everything we could do like gentlemen and statesmen. It hasn't worked, and something has got to shake before it's going to give.

THE CHAIRMAN: I think we should be ready with three candidates to fill that Littleton office. All I'm saying is we can get a hell of a lot more impact if we consider a lot more factors.

A SPEAKER: I hope I didn't cause you to misunderstand me. I agree that if the problems are administrative, we take it through administrative procedures; and if the problems involve case law, we take it to the courts. But I just hate to think that the whole existence of our position should be thrown into the courts, where we have only a 50-50 or less chance of winning. The question is: Are we going to survive or not? Otherwise, I agree with you. I think the treaty issue is not a court question, and nobody has any right to say that all of a sudden you no longer exist, just because the government which has a contract with us, wants to break it. My answer is that we existed before they came here and they have taken advantage of us. We haven't changed anything, and we still stand west looking east, watching more and more people coming west. Now they have cars instead of wagons, but we still exist as people, and we shouldn't let their judges and courts decide we no longer exist.

THE CHAIRMAN: I'm not saying everything can be resolved in court, but 95% of the problems are administrative. But, let's not trade slight progress at Littleton for a real racist administration at Littleton. We have to fill those 48 openings in the BIA with Indians who can make it and want it. Of course the white man wants to beat you out of it.

The fact is, that until we resolve the competition and leadership in the Indian community, we are not going to progress. That is the reason why nothing has been filled, because every list that is brought up, the Indians attack. These are not white men who are attacking; it's not white men who are doing it. It's Indian.

Well, we are way over our time. I'd like to thank all of you who participated in this panel, and all the panelists, for giving us their views. We now close this panel on the *Urban Scene and the American Indian.*

Two participants at dinner before Convocation

John Winchester, participant, at panel

Two Special Sessions were held as evening events at the Convocation. One session considered the role of Foundations in funding Indian programs. The second was concerned with publishers and the publishing of textbooks as they deal with the American Indian. Both sessions were largely experimental, and were planned as an effort to develop a better understanding of mutual interests and concerns; and to bring forward the position of many Indian people, both to Foundation representatives and to publishers. It was hoped that a free and unrestrained discussion would evolve. Thus, no stenographic records were taken of the proceedings, in the interest of stimulating such an open discussion. In this report, the Presentations for both Sessions are given verbatim. The discussion is in the form of a general digest of the remarks made.

No names are listed due to the sensitivity of some Foundation representatives and some publishers' agents. As a first small step in the right direction, the ideas, conflicts, and problems expressed herewith—even in so tentative a form—are valuable in themselves. The names of discussants are withheld by request.

14

Special Session:

Responsibilities of Foundations in Native American Programs

Presentation by
BEA MEDICINE

(Note: Ten Foundations were invited to send representatives. Four responded, largely due to insufficient time allowed for the Foundation representatives to make proper arrangements. These four, however, were those Foundations which are most involved in funding Indian programs.)

This Presentation begins with the premise that Native Americans are entering the private sector to seek funds for Indian projects and "problems." By becoming increasingly involved in fund-soliciting activities, Indians must necessarily be cognizant of the expectancies and regulations of the Foundations. At almost any gathering of Indian people—urban, reservation, and non-reservation—one hears such phrases as "funding," "writing proposals," "expertise," and "getting grants." More emphatically, many Native Americans reiterate the fact that Indians are "in the numbers game," and are indeed entitled to their fair share of "Foundation give-aways."

Proposal writing is included as part of the "communications skills" segment of at least one Native American Studies program.

This invasion of the private sector for financial resources might cause us to pause and to evaluate our position in the contemporary scene. A tentative stance to determine involvements, and responsibilities to Foundations and native population aggregates, seems essential at this time. No attempt shall be made to deal with federal programs, except to state that in general, "guidelines" tend to be usually explicit and detailed. Too, Indian groups appear to have more experience with funding through the Office of Economic Opportunity programs. Approaches to government have been varied, from initially employing non-native professional proposal-writers to the utilization of indigenous peoples presenting their own socio-economic data and "being funded."

Because of the cursory and speculative character of this presentation, concrete examples shall not be presented but could possibly arise in the discussion.

Our concern here is precisely because the American Indian is so constantly in the media. Radio, television and national newspapers and magazines relate his plight as being "deplorable." This projected image does undoubtedly have an effect upon private foundations and their decision-making processes. Therefore, it behooves us to ask such questions as—what do those Indian scholars, students, and tribal activists feel is crucial to developing beneficial and realistic transactions between those two groups?

We who are concerned with the general enhancement of Native American socio-economic, educational, and cultural arenas of the present day Indian society, feel that this presentation, though tentative, is necessary. We hope to evoke and crystallize queries and dialogue on the dimensions of this venture into Foundation structures. We feel that Foundations set up programs without knowing the realities of the Indian situation. There can be a possible retort from Foundations—"Yes, we do have an Indian expert," or "we have gone to various reservations. Thus, we did have consultation from the tribes." This may be true. However, the view from the inside seems pertinent and remains persistent.

In general, the majority of the Indians on reservations (and in urban centers) have little awareness of the "funding game" as far as private Foundations are concerned. This should not surprise us when we realize the level of educational achievement which is so pronounced in the media and reflects the minority position of the average Native American. Monies received for social action programs are usually thought of as being "from the government" or that "the tribe got money from some place." This seems logical in context, for proposal writers may be consulted elsewhere, or imported. This unawareness also speaks tellingly of the inadequate communications network of the "tribal leaders" and the rest of the tribe on reservations. A similar corollary could be presented for "Indian leaders" in urban centers. Only recently have Indians in the hierarchy of tribal government begun to write proposals. These have generally been directed to the public sector and have proved to be exceedingly acceptable. This has also resulted in a new breed—"the degreeless expert." The social action programs funded by foundations have not been completely explored by these indigenous proposal writers.

Generally speaking, private foundations tend to fund "palatable natives" who present proposals. Those individuals representing organizations or tribal aggregates tend to be judged by the external cultural cues of the dominant society which makes them acceptable. Obviously, these natives dress, drink, dine, and dance well.

Essentially, directors of programs seem to be funded on the interactional (and often, dyadic) level of the director of the native organization (or tribe) and that person specifically assigned to that aspect of Indian involvement, i.e., "community development," or "leadership training" in the foundation structure. This transaction often precludes awareness of the total picture of the Indian organization or tribe. Further, this dyadic interaction often includes pressures from foundation persons to native organizations or activities to include this "pet Indian" in certain activities. It would appear that personal charisma had great influence upon the granters of funds. Once a charismatic character is captured he seemingly continues as a "consultant," no matter how a previous program in which he was involved has failed. This fact often causes wonder among the native peoples.

Funds for economic development on reservations seem to be of prime importance to the granters. This may seem legitimate in terms of Indian poverty, but very often the cultural values of reservations may not presume that this involvement is necessarily useful for this type of tribal background and its development. Questions of utilization of land, restoration of land, or cattle economy or training management for food cooperatives that may more realistically come to grips with the socio-economic conditions in Indian country are seldom considered. Why should they be? The "pet Indian" (consultant) has all the facts. (This was attempted at one time, but personal idiosyncratic behavior caused failure.)

Another aspect of funding agencies hinges upon the premise that American Indians are too inept and incompetent to handle their own affairs. Thus, money is readily available for "workshops for leadership training for Indians." Leadership in workshops and the attempts to induce changes in *the* Indian community are often of dubious value. Assessment and "follow-through" of the effects of such workshops are often sadly lacking.

In the field of education, one foundation set up a program

for advanced degrees. Although this private agency had experience in funding Indian programs, there appeared to be little dialogue between persons "experienced" (or exposed) to "Indian work" in that agency, with persons running this new program. What evolved was a very unrealistic plan for doctoral candidates. A member of the Foundation staff visited various Indian academicians after the program had been firmly established. This did not produce a change in criteria previously set up, however. This type of consultation reverberates with tokenism.

To complicate matters, those judging applicants were of dubious Indian backgrounds. Final decisions on the applicants were made by two Native Americans, it seems.

Many foundations are still giving grants to nonIndian "do-gooders" who are supposedly helping the Indians or building Indian self-image in a "positive fashion."

Earlier involvements by Foundations in the realm of funding students (on scholastic achievement) has produced several Native American academicians and leaders involved in all levels of Indian affairs. It is too early to postulate the present trend of larger foundations funding potential university teachers. It seems a step in the right path, however.

Other private funding coalitions have established "Indian Task Forces" who make the decisions on grant proposals. Unfortunately, one agency has funded NO programs for Indian tribes or organizations but has given a small fund for a social movement to radically change the urban community.

Other funding conglomerates have selected one Indian to pass on proposals, and very often decisions are whimsical (or appear so) and/or are used as a chastising mechanism by the native person.

The expectancies of foundations are seldom spelled out clearly—i.e., published reports, quarterly reports, etc., by the Indian recipients. A statement by a Native American scholar contained an observation that "The Indians believe in the spoken word." Thus, many do not make reports on activities of their personnel or summary publications on the use of the monies. Another factor may be pertinent here. Speaking and writing in the English language is rather difficult for most Native Americans. Often, dialogue seems clear when a face-to-face transaction occurs. However, when the Indian individual reports his encounter to his "constituency" he may not be too clear about what the commitments are on both sides.

Funds searched for by Universitites for the "good" and "welfare" of the indigenous peoples in the state are often utilized for university development, salaries of professors in certain fields, or setting up book rooms in libraries. If this is opposed, very often the higher echelons in university bureaucracies state that "Foundations have no control over funds." Using Indians to get funds is fair game in Indian country . . . North and South Dakota, New Mexico, etc.

In one commitment to several universities, in the collection of data from tribes, no provision or control was made to protect the informants or the ultimate utilization of the data in an oral history project. Do the tribal groups have a vested interest in the data obtained? How can the information be used for their benefit? How can tribes control or direct investigations into their lifeways?

A criticism that the native American communities suffer from the lack of relevant information funneling back into the community is appropriate here. Effective evaluations of such projects seem not to pinpoint weaknesses of the action programs that could be directed for tribal benefit.

What do some foundations think about Indian programs? From Carnegie Quarterly, Spring, 1969, "To the foundations, they suggest that support should be given to responsible groups of local Indians rather than primarily to large national organizations, where a good deal of the money tends to get chewed up in administrative costs. They recommend also that foundations provide funds for the training and placement of young Indian leaders in research and development projects, and fund a central clearing house for information on research and action projects in Indian communities across the country."

As far as research itself goes, they cite the enormous and growing resentment among Indians because the vast amount of research done in their communities has not been communicated to them in such a way as to be of benefit to them.

In summary, we suggest that responsibilities and expectancies on the part of the foundations and more precisely, of the Indian groups, tend to be obscured and misunderstood. Mutually understood articulations and frames of reference could greatly enhance the communication process.

We feel that this presentation, though pessimistic, begged to be made. Although diffuse and general, it hopefully may cause both Indian aggregates and foundations to begin serious stock-taking of current and future commitments on both fronts.

As a measure of the much-touted "self-determination," American Indians would like an active part in their destiny as it is affected by foundations (and other groups).

We, too, watch the stock market, and we wish you well.

DISCUSSION

Foundations and Indian Programs

The discussion was opened by a Convocation participant who expressed surprise and dismay that the Donner Foundation had recently awarded the University of Utah a large grant for work in an Indian program. Several Participants expressed the belief that Indian people generally do not support the Mormon Church in its Native American activities, that the Natives felt the Mormon Church should not be funded for such purposes, that the church has ample funds of its own, and that such foundation funds would be better utilized in programs conceived by, and directed by Native Peoples themselves.

"Money gives power," said one Indian leader. Too much power is given to a religious group which then insinuates its proselytizing influence into Indian affairs. "This has been done for hundreds of years, and the Native Peoples have lost thereby," said one Indian Participant. Several speakers stated the Donner Foundation should be made aware of such Indian opposition.

A representative of the Donner Foundation replied, to the effect it's their money, and it would be distributed as the Fund trustees saw fit; that the animosity shown in the present speaker's statement was unfair, that the amount involved was only $80,000, and that no effort to support the Mormon Church was implicit in the funding "of a good program in Indian education."

A second Convocation Participant spoke about priorities, and expressed the view that funding of Indian programs should go only to Indian-directed activities. The speaker said, "We must take special measures to insure that recipients of Foundation grants shall not become cripples with built-in crutches, depending upon "grants" for its very life. Each program should be required to prove the possibilities for continuance of a program under its own fund-generating power."

A Participant stated that "Foundations should consider priorities, and what the Indian people themselves want. It is true that these funds are private funds, and private individuals have the right to expend such funds as they see fit. But when a Foundation begins to influence activities, leadership, and policies by means of money, then it is time the People themselves began to exercise some type of influence." A speaker stated that "Our priorities are such programs as the Rough Rock Demonstration School, the Many Farms Community College, scholarships for our capable and talented young people, and particularly scholarship aid for those of our people who are preparing their Doctoral dissertations and are held back because of lack of money."

A speaker raised the question of the Rocky Boy school district, which "Indian people are trying to install their own Board of Education in, since most of Rocky Boy is populated by Indians." These people need financial help to do it, since it is innovative and does not receive widespread aid.

A Participant raised the question about "follow-up in funded programs." This speaker stated that the program usually begins well, goes into activity, and then is left hanging high and dry because there is no more money, there is no consideration about following up the program, and as a rule the results are meager and do not help generally the Indian people. The Participant suggested that perhaps Foundations should have a special department for follow-up purposes, helping to determine whether a particular program should be eased into completion, or even refunded in order to fulfill the goals of the program. This speaker stated that as things are today, the funded programs suffer as a result of such indifference on the part of the Foundations.

Replying to this point of view, another Paritipant stated that if this were done, then the Foundations could well be accused of attempting to influence Indian affairs, to influence the programs, to exert leadership where they had no business to do so, and ultimately would be subjected to severe criticism for attempting to "influence Indian affairs."

One speaker raised the question of the Ford Foundation. This Participant said that it was rumored that the Ford Foundation representative was exerting undue influence over programs funded by this Foundation. Replying to this, another Participant said, "We should not forget that if it were not for the Ford Foundation, we would not be here in this historic Convocation. In my experience during the past four months, as the Convocation was being prepared, no influence was brought to bear upon the organizers in any way."

A Ford Foundation representative stated that the Foundations could not "advise, or act as a follow-through agency. We would be charged with attempting to undertake leadership, or influence Indian affairs. We can only propose that funds be granted if we are convinced, to the best of our knowledge, that the particular program is a good one, a solid one, and that it has a possibility of giving aid where aid is needed."

A representative of another Foundation explained that he had no knowledge of Indian affairs, history, or cultures, and that he was grateful for the privilege of listening to the presentations and discussion. The speaker said that his Foundation was attempting to set up a program which would make funds available, although in limited quantities since this is a small and new Foundation, to worthy Indian programs.

Some discussion took place as to programs funded by the Foundations which were so highly unsuccessful that their merit could have been challenged at the very beginning of negotiations for the grant. "Consultants do not help in such cases. It would require a completely objective, disinterested Indian person to advise. The best way is to let the Indian people themselves decide, those who would be affected by the program," was the comment.

Replying to this comment, a speaker said that if this were done, the jealousies inherent in any society and even in the Native American societies, would lead to a situation in which no program would receive aid. This led to a remark by one speaker that "in the end, much depends upon the solid judgment of the Foundation people themselves."

The consensus, in every case, and in the view of every speaker, was that no programs should be funded "for or about Indian or Native affairs, which is not planned and directed by the Native Peoples themselves." This point of view appeared to be unanimous among all the Participants present at this Special Session, and indeed it was the view held by all the Native Peoples present at the Convocation as a whole.

Views expressed by many Participants appeared to give substance to the belief that such conferences, although perhaps some unpleasantness might emerge, were necessary, and should be held from time to time. As one Participant expressed, "Some way is needed in which both the Foundation representatives and the Native Peoples involved in any program, whatever its nature, can get together and talk off the cuff, with no holds barred, leading to better mutual understanding." A Participant asked, "Will this help?" Another Participant replied, "Not really. What must be done is to make the Native Peoples, their tribes and organizations, fully self-reliant, completely independent, knowledgeable as to how to generate funds through their own programs and activities. Anything else is guaranteed intellectual and practical bankruptcy, sooner or later."

15

Special Session:
Native Americans in the
Textbook Literature

Presentation by
JEANNETTE HENRY

The second Special Session of the Convocation
of American Indian Scholars was held Wednesday evening, March 25, 1970, at 8 p.m. Eleven
publishers were invited to send representatives.
Seven responded, and there were a total of fourteen representatives of these seven publishing
houses present at the session. The representatives of
four publishers took part in the discussion. The
others remained silent. Attendance at the session,
for the Convocation Participants, was not obliga-
tory. But approximately 30 of the nearly 200 Participants chose to attend the session. Discussion
was spirited, and the session did not break up
until after 11 p.m. As in the first Special Session
names of the invited guests who attended remain
anonymous. Discussants are not named, and the
reasons for this emerge in the discussion itself.

The Session which we now open as part of the extra-curricular
activities of the First Convocation of American Indian Scholars
cannot be said to have a "purpose." But it does have a *reason*
for being held. To have a purpose, or a goal, one must be
reasonably certain that something can come out of an event.

In this case, all we could hope for was to bring to light a situation which can best be described as a chronic disease in our society—the persistent and continuing degradation and misinterpretation of the history of our Native people in the textbooks.

The textbook, as a most important and universally accepted instrument of learning, has carried an aura of respect and even reverence among students the world over. This inherent "acceptance" has now become a mere hypothesis. Textbooks, their authors, and the contents between the covers of these often formidable tomes, are now being subjected to intensive scrutiny, careful questioning, and even irreverent laughter. It is true, as many educators believe, that new instruments of learning are developing for classroom use. Visual aids, maps and charts, sounds and sound effects, films and their various offspring— all contend for equal place today in the classroom. Textbooks, it is said, will soon be a thing of the past. I don't believe this. Besides, the new modalities offer little change as to inaccurate content. We still have a deep regard for learning found in the great books. We still believe that unless a person can read, and read well, he cannot become well educated. We still try, with all our energies, to make some changes in the morality of the publishing business, so that the complete and authentic story of our People may be told, and in that way the history of this entire country be enriched.

But the textbooks themselves do not tell this story; rather they falsify it in so many ways that we have written a book about it: *Textbooks and the American Indian.* We view the *publishers* as those who are solely responsible for textbooks which are inaccurate, degrading to our people, and tilted to the politically dominant group of our society. It is the thesis of this paper that the publishers of textbooks, their authors, and the contents of these learning tools should be subjected to searching and scholarly examination. Freedom of speech has no meaning when schoolchildren are forced to read books that lie. A book for public consumption gives the reader a choice. Textbooks do not, and have no right to lie, or to falsify history, or to demean and insult a whole people. The Native American has suffered more than any, because of textbook distortions, slanders, degradatation, and misconceptions. We American Indian scholars propose that there is an open door leading to correction of this situation, and that an irreverent approach is the first step in this direction.

What would you say to a fourth grade book, utilized on a one-to-one basis in the classroom, which states the "Indian was degraded, filthy, refused either to wash or work, and lived on the lowest stage of man's development." What would you think of a textbook which referred to the Native peoples of this land as "primitive beings who barely could be called human." How would you like it, if you were a Native American, to have forty children in a classroom, and this classroom multiplied in the tens of thousands, all of them learning that the Native American was a savage, without culture or technology, who scrounged among the roots and grasses of the earth, and lived from hand to mouth, from area to area, travelling wherever the whim took him. These are only some of the thoughts put into the heads of our young people about the Natives of this land—our land. If you want authentication, why don't you read *Textbooks and the American Indian*, where authentication is given, books and titles are named, and publishers are listed for inaccuracies we found in those 176 books evaluated as only one small part of the whole. That these things are inaccurate at best, and utterly insulting at least, goes beyond saying. Any scholar . . . any serious student . . . can tell you the story is entirely different: that the Indian had complex and well developed cultures; that he worshipped God as citizens of this country do not do today; that he had a technology and built trails and girdled trees; knew conservation and practiced it; and that he made life beautiful through his arts which were a daily part of his life. That the Native had his land stolen from him, was massacred, his homes and food stores destroyed, and made to live a life of serfdom in the missions. Not one textbook tells about our trailblazers, path-finders, the original pioneers and settlers of this our Native land. Not one textbook tells about our Native heroes and heroines, but rather tells the saccharine phony story of heroes who never were heroes—men like Andrew Jackson and Custer and Chivington. No textbook relates the story of the Native knowledge of the land's ecology—a new word you have popularized, which was a way of life with us. And no book will tell you that the successors to the Indian have violated the land, made a world of greed, filth and inhumanity. These are facts well known to scholars, except those who write and publish textbooks, and do it in a dark room with blinders over their eyes, earplugs in their ears and shades drawn tight over their intelligence.

The American Indian Historical Society began a serious evaluation of the textbooks seven years ago. We have appeared before Boards of Education and Curriculum Commissions. We have won victories on many fronts, and have had some books rejected for reasons of inaccuracy and slander against our people. Still, the situation does not change. The new textbooks now being submitted for use in the classrooms are just as bad, and some are even worse . . . although in a more sophisticated way, than the old ones.

What kind of people are those who author such textbooks? Indeed some of them have long and awesome pedigrees in the world of Academia. One might think they should know better, for some of their inaccuracies are so brazen and so blatant as to make the intelligent reader blush for them. Do they really believe these things they are writing about the American Indian? I am inclined to give them more credit for common sense, if not for scholarship. Then why do they do it? Why do they propound these lies and falsifications; why do they peddle these misconceptions and perpetrate these slanders? It was relatively easy to correct the situation as to the Black history in the textbooks. The Negroes got hold of a lot of money, demonstrated, put the pressure of their millions of people to bear upon the situation, and obtained the sympathetic support of the whites. Finally, they wrote, or hired people to write, their *own* histories. We are too few for that kind of a campaign. Yet, our story is so much more a part of America and her origins. Our history is so much more *original* Americana, that it is to wonder the authors and publishers choose to tell it slanted instead of truthfully. It is difficult not to believe that the demands of truth, the requirements of scholarship, might compel authors and publishers to change their ways, and yet this does not happen. I must tell you, however, that we have gone one step further than the Blacks. We have organized our own publishing house, and will now be producing books for use in the classrooms about our own people.

The story of the American Indian is one entirely different from that of other so-called "ethnic groups." We are not just one more complaining minority crying in the wilderness for justice. We are the original peoples of this land, the only original peoples, and the time has come for us to be heard . . . and not merely to be heard, but to insist that this ugly situation be changed. We have held many workshops and seminars with teachers . . . teachers of all races, in an effort to bring some light to bear upon this evil situation. Invariably, after presenting the facts, there is a reaction of sheer disbelief, and then the question is asked: "To what do you ascribe such a wholesale destruction of truth, such a system of misconception and falsification?" We can only say that the cause of it is that the dominant society finds it necessary to obtain justification for the crimes they have committed against the Natives of this land. The philosophy of historiography is tainted with this purpose; and given such a purpose, scholarship becomes a jungle of propaganda and proselytizing.

I will not belabor this point further. Suffice it to say that we believe the publishers are well aware their books are bad, as to the role of the Indian in the history of this country. We come now to the point where the prick of truth can produce an extreme twinge of intellectual pain, at which time both the publishers and their paid authors turn away from us, making believe we don't exist, trying to place our history in the shadows of ancient memory alone, and at best attempting to explain away their falsification of history with such an ideology as this: "Well, we are one people now. The past should be forgotten. We should learn to live together now and let bygones be bygones." That's not good enough for us. We have lost our land, or most of it. Our people are in poverty. Our youth have the least chance of all for a decent life. Our culture has been degraded and only the remnants remain. Still we are striving to preserve those pitiful remnants, and what remains of our languages. We want moral and intellectual justice. I say to you, that if once the beauty and fascination of our people becomes known, once the truth is told, and once the accurate history is related . . . this country will see a revival of interest and excitement such as it has not known before. There is not one ethnic group in this land whose story has more interest and excitement. Not one so-called ethnic group can hold so much fascination, particularly for the young and the student, as the Native American story can.

Your trouble, my publisher friends, is that you don't think the truth about the Native American can make money. I am sorry to be so blunt, but that is the sordid truth. What is more, you have a stockpile of books now loaded in your warehouses, and you have got to sell those books. If the school districts and universities of the country once fully understand how bad your books are, how truly indigestible they are, you would (many of you) be confronted with serious financial loss. We have been in close contact with the publishers and the publishing business ever since we began this arduous program of textbook correction. I can tell you what you probably know better than I, that the publishing business is one of the most powerful in this nation, that it controls more of the property and finances of this country than most people believe, and that it has controlled the minds and thoughts of our youth as well as that of much of our adult population.

You have too much power.

You control book production, visual aid production, instructional materials production, dissemination of information, films and film strips, photographic media and multi-media. You also control television and newspapers. At least two of you have huge international interests and enormous world-wide contacts, with the resultant control over the minds of other peoples in other lands. You have a lobby in Congress which is one of the most powerful in the country. You have an educational publishers' organization to which one must pay a minimum of $500 annually in order to be a "member" of it, and then must pay dues according to the income of your business. This smacks of that rarefied air-space in which only the rich and powerful may operate or have a voice. You have a network of agents bigger than the FBI, more huge than a police state, more potent than the food industry. They are part of that monster of a book distributions industry which makes it practically impossible to fight you. You can put a small book publishing house out of business, or you can choose to swallow it up (as at least one of the big publishing monsters has already done). You can stop or start publicity on any issue you choose; some of you own great newspapers and television stations as well as the publishing firms you represent. If you do not own them as a corporate body, then among your directors can be found *individuals* who do. The only grim feature of this power is that quite often you "choose" to stimulate publicity inimical to you, because after all, it sells books and newspapers. That's what counts, isn't it? I know for a fact that some of the publishing houses print the same book in two editions: one for the north and one for the south. What kind of an author would stand still for this kind of pimping? The publishing business in the United States of America is the greatest promulgator of falsification and misconception the world has known, and it has greater power than any other industry in this land. Only Russia and China can compete with you in control over the minds of the people.

Now this, however, needs to be said. In this country, we still have an "out." We still have some methods with which to fight, and some routes yet exist by way of which we can fight. There are scholars who have (and still do) write the truth about our people and about American history. Sadly, their words are hidden in scholarly tomes and written in highly specialized language, which no ordinary person would find "fascinating." Nor would the usual American citizen, intellectually depraved as he is, pick up such a book for information and pleasure. These books are usually written by anthropologists, by responsible and scholarly historians, by researchers and other scholars who are interested in some highly specialized aspect of ancient history or archaeological and scientific discovery. They cannot fight you. They cannot remedy this outrageous and immoral situation. I must say as well, that some publishers are now manufacturing books which *do* speak the truth . . . such as Macmillan's issuance of "Custer Died for Your Sins." These are few indeed. But on the one hand, the itch to make money is a powerful reason for such publishing. On the other hand, such books do not usually find their way into the classrooms as textbooks. . . .

We believe that the situation can be changed. And I believe that people such as those who are participants in the Convocation of American Indian Scholars can change it. It is not impossible. After all, wasn't it David and his slingshot who managed to change history?

Let us raise another question. When you decide to publish a book in American history, why do you invariably assign the work to a nonIndian when it involves authentication of Indian materials. . . . one who knows little or nothing about Indian history or cultures. When you decide upon a book for production, in Indian history, or "Indian stories," you also go to a nonIndian. In our offices, we have hundreds of letters from these so-called authors who have been assigned to write either sections dealing with Native Americans in general history books, or books of which the main subject is the American Indian. These people are asking *us* for information. They are requesting *us* to do their research; they ask for materials and information; they come to us for authentication of drawings and primary as well as secondary sources. Now this is quite flattering, that the American Indian Historical Society can be considered as authorities in our own history, with expertise of value. But why should we do the work of the authors who are being paid by you for knowledge they ought to have as part of their scholarly training? I had one of these authors call me long distance from the East. He was writing a history of California, and had a section on the Indians. He wanted corroboration that the Yokuts lived in the Bay area. I couldn't give him such corroboration, because they didn't live in that area at all. In very general terms, this tribe lived along the lower Sierra Nevada to the Coast range, and from Mounts Pinos and Tehachapi to Fresno and Chowchilla rivers. Some lived along the San Joaquin. Now this is common knowledge among scholars. Certainly we are glad to cooperate with any responsible scholar, and have always provided materials and information, sources and authentication. But when it comes to the publishing business, and the authors (usually without claim to knowledge in this highly specialized field) we must make some exceptions.

We think the publishers, if they really want an objective and scholarly work, should contract out such work to Indian scholars, or at least to scholars who have expertise in these fields. We have many distinguished men and women who could do a remarkable job. We have poets, writers, scholars, who are never approached by the publishers. It is always a white man or woman, and very often it is the little old lady in tennis shoes . . . the retired schoolteacher, who is engaged to write the books for children about the Native Americans. What they have produced through the years, is the sickliest pablum—a travesty of the real thing. I say to you that this Convocation and those of us who are meeting here together for the first time in history, is evidence of the fact that we have the scholarship, the talent, and the people. We can write our own history. In fact, there is no reason why we cannot write the history of the *nation*. Certainly we can be far more objective than the current historians who are making a farce of the writing of books for classroom use.

The publishers pay evaluators, readers, consultants . . . when these are utilized in the production of textbooks. But we have done this work for seven years now, without charge. I can tell you we are not going to do it any longer. If you want our services as consultants, readers, evaluators, you will have to pay for it. We have an expertise and a knowledge born not only of book learning (and we certainly have that too), but born of our inmost beings, part of our hearts and spirit, part of our own Native history.

One of the most ignominious results of your control over the publishing business is that you sell such books to the Bureau of Indian Affairs, for use in classrooms where Indian children are taught. We examined nearly two hundred books used in history schools. Indian children are being taught the same lies that schools. Indian children are being taught the same lies that public school children are taught. These are *your* books; they are peddled by your sales departments. They are an insult to the Indian people. One can ask: How does this happen? Well, the answer is really quite simple. Who buys the books? The upper echelon of school districts, agencies, boards of education. The Curriculum Commissions may evaluate and study the proposed books to their heart's content. But the books *that are finally adopted*, are what the upper strata people want, and this is an obscene joke upon the entire educational community. Let me give you an example. The American Indian Historical Society succeeded, in the State of California, in having four books for fourth grade classes *rejected* by the State Curriculum Commission. These books degraded the history of the Native Americans, and their rejection was fully justified. But, one week following this rejection, we found to our outrage that these four books were immediately adopted *following this rejection*, by the Los Angeles School District . . . perhaps the largest school district in the entire nation. These four books are now being utilized, on a basis of one-to-one ratio, in the classrooms of that school district. The books are published by Doubleday. They were well aware of our criticisms and our opposition to the books. They knew of the rejection by the commission. Yet, their sales department proceeded, in violation of the law in fact, to sell the books. How do you fight such things? You would have to spend your entire life in combatting these maneuvers, and we don't have all that time. In some school districts, elsewhere in this country, we are getting a fair hearing and things are changing for the better. But largely, the situation remains utterly outrageous.

Finally, I believe the publishers ought to do something very concrete to actually stimulate Indian writers. This is done for all other groups, why not for Indians? It should be possible for the publishers to get together and put up a purse for a large award for the best novel, the best poetry, the best nonfiction, in Native American literary works. The Native American has a talent so unique that it makes your heart ache when you realize how much of it is going unrecognized, unpublished, unknown. Why is this so? Because my people are too busy scrounging for a mere existence. My people who are writers and have natural talent if not genius, don't have a chance. These days, one needs money, if ever so little, to take the time to write. I believe the publishers might do something to make it possible for the Indian to write professionally. It would be nothing for you to get together and put up a $10,000 award for the best book in the history of Native America, written by a Native American.

I would like to say that when we set up this special session, we had little hope of anything concrete coming out of it. We did want to have a chance to meet you face to face . . . to talk with you and listen to you, and have you listen to us. And, to find out if there is really any chance for something good to come out of the publishing business in America, so far as developing accurate and authentic materials about the Natives in the textbooks.

Perhaps, when you discover that there is money in good books about the Natives, you will finally do something about it. So far as we are concerned, in the American Indian Historical Society, we are not commercially motivated. Very few Indian people are, in fact. We have given and given, all our lives, for the work among our people, and we will give more. This is our pleasure, and we are joined in this by thousands of other Native peoples who have the same philosophy. But as far as you are concerned, as people in the publishing business, we know that money talks. Whatever the reasons, and whatever the justification for the falsification of history which has been developed by the publishing business in this nation, I say to you that the time has come when it must stop. There are millions of people in this country who are listening to us now. We have more intellectual and ideological power than you might think, small in numbers as we are. And we are saying now, that your falsification of history and slandering of our people must stop—or we will make you stop.

DISCUSSION

The Native American in Textbook Literature

A representative of one publishing firm made the following observations: It is true that there is not enough material in the textbooks about the Indians. We would certainly like to remedy this situation. After all, we are in the business of publishing books for educational purposes. But how do you distinguish between fact and fancy? Who is to say what is true and what is false? I think the authors who write for us are sincere in their efforts to present the truth. How do you authenticate that those facts you say are false are really false? I think it is a matter of opinion, and maybe one man's opinion is as good as another's.

A Convocation Participant responded by stating that the "facts" are present in the findings of many scientific workers, such as anthropologists and archaeologists and even many historians. But these scientific works are not usually drawn upon for background material in the writing of the textbooks.

The representative of another publishing firm stated that: His firm was indeed interested in producing books that are truthful and interesting as well. It is not true all publishers want to color the facts. That, in his view, his own publishing firm was not interested solely in making money, and wanted to help bring the true story of the Native American into the classroom, and into the public book stores also. He would be willing to propose that his publishing firm actually decide that money would not be the main objective in producing books such as told the truth, whether they made money or not, and that Indian writers should receive encouragement in writing about their own people, in telling the story of their own history.

A Convocation Participant observed that his people needed books written in their own language, so that the children could be taught their language, and learn their own history. This speaker related how the school district in his area taught the children that their grandfathers wre savages, dirty and unkempt. "There is prejudice in my area," he said, and "there is no doubt about it. The whites want things taught so that they come out bright and shiny. They talk about the frontiersmen and the settlers and how much they suffered to tame the wilderness. That wilderness was our home, and they are the ones who defaced it and made it into a place so crowded and dirty that even they don't want to live there anymore."

A speaker explained how some of the books and the ideology propounded in them are insidious falsifications of the truth. In one book, he said, in describing Indian homes, the book says they are "huts." But when describing homes lived in by white settlers at the same era in time, they are said to be "homes," or "houses." Indians are said to "roam" in their land, instead of "travel." Indians "wander" instead of travel, in these books. The Native people are made to appear as "simple, primitive stone-age people," when indeed they had a technology, a complex culture, and lived well in their various regions, according to their environment and the needs of their lives.

A publishing firm representative, who refused to state his name or his firm, said this: You can have no idea how competitive the publishing business is. We print books not for love, but so that we can continue to print books. It's a business, face it. Still, the demands upon excellence are great, and we compete with all other publishers. This business is so competitive, and one publishing house is watching the others so closely, that in our office the boss has arranged for a maintenance man to come around after working hours and pick up even the memoranda that we make during the day, and see to it that these memoranda are destroyed, if they have not been put in a safe place. The publishers steal ideas from each other; they steal writers from one another; they even steal manuscripts in some cases. It's a very, very competitive business, and if you are not aware of it, you are very foolish. I think it is a very foolish idea to believe that the publishers could possibly get together, even in such a thing as an award for the best poets or writers who are Indian. It will never happen. There is too much competition, and we are in business not only for today . . . but so that we can remain in business.

Another publisher's representative rose to object to the above statements. He said that it was wrong and immoral to hold such views; that he would retire from the publishing business if he could believe such an immoral ideology. He believed that publishers should indeed get together to encourage writers, and that if the others did not, then he would propose to his company that it should be done.

A publisher stated that the "educational business" was very complex, that it was not for amateurs, and that "we want the best books, but also want to be competitive. The publishing business is not for humanitarians." At this point, a representative of this man's firm replied in these words: "I disagree with that. I think we have a moral duty to perform. I think we should perform that moral duty. Publishing is not like selling automobiles or any other products. We are selling ideas, information, and education. And we have a duty to perform, a duty to education and a duty to the citizens of America." To which the first speaker here referred to, replied: "You are in the editorial end, and that's different. We sales people have to sell the books, and I can tell you that many school districts won't buy that kind of thing you call a humane attitude. Facts are facts, and the fact is that we have to sell the books and the school districts are controlled by higher boards and commissions. They buy what they think is best for their area. Certainly we have salespeople going around to all the districts. They cover every area like a blanket. I think my firm does a good job. Our books are beautiful and the districts like them, or they wouldn't buy them.

A publisher stated that: "We take our jobs in our hands even to be here in such a meeting, where competing publishers can learn things they have no business knowing, and where random ideas can be spilled out to the detriment of our own firms. When publishers and their representatives get together, it is on a very different level. We don't talk about content of books, or such things. We talk about the markets, what is needed in methodology, production costs and means, and our general business problems. Sure, there are occasions when complaints about contents are heard, but we are very careful not to divulge our own plans and ideas. Publishers even steal each other's authors."

This person was asked: Is it possible to change this? To which he replied, "Well, anything can change. But is it necessary? It's a very competitive business, and the best stay on top, which is no more than right. We like the dreamers too. They make our business the exciting thing it is. But when it comes right down to brass tacks, we have got to sell those books. Perhaps you should first educate the general public and the educators; then when there is a demand for books like you describe, we can give it to them. We can produce any kind of a book that there is a demand for."

The chairman then observed, "I think that approach is not only immoral, but positively obscene, and if this is the situation, then perhaps we need a different level on which we can talk— perhaps a legal level. Or, at the very least, a level on the highest rung of the academic professions."

A speaker who identified herself as a teacher, observed: "We need instructional materials about the American Indians so badly, and the current materials are so inadequate, that I wonder why the publishers themselves don't see this." To this, a Convocation Participant replied: "We should, perhaps, proceed to develop our own publishing facilities. In that way, we can be certain the materials will be published for the best interests of the student and the educational community, instead of being solely a question of "business and monetary gain."

Another speaker referred to an eminent historian, author of many books about American history, and asked, "How could such a man make such errors? If indeed he is wrong in his facts, and is promulgating falsification of history, then upon whom can we depend for truth in education, truth in history, and truth in historical analysis?" To this, the chairman replied, that historians as well as other citizens and other scholars, are subjected to the same influences and the same dominant ideologies—all of which colors their philosophy and all of which ultimately colors their writing. We might ask, then, is there such a thing as truth? And perhaps this is a question of a point of view. But we believe there is such a thing as truth, objectivity in scholarship, and we will not relinquish this belief. We also don't believe that the truth can hurt little children.

To this, a publisher replied: You are forgetting the fact that school districts set up criteria for the adoption of books. In California, the whole state buys books for all the districts, and let me tell you that is big business. If the curriculum commission sets up a criterion that gory stuff shall not be produced for the education of fourth grade children, how are you going to write about the massacres of Indians by whites, by the army, by Custer for example? In California there is a 40-page report by one of the country's distinguished scholars who says you must not have such ideas in the textbooks as "would impair the self-image of the white child." We publishers are up a tree, between what you people want and what the school districts decide they are going to get.

A speaker replied: It is just too bad about the little white children having their self-image impaired. This report to which the former speaker has alluded, was torn apart and we criticized the hell out of it. It was proven to be unscholarly, inept, and lacking in educational value. After all, you are writing and producing books for these so-called "innocent little children," who have seen a President of the United States shot down in cold blood before their very eyes; who have seen a presidential aspirant massacred right in front of their eyes, who daily read about and see murder, mayhem, sodomy, and sexual freedom. The child of today is not the child of yesterday. He is utterly sophisticated, and the truth can only help him, not hurt him.

At this point, the chairman observed that the time was running out, and that the discussion should end. Four of the publishers' representatives had already left the hall; they had remained silent throughout the session. The session was then adjourned. Still, at least eight of the participants and publishers remained in the outer hall to continue the discussion. At its end, several publishers stated to the chairman: "We have all sorts of sympathy for you and what you are doing. We certainly believe you are doing a wonderful job, and all power to you. If there is ever anything we can do for you, let us know. We can't do anything openly, but we certainly can do all sorts of little things to help." The Special Session was then ended.

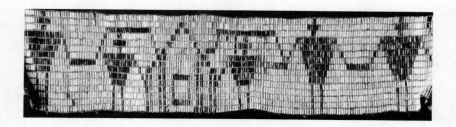

16

Report on Resolutions

RESOLUTIONS

DURING the last days of the Convocation of American
Indian Scholars, the airline controllers engaged in a slow-
down and strike. Consequently, the matter of returning the
Participants to their home bases became an urgent problem.
Many of the Participants were needed at home, and could not
take chances that would make them stranded at Princeton.
As a result, these were returned on the last day of the Convocation, giving the Convocation a bare quorum with which to
conduct the business of considering Resolutions. In spite of
these difficulties, 22 Resolutions were introduced, discussed, and
passed by the Convocation.

These Resolutions, as well as the proposals and suggestions
for further activities, were passed by the Convocation, despite
the difficulties of the strike situation. In the interests of space,
only the sense of the Resolutions is presented here.

> Dr. Alfonso Ortiz, Convocation
> Chairman, turned over the chair-
> manship for this session, to Bea
> Medicine, Resolutions Committee
> chairman.

RESOLUTION #1

To continue the Convocation as an annual event under the leadership of the American Indian Historical Society.

> This Resolution was originally proposed by the entire
> Navajo group, and was adopted unanimously by the
> Convocation.

RESOLUTION #2

To support the Native Americans at Littleton, Colorado, who have attempted to institute fair hiring practices for Native employees by the Bureau of Indian Affairs. This Resolution was proposed by the students at the Convocation, proposed in the form of a petition, and was adopted unanimously by the Convocation.

RESOLUTION #3

Since the Iroquois wampum belts, now held illegally by the State of New York, are sacred and irreplaceable in performing the rites and ceremonies of the Iroquois Confederacy, that the Convocation support the demand of the Iroquois people for the restoration of the wampum belts to their proper keepers, the Iroquois Confederacy. Adopted unanimously.

RESOLUTION #4

The Convocation shall take the position that the Native American tribes, through their governing bodies, be consulted on any proposed studies involving research, information concerning religions, cultures, languages, and ceremonial activities, and that no such studies be made without the consent of such governing bodies. The reasons for proposing this Resolution include a past history of such studies being made without either knowledge or approval of Indian tribes and groups, and it is generally ignored that the Native peoples are not an extinct race, but a living People and consequently entitled to the respect and concern shown for all living peoples. Professional societies, the Bureau of Indian Affairs, and Foundations granting funds for such purposes, shall be informed of this Resolution. Passed unanimously.

RESOLUTION #5

This Resolution stated that one of the greatest needs of the Native American is immediate and easy access to all parts of the Indian world, a condition that does not now exist. Inter-communication of tribe to tribe, organization to organization, and group to group, does not now exist, and has always been difficult to develop. The Resolution asked the Convocation to go on record as demanding the Bureau of Indian Affairs immediately provide an accurate listing of all tribal council members, officers, and Indian schools with teachers and administrators thereof; and that such a listing be maintained on an annual basis, and be made available automatically to every Indian tribe and Indian organization in the country. Adopted unanimously.

RESOLUTION #6

The Convocation of American Indian Scholars endorses the continued development of the Navajo Community College and urgently demands that the Department of the Interior provide operational funds for the College, and that Foundations, Indian tribes and groups, and the general public be asked to support the concept of Indian-administered community colleges. Adopted unanimously.

RESOLUTION #7

This Resolution involved support for a demonstration project in higher education of American Indian Studies at Oklahoma City University. A discussion was held on the proposed program. It was felt that the Convocation paricipants had not had an opportunity to study the proposed program. It was also found that the two writers of the proposed program, Dr. Trimble and Mr. Sahmaunt, had been compelled to leave for home due to the controllers' air strike, and could not be called upon to answer questions. In the discussion, there was a division of opinion, primarily due to the fact that the program had not been examined prior to presentation. A student from Oklahoma opposed the adoption of a resolution approving the program, on this basis as well. The final action on this proposed program was to table until further study could be made.

RESOLUTION #8

That the Convocation give full support to the Rocky Boy Band of Chippewa-Cree in their efforts to obtain quality education for their children by forming their own public school district. Adopted unanimously.

RESOLUTION #9

That in the case of federal programs, programs sponsored by agencies, foundations, or organizations, involving such Indian programs as leadership development, higher education, scholarships, American Indians be involved in the actual planning and implementation of such programs. Adopted unanimously.

RESOLUTION #10

The Resolution observed that the United States and certain foreign countries are engaging in activities threatening to the sensitive balance of the natural environment, are not maintaining the quality of life, are not making efforts to prevent famine and plague, are not making efforts to avoid an over-population. That the consequences of such a lethargic attitude lead to catastrophe, and the Indian has a unique affinity to the land and his people, and has his roots in the natural balance of the environment. The survival of the Indian culture as well as that of the Indian himself cannot be separated from the preservation and restoration of the environment. This increasing ecological problem causes deep concern to the Native about himself, his land, and water. The Resolution called for a commitment to avoid this ''ecocatastrophe'' and bring about rapid measures to stabilize the population explosion and exert strong control to return the environment to a more harmonious state. Adopted unanimously.

RESOLUTION #11

The proposed resolution took recognition of the fact that there is today a strong movement for Indian rights, better conditions, and increased educational opportunities. This movement involves a most important effort to reclaim Indian land, preserve existing land bases, and resist the oppressive actions of the Bureau of Indian Affairs. It stated that the only strength owned by the Indian people is one of unity, and it called upon the Convocation to go on record as supporting actions not resulting in harm to innocent persons, leading to the goals expressed, and for support to all actions representing an effort of the Indian people to act in their own behalf and for their own betterment in every area of their lives. Adopted unanimously.

RESOLUTION #12

This Resolution called for a conference or workshop to be organized to undertake an examination of the current and proposed Native American Studies programs in the universities of Canada and the United States, composed of both Indian and nonIndian representatives of the institutions of higher education involved in such programs. Adopted unanimously.

RESOLUTION #13

Support to the newly formed Indian Historian Press was given in this Resolution, in order to develop a body of literature about and for the Native American, independently created and produced under the supervision of competent and responsible Native scholars. Adopted unanimously.

RESOLUTION #14

That the Convocation give its support to the creation of a national center for Native Arts, both visual and performing arts, planned and directed by the Native people. Adopted unanimously.

RESOLUTION #15

Since there is no authentic, All-Indian association of American Indian and Native artists, controlled and directed by Natives themselves, and since there is no known national source of information concerning Native arts, be it live arts, drama, sculpture, painting, or any Indian art or craft, an up-to-date listing should be composed of such information, a chain of Indian-owned art galleries should be encouraged, and a Theater of Native Performing Arts be organized. Adopted unanimously.

RESOLUTION #16

That a National Society of Indian Artists be organized, under the auspices and with the help of the American Indian Historical Society. That a definitive book be prepared on the arts of the Native American. This Resolution was amended upon recommendation of Jeannette Henry Costo, to state that the Indian Historical Society would *help* organize such a group. Adopted unanimously.

RESOLUTION #17

The Convocation was asked to support a Resolution calling upon Foundations not to support with funds any program or activities for or about American Indians and Native Peoples, which are not directed and controlled by Indian groups, organizations or tribes. Adopted unanimously.

RESOLUTIONS OF THANKS

Resolutions of thanks were submitted and adopted unanimously: to the Ford Foundation for funding the Convocation; to Princeton University for supplying certain physical facilities; to the various hosts who entertained as their guests, the participants to the Convocation; and to the donor who provided funds for the pre-Convocation dinner.

17

The Convocation Participants

PARTICIPATION in the Convocation of American Indian Scholars was by invitation, and approval of the Steering Committee. A maximum of 200 participants were anticipated, due to the limitation of facilities at Princeton University, and also due to the fact that a small group was considered a better working format. Ten nonIndian scholars were invited and attended the Convocation. Four observers were in attendance. The Criteria for participation, as set up by the Steering Committee and approved by the American Indian Historical Society, were:

Scholars must be at least college graduates. Students shall be attending their institutions of higher education full time. Evidence must be shown that the student or scholar intends to pursue some professional or academic calling. Professional people were in attendance from the fields of the arts, medicine, social sciences, exact sciences, natural science, and the law. Native American historians were present from various tribes. These latter individuals were not required to have formal education, but it was required that they speak their Native language, be active in their tribe, and have a knowledge of their history.

A listing of Native American participants follows. It should be remembered that the academic status, where such information is given, described the individual situation as of March, 1970. Many participants have since graduated, or received higher degrees, moved into fields of higher qualification, or changed their institutions of learning.

The following nonIndian scholars were invited guests at the Convocation:

Lowell J. Bean, California State College at Hayward; William Brandon, author and educator; Edward M. Bruner, University of Illinois at Urbana, anthropologist; Harold E. Driver, Indiana University at Bloomington, anthropologist; Bernard L. Fontana, University of Arizona, ethnologist; Richard I. Ford, University of Michigan at Ann Arbor, professor in prehistory; Kenneth Hale, Massachusetts Institute of Technology, linguistics; Edward H. Spicer, University of Arizona at Tucson, anthropologist; William Sturtevant, Smithsonian Institution, anthropologist, Gary Orfield, Princeton University, Woodrow Wilson School of International Affairs.

GEORGE H. ABRAMS, 30, Seneca, University of Arizona, Tucson, applied anthropology, Ph.D. candidate.

ANDREW ACOYA, 26, Laguna Pueblo, Massachusetts Institute of Technology, architecture, graduate student.

LEE ANTELL, 27, Chippewa, University of Minnesota, Minneapolis, graduate student.

RUSSELL AYERS, 67, Oklahoma Cherokee, Dartmouth College graduate, electronics and automation engineer.

LEE R. BACON, 41, Choctaw, Mississippi Choctaw Reservation, Philadelphia, school counsellor.

BENJAMIN BARNEY, 24, St. John's College, Santa Fe, N.M., medicine.

LEW BARTON, 52, Lumbee, Pembroke, North Carolina, teacher, author.

JOHN W. BATES, 19, Omaha, Central State College, Edmond, Okla., business management.

LINDA BELARDE, 22, Tlingit, University of Washington, Seattle, special education.

EUGENE BENALLY, 21, Navajo, Eastern New Mexico University, Portales, finance.

ROBERT L. BENNETT, 57, Oneida, University of New Mexico, Albuquerque, law.

SAMUEL BILLISON, Navajo, University of Arizona, Tucson, Ph.D. candidate in educational administration.

HERB BLATCHFORD, 42, Navajo, Gallup Indian Community Center, leadership training.

HENRIETTA BLUEYE, 22, Seneca, Radcliffe College, pre-medical.

JOSEPH BROWN, S.J., 53, Blackfeet, Gonzaga University, Spokane, Wash., history.

W. ROGER BUFFALOHEAD, Ponca, University of Minnesota, Minneapolis, American Indian history.

MARY GLOYNE BYLER, Cherokee, Editor, Indian Affairs.

PHILIP CASSADORE, 37, San Carlos Apache, University of Arizona, Tucson, linguist, singer, lecturer.

HERMAN LALUZ CATA, 35, San Juan Tewa, University of New Mexico, Albuquerque, graduate student, guidance and counselling.

RACHELLE LALUZ CATA, 28, Cochiti Pueblo, University of New Mexico, Albuquerque, graduate student, education.

ROSEMARY CHRISTENSEN, Chippewa, Upper Midwest Regional Educational Laboratory, history.

EDWARD L. CLARK, Comanche, Arizona State University, graduate teaching assistant.

SOLOMON COOK, 50, St. Regis Mohawk, Cornell University, Ph.D., teacher-counsellor; farmer.

JOHN H. COMPTON, 40, Sioux, University of Iowa, Iowa City, assistant professor, social work.

MARIA DE OCA CORWIN, 28, Seneca, Smith College School for Social Work graduate student.

JEANNETTE HENRY COSTO, 52, Eastern Cherokee, Ph.D. history, editor, The Indian Historian.

RUPERT COSTO, 63, Cahuilla, President, American Indian Historical Society; spokesman Cahuilla Indian Tribe of Southern California, engineer.

RAYMOND CROSS, 21, Mandan-Hidatsa, Stanford University senior, political science.

GEORGE M. CROSSLAND, 33, Osage, University of Chicago Law School.

DOROTHY DAVIDS, 46, Stockbridge-Munsee, education and human relations specialist.

PHILIP SAM DELORIA, 28, Standing Rock Sioux, Yale Law School.

VINE DELORIA, JR., 36, Standing Rock Sioux, University of Colorado School of Law.

WILLIAM G. DEMMERT, JR., 36, Tlingit, Klawock public school, Alaska, administrator.

DENISE DEANE, 19, Arikara, Oberlin College, Ohio, government-history-law.

LOUISE DESCHEENY, 21, Navajo, Northern Arizona University, Flagstaff, Indian education.

LIONEL H. DEMONTIGNY, 34, Chippewa, University of Oregon Medical School, professor.

BRIAN DEERING, 25, Iroquois, Caughnawaga Reservation, teacher, education.

ADOLPH L. DIAL, 47, Lumbee, Pembroke State University, chairman of the Department of History and Political Science.

PATRICIA ANN DIXON, 21, Luiseno of Southern California, University of San Diego.

WILBUR V. DIXON, 43, Navajo, Navajo Community College, Edmond, Okla., associate professor, elementary education.

JOHN E. ECHOHAWK, 24, Pawnee, University of New Mexico School of Law, Albuquerque.

EMERSON ECKIWARDY, 41, Comanche, social worker.

JACK EDMO, 29, Shoshone-Bannock, Idaho State University, history.

GLORIA EMERSON, 30, Navajo, Harvard University, education.

DUANE EVANS, 33, Potawatomi, Kansas public schools, co-ordinator.

P. MICHAEL GALVAN, 19, Ohlone of California, St. Patrick's College, Calif., history.

VELMA M. GARCIA, 24, Acoma Pueblo, University of Arizona, Tucson, cultural anthropology.

GEORGE A. GILL, 44, Omaha, Arizona State University, Tempe, assistant professor of education.

JESSE GREENE, Nez Perce, Lapwai Nez Perce Reservation.

RONALD HALFMOON, 37, Umatilla, Washington State University, Pullman.

BENJAMIN HANLEY, 28, Navajo, Arizona State University Law College.

KATHRYN HARRIS, 20, Comanche, Radcliffe College, sociology.

ANNIE LEE HENRY, 32, Choctaw, University of Southern Mississippi, Hattiesburg, education.

FRANK HENRY, 40, Choctaw, University of Southern Mississippi, Hattiesburg, education.

JERRY M. HILL, 31, Oneida, University of Southern Mississippi, Hattiesburg, education.

BERNARD A. HOEHNER, 46, Standing Rock Sioux, veterinarian.

PARE HOPA, 34, Maori (observer), New Zealand, assistant professor in anthropology.

KATHY HURST, 20, Creek, Central State College, Edmond, Okla., business education.

CALVIN J. ISAAC, 36, Choctaw, Sequoyah High School, Tahlequah, Okla., teacher.

WANDA JANIS, 21, Oglala Sioux, Augustana College.

ARTHUR S. JUNALUSKA, Cherokee, dramatist, playwright, director.

ROBERT KANIATOBE, Choctaw, San Francisco State College, anthropology and Native American Arts.

GARY KIMBLE, 28, Gros Ventre, University of Montana Law School, Missoula.

TRAVIS F. KINSLEY, 19, Papago-Hopi, Dartmouth College, psychology.

VINCENT L. KNIGHT, 24, Ponca, University of New Mexico Law School, Albuquerque.

EDMUND D. LADD, 44, Zuni, archeologist, Hawaii National Park Service.

FRANK LAPENA, 32, Wintun, Shasta College teacher, Calif.

MARIGOLD LINTON, Cupeno, San Diego State College, professor psychology.

JOSEPH LITTLE, 20, Mescalero Apache, University of New Mexico, Albuquerque, English.

PETER LITTLE, 33, Apache-Tewa, New Mexico State University, Las Cruces, social welfare.

CHARLES LOLOMA, 46, Hopi, artist.

SIMON LOOKING ELK, 32, Sioux, University of Dubuque, Iowa, ministry.

EDWIN L. MADSEN, 33, Flathead, University of Idaho, Moscow, administration.

LAVERNE MASAYESVA, Hopi, University of Arizona, Tucson, anthropology, liguistics.

N. SCOTT MOMADAY, Kiowa, University of California, professor of comparative English, author.

BUD MASON, 33, Arikara-Mandan, Black Hills State College, Spearfish, S.D., social psychology.

BEA MEDICINE, 30, Standing Rock Sioux, San Francisco State College, assistant professor, anthropology.

ILARION MERCULIEFF, 20, Aleut, University of Washington, Seattle, law.

MRS. ARLENE MILLICH, 31, Southern Ute, Ft. Lewis College, Durango, Colo., education.

MICHAEL A. MISIASZEK, 24, Colville, Gonzaga University, Spokane, Wash., business.

WILLIAM MORGAN, SR., 51, Navajo, Navajo Community College, linguistics instructor.

MRS. JOANN S. MORRIS, 25, Chippewa, University of California, L.A., anthropology.

HARRIETT MARMON, 29, Laguna Pueblo, University of New Mexico, Albuquerque, bilingual education.

SOLOMON MCCOMBS, 54, Creek, artist.

HARVEY MCCUE, 25, Ojibway, Trent University, Canada, assistant professor, sociology.

TAYLOR MCKENZIE, 38, Navajo, Indian Hospital, Shiprock, N.M., physician.

STEVE MCLEMORE, 33, Cherokee-Pima, University of Oklahoma, Norman, environmental science.

CHRIS MCNEIL, 21, Tlingit, Stanford University, political science.

D'ARCY MCNICKLE, 65, Flathead, University of Saskatchewan, professor in anthropology, chairman of department.

MARY F. NELSON, 36, Colville, Eastern Washington State College, Cheney, assistant professor, art/anthropology.

BARRY NICHOLAS, 27, Malecite, teacher, Indian education.

ROSALIE NICHOLS, Miwok, University of California, Davis, graduate student, history.

SPARLIN W. NORWOOD, 32, Cherokee, Central Jr. High School, Bartlesville, Oklahoma, teacher.

DALE OLD HORN, 24, Crow, Montana State University, Bozeman, counselling.

EMMETT OLIVER, 55, Quinault, University of California, Los Angeles, Indian Culture Program.

ALFONSO ORTIZ, Tewa, Princeton University, associate professor anthropology.

SIMON J. ORTIZ, 28, Acoma Pueblo, Rough Rock Demonstration School, Poet.

HURLEY PARKHURST, 35, Oneida, University of Minnesota, St. Paul, graduate, soil science.

MICHAEL M. PAUL, 34, Colville-Salish, artist.

ROBERT PENN, 22, Sioux, University of South Dakota, Vermillion, art.

JAMES C. PETERSON, 35, Blackfeet, Brigham Young University, Provo, sociology.

MRS. KAREN S. PETERSON, 27, Cherokee, Western Carolina College, science.

ROBERT L. PIERCE, 18, Seneca, State University of New York at Buffalo, social welfare.

DILLON PLATERO, 43, Navajo, director, Rough Rock Demonstration School.

CHARLES A. POITRAS, JR., 31, Sac and Fox, Shawnee Reservation, leadership development.

ANN P. RAINER, 28, Taos, Stanford University, anthropology, pre-med.

VINCENT E. RANDALL, 29, Camp Verde Apache, tribal government, education.

COEY REAL BIRD, 23, Montana State University, Bozeman, elementary education.

HELEN MARIE REDBIRD, Cherokee, Oregon College of Education, Monmouth, professor, social science.

DAVID J. RED FOX, University of Oregon, Eugene, history, law.

JACOB REYNOLDS, 19, Cheyenne-Arapahoe, Colorado State University, Ft. Collins, sociology.

MONTANA H. RICKARDS, 57, Cherokee, Oregon College of Education, Monmouth, associate professor, humanities-education.

JACK R. RIDLEY, 35, Shoshone, University of Idaho, Moscow, assistant professor, physiology.

DAWN GOOD ELK RIEKER, 21, Sioux, University of Oregon, Eugene, public affairs, arts.

LEONARD ROBBINS, 23, Navajo, Utah State University, Logan, natural resources, wildlife.

DONALD D. ROSS, Sioux, University of Omaha, Nebraska, education.

HERSCHEL SAHMAUNT, 36, Kiowa, Oklahoma City University, consultant.

MARLENE SALWAY, 24, Blackfeet, University of Montana, Missoula, social worker.

MRS. CATHERINE B. SANDERS, 51, Cherokee, Cherokee Elementary School, North Carolina, teacher.

JOE SANDO, 46, Jemez Pueblo, Talent Search Program, Albuquerque, N.M., history.

BUFFY SAINTE-MARIE, Cree, singer, composer.

KENNETH L. SAUPITTY, 32, Comanche, Oklahoma College for Continuing Education, Norman.

FRITZ SCHOLDER, 32, Luiseno, artist, Santa Fe, N.M.

JOSEPH SENUNGETUK, 30, Eskimo, artist, writer.

JACKIE SINE, 20, Oklahoma State University, Stillwater, education.

FRED SMITH, 30, Seminole, education, Hollywood, Florida.

THELMA STIFFARM, Gros Ventre-Cree, University of Montana, Missoula, law.

WILLIAM A. THACKER, 28, Paiute, rancher, farmer, Owyhee, Nevada.

BOBBY THOMPSON, 24, Choctaw, University of Southern Mississippi, education.

DONALD W. WANATEE, 37, Mesquakie, Central College, Pella, Iowa.

KENT. C. WARE II, 28, Kiowa, Arizona State University Law School.

WILFRED C. WASSON, 45, Western Washington State College, Bellingham, education, anthropology.

JAMES L. WEST, 24, Southern Cheyenne, Andover Newton Theological School.

DICK WEST, JR., 27, Southern Cheyenne, Stanford University Law School.

BARRY WHITE, 19, Seneca, State University of New York at Buffalo.

DENNIS R. WHITE, 23, Chippewa, University of Wisconsin, Madison, graduate student, mathematics.

ELIZABETH WHITEMAN, 22, Crow, University of Montana, education.

RICHARD N. WILSON, 33, Santee Sioux, University of Oregon, Eugene, education.

SAUNDRA WILSON, 20, Sioux, Augustana College, Sioux Falls, S.D., special education.

JOHN R. WINCHESTER, 48, Potawatomi, Michigan State University, Lansing, instructor.

BARBARA WOELK, 21, Kiowa, Kansas University, Lawrence.

FLOYD M. WYASKET, 23, Ute, University of Utah, Salt Lake City, education.

FREDERICK YOUNG, 37, Navajo, University of New Mexico, Albuquerque, physicist.

THESE ARTISTS EXHIBITED THEIR WORK AT PRINCETON UNIVERSITY DURING THE CONVOCATION OF AMERICAN INDIAN SCHOLARS.

Fred Beaver

Larry Bird

Blackbear Bosin

George Burdeau

T. C. Cannon

Robert Chee

Jimmie C. Fife

Henry Gobin

Barbara Goodluck

Joan Hill

Patrick Swazo Hinds

Allan Houser

John Hoover

Oscar Howe

Peter Jones

Fred Kabotie

Mike Kabotie

Yeffe Kimball

Otellie Loloma

Solomon McCombs

Leatrice Mikkelsen

Al Momaday

George Morrison

Lawney Reys

C. Terry Saul

Fritz Scholder

Bill Soza

Willard Stone

Jose Rey Toledo

Pablita Velarde

Dick West